Robertson —

Thank god one of
us gets pleasure
doing crossword puzzle

love me!

S J.

4/20/85

A Pleasure in Words

BY

EUGENE T. MALESKA

WITH A FOREWORD BY
DAVID B. GURALNIK

SIMON AND SCHUSTER
NEW YORK

Library of Congress Cataloging in Publication Data
Maleska, Eugene T
A pleasure in words.

Bibliography: p.
1.   English language—Etymology.   I. Title.
PE1574.M26   422   80-20347

ISBN 0-671-24881-2

Grateful acknowledgment is hereby made to the following:

George Braziller, Inc., Publishers, for permission to quote passages from *A Dictionary of Colorful Italian Idioms* copyright © 1965 by Carla Pekelis.

Holt, Rinehart and Winston, Publishers, for permission to use text from "The Bear," copyright © 1956 by Robert Frost, which is included in *The Poetry of Robert Frost,* edited by Edward Connery Latham, copyright © 1928, 1969 by Holt, Rinehart and Winston.

Harcourt Brace Jovanovich, Inc., for permission to use text from "Primer Lesson," which is included in *Slabs of the Sunburnt West* by Carl Sandburg, copyright © 1922 by Harcourt Brace Jovanovich, Inc., copyright © 1950 by Carl Sandburg.

Dover Publications for permission to use text from "The Tutor" by Carolyn Wells, which is included in *The Home Book of Quotations,* edited by Burton Stevenson, copyright © 1967 by Dodd, Mead & Company.

*This book is dedicated with love
to my children
Merryl and Gary*

OUTLINE OF CHAPTERS

FOREWORD

It has become fashionable these days to bemoan what is termed "the decline in literacy," and new books and articles filled with Cassandran alarms about the imminent demise of English keep rolling off the presses. The fact that a number of these books immediately become best sellers and that the articles stir up vigorous and literate debate would seem to give the lie to that notion. Even more encouraging is the warm welcome given the many less ominous but more informative books about the language that have been written and compiled in recent years, among them the one you hold in your hands.

Those of us who toil in the vineyards of English linguistics and lexicography approach our tasks in a general spirit of sobriety, but we know very well that language does not serve humankind only for communication any more than food serves only for nourishment. The pleasure derived from a well-prepared *saltimbocca,* that Italian enhancement of veal, is no greater than the joy of discovering that the name for the dish means literally "jump into the mouth." Eons ago, people huddling around a fire in a cave somewhere must have learned that language is, *inter alia,* for playing with. And so arose puns and comic verse and charades and anagrams and crossword puzzles.

Which brings me to this delightful book and its author. Eugene Maleska, a former teacher, a writer, and one of the great crossword-puzzle constructors, has spent a lifetime compiling oddments about the lexis that makes up the vocabulary of English. And in this lively work he shares with us his exhilaration at discovering the relationship between words that on the surface appear to have no connection whatsoever (as between *apothecary* and *boutique* or between *pawn* and *pioneer*) and the strange and varied routes by which the words we use have found their way into our language.

This rich olio (a word well-known to crossword-puzzle fans) of little etymologies, interspersed with literary allusions, personal anecdotes, pungent puns, and witty couplets, quatrains, and what Maleska calls his "cursed tercets," offers a painless method for learning about the ways of language and for expanding one's vocabulary. As a special bonus, the author initiates us into the mysteries of crossword-puzzle construction, offering tips to the would-be constructor as well as to the solver, capped with several sample puzzles.

Start at the beginning of this book and follow the author's logical connections, or dip at random in the treasures that abound. Either way, if you have any interest at all in the luxuriant and eclectic vocabulary that has made the English language one of humankind's most effective and flexible tools for transmitting knowledge and feelings, you will be enriched. This is a particularly lovely book to browse in, in the etymological sense of that term, for it does offer nourishment as well as pleasure.

DAVID B. GURALNIK
Editor in Chief
Webster's New World Dictionaries

TO THE READER

This book has been simmering on the back burner for decades. It probably stems from my ancestral genes, because words have fascinated me ever since I can remember. But the impetus was first provided on a New York City subway when I was a teenager traveling from New Jersey to Regis High School, in Manhattan. One day I picked up a discarded newspaper on the seat next to me and happened upon the crossword puzzle. Since English was my favorite subject, I figured I could easily solve the puzzle.

What a surprise awaited me! One four-letter word was defined as "Very long time." It seemed to begin with AE. *What could it be? The answer to the puzzle was on another page. Impatient, I peeked.* AEON! *I had never come across that word before. In the same puzzle a feudal serf turned out to be* ESNE, *a trout worked out as* CHARR *and a card game evolved as* SKAT.

When I got home I checked my dictionary just to see whether the creator of the puzzle hadn't made up those strange words. They were all listed. My ego had been deflated but I had learned four new words. I was hooked!

Subsequent pursuit of my addiction expanded my vocabulary with more than mere "crosswordese"—such as coins of Macao or three-toed sloths. I remember learning AERIE, PERIDOT, ANSERINE, CACHINNATE *and hundreds of other useful and interesting words. I also found new meanings for familiar words. A gem, for instance, could be a kind of muffin, and the game of* euchre *could also be a verb meaning "to cheat or trick." Exotic synonyms also kept popping up. The puzzles taught me that a* hermit *might be an eremite, an anchorite or even an anchoret. In various puzzles I found such a simple word as* ode *defined as "monody; canticle; canzone; parabasis; epicede; serenata" and—my favorite— "genethliacon."*

The above are only a few examples of the many terms by which my vocabulary was expanded. At any rate, I began to keep a notebook—a kind of personal thesaurus—and during my years in college I became an expert solver.

At that point I met a lovely coed. Aside from being a Latin major like me, she shared my interest in solving crosswords. So I courted her with original puzzles. The first of the series contained her name (Jean) at 1-Across. The clue read: "Most beautiful girl on campus."

One day she showed the puzzles to her roommate, who happened to be a go-getter type. "Your boyfriend can make money with his puzzles," she stated. "The HERALD TRIBUNE *pays five dollars for those in the daily papers."*

And so, after many rejections, I finally became a pro—well, maybe a semipro. My early publications were not the works of a master puzzler.

But the hobby, as well as the notebook, expanded as the years flew by. Simultaneously I had developed a profound interest in the derivations of English words. It fascinated me to learn that the scallion *is probably a corruption of "Ascalon," a seaport in southern Palestine. I chuckled when I learned that William de la Pole, Duke of Suffolk, was nicknamed Jac Napes and willy-nilly handed down the word* jackanapes. *And I felt sorry for the people of Wales when I discovered that the verb* welsh *is an opprobrious reference to their alleged propensities for swindling or failing to pay their debts.*

A second notebook labeled "Etymology," emerged. Others followed: "Words from Mythology," "Spelling Demons," "Nice but Naughty Words," "Eponyms," and so on.

Such was the genesis of A PLEASURE IN WORDS. *The book evolved gradually and naturally from years of scanning dictionaries, mainly in connection with my work as a crossword puzzle constructor and editor. It is an attempt to share the results of somewhat haphazard and perhaps dilettantish research in the wonderful world of words.*

Let me emphasize that I am not a lexicographer and that I have tremendous respect and admiration for the experts who put together excellent dictionaries. But I do claim to be a philologer in the literal sense of that noun—"lover of words"—and I hope that I shall manage to transmit to the reader the feeling of personal joy that I experience each time I make a new linguistic discovery in a lexicon or elsewhere. Naturally, it would be even more delightful if some of my feelings should rub off on those who browse through these pages.

Another point to be stressed is that I have not attempted to be all-encompassing. The book provides eclectic samplings in etymology and related fields that I hope will whet the reader's appetite for further explorations on his own. Incidentally, such areas as grammar and dic-

tion are deliberately omitted, and the general history of our language is discussed only in brief terms.

A chapter called "How to Construct Crossword Puzzles" is included chiefly because so many people have asked me to reveal the stratagems used by expert puzzle-makers.

Finally, I wish to thank Paul and Carl Angiolillo and my daughter Merryl for contributing a few stories to the chapter called "Twice-Told Tales." I am also grateful to Peter Cancro and Lois and Robert Hughes for typing and proofreading the manuscript. Last, but certainly not least, I am indebted to the lovely coed whom I married. Without her patience, encouragement and help with research I never could have produced this book.

Pax, amor et felicitas,
Eugene T. Maleska

CHAPTER 1

Our Hellenic Heritage

Are you a *misocapnist?* Have you recently written to a *thesmothete* or a *diaskeuast?* At dinner are you a *deipnosophist?* Do you enjoy gazing on *callipygian* beauties in centerfolds?

All of the foregoing esoteric words can be found in unabridged dictionaries. Like many others that are unfamiliar to most people, they have come down to us from the ancient Greeks.

But we have also inherited many commonly used words from the Athenians. *Atom, criterion, tyrant, cyclone, hippopotamus* and *strategy* are just a few examples. The last two, by the way, are especially interesting. The "hippo" is literally a river horse, and *strategy* comes from the Greek word for a general. Naturally, he would have to be versed in *stratagems!*

About 15 percent of our words have a Hellenic origin. They have been transliterated into English largely because of the influence of the Romans and the scholars. When the Roman legions conquered Greece, they enslaved the Athenians and brought back the bright oldsters to act as teachers for their children. These *pedagogues* (another borrowing from the Greeks!) taught the little *pueri* to read Plato, Aristotle, Aristophanes and other great writers.

At Alexandria—a city founded by Alexander the Great in 332 B.C. —a Pharaoh named Ptolemy I established one of the world's most famous libraries. It included not only collections of Greek literature but also the finest works of Rome, India and Egypt. The museum at Alexandria became a sort of ancient academy in which sages from various realms were fostered at the expense of the state. The existence of that institution helped to preserve a treasury of words that have eventually enriched our own language. But enough of history for a while. Let's return to the words in the first paragraph.

One of my fantasies is to own a bus line. In each vehicle a prominent sign would read: "NO SMOKING. HAVE REGARD FOR THE MISOCAPNISTS." Yes, a *misocapnist* is one who has a hatred of tobacco smoke! Lately he and his colleagues have organized a drive against smoking in public places. Cigars are the special targets of this group. In fact, as the Greeks would say, havanas are *anathema.** My friend Will Weng and I are habitual cigar smokers. At times we feel like *pariahs†* and would like to form our own group—the *Misomisocapnists.*

Miso, as you can readily ascertain, is a Greek form meaning "hatred." Another example is *misanthrope,* a person who hates mankind. Note that *miso* has been shortened to *mis.* It should not be confused with the prefix *mis,* which means "wrong" or "incorrect."

Thesmothete literally means "a person who lays down the law." Your congressman is one, because today the word is defined as "a legislator." It would be interesting to know how many of our politicians on Capitol Hill realize that they are *thesmothetes.* Certainly, many of them are not *solons.* That's a word that has been debased to indicate any lawgiver. Purists hold out for one definition only: "a wise and skillful legislator or statesman." The reason is simple enough. Solon was an eminent reformer of Athenian statutes. Known as one of the Seven Wise Men of Greece, he was a master at undoing legal knots and simultaneously tightening loopholes. Even today conscientious lawyers are indebted to him.

Thesmothete has a crazy cousin called *Thesmophoria.* The Greek goddess Demeter had an alias—Thesmophoros. The Greek women celebrated her festival in the ritual of *Thesmophoria.* On that occasion they would throw pigs into chasms and later carry up the decaying flesh. Then they would mix it with seed to guard against sterility. Demeter, as you can guess, was the goddess of fertility.

Diaskeuast was a word I discovered when I began to construct crossword puzzles. In search of a new definition for *editor,* I leaped with joy when I came across this gift from the Greeks. Previously our clues had read as follows:

> Newspaper official
> Magazine official
> Film cutter
> Maxwell Perkins was one
> Redactor (an interesting word too!)
> One who corrects or revises MSS

You can imagine my excitement when I first used my new word as a clue! Margaret Farrar was a NEW YORK TIMES *diaskeuast* then, and she confessed that it was an addition to her vocabulary. Incidentally,

---

* *Anathema* (from a Greek word meaning "anything devoted to evil, a curse"). Today one of its principal meanings is "anything intensely disliked or loathed." It also means "a curse or ban" or "a vigorous denunciation."

† *Pariah* (from Tamil, a language of India; literally, it means "drummer"). The pariahs were a low caste; hence the word has come to mean "an outcast."

she deleted the definition because the crossings were too difficult. But I used the clue later when it appeared to be fair to the solvers.

———

A *deipnosophist* to the Greeks meant "a wise man at a meal." By the way, it's interesting to observe that the classical words often seem to read backward. *Deipnon* is the "meal" part. The same is true of *hippopotamus,* which was mentioned earlier. If you translate sequentially, it's a "horse river" rather than a "river horse."

(The same is sometimes true of Latin. Take, for instance, an M.A. degree. To the Romans it was *artium magister.* Another example is *Omnia vincit amor*—Love conquers all.)

At any rate, a *deipnosophist* is a person skilled in the art of table talk. One can picture a Radcliffe girl telling her dorm mates that her dinner date was an arrant bore and certainly no *deipnosophist!* Or, to give the image an Attic flavor, how about Acis facing Galatea over supper?

———

Callipygian, or *callipygous,* is one of the eyebrow raisers to be discussed in another chapter. "Having shapely buttocks" is the definition. A lovely ancient statue, now located in a museum at Naples, is called the Callipygian Venus. It is rumored that the guards have a difficult time preventing Neapolitan males from pinching the sculpture.

Let's take our minds off Venus for a while and consider *calli.* It's sometimes abridged to *cali,* and in either case it translates into "beautiful." *Calisthenics* is a case in point. To Athenians it meant "beautiful strength"—an instance of a nonbackward word.

But *calli* and its opposite, *caco* (meaning "bad, unpleasant"), tell us something fascinating about ourselves. For some reason we humans tend to dwell more on what is evil than on what is good. Take *smell,* for instance. To most people the word has an offensive connotation. They immediately think *stink!* Of course it can mean "perfume," "fragrance," "bouquet" or any other delightful olfactory synonym. But the word has decayed into rottenness through the years. *Aroma* and *scent* have taken its place in positive thinking.

We say, "Ah, the wonderful aroma of coffee!" or "The scent of roses pervaded the air." We also say, "That house has a peculiar smell" or "I smell a rat" or "Do you smell gasoline?" In that connection, an anecdote about Samuel Johnson seems apropos. A dowager next to him in a public conveyance said, "Sir, you smell!" Johnson replied, "No, madam. *You* smell; I stink."

Another instance of our tendency to accent the negative is the abundance of synonyms in our language for thief, rogue and other such criminals, as opposed to words applying to decent people. Think about it! How many "evil" words can you come up with vis-à-vis "good" ones? The moral seems to be that wickedness intrigues us more than virtue.

Let us get back to the *calli-caco* contrast. On the one hand we find *calligraphy* as one of the few remaining vestiges of the bright side. It means, of course, "elegant penmanship." A *calligrapher's* handwriting is beautiful. However, in this age of the typewriter and neglect of the Palmer method in schools, even *calligraphy* seems to be doomed to extinction.

But the *caco* words retain their vigor and grow more popular with every new generation.

> *cacophony*—harsh or discordant sound; dissonance. (Incidentally, why isn't there a *calliphony,* meaning "sweet harmony"?)
> *cacodemon*—an evil spirit
> *cacodemonia*—insanity in which the patient has the delusion of being possessed by an evil spirit
> *cacodoxy*—perverse teachings. (What, no *callidoxy?*)
> *cacoepy*—bad pronunciation. (Here the opposite is *orthoepy.*)
> *cacoëthes*—a habitual and uncontrollable desire; a mania or itch. (What an interesting word!)
> *cacoëthes scribendi*—an uncontrollable urge to write. (Dickens' problem?)
> *cacography*—bad handwriting. (My problem.)
> *cacology*—bad diction or pronunciation

There's another *calli* word in the dictionary that deserves attention, although it has nothing to do with what is beautiful and lovely. It's *callithump,* a hand-me-down from dialectic English and a distortion of *gallithumpian*—a disturber of the peace at elections back in the eighteenth century. In fact, the word may be related to *gallows.*

What's a *callithump?* Well, it's the same as a *shivaree* and similar to a *charivari*—it's a noisy, boisterous parade. My Irish ancestors on my mother's side (Kelly was her maiden name) participated in many a *callithump* on March 17!

A *shivaree,* by the way, is a clamorous mock serenade to a newly married couple—complete with kettles, pans, horns and other noisemakers. It's an offshoot of the French *charivari* (which originally meant "headache" in its Low Latin form). A charivari is a confusion of discordant sounds.

———

Charivari is one of those words that appeal to our sense of rhyme. One of my favorite crossword puzzle topics is called "Terse Verse" or "Rhyme Time." To make such a puzzle I gather a whole list of words and phrases such as the following:

hifi	hotshot	bedstead	backtrack
kiwi	hot spot	claptrap	bandstand
Pogo	humdrum	cookbook	blackjack
bigwig	ill will	deadhead	chalk-talk
boohoo	layaway	downtown	eeny, meeny
bowwow	Oshkosh	Hong Kong	etiquette
fan-tan	pie-eyed	I like Ike	fair share
heyday	rat-a-tat	jingling	handstand
hoodoo	redhead	locofoco	handy-andy
hubbub	rub-a-dub	maintain	hoi polloi
jet set	slumdom	packsack	itsy-bitsy
May Day	whatnot	Pall Mall	okey-dokey
Seabee	wise guy	Pickwick	prime time
		wingding	rigamajig
		zoot suit	sentiment
			sweetheart
			ting-a-ling

Once the list has been put together, the next step is to choose words from it and place them into the diagram as the main entries. After that the chief task is to make the crossing words fit the "Rhyme Time" entries.

Rhyme and its cousin *rhythm* can also be traced back to the Greeks. Their word was *rhythmos* ("measure, measured motion") and was related to the verb *rhein* ("to flow").

The rhythm of Homer's twenty-four books of the ILIAD flows along smoothly in *dactylic hexameter.* Now let's pause a while and examine those two words.

Dactyl was the Athenians' word for finger. Looking down at their hands, they noticed that, starting at the knuckles, the first joints of the fingers are much longer than the other two. Hence, to a poet, a *dactyl* became a metrical unit beginning with a "long" (or stressed) sound and ending with two "short" sounds. The symbol for a dactyl is —∪ ∪.

Longfellow used *dactylic hexameters* in EVANGELINE. Consider the opening line:

> "This is the forest primeval. The murmuring pines and the hemlocks . . ."

But the original nonpoetic meaning of *dactyl* has been preserved in several interesting English words:

dactyliomancy—divination by means of finger rings
dactylion—the tip of the middle finger. (When a person makes a commonly known vulgar sign, he is giving someone else the *dactylion!*)

dactyliotheca
> a. a case for a collection of such items as rings and gems
> b. an illustrated catalogue of rings and gems

dactylogram or *dactylograph*—fingerprint

dactylography—scientific study of fingerprints. (Note that a *dactylographer* becomes a *dactyloscopist* when he classifies or compares fingerprints!)

Most interesting of all the *dactyl* words is *dactylology*—the art of communicating by signs made with the fingers. I first learned this word when I visited Gallaudet College—an institution for the deaf. (At that time, I was head recruiter for the New York City schools and we needed teachers for our School for the Deaf.)

Finally, let us not forget the *pterodactyl,* that grotesque flying reptile of yore. The creature's name literally means "wing finger"— and the appellation is apt. The wings were attached to greatly enlarged fourth digits at the ends of two skinny arms.

All the cousins of *dactyl* come from the Greek too. It's somewhat ironic that it should be defined as "metrical foot" rather than "hand" or "finger."

iamb   ∪ —
trochee   —∪
> This word is often confused with *troche*—a medicinal tablet or lozenge, usually having an oval shape. *Troche* comes from the Greek word for "wheel." The metrical foot comes from *trochos,* "a racecourse" —perhaps because this form allows our minds to run along as we read!

spondee   — —
> What an interesting history this word has! It's derived from the Greeks' term for "libation," because it was the form used in the solemn music accompanying sacrificial rites, when it was the custom to pour wine either on the ground or on the victim. In the latter case, I surmise that the "sacrifice" would then become more palatable to the denizens of Olympus.

anapest or *anapaest*   ∪ ∪ —
> This direct opposite of the *dactyl* is derived from *anapaistos*—struck back. Byron "struck back" perfectly in such a line as: "And his cohorts were gleaming in purple and gold."

Hexameter is derived from *hexa* ("six") and *metron* ("meter, measure"). We're all familiar with *hexagons,* but did you know that ants, bees and flies are *hexapods?* And, of course, *hexapody* is a poetic line or group of verses containing six feet. Anyone who knows that an octad is a group of eight can readily guess the meaning of *hexad.*

What about *hex* itself? Well, it can't be blamed on the Greeks. Instead it has a Germanic history. *Hexe,* to a Berliner, is a witch. *Hexen* means "to practice witchcraft." All wordmongers will love *hexenbesen,* a word we borrowed from the Teutons. It's defined as "witches'-broom: an abnormal tufted growth of small branches caused by fungi, viruses, mistletoes, insect injury or physiological disturbances."

But if *hex* is not of Greek descent, *jinx* probably is. Lexicographers assume that it's an alteration of *jynx* or *iynx,* which meant "a wryneck genus" to an Athenian. That bird was often used in ancient witchcraft and other occult practices.

At this point let me digress a moment and tell a *jynx* story. Early in my career as crossword puzzle editor of THE NEW YORK TIMES I published an excellent April 1 "daily." Unfortunately the word *iynx* appeared in the puzzle, but since it crossed with easy words, I foresaw no problems. The definition was "wryneck."

Lo and behold, a flood of letters arrived. Many wary solvers asked if I had perpetrated an April Fools' joke by including a made-up word. One writer declared, "The iynx stynx!"

But the bulk of the letters came from bird watchers. They entreated me to give them more information on this unfamiliar feathered friend. What were its habits? Where could it be found? Was the iynx extinct, like the moa and the dodo?

To all of these would-be ornithologists I replied: "The iynx, which is a wryneck (which is a type of woodpecker), is of the genus jynx. I do not know where it can be found, but since the word is of Greek origin, I suspect that there may be a flock of iynxes flying around Athens."

Another time I got into a peck of trouble with bird lovers when I defined a *hoopoe* as "a filthy bird"—a definition taken right out of an encyclopedia. How could any bird be "filthy," the ornithophilous crowd demanded to know.

But to return to Greek numbers such as *hexa,* all we need do is drop down one notch and we find *penta*—a source for a score of words that deserve attention. Here are some of them.

pentacle
    a. a five-pointed star
    b. an occult symbol (For some strange reason the occult symbol is really a six-pointed star, equivalent to a hexagram.)
pentacular—the adjective for the above
pentact—having five rays
pentadactyl—having five digits on hand or foot; or five fingerlike parts
pentaglot
    a. using five different languages
    b. a *pentaglot* work
pentagon—a polygon having five angles and therefore five sides. (The building containing U.S. Defense Department offices was aptly named because of its shape. But a *pentagon crab* is not one of the bureaucrats therein; it's just another crustacean.)

pentalogy
>   a. fivefoldness
>   b. a series of five closely related works

pentameter—a line of five metrical feet. (Iambic pentameter is a form favored by many English poets.)

pentarchy—government by five persons

Pentateuch—the first five books of the Old Testament. (*Teuchas* is the Greek word for "tool" and, in a scholarly sense, "book." The *Pentateuch* is also called the Five Books of Moses.)

pentathlete—an athlete in a pentathlon

pentathlon—athletic contest involving participation by each contestant in five different events. (Today the most grueling of all Olympic events is the *decathlon*. This doubles the number for a *pentathlon*. Here are the contests: 100-meter, 400-meter and 1500-meter runs; the 110-meter high hurdles; the javelin and discus throws; the shot put, the pole vault, high jump and broad jump. No wonder Bruce Jenner found it helpful to eat a certain breakfast food!)

Pentecost
>   a. a solemn Hebrew festival, so called because it is celebrated on the fiftieth day after the second day of Passover
>   b. Whitsunday, a Christian festival. (Note the ecumenical flavor of this word. Why fifty? The reason is that the second part of *Pentecost* originally meant "ten times.")

Before leaving *penta* let me point out the *pentagamists*. They are people who have been married (sometimes bigamously) five times. I wonder if Mickey Rooney, Zsa Zsa Gabor, Elizabeth Taylor et al have ever heard of "pentagamy."

In that connection, I recently learned the difference between *bigamy* and *digamy*. The former is illegal, but the latter is licit. In other words, if one's spouse has died or if there is a divorce followed by a remarriage, it's a case of *digamy*.

Yes, Virginia, there is a *trigamy* and a *tetragamy,* but no lexicon at my command lists *hexagamy*. From there on up, *polygamy* seems to be the proper terminology.

———

Tetra (meaning "four") has given us its own legacy. Any reader who has hung in there up to this point can easily evolve the meanings of *tetrad, tetraglot, tetragon, tetralogy, tetrapod* and *tetrarchy*.

But pornographers may be surprised to learn that a *tetragram* is a four-letter word. And urban dwellers may be interested to hear that a *tetrapolis* is a group or confederation of four cities. *Tetraphony* is not the art practiced by fourflushers but a term equivalent to dissonance in Greek music.

———

Poly (meaning "many, much, diverse") is a combining form coming from the Greek word *polys*. It has supplied us with a Golconda of interesting entries in our dictionaries. Here is only a sampling:

polyandry—a marriage form in which one woman has two husbands at the same time. (This is a counterpart of *polygyny,* in which the male has two wives. Both are forms of *polygamy.* Incidentally, *monandry* is the commonly accepted practice today.)

polyacoustics—the art of magnifying sounds. (Rock 'n' roll groups today seem to have perfected this skill almost beyond human endurance!)

polyarticular—affecting many joints. (This adjective is often applied to *polyarthritis.*)

polychord—having many strings

polychrest—a drug or medicine of value as a remedy for several diseases

polychresty
    a. a thing that has several uses
    b. same as *polychrest*

polychromatist—one who advocates the use of many colors, as in painting

polydactyl—having more than the normal number of toes or fingers. (Note how *dactyl* is here extended to pedal digits.)

polydipsia—excessive or abnormal thirst. (In this connection, a *dipsomaniac* is a candidate for A.A. Literally, he's a madman with a certain form of *polydipsia.*)

polydomous—inhabiting several nests. (Zoologists use this adjective for a group of ants that spread their colony in various directions. Their opposites are *monodomous.*)

polyethnic—formed or inhabited by people of many races

polygraph
    a. a voluminous or versatile writer
    b. an apparatus for producing copies of a drawing or writing
    c. an instrument for receiving and recording simultaneously variations in pulse, blood pressure and other pulsations
    d. a lie detector

polyhistor—person of encyclopedic learning. (*Histor* means "judge" or "learned man" in Greek. From this root we also get such words as *history, historian, historic.*)

Polylemma—an argument in which there are usually at least three alternatives. (*Lemma* is the Greek word for "proposition." In logic today a *lemma* is a preliminary proposition or a premise. *Dilemma* of course is the most commonly used descendant of the root. When you're on the horns of a *dilemma,* you have a choice between two alternatives.)

Polynesia—large number of islands in the central Pacific Ocean (*nesos*—island)

polyonymous—having many names; known by many names. (It tickles me to think that gangsters with several aliases probably don't realize that they are *polyonymous.* Imagine what would happen to you if you called them by such a term!)

polyonymy—plurality of names; the use of various names for one thing. The root word, *onyma,* means "name." From it we have also inherited *anonymous*—without a name. Other cousins in this family are *synonym, antonym, homonym, pseudonym* and *eponym.* My own favorite is *cryptonym*—a secret name. *Heteronyms* also are fascinating. They are words spelled the same but having two meanings. The noun "sow" (pig) and the verb "sow" are examples. *Paronymous* words contain the same root or stem. "Wise" and "wisdom" fit into this category. *Polynym* and *mononym,* two opposites, seem to be dropping out of our language. *Autonym,* too, appears to be obsolescent, but I hate to see it go. In contrast with *pseudonym,* it literally means "one's own name," but it can also be defined as "a book published under the author's real name."

polyphage—one eating much or many kinds of food

polyphagia—excessive desire to eat. (This Greek root for "eating" has given us several other intriguing words. For example, if your diet is oysters, then you're *ostreophagous.* The starfish, by the way, is a voracious *ostreophage.* And then there are those *xylophagous* little creatures that feed on wood.)

polyphony

    a. in music, counterpoint

    b. a multiplicity of sounds; reverberations caused by an echo

polyphyodont—having several or many sets of teeth in succession. (Sharks are *polyphyodonts.* The *odont* root obviously means "tooth." Related words are *polyodontia* and *odontologist.* And when Socrates had a toothache, he suffered—as we sometimes do—from *odontalgia.*)

polypragmatic—meddlesome; overbusy; officious

polypragmatist—busybody or fussy person. (*Pragma* means "deed" or "affair." Hence it's easy to see how the delightful duo above came into existence.)

polytheism—belief in a plurality of gods

polytropic—visiting many kinds of flowers for nectar. (*Tropos* means "turning" or "changing." Another marvelous word from this root is *heliotrope,* a garden plant that turns toward the sun.)

Most readers will be familiar with *polyclinic, polyglot, polygon* and *polytechnic.* And it's relatively simple to educe the definition for *polydaemonism.* But it's also easy to confuse that word with *polydemic.*

Demos was the ancient Greek word for "the populace." From it we get such words as *democracy, demography* and *demagogue.* Literally, *polydemic* means "of many peoples." As its usage has evolved through the centuries, the present definition is "native to or occurring in several regions or countries."

Endemic is a close relative. It means "restricted or native to a particular area or people." Medical men breathe a sigh of relief when a disease is *endemic* rather than *epidemic* (spreading widely). And when the disease is of foreign origin it is said to be *ecdemic.*

But the most all-embracing member of this family is *pandemic*—
affecting the majority of the people. Actually *pan* is another borrowing
from those remarkable old Greeks. It means "all," and it has nothing
to do with a kitchen utensil or—to the best of my knowledge—with a
certain playful Greek god of the forests and pastures who gave us the
term "panic." But it has bequeathed us a cluster of charming words.
Before presenting some selected examples, let me point out that the
greatest number of our words from Greece are scientific in nature.
Botanists, biologists, chemists, physicists, zoologists et al seem to be
confirmed Grecophiles. This is only natural because of the historical
fact that Greek became the language of the learned in ancient times
and its study was intensified during the Renaissance. However, since
most readers would rightfully find technical terms boring, I am deliberately omitting most of them from this chapter.

panacea—a cure-all. (The last part of this word comes from *akeisthai*—to heal.
　　　Quacks, charlatans* and mountebanks† are notorious for offering
　　　panaceas to ailing dupes.)
panchromatic—sensitive to the light of all colors in the visible spectrum
pancratic—giving mastery of all subjects
pancyclopedic—pertaining to the whole range of knowledge
pandect
　　　a. any complete code of laws
　　　b. a treatise covering an entire subject; a complete digest
Pandora
　　　a. first woman of Greek mythology. A creation of Hepaestus, she was
　　　beautiful and gifted.
　　　b. a mollusk or its genus
　　　(*Doron* is the Greeks' word for "gift." The plural is *dora*. Thus *Pan-
　　　dora* was well named, because she had "all gifts"—beauty, intelli-
　　　gence, charm. However, she was also given a box in which
　　　Prometheus had confined all the world's evils. Zeus commanded her
　　　not to open it, but curiosity got the better of her—in some versions—
　　　and all the ills flew out. Thus a *Pandora's box* is a source of extensive
　　　but unforeseen troubles. Incidentally, it's distressing to note that such
　　　a lovely name as Dora has acquired the adjective "dumb." The term
　　　was popularized by a comic strip, "Dumb Dora," which lasted from
　　　1925 well into the thirties. Also, it should be mentioned that Theo-
　　　dore, Dorothy and Dorothea come from the same root. Such people are
　　　"gifts of the gods.")

* *Charlatan*—a quack or imposter (from the French). Our Gallic friends borrowed the word from *ciarlatano,* an Italian variant of *cerretano.* The village of Cerreto
was known for its quacks. A related Italian word is *ciarlare*—to chatter.

　† *Mountebank*—a hawker of quack medicines (from the Italian words *montam-
banco* or *montimbanco*—literally, "one who climbs on a bench")

panegyric—a eulogy or laudatory discourse. (The word can be traced back to *agora,* the Greek marketplace familiar to crossword puzzle fans. It originally embodied the idea of a festival where all the people were assembled. This was a natural place for orators to deliver commendations to V.I.P.s whose favor they wished to curry.)

panentheism—the doctrine that God includes the world as only a part of his being. (How many "theisms" can there be?)

Panesthia—a genus of subsocial burrowing cockroaches. (I couldn't resist this one! If we break down the word, it means that these insects "eat all." Actually, their habit is to eat each other's wings.)

panoply—a full suit of armor. (*Hopla* was the Greek word for "armor." The initial letter got lost sometime between now and then—an elision that occurs often. A related word is *hoplite*—a heavily armed infantryman of ancient Greece. This poor soldier was weighed down with a helmet, cuirass, greaves, shield, spear and sword! Could that be one of the reasons for the Romans' conquest of Greece?)

panoptic or *pantoptical*—all-seeing. (It also means "allowing everything to be seen." In that sense the temptation to think of ecdysiasts* is irresistible.)

panorama—comprehensive view. (The *orama* root leads us to *myriorama*—an exhibition of views in quick succession. A *cyclorama* is a large pictorial representation encircling the spectator. A *cosmorama* presents scenes from various parts of the world. *Dioramas* are often three-dimensional, spectacular and translucent.)

Pan-Satanism—doctrine that the world is an expression of the personality of the Devil. (Well, when you listen to TV news programs, you can't help but wonder.)

pansexualism—the view that all desire and interest are derived from the sex instinct

pansophy—universal wisdom or encyclopedic knowledge.

pansophist—one claiming universal knowledge

pantarchic—cosmopolitan

pantheon

    a. a temple devoted to all the gods

    b. a treatise on pagan gods

    c. the gods of a people

    d. a building serving as a burial place for national heroes or containing memorials to them

    e. the person most highly esteemed by an individual or group

      (Take a second look at the above definitions and you'll receive a lesson in the evolution of the meanings of a word.)

pantocrator—the omnipotent lord of the universe (epithet applied to Christ)

pantology—a systematic view of all knowledge

---

* *Ecdysiast*—a strip-teaser (from *ecdysis*—act of getting out). This noun stems from the verb *ekdyein*—to take off or strip off.

The words *pansophy* and *pansophist* remind me of another interesting noun from the same root—*sophos* ("wise"). The word is *sophomore*. The last four letters of that term come from *moros* ("stupid"). Thus a second-year student is wise, yet stupid. In other words, he thinks he's smart but he still has a lot to learn. He's *sophomoric*.

Sophia is an English word handed down from the Greeks. It means "divine wisdom." As a proper noun it's often changed to Sophie or Sofia.

Sophistry has a fascinating history. It means "reasoning that is superficially plausible but is really fallacious or deceptive." *Sophists* were a group of teachers of philosophy and rhetoric in ancient Greece. Actually, they were learned men, and that definition for *Sophists* still applies. But their unorthodox ideas and the fact that they accepted money for their instruction caused them to fall into disrepute. Their detractors labeled their arguments as specious, and this connotation persists today. *Sophistic* means "fallacious."

The Romans took it up from there, and as a result we have been given the adjective *sophisticated*. The most common definition is "worldly-wise," but the word also means "adulterated; not in a natural state; many-sided; complex."

To *sophisticate* means "to alter deceptively or to adulterate." What a far cry from *sophos!*

———

Let's return to *sophomore:* the second root in the word is the basis for *moron*. In some unabridged dictionaries you can also find *moronity* and *moronism* as synonyms for stupidity or feeblemindedness.

Erudite psychologists use a different term—*oligophrenia*. This word combines two Greek roots, *olig* or *oligo* ("little" or "few") and *phren* ("mind"). Literally, an *oligophrenic* has a little mind.

Many people are familiar with *oligarchy* ("rule by the few"), but *oligopoly* is not so well known. It's a sort of standoff in industry. Specifically, it's a situation in which each of a few producers is strong enough to influence the market but cannot disregard the reaction of his competitors. The word is related to *monopoly* and is next of kin to *duopoly*. Another sibling, by the way, is *oligopsony* ("purchase by the few").

If you started at the beginning of this chapter, you will surely be able to evolve the meaning of *oligodactylism* (and don't forget that toes must be included). And it's not difficult to define an *oligochronometer*. Well, to save you precious seconds, it's an instrument for measuring very small intervals of time. It's certainly not an *oligosyllabic* word.

Have you ever seen a *chronogram?* Literally, it means "time writing," but it's also a kind of numerical stunt or puzzle. *Chronogrammatists* concoct inscriptions, phrases or sentences in which the Roman numerals form a certain date when put together.

King Gustavus Adolphus of Sweden had a medal struck in 1632 with the following *chronogrammatic* motto: ChrIstVs DVX; ergo trIVMphVs. Now, if you take each capital letter separately and translate it into a number, you will come out with 1632 when you add up all the numbers. Don't forget the first capital letter, C, equal to 100!

Believe it or not, there is also a *chronanagram*, which is an anagram of a *chronogram*. That sounds like a pastime for superintellectuals.

Most of us are familiar with *chronic, chronicle, chronological* and *chronometer*. But leave it to the French to borrow the root and then hand us *chronique scandaleuse*—a history or biography that reports shocking, sensational details.

A polysyllabic modern offshoot of *chron, chrono* is *chronocinematography,* in which measurements of intervals of time are made via motion pictures.

––––––

Cinema may sound like a Spanish or Italian derivative, but it has a Greek ancestry. It's a shortening of the invention called a *cinematograph* or *kinematograph* (a motion-picture projector). In Athens *kinema* meant "movement."

In recent years, several new and exciting words have sprung up from this root. Consider the following:

cinedance—a dance composition or performance devised for motion pictures
cine—a movie or movie theater. (This is a shortening, of course, used by smart-alecky columnists. It's interesting to note that the word is now an integral part of the Italian and Spanish languages. As far as I can tell, the French still use *cinéma*.)
cinemagoer—person frequently attending movies
cinéma vérité—motion-picture art (as a documentary) with candor and realism

The medical profession has latched onto this root with a vengeance. In typical jawbreaking style, the good doctors have coined *cineangiocardiography*. This is the use of motion pictures on a fluorescent screen to record passage of a contrasting medium through the chambers of the heart and large blood vessels. *Cinemafluography* is a cousin of the above. In this case X-rays are used.

But let us not forget that the old Greek root was *kinema* (not *cinema*). When the original letter is retained, we are greeted by a cluster of beauties, especially if we are aware that *kinema* itself is an offshoot of the verb *kinein* ("to move").

kinematics—the branch of mechanics or dynamics that deals with pure motion

kinesalgia—pain occurring in conjunction with muscular action. (Beware, you joggers, wrestlers, and other athletes!)

kinescope—the recording of a TV program on motion pictures for subsequent use; also a tube used in television receivers and monitors

kinesimeter—an instrument for measuring bodily movements. (It boggles the mind to think of how many "meters" mankind has invented. Readers who are measure-conscious are invited to turn to p. 432 in the Appendix. A sampling of *meters,* most of them of Greek origin, is presented therein.)

kinesiology—the study of the anatomy with respect to movement

kinesthesia—the sensation of movement or strain in muscles, joints or tendons; "muscle sense"

kinesthetic—of bodily reaction or motor memory. (We get a *kinesthetic* feeling from watching an Astaire cinema.)

kinetic—active or lively; dynamic

kinetosis—motion sickness. (This is a synonym for *mal de mer,* or seasickness. Can you imagine a seasick passenger on an ocean liner being told by the ship's doctor that he was suffering from *kinetosis?* The poor fellow would probably faint from fright.)

To return to the *cine* alteration, a brand-new word for a movie buff is *cineast.* The last part of that word eventually comes from the Greek *astes,* an equivalent of our familiar suffix *ist.* Now let's take a look at some of the engrossing offshoots:

chiliast—one who believes in the millennium. (This word deserves careful consideration. It stems from *chilloi*—the Greeks' equivalent of the Romans' *mille,* meaning "thousand." *Chiliasm* is the doctrine that Christ will come to earth and usher in the millennium. Those familiar with the Bible know that in Revelations 20:1–7 the millennium is the period of a thousand years during which Christ will reign on earth.

The French changed *chilloi* to *kilo.* Thus a *kilowatt* is equal to one thousand watts, a *kilometer* is a thousand meters, and so on.

Chiliad and *millennium,* by the way, are synonyms.)

dynast

a. hereditary ruler

b. one of a line of kings or princes

c. member of a family powerful in a particular field

(Thomas Hardy helped to popularize the word when he wrote his most ambitious poetic work, THE DYNASTS, an epic drama on the Napoleonic Wars. The noun is only one of a whole host of words that eventually can be traced back to a Greek verb, *dynasthai* or *dunasthai* —to be able. The concept of ability soon came to mean "power." Today most of us never think of the Greeks when we use such words as *dynasty, dynamic, dynamite* and *dynamo.* For the benefit of physicists and crossword puzzle fans, let me not forget *dyne*—a unit of force.)

encomiast—one who praises; a panegyrist. (An *encomium,* of course, is an expression of praise. It has a fascinating background, similar to that of *panegyric.* Literally, it means "in a revel or celebration." *Comus* was the god of festive joy and mirth in late Greek and in Roman mythology. Milton wrote a poetic masque about that Olympian.)

enthusiast—a fanatic or zealot. (*Theos* meant "god" in Athens. *Enthusiasm* once meant "inspiration by a god." Incidentally, I wonder how many people are aware that *fan* is a shortened form of *fanatic.* Sometimes when wrathful crossword puzzle fans reprove me, I can't help but think of the longer version.)

fantast—a visionary or dreamer. (This word is related to *phantasy, phantom, fantasia, fancy* and others of that type. All of these come from a Greek root meaning "idea." Most delightful to contemplate is *phantasmagoria*—a constantly changing succession of scenes or things observed or imagined, as in a dream. Words like that send a shiver of joy up and down my spine!)

gymnast—an expert in calisthenics and bodily exercises. (Here is another word with an exciting history. It stems from *gymnastes*—a trainer of athletes. Obviously it's an offshoot of *gymnasium*—a school where Greek youths were given athletic training while naked. Yes, the root *gymnos* meant "naked." Now you should be able to identify the Hindu sect called *gymnosophists.* But you may have trouble with *gymnogyps.* They are not chiselers in the buff or nude gypsies but a genus of very large carrion-eating birds. *Gyps* meant "vulture" in Greece.)

scholiast—an annotator or commentator on the classics. (Sad to say, the *scholiasts* are a dead or dying breed in a society that pays less and less attention to Homer, Vergil et al. But the word itself has some very familiar relatives: *scholastic, scholar* and *school.* It's interesting to note that the Romans borrowed the Greek word *scholē* or *skholē* and changed it to *schola.* This is just another instance of the cultural influence of the Greeks upon the belligerent but bright descendants of Romulus and Remus.)

In connection with the foregoing statement, let us take another look at *pedagogue,* to which reference was made in the fourth paragraph of this chapter.

As Arthur Miller said in THE DEATH OF A SALESMAN, attention must be paid! The reason is that the Greek root *paed* (for "child") became shortened into *ped* as the centuries flowed on, and got confused with a Roman root with the same spelling. The Roman *ped,* however, meant "foot." It will be dealt with in a later chapter.

Pedagogue is a combination of *paed* and *agogos* ("leader" or "escort"). Literally, this person is a leader of children. *Pedagogy,* of course, is instruction or teaching. Since schoolmasters sometimes tended to be pompous, the word *pedant* soon took on a pejorative* connotation. A fault that I'm trying to avoid in this book is *pedantry,* but when you try to share something you've learned, there's a temptation to become *pedantic.* At least I trust I'm not indulging in that gobbledygook of educationists, *pedagese.*

When I was a student at Regis High School the teacher I had for Latin I had a mean streak in him. He had taught us *pes, pedi.* Then he turned to me and asked, "Okay, Maleska, what's a *pediatrician?*" I fell for his trap and promptly answered, "A foot doctor!" Luckily the joke fell a bit flat because most of my classmates thought I was right. We didn't take up Greek until we had become "wise dumbbells." Then we learned that *pod* was the Athenians' root for "foot," and a *podiatrist* is the specialist in that part of the anatomy.

To make matters worse, there is a similar Greek word, *pedon* (meaning "ground" or "earth"). Now, if you met a *pedologist,* would he be a specialist in the study of soil or of children? The answer is both! This is one of quite a few words in our language that can be interpreted, according to the context, in different ways. Egregious† examples are *cleave* and *ravel.* Cleave means "to sever or split," but it also means "to adhere firmly." Ravel means "to tangle" or "to untangle."

————

Returning to *pedagogue,* we find that the second part of the word is rooted in the Greek verb *agein* ("to lead or drive"). It has also given us *synagogue,* originally a place where Athenians were brought together—an assembly, if you will. Perhaps some erudite reader can inform me why this word has come to mean only a Jewish house of worship.

A *galactogogue* is the answer to every dairyman's prayer; it's an agency for increasing the flow of milk. A related word from the Greeks is *galaxy.* Hence, the Milky Way.

Finally, let me lay this one on you: *mystagogue.* This is an expert in religious mysteries who instructs neophytes in the sacraments.

————

* *Pejorative*—depreciatory or disparaging. For a change, here's a word that doesn't come from the Greeks. Its origin lies in *pejor,* the Latin adjective for "worse." But *pejor* itself is related to *ped* ("foot"). Apparently when a Roman made things worse, he put his foot in it.

† *Egregious*—extreme; flagrant; notorious. This adjective comes from the Latin word *grex-gregis*—flock or herd. Its literal meaning is "out of the flock or herd." On the other hand, a *gregarious* person prefers to be with the group. Incidentally, *gregge* is the modern Italian noun for "flock" or "herd."

Neophyte itself is a word with two ubiquitous* Hellenic progenitors combined—*neos* ("new") and *phytas,* from the infinitive *phyein* ("to grow or bring forth").

––––––––

Phytos provides us with a cluster of botanical words. The *epiphytes* and *aerophytes* are plants that grow chiefly in the air. The *lithophytes* are corals (growing on stone) and the *thallophytes* or *protophytes* are algae and fungi. A *hydrophyte,* naturally, flourishes in water, but a *saprophyte* lives on dead or decaying organic matter. Ugh!

Incidentally, the admen who discovered *halitosis* ("condition of having bad breath") in the lexicons missed out on the adjective *saprostomous* ("having a foul breath"). The last part of that word is derived from the Greek noun for "mouth."

A *zoophyte* is easy to define, even if you never saw one. Yes, it's an animal resembling a plant.

Stay away from *dermophytes*. They're fungi parasitic on the skin. *Microphytes,* as you can guess, are minute plants or bacteria. A *pteridophyte* (another spelling demon!) is a flowerless plant, such as a fern.

––––––––

But enough of the fauna! Although I had firmly intended to eschew those horticultural terms, they were just too enticing. Turning our attention to the first part of *neophyte,* we are rewarded with a dazzling array of arresting words. Let's skip such obvious ones as *neoclassic, Neo-Impressionism* and *Neoplatonism.*

Neo-Dada—junk art. (This was an anti-art movement of the fifties and sixties.)
neolalia—speech, as of a psychotic, that includes strange words
Neolithic
    a. of the latest period of the Stone Age
    b. of an earlier, outmoded age
    (*Lithos* meant "stone." When Zeus turned Niobe into stone because she had taunted Leto about her children, he *lithified* her!)
neologism—a new word or expression; a new usage of an established word or expression. (Years ago, when I taught in Harlem, the boys would talk about a "rumble" on the playground. I had no idea what they meant. Had a clap of thunder frightened them? No, they were referring to a fistfight. Today that neologism is listed in unabridged dictionaries and defined as "quarrel or disturbance." At the same time, baseball announcer Red Barber was introducing another neologism. When an argument or row started on the diamond, he called it a "rhubarb"—a word I'm assuming he picked up during his boyhood in the South. At any rate, the new meaning for that old plant is now acceptable.)

* *Ubiquitous*—existing everywhere; omnipresent. Again, this is a Latin inheritance. *Ubi* means "where," *qui* means "who." Those who seem to be everywhere at once are *ubiquitous.* I first ran across the word in a sports column by Red Smith. I think he was talking about shortstop Marty Marion, who covered so much ground that he was indeed *ubiquitous.*

neomenia—the time of the new moon

neomycin—an antibiotic. (Here's another surprise. *Mycin* is a combining form meaning "substance derived from fungus." The Greek word *mykes* meant "fungus." *Mycosis* is a disease caused by fungus, and a *mycologist* studies fungi.)

neon—inert gaseous element. (This gas was discovered in 1898 by Ramsay and Travers. Their reason for giving it that title is obvious.)

neophilism—morbid or excessive desire for novelty. (To coin a word, or use a neologism, people afflicted with this craving are *neophilistic*. They're faddists. And do you know what a fad is? It's something that goes in one era and out the other. To understand that joke, you must be able to pronounce *era* correctly—unlike most of our TV and radio announcers. I often feel like writing to them and saying, "To pronounce *era* as though it were *error* is an error.")*

neoteric—modern; new

A current neologism is *neonate,* defined as "a newborn child." It's a shortening of another English word, *neonatus.* Both are interesting hybrids. As we know, *neo* is from the Greeks; but *natus* is from the Romans. It means "born" in Latin. From the same root we get such words as *nativity, native* and *nation.*

In the past, neologists were careful not to create hybrids lest they be scoffed at by scholars. When Edison invented the *phonograph* in 1877, he used two Greek roots *phone* ("sound") and *graphein* ("to write"). His device actually wrote the sounds. And when Emile Berliner came up with his Gramophone ten years later, he just reversed the roots. In ancient Greece *gramma* was a letter or piece of writing and was closely related to *graphein.*

TV viewers who listen annually to the ceremonies of the Grammy awards for notable achievement in phonograph recording may not know that the title for this statuette is derived from Berliner's *Gramophone.* (It's still a trademark, so I'm obliged to capitalize the word.) And that other prize, the Emmy, also has Hellenic overtones. It's an alteration of "Immy." So what's an "Immy"? Well, it's a shortening for *image orthicon*—a certain camera tube used for TV.

To get back to the inventors, Morse had no problem with terminology when he devised the electric *telegraph* (*tele* means "far" or "afar"). As early as 300 B.C. those amazing Greeks had already developed the first systematic method of telegraphy!

Bell's *telephone* (exhibited in 1876) and his *photophone* did not violate any nonhybrid rules. Nor did Edison's *mimeograph.* In Athens a *mimos* was an imitator. From the same root we are given such words as *mime, pantomime* and *mimesis* ("imitation, mimicry"), among oth-

---

* Unfortunately the lexicographers are now condoning "erra" as a second pronunciation.

ers. The sage of Menlo Park also adhered to tradition when he brought forth his *cinematograph*. Ironically, this term for a motion-picture camera is now chiefly British.

Even the *typewriter* can be claimed to be all Greek in origin as far as roots are concerned. *Typos* was an Athenian word for "blow, impression, image or model." *Writer* can be traced back to a Greek word, although it gets all mixed up with German and Icelandic heritages.

The *telescope* (actually invented before Galileo improved the instrument) adheres to the conventional rules for neologists' nomenclature.* *Skopein* was the Greek infinitive for "to view."

When the Wright brothers astounded the world with their *aeroplane* or *airplane,* they were right on the mark. The first Greek root is easy to ascertain; the other is from *planos,* meaning "wandering." Think of that word for a moment. An airplane wanders in the air! So does a *planet*—from the same root.

The *locomotive,* on the other hand, is a "pure" neologism from the Romans. It combines two Latin words, *locus* and *motus* ("place" and "movement").

But tradition and meticulous concern for details have been put aside in our free-and-easy twentieth century. Let's start with the *automobile. Auto* is a Greek root meaning "self." But the last half of the word is from the Romans. *Mobilis* is a form of *movere* ("to move"). Thus an automobile moves by itself, but it will always carry the stigma of having parents from two different word groups.

The same goes for *television*. The pioneers in that field probably avoided *telescopy* because it was already a word meaning "the art or practice of using or making telescopes." *Tele,* as we have already noted, was the Greek form for "far." But *vision* comes directly from the last principal part of *videre* (the Romans' infinitive for "to see"). In fact, *video* is a synonym for television. As most people know, that word means "I see" in Latin.

Readers can probably dredge up many more examples of modern hybrids, but I don't wish to labor the point. Really, I am not against this neoteric trend; it's interesting to see it happening and to be aware that the times are a-changing!

In this connection, mention was made earlier of slangy words, such as *rumble* and *rhubarb,* that have become part of our accepted speech. I for one do not take up the cudgels against slang. I think that *shiv* is

---

* *Nomenclature:* 1) name; appellation; 2) a set or system of names. This noun comes from two Latin words—*nomen* and *clator.* The former means "name" and the latter means "caller." Rather than "name-caller" it has come to mean "name-calling" because of the change in the suffix.

a perfect word for a daggerlike knife, and *slammer* aptly describes a jail. Thousands of other expressions in the vernacular intrigue me, because they hit the nail on the head, so to speak. *To raise Cain* (to become angry or violent) or *to hit the roof* (to lose one's temper) are still considered to be non-standard expressions. Ridiculous! These phrases, and legions of others, have added a certain zest to our language which we should all applaud.

I am reminded of *blizzard*. In New England, where I live, we are all afraid of such storms. In January 1978 one of them devastated towns on the Atlantic coast. Well, *blizzard* is an accepted word that once had a slangy origin. Actually, some lexicographers and philologists trace it back to "blaze"—the exact opposite of a severe snowstorm. In 1770, Colonel Landon Carter referred in his diary to "a mighty *blizz* of rain." In his day a *blizz* was any kind of storm. Meanwhile Davy Crockett was alluding to a volley of shots at bucks as a *blizzard*. Somehow the noun lost its connection with marksmanship and followed the course suggested by Colonel Carter. Rain? That was nothing compared with snow! A *blizzard* had to be a terrible invasion of what the C.B. (Citizens' Band) operators call "fluff stuff."

I mention the above only as one example of how our language has become a melting pot for neologists of all sorts, whether they come from rural or urban environments in America or from foreign lands, either ancient or modern. Sociologically, we embrace all kinds of people. And simultaneously we do the same thing in a linguistic sense. We have borrowed slang words and legitimate words from practically every other language in the world, and my contention is that each addition has enriched us tremendously.

But let me get off my soapbox and return to those astonishing Greeks. By this time every reader should be convinced that we owe them a debt that is beyond comprehension. This chapter has touched only the tip of the iceberg. Reserved for special consideration are such Greek roots as *crat* or *cracy*, *arch* or *archy*, *phag*, *phobia* or *phile*, *mania* and *logue* or *logy*. Obviously, volumes could be written on the wonderful vocabulary we have inherited from Homer, Euripides, Aristotle, Aristophanes, Pericles, Socrates, Plato and all those other remarkable people who flourished more than two thousand years ago. I wouldn't be surprised if scholars have already produced such tomes, but in this book we can afford only a scattered smattering.

Finally, allow me to present you with a creative challenge. Below I have listed a number of Greek roots. The idea is to unite them to make words. If some of your combinations are neologisms, all the better! A sampling of my own results can be found on pp. 431–32, in the Appendix. Combining *only the roots below,* I found 67 words in various lexicons. If you're an expert, you should be able to form at least 20 words without consulting a dictionary.

anthrop	man, mankind
astr, aster	star
bibli	book
bio	life
cosm	world
crypt	hidden
cycl	wheel, circle
derm	skin
dox	belief, teaching
gen	race; sex; offspring; causing to be
geo	earth
gram or *graph*	writing
hetero	other
homo	same
hydr	water
latr	worship
mega, megalo	large, great
metr, meter	measure
micr	small
nom	law, rule
onym	name
phot	light
polis	city

CHAPTER 2

Latin—A Living Language

Latin was my major subject at college. The English majors used to say with a sneer: "Why do you bother with Caesar and Cicero, or even Vergil and Ovid? It's a dead language. Nobody speaks it except a few scholars and monks."

And what were my scoffers studying? Chaucer and Shakespeare, among others. Chaucer! Who speaks Chaucerian English? Those English majors needed a trot to translate even the first line of the Prologue to the CANTERBURY TALES:

> "Whan that Aprille with his shoures sote
> The droghte of Marche hath perced to the rote."

That one happens to be relatively easy to fathom, especially if you supply "sweet" for "sote." But how about the following lines from the various tales?

> "So was hir joly whistle wel y-wet."

> "Men loven of propre kinde newfangelnesse."

> "This wol be doon at leyser parfitly."

> "Therefor bihoveth him a ful long spoon."

If the reader is asking, "How's that again?" I think I have scored a point. As for Shakespeare, it's almost impossible for even an English major to read an entire act without becoming befuddled somewhere along the line. Not that I have anything against the Bard or his fourteenth-century predecessor. Quite the contrary! But, in a way, theirs is no more a living language than Latin, because usage changes as the centuries come and go. Some words become archaic; others arise to take their place. Modifications of meanings of words continually occur too. For example, today the verb *to tent* generally means "to encamp." But Hamlet, when planning to catch his wicked uncle off guard, says, "I'll tent him to the quick." Translated, that line means "I'll probe to the very center of his mind and emotions."

The only living language is the language of now. And Latin is alive and well in all English-speaking countries. It also breathes vitally in Italy, France, Portugal, Spain and Rumania—the lands of the Romance languages.

Most scholars conclude that at least 60 percent of our words come directly or indirectly from the ancient Romans. It's also been estimated that a person combing an unabridged English dictionary and copying every word of Latin origin would take more than forty years to complete the task if he jotted down forty words each day.

In daily speech we depend more on our Anglo-Saxon heritage than on words of Latin ancestry. But most writers lean toward the classical and Romance languages. Essayists are especially prone to follow this course. One of the great ones was Sir Francis Bacon, a contemporary of Shakespeare's. Here's an example from "Of Youth and Age":

> "Young men are fitter to *invent* than to judge, fitter for *execution* than for *counsel,* and fitter for *new projects* than for *settled* business."

The words in italics are of Latin origin, although it must be added that "new" and "settled" are a mixed breed.

Shakespeare is quoted as having said that he had learned "a little Latin and less Greek." His plays reflect that statement, not because he was unacquainted with English words descended from those languages but for the good reason that his instincts as a playwright told him to communicate as clearly as possible to the audience in the pit. Hence he adhered greatly to words of Middle English background. But once in a while Latin was given its due. Witness the following passage from TROILUS AND CRESSIDA (Act I, Sc. 3):

> "The heavens themselves, the *planets,* and this *centre*
> *Observe degree, priority,* and *place,*
> *Insisture, course, proportion, season, form,*
> *Office,* and *custom,* in all *line* of *order.*"

Fathership of "planets," "centre" and "place" can also be claimed by the ancient Greeks, but all the other italicized words originated in old Rome.

Unlike Shakespeare, I was exposed to eight years of Latin and three years of Greek—and I consider myself fortunate. Caesar and Xenophon, with their descriptions of battles and military tactics, excited the imagination of a teenaged boy. The lofty lines of THE AENEID and THE ILIAD supplied not only inspiration but also the delightful feeling of being made privy to strange and important events that occurred ages and ages ago. Ovid was surprisingly sexy, and Lucretius astonishingly up-to-date, especially in his discussions of the power of the atom or his views on psychology.

But, as the saying goes, One man's meat is another man's poison. I hated most of my math courses, and I still get a headache when it's time to fill out an income-tax form. To this day I resent the fact that I was forced to take algebra, plane geometry, solid geometry and trigonometry. To me those subjects were excruciatingly painful and a waste of time. My point is that we are all born with certain hereditary bents, and high schools should allow more opportunities for elective courses.

Also, I deplore the fact that Latin I is taught less and less frequently in our schools today, and that etymology is practically a forgotten subject. In the eighth grade my classmates and I were taught roots, prefixes and suffixes for one hour each day. What a joy it was to learn new words in that fashion!

Note that I have singled out Latin I. Many of my contemporaries who took that course declare that it not only increased their word power tremendously but also gave them their initial insights into sentence structure, grammar and syntax—all invaluable assets in speaking or writing. When I hear a TV announcer say "between you and I," the error makes me shudder. I think of the accusative case in Latin and the phrase "inter nos," and I remember why I have no trouble with pronouns preceded by prepositions.

As for Latin II, III and the more advanced courses, I'd like to quote the boys from Madison Avenue. Their slogan is: "Let's run the idea up a flagpole and see who salutes it." Some of the Latin I students, if they have a good teacher, will salute it and opt for more. Others will say, "That's enough! On to French or Spanish or Italian!" A few will think this area of learning isn't their thing and drop foreign languages altogether. But it's hard to believe that, even for them, no residue of comprehension of the nuances of language usage and vocabulary building will remain.

Lawyers and physicians use Latin every day. When the Spiro Agnew case hit the headlines, Agnew's attorneys pleaded *nolo contendere* (literally, "I am unwilling to contend"). In other words, Agnew did not admit guilt but subjected himself to punishment as though he had pleaded guilty. In the slanguage of today, the Veep copped a plea. Sometimes the defense argues that the punishment is *ex post facto* ("formulated after the fact"). And all those lawyer-senators on Capitol Hill agree to adjourn *sine die** ("without a future day being designated for resumption"). These are only a few instances of the many uses of the so-called dead language in the legal profession.

---

* *Sine die* is a perfect example of how some Latin expressions become Anglicized in pronunciation. In ancient Rome the phrase sounded like this: "see-nay dee-ay." Today it is pronounced "sign-nee die-ee"!

As for the A.M.A. members, their prescriptions are sometimes scrawled in Latin abbreviations. In their anatomy courses they learn that a vein is a *vena* and the *venae cavae* are the large veins that discharge blood into the right atrium of the heart. *Atrium* itself is a word they borrowed from Caesar's compatriots. It was originally the central hall of a Roman house.

To an M.D., *cordia pulmonalia* is heart disease stemming from lung trouble, and *corpus callosum* is a great band of fibers in the human brain. Again, examples could be cited *ad infinitum* regarding the usage of Latin in the medical profession, but it behooves me not to elaborate on the argument *ad nauseam*.

Actually, Latin phrases flourish abundantly in our language and have many applications. Consider our abbreviations alone:

A.D.	(Anno Domini)	in the year of our Lord
A.M.	(ante meridiem)	before noon
P.M.	(post meridiem)	after noon
e.g.	(exempli gratia)	for the sake of the example; for example
Q.E.D.	(quod erat demonstrandum)	which was to be demonstrated
i.e.	(id est)	that is
M.O.	(modus operandi)	manner of operating or working. This abbreviation has been popularized by mystery books and TV programs. Its sister is *modus vivendi* ("manner of living or getting along"). A compromise between disputants is called a *modus vivendi*.
N.B.	(nota bene)	Note well.
D.T.'s	(delirium tremens)	violent state caused by prolonged alcoholism. Victims are often said to be *non compos mentis* ("not of sound mind").
R.I.P.	(requiescat in pace)	May he or she rest in peace. Associated phrases are *in memoriam* and *hic jacet*.

And, of course, many who graduate from their *alma mater* (fostering mother) receive an A.B., or B.A., degree (Artium Baccalaureus or *vice versa*). The M in M.A. stands for *magister*. From this Latin noun for "master" we have inherited *magistrate*.

Those same graduates may be given such honors as: cum laude—with praise; magna cum laude—with great praise; summa cum laude—with the highest praise.

In some colleges the "summa" distinction is conferred on a *rara avis* who is *sui generis* (unique). In others the honor is *pro forma* and should be taken *cum grano salis* (with a grain of salt). Sometimes it is bestowed as *quid pro quo* for a donation by a wealthy *pater*. But since such practices are *contra bonos mores* and not *pro bono publico,* favors to students are often granted *sub rosa.**

But not all who enter the groves of academe are successful. For some the hope of graduating is an *ignis fatuus* (delusion). *De novo* they are plunged *in medias res* and cannot compete. Their agonizing *de profundis* is never heard! No *deus ex machina* or *amicus curiae* comes to succor them. They do not even have a *fidus Achates* (trusty friend) on campus. Their chances of hearing *"Gaudeamus Igitur"* sung at graduation are nil. Like gladiators before Caesar, they whisper hoarsely to their eminent professors, *"Morituri te salutamus!"* And in turn, like Pilate, does each *Philosophiae Doctor* declare, *"Ecce homo"*?

Sometimes a classmate will reach out *sponte sua* (of his own accord) and try to help. *"Nil desperandum!"* he will advise, or *"Carpe diem!"* In vain he will tell the poor soul to make this year his *annus mirabilis* and explain that the *ne plus ultra* is to score an A on all exams by cramming for weeks beforehand. But, confused and discouraged, the future dropout will reply with *non sequiturs* or resign himself to the *status quo*. Ah, what a contrast between *Homo sapiens* and *homo faber* (man the creator)! And when such a paraclete finally gives up, it often happens that the failing student will cry, *"Et tu, Brute!"* instead of *"Mea culpa!"*

In college I knew such a person. Felix Fargonne was his name. He was always in a hurry. *"Festina lente"* ("Make haste slowly"), I would tell him, but he never listened. *"Cui bono?"* was his usual reply. Instead of studying (the *sine qua non* of success) he would go out at night and gaze up at *Canis Major, Canis Minor, Ursa Major, Ursa Minor* and even the *Aurora Borealis*. I tried to impress on him that our *summum bonum* was to graduate and get good jobs in which we could draw high salaries *per annum*. Stubbornly, he declared, "That's an *argumentum ad hominem!"* *Noli me tangere* (Don't touch me) seemed to be his motto.

Well, I could have defeated him with some *bona fide* statements that would have fallen into the category of *reductio ad absurdum,* but I refrained.

All of this happened in the *ante bellum* period before F.D.R. found

---

* *Sub rosa* (literally, "under the rose")—covertly; secretly; privately. This phrase stems from the ancient custom of hanging a rose over the council table to indicate that everybody is sworn to secrecy. It is probably connected with the legend that Cupid gave a rose to Harpocrates (god of silence) to stop him from exposing Venus' indiscretions. Incidentally, note the similarity between Harpocrates and Harpo Marx! Both were silent!

a *casus belli* at Pearl Harbor. Then, one day, it happened! While reading Horace's *"Ars Poetica"* (or was it Ovid's *"Ars Amatoria"*?), Felix drank too much *aqua vitae* (brandy). Would that he had stuck to *aqua pura!*

De gustibus non disputandum est, but I always preferred to stay away from the stuff. I wanted to keep my mind a *tabula rasa* (clean slate) on which the professors could imprint their ideas. But you know the old saying: *In vino veritas* (In wine there is truth). Like Julius Caesar at the Rubicon, Felix cried out, *"Jacta est alea!"* ("The die is cast!") and began *nolens volens* (willy-nilly) to curse the faculty and administrators. He was caught *flagrante delicto* (red-handed). Later the dignitaries met *in camera.* Though recognizing that he had anathematized them *in extremis,* nevertheless an *ad hoc* committee declared him *persona non grata.*

Felix argued that he had suffered a *lapsus linguae* and even a *lapsus memoriae,* but to no avail. *Inter nos,* I believe that the committee decided against him because he was a *nullius filius* (bastard) and there was no one to defend him *in loco parentis.* By the way, as an *obiter dictum,* the faculty wrote a derogatory statement on his transcript. This calumniation prevented him *de facto* from enrolling elsewhere. It was really a case of *post hoc, ergo propter hoc* (illogical reasoning) on their part, but I suppose he was destined *ab initio* to be a failure in that institution.

Quid novi re Felix? Well, the faculty's *ipse dixit* (dogmatic statement), which was really not made *bona gratia* (in all kindness), proved to be his good fortune. He started a rock group in New Orleans and raked in a million. Naturally, a *curriculum vitae* (resumé) is not important for that kind of work. In his last letter to me he wrote: *"Vox populi* has triumphed! They've made me a star, at least *pro tempore!* And by the way, *mirabile dictu,* at the next Mardi Gras I'll be the *rex bibendi* (king of the revels)! *Bene vale!"*

———

Aside from the above, Latin phrases are often used in mottoes. Here's an *omnium gatherum* ("miscellaneous collection") of such sayings. You are asked to match the mottoes on the left with the places or groups on the right. The answers appear on p. 434, in the Appendix.

1. E pluribus unum (One out of many)	a. Queen Elizabeth
2. Deo juvante (With God's help)	b. U.S. Coast Guard
3. Semper eadem (Always the same)	c. Virginia
4. Crescit eundo. (It grows as it goes.)	d. Monaco
5. Per ardua ad astra (Through difficulties to the stars)	e. Yale
6. Sic semper tyrannis (Thus ever to tyrants)	f. Kansas
7. Lux et veritas (Light and truth)	g. U.S.A.

8. Ad astra per aspera (To the stars through h. R.A.F.
   hardships)
9. Semper paratus (Always ready) i. Constantine the Great
10. In hoc signo vinces. (In this sign thou shalt j. New Mexico
    conquer.)

Since the Roman Catholic Church and others held onto Latin for so many centuries, naturally a number of hymns in that language have become familiar. Can you translate the following into English? The answers appear on p. 434, in the Appendix.

1. "Adeste Fideles"
2. "Agnus Dei"
3. "Asperges"
4. "Ave Maria"
5. "Dies Irae"
6. "Gloria in Excelsis Deo"
7. "Gloria Patri"
8. "Nunc Dimittis"
9. "Stabat Mater"
10. "Tantum Ergo"

The use of "Gloria" in two of the preceding hymns reminds me of another Latin saying that is used when someone who is rich or famous suddenly comes upon misfortune. "Sic transit gloria mundi," we say. It literally means "So passes away the glory of the world."

In jest I once wrote a couplet punning on that expression:

"Gloria rode the subway Sunday;
Sic transit Gloria mundi!"

Those lines were triggered by a real experience. For six years I had to hang onto a subway strap for almost an hour in order to get to work. And then the awful trip back home! It really made me sick in transit from Monday through Friday.

In the New York City high school that I attended, the custom was to buy your textbooks from a student in the class just above you. It was also customary for the seller to inscribe some verses for the edification of the buyer. One of my English books contained this gem:

"The wind blew down the avenue;
The women's skirts flew high.
But God is just; He blew the dust
Right in the bad man's eye!"

That titillating bit of theological philosophy was easy to understand. But the inscription at the front of my Latin I text really puzzled me for months. It read:

> "Isabile haeres ego,
> Fortibus es in ero.
> O nobile, themis trux!
> Vaticinem? Pes in dux!"

You can imagine how I combed my Latin dictionary in an effort to translate the jingle. Desperately I sought out my seller, Peter Reilly, and asked what it meant. But, like any supercilious* sophomore, he just grinned and advised me to study harder. I cannot recall how and when I finally solved the mystery. Maybe it started to unravel when I perused that last line. "In dux?" No, it had to be "in ducem" or "in duce." Reilly's inscription was a put-on!

Now, dear reader, if you haven't figured out the translation already or if it continues to baffle you, turn to p. 434, in the Appendix, and you'll get a surprise.

Incidentally, Reilly's verse was not pig Latin. Isthay isnay igpay atinlay! For the uninitiated, that sentence reads: "This is pig Latin!" As far as I can determine, nobody seems to know who invented that linguistic trick. But in my high school days it provided my friends and me with a merry release from Caesar and Cicero. We also got our kicks making up monstrous Latin-English sentences, such as "Tempus fugits; non cumbaccibus."

Speaking of monstrosities, have you ever heard of a *circumbendibus?* It's a roundabout way. And if a speaker uses a lot of words to say very little, his circumlocution can also be called *circumbendibus.* Of course it's not a legitimate Latin word. Some wag placed an ablative suffix on *bend* and attached his neologism to *circum.*

This reminds me of the funny thing that happened to *asparagus* in the seventeenth century. Some folks started to call it *sparrow grass* because of the similarity of sounds. For a while the term caught on, but in the 1800s educated people returned to the original. Now *sparrow grass* is considered uncouth. By the way, our spelling of *asparagus* is exactly the same as that of the Romans.

---

* *Supercilious.* The derivation of this word tickles me. *Super* means "above" and *cilious* is from the Latin word *cilium,* meaning "eyebrow." When people raise their eyebrows in haughty fashion they are indeed *supercilious!*

CHAPTER 3

As the Romans Said It

T he last sentence of the previous chapter has generated this one. It is indeed amazing how many Latin words have come down to us *in toto*, or completely unchanged. Since so many of them end in *um, us, a* and *or,* let us concentrate on those words.

Rather than give a complete list, it seems best to divide them into alphabetical segments and comment on the meanings and histories of some of them.

Let's start with words ending in *um,* because there are so many of them that we have inherited either from the early Romans or from Medieval Latin.

Herewith begins a partial list:

addendum	atrium	curriculum	encomium
album	auditorium	datum	erratum
alluvium	bacterium	decorum	exordium
aluminum	candelabrum	delirium	factotum
antrum	cerebrum	desideratum	forum
aquarium	chrysanthemum	dictum	fulcrum
arboretum	colosseum	effluvium	
asylum	consortium	emporium	

Let us examine a few of the above words.

Album is the neuter form of *albus,* the Latin adjective for "white." Since the tablet on which Roman edicts were written was white, it was called an *album.* Fittingly enough, today most photographic albums for weddings have white covers.

Consortium means "association; fellowship." From this same root we get *consort,* which can be a verb or a noun. As the former it means "to associate." The noun carries the idea of "mate or spouse."

Curriculum is "a body of courses offered by an educational institution." Once more we encounter a noun taken bodily from Latin but changed in meaning through the years. The early Romans called a racecourse a *curriculum*. Later it became the running itself, and finally a career. Anyone who has tried to keep up with competitors in his vocation will understand how appropriate that particular definition is! And college students will agree that their *curriculum* keeps them running. This word, by the way, has a slew of relatives—all coming from *currere* ("to run"). Consider *current, currency, concur, occur, recur,* and even *course, concourse, discourse* and *recourse.*

Exordium today means "the introduction to a speech or composition." The Latin noun is an offshoot of *exordiri* ("to begin a web"). Thus when an orator or writer starts off, he is beginning to spin a web of words in the hope that his *exordium* will catch the interest of the listener or reader.

Factotum literally means "do everything." An employee who has a variety of tasks and responsibilities is called a *factotum.*

Fulcrum in Latin came to mean "bedpost." The noun was derived from *fulcire* ("to support or prop up"). Today it is defined as "the support on which a lever turns."

As we continue with the *um* category, it should be noted that the Romans borrowed some of these words from the Greeks and usually changed an *on* ending to *um*. Also it's interesting to observe how many of these words today retain the Latin plural ("a") instead of adding an *s*. For example, misprints are called *errata,* not *erratums.*

geranium	labium	memorandum	museum
gymnasium	lustrum	millennium	nostrum
helium	magnum	minimum	odium
herbarium	mausoleum	modicum	opprobrium
honorarium	maximum	momentum	
interregnum	medium	moratorium	

A second look at some of the words in the above columns will be rewarding.

Geranium is one of the Latin words borrowed from the Greeks. To the Athenians a *geranion* was a small crane. Its resemblance to a crane's bill gave the flower its name. In fact, a modern synonym for geranium is cranes-bill.

Helium is a New Latin word. The gas was named for *helios,* the Greek noun for "sun." The reason is that the element was discovered during an examination of the solar spectrum.

Lustrum has a fascinating history. Today it means a period of five years, or a *quinquennium*. It's related to *lucere* ("to shine"). The Romans' lustrum was a ceremonious purification of the populace. It was conducted after the census, which was taken every five years. Thus the Romans were forced to "rise and shine" twice each decade!

Magnum is a wine bottle holding twice as much as the usual vessel does. It contains about two-fifths of a gallon. In other words, it's large. The noun comes from the neuter form of *magnus,* the Latin adjective for "great." *Maximum* is the superlative form. (See *Circus Maximus,* later in this chapter.)

Mausoleum is also a derivative of a Greek word. The original *mausōleion* was the tomb of King Mausolus at Halicarnassus.

Medium meant "middle" to Cicero. One use of the word today applies to a person through whom communications are supposedly sent to the living from the spirits of the dead. A *medium,* then, is a middleman—or should I say middleperson? Incidentally, Robert Browning once found a medium at his home and irately chased the spiritualist away. 'Tis said that this was a unique example of an *unhappy medium.*

Moratorium today means "an authorized delay." To the Romans a *mora* was a delay. In legal terminology today it retains that sense.

Museum once was *mouseion* in Athens. It meant "a place for the Muses to study." The Romans altered the spelling, and soon the Muses were left out. It became a place for any would-be scholar to study or learn. The word is a first cousin of *music.*

Nostrum is the neuter form of *noster,* the Latin word meaning "ours." How did it come to mean a patent medicine? Lexicographers guess that it derives from the sellers' cries, meaning "our drug." Perhaps they cried: "Nostrum medicamentum est optimum!" ("Our remedy is best!")

Now let's conclude our list of those intriguing *um* words.

pabulum	quorum	simulacrum	sudarium
pendulum	referendum	solarium	trivium
petroleum	residuum	spectrum	tympanum
podium	rostrum	stadium	ultimatum
proscenium	scriptorium	stratum	vacuum
quantum			

Most of these nouns deserve our close attention. In my opinion, some of the most exciting words in this book are contained in the above grouping.

Pabulum was the Romans' word for "food or fodder," and it still retains the same meaning. But along came a company that called its cereal for infants *Pablum,* and the name stuck! Today many writers use that spelling in place of *pabulum* to mean "oversimplified or tasteless ideas, or insipid intellectual nourishment." This is just one of many instances of how we latch onto the catch words in commercial advertisements and are led to accept them into our language. Consider Silex, Saran and Kleenex as just a few examples.

Pendulum is the neuter form of *pendulus* ("hanging"). The eventual source is the verb *pendere* ("to hang"). From this root, and its sister verb ("to weigh"), we also obtain such words as *pendant, pendent, dependent, impend, compendium, compensate, pension, pensive, propensity, expend, expensive, dispense, dispensation, perpendicular* and a host of others.

Petroleum is one of the most vital sources of energy in this modern era. The word was not known to the ancient Romans, but it comes to us via Medieval Latin. Actually, it's a sort of hybrid. The Romans acquired *petra* ("rock") from the Greeks. *Oleum* was the Latin word meaning "oil." Sometimes, by the way, it meant "olive oil." At any rate, *petroleum* literally means "rock oil."

Podium is another Latin borrowing. The Greek word was *podion,* and it meant "a small foot." Even today zoologists retain some of the original import. To them, a *podium* is "a foot or hand, or footlike structure." The noun can also mean "a low wall or bench projecting from a wall." But most of us think of it as a synonym for dais.

Kinship of words always intrigues me. It's somewhat exciting to discover that podium is related to *podiatrist* ("foot specialist") and *chiropodist.* It's even a cousin of *pew.* That word was altered in Medieval French and English.

Proscenium literally means "the place before the scene." If you substitute "set" for "scene," you'll see how today it is the apron of a stage, or the area in front of the curtain. But the most delightful aspect of the noun is that its main root can be traced back to *skēnē,* the Greek word for "tent." Such words as *scene, scenery, scenario* and *scenic,* for example, are in the same "tent," so to speak. But not *obscene.* Appropriately, that adjective eventually stems from *caenum,* the Latin word for "filth."

But you may ask what connection "tent" has with "stage." Well, the ancient actors used the *skēnē* as a dressing room. Incidentally, every summer in Hyannis, Massachusetts, for many decades, top entertainers have been performing at an airy structure called the Melody Tent.

―――――

Quantum is the neuter form of *quantus,* a Latin adjective meaning "how great or how much." It is related to *quantity* and means exactly that. But physicists have taken over the word. Their *quantum theory* is based on Max Planck's concepts concerning radiant energy. To them a *quantum jump* or *leap* is an abrupt transition of an atom or other particle from one energy state to another. The phrase has become popularized to mean "any sudden or extensive change or advance in a program or policy."

―――――

Rostrum has an intricate history. In ancient Latin it took on many meanings:

1. the accomplisher of gnawing; hence the bill, beak, snout, mouth or muzzle of an animal
2. the curved end of a ship's prow; a ship's beak
3. structure for speakers in the Forum (usually *rostra,* plural form)

The first definition evolved because the word stemmed from *rosus,* the past participle of *rodere* ("to gnaw"). Thus *rostrum* is related to *rodent* and even to *rat.*

The second definition developed because the ancients often carved the bows of their ships to resemble the beaks of huge birds.

The third definition is one we recognize today. After a war the victorious Romans would decorate the Forum platforms with the beaks of captured ships.

But it should be noted that modern biologists still consider *rostrum* to mean "a beak or beaklike process or part."

―――――

Simulacrum has a nice ring to it. Today, as in ancient Rome, it means "an image or likeness." A second definition is "mere pretense; sham." *Simulate* and *dissimulate* ("to hide one's feelings") are members of the same family. The mother root is *simulare* ("to imitate or feign").

―――――

Solarium originally meant "a sundial or a water clock." In Cicero's day it came to mean "a flat housetop, a terrace or balcony exposed to the sun." *Sol,* as you may know, was the Latin word for "sun." Today a *solarium* is a sun parlor.

―――――

Spectrum and *specter* are sisters! Both can mean "an apparition." In fact, that was the definition given to *spectrum* by the Romans. In 1671, Sir Isaac Newton's special use of the word caught on. Now we consider it as a series of colored bands diffracted by the passage of white light through a prism. In school we had a mnemonic for the colors: ROY G. BIV (red, orange, yellow, green, blue, indigo, violet).

Today the meaning of *spectrum* has been considerably broadened, probably as a result of that wide array of colored bands. We use the word to indicate a continuous range or entire extent or broad sequence of ideas. Recently I read that Thomas Wolfe was "eager to grasp the whole *spectrum* of knowledge."

The word has its origin in *specere* ("to look at"). What a large clan has developed from that verb and its cousin *spectare!* Here are only a few examples: *specimen, spy, spectacles, spectator, respect, inspect, conspectus, prospector* and *expectation.*

Two that appeal to me are *suspect* and *suspicion.* When you *suspect* something or someone, you literally look underneath! But my favorite is *circumspect* ("careful or cautious"). A *circumspect* person will look about before he leaps.

Stadium is another of those words that the Romans took over from the Greeks. In Athens a *stadion* was a measure equaling 600 feet. And so it became a Roman measure too. But the Greeks had enlarged the meaning of the word. Since their courses for footraces were 600 feet long, they called the grounds for such races *stadia.* Again the Romans followed suit. As time went by, seats for spectators were installed and walls were erected around each *stadium,* or athletic event. Thus today when we speak of Yankee Stadium, we think of the entire structure. The measure of length and the footraces are long forgotten.

Sudarium may be unfamiliar to most readers. In Suetonius' day it meant "handkerchief." It came from *sudare* ("to sweat"). Hence it was an object used to wipe off perspiration.

Today *sudarium* is used as a synonym for a *Veronica.** This comes from an old legend that Saint Veronica gave Christ a cloth with which to wipe his face as he carried the cross. Miraculously, his image appeared on the cloth. Thus any cloth containing a representation of Christ's countenance is called a *Veronica* or *sudarium.*

The noun also is sometimes equated with *sudatorium* ("a hot-air room used for sweat baths"). Etymologically it is not related to *sauna*

---

* A *veronica* is also a bullfighter's maneuver, but in that sense it is apparently not directly related to the saint. See Chapter 7. Finally it is a lovely flower; as such, it is often called a speedwell.

—a word of Finnish origin. But it is definitely a cousin of *exude*. That verb stems from *exsudare* ("to sweat it out").

Tympanum was a drum to Caesar. Originally it was a Greek word, *tympanon,* with the same meaning. In modern usage it means the "eardrum or middle ear."

From that same Greek root we get *tympany* ("resonance obtained by percussion") and *tympanist* ("drummer").

But the most thrilling discovery I have recently made is the fact that *tympanum* can be finally traced back to *typtein,* a Greek verb meaning "to strike or beat." From that source we derive such words as *typography, prototype, archetype, typical* and others. And since *tympanist* and *typist* are related, the latter can certainly be considered as a sort of drummer.

Ultimatum in Latin means "the last part." We use the word to signify a final offer or demand. In plural form both *ultimata* and *ultimatums* are acceptable.

There's a funny story connected with *ultimata.* An educated woman was berating her local fruit dealer for his high prices. In exasperation, he ultimately told her to get out or he would throw her out. She replied, "Don't give me any of your *ultimata!*" The dealer was shocked for a moment. Then he retorted, "My tomaters are fresh, lady —just as fresh as you!"

Vacuum, to the best of my knowledge, is one of three bona fide English words that contain successive *u*'s; the other two are *residuum* ("remainder") and *menstruum* ("a solvent"). Maybe some reader can tell me if there are any others.

I am reminded of the question that is going around among word lovers: "Can you name three words that end in *gry?*" Everybody immediately answers: "Angry and hungry." But what's the third one? Well, it's not to be found in any abridged lexicon. The word is "aggry," which *Webster's New International Dictionary* (Second Edition) defines as "Designating a kind of variegated glass beads, of ancient manufacture, found in the Gold Coast, West Africa."

Now is there any other *gry* ending that has escaped me?

To get back to *vacuum,* it is the neuter form of the Latin adjective *vacuus* ("empty, void"). Our own adjective is *vacuous,* from the same root. Like the Romans, we have extended the scope of the word to mean "vain or inane." But *vacuum* itself means "the absence of matter" or "empty space." A device creating or utilizing partially empty space is, naturally, a *vacuum cleaner.*

The parental verb is *vacare* ("to be empty"). Thus when a position is *vacated,* it is emptied, and when people are *evacuated* from a house, they are literally emptied out. The Romans also defined *vacare* as "to be free from labor or unoccupied." And so *vacationers* truly live in a *vacuum!*

———

Just as some scientists and similar learned persons have always been enthralled by Greek, others have been entranced by Latin. When they coin words, they use what we call Modern Latin. Some examples are: *planetarium, platinum, radium, sodium* and *uranium. Linoleum* is a word coined in 1863 by an English manufacturer named Walton. He combined *linum* ("flax") with *oleum* ("oil"). Linseed oil (used in the product) does come from flax, so I suppose his neologism was not amiss.

———

Tedium, premium and *equilibrium* can be linked for one special reason. They are typical of Latin words that have come down to us with one slight change: the *a* in front of the *e* has been dropped. For instance, when **Vergil** was weary, he suffered from *taedium.* Ovid talked of *praemium* when he was referring to profit taken from booty (Insurance companies, take note!), and Seneca's *aequilibrium* was a level or horizontal position. The poor fellow found it when Nero ordered him to commit suicide!

———

Sanatorium and *sanitarium* are New Latin words. If the ancient Romans had places to care for physically or mentally ill people, it's news to me. At any rate, both words are descendants of *sanitas* ("health"). Some other members of the family are *sanitary, sane, insane* and *sanity.*

———

Have you ever heard of a *teetotum?* It's a small top inscribed with letters and used in put-and-take. My parents and I often played that game. We would spin the tiny metal top and wait until it fell on its side. Sometimes its message would read *P-1* (meaning "Put up one coin or other object"). *T-1* was better and *T-All* was best! Of course the top could have been named *peetotum* (for "put all"), but I guess the inventors of the game were wary of other connotations. Anyway, *tee* stands for "take" and *totum* (from Latin) means "all."

———

What about *bunkum, hokum, hoodlum, panjandrum, tantrum* and *wampum?* Well, it's obvious that those words never reached the ears of Brutus or Caesar.

Bunkum has made Buncombe County, North Carolina, famous— or infamous, if you will—ever since 1820. Felix Walker, a congressman from that county, took the floor and prattled on and on about matters that had no relation to the question being discussed. When asked to yield, he refused and said that the people of his district expected him to "make a speech for Buncombe."

After that the phrase "to speak for Buncombe" became a joke. It carried the idea of babbling away just to be heard or to gain popularity back home. Soon the word *buncombe* became a synonym for nonsense or humbug. Later it was shortened to *bunkum,* and finally it became just plain *bunk.*

Does *bunco* or *bunko* (meaning "a swindle or con game") come from the same source? Some philologers think it does. Others surmise that it's a variation of *banca,* the Italian or Spanish word for "bank." This seems logical, especially because "bank" is a sum of money in certain gambling games. By the way, I was once swindled out of ten dollars by a *bunco steerer* in Milan. After I realized that I'd been duped, I felt punco!

Hokum is thought to be an abridged combination of *hocus-pocus* and *bunkum.* As for *hocus-pocus* itself, it's believed that the term was invented by jugglers in imitation of Latin (something like *circumbendibus*).

Hoodlum may have come from a Swiss word *hudilump* ("wretch, miserable fellow"). The slang word *hood* is a curtailment of *hoodlum.*

Panjandrum is a mellisonant word for a "self-important, pretentious official." It was invented by Samuel Foote, an eighteenth-century actor-playwright. In some nonsense lines he called an imaginary character *Grand Panjandrum.*

Nobody knows the origin of *tantrum,* but *wampum* comes from a compound Algonquian noun *wampumeage* ("white string of beads"). Since the Indians sometimes used beads for money, *wampum* has become one of the slangy synonyms for currency—along with *greenbacks, moola, dough, bread, jack, shekels, cabbage, lettuce,* et cetera, et cetera.

Interesting, isn't it, that so many items of food are synonymous in the lingo of the street with money? I think this is an example of *metonymy*—the practice of using one name for another with which it is associated.

But it's time to return to those Latin words that have come down to us unchanged in spelling, and often in meaning too. Next on our list is the category that ends in *us,* such as *afflatus, arbutus, citrus* and others below.

abacus	angelus	bacillus
acanthus	animus	bolus
alumnus	apparatus	bonus

cactus	colossus	fetus
caduceus	consensus	focus
calculus	conspectus	fungus
callus	corpus	genius
campus	crepitus	genus
census	crus	gladius
cestus	cumulus	Hesperus
chorus	discus	hiatus
circus	emeritus	humerus
cirrus	exodus	humus

Now let's take a hard look at some of the words in the above list before we go on to another group of *us* inheritances.

Acanthus was described by Vergil as a thorny Egyptian evergreen tree. This is one of the many words that the Romans borrowed from the Greeks and transliterated. To the Athenians it meant "a thorny plant," and that's what it means today. The flower grows naturally in Mediterranean regions and has been brought to America as a garden adornment. Have you ever noticed the ornamentation atop a Corinthian architectural column? It represents or suggests the leaves of the *acanthus*.

Alumnus meant "pupil or foster son" in Horace's heyday, and an *alumna* was a foster daughter. Both words stemmed from *alere* ("to nourish"). The British still retain the original idea, but we Americans have altered it to mean "a graduate" or one who has been intellectually nourished by his alma mater.

Angelus is a form of devotion for Roman Catholics. It has the same roots as angel. My own devotion to this word comes from my early love for Millet's painting *"The Angelus."* I didn't understand that the two peasants were bowing their heads in prayer because of the ringing of the *Angelus bell,* but I was moved by the entire scene. How did I come across it? In a jigsaw present at Christmastime!

Animus fascinates me. It originally meant "soul, aim, mind, will, desire, passion." Plautus used it to signify affection; but Tacitus described it as "haughtiness or arrogance," and to Terence it was a synonym for anxiety. As so often happens in linguistic history, evil triumphed. Today most people think of *animus* as ill will or hatred. *Animosity* ("enmity") and *animadversion* ("censure") come from this same root. However, there is still some hope left. In many dictionaries the first meaning of *animus* is "intention or objective," and another definition is "inspiration." May the Force be with those connotations in the future!

Apparatus literally means "a making preparation." If you have the right tools, you are prepared. Incidentally, a city in New Jersey that has recently grown by leaps and bounds is called Paramus. I wonder how many of its residents know that it means "We get ready."

Bacillus is one of the rod-shaped bacteria. In Low Latin (of medieval origin) it meant "little rod." The parental word is *baculus* ("stick").

Bonus has an obvious history. If your boss gives you a *bonus,* that's good!

Caduceus lives today because it is one of the symbols of physicians. This staff with two snakes wound around it is also an emblem of the U.S. Medical Corps. Originally it was a herald's staff. But those serpents are two of the reasons the A.M.A. has adopted it. To the ancients a snake was a sort of token of reincarnation, because the reptile could slough off its old skin periodically and produce a new covering. Thus word eventually got around that it had the power to ferret out medicinal herbs.

The *caduceus* was also the staff toted by Mercury (or Hermes) the wing-footed messenger of the gods. Would that today's physicians were as speedy when asked to make house calls!

Calculus to a Roman meant "a pebble." The ancients used little stones when they *calculated.* Q.E.D.

Callus is a Latin variation of *callum* ("hard, thick skin"). From it we derive the adjective *callous.* If you know a person who fits that description, he is literally thick-skinned.

Campus originally meant "plain or field." The *Campus Martius* (Field of Mars) was a grassy area in which the Romans held contests, military exercises and assemblies.

Census comes directly to us from Caesar's time. In those days it was a registering and rating of Roman citizens and their property. The parent verb was *censare* ("to assess"). From it we also derive *censor, censorious* and even *censure*—another example of how evil connotations seem to thrive.

Recently I heard a joke about *census* that you may enjoy:

> STOOGE: Do you know that China hasn't calculated its population for the last twenty years?
> COMEDIAN: It's about time that country came to its *census!*

Chorus is another word lent by the Greeks to the Romans. The Athenian word was *choros.* In ancient days it meant "a dance in a ring" and later "a band of people singing and dancing." Thus we can see that this word has retained its pristine denotations. Incidentally, *choir* is from the same root.

Circus meant "ring" to ancient Romans. Their *Circus Maximus* was literally the largest ring. You can still see it today if you visit Rome.

Cirrus in modern times is associated with cloud. A *cirrus* cloud is wispy. In Latin the word means "tuft of hair." Enough said!

Colossus still means "a gigantic statue," as it did in Pompey's period. Now it also carries the idea of any huge or important person or thing. Again, the Greeks were originally responsible for this word. Around 280 B.C., Chares of Lindus designed and built the *Colossus of Rhodes,* one of the Seven Wonders of the World. 'Tis said that ships could sail between its legs. Unfortunately an earthquake toppled the huge creation in 224 B.C.

Shakespeare makes reference to this work when Cassius is trying to entice Brutus into a conspiracy against Caesar. He says:

> "Why, man, he doth bestride the narrow world
> Like a *Colossus;* and we petty men
> Walk under his huge legs, and peep about
> To find ourselves dishonourable graves."

What a persuasive argument! If I had been Brutus I probably would have succumbed on the spot.

Finally, I should mention that the Roman Colosseum and the Coliseum in New York City owe their titles to the same Latin word. And, of course, *colossal* is a derivative.

Consensus literally means "feeling together." Hence its present usage as a synonym for unanimity or accord is certainly appropriate. It's interesting to note that many people spell this word incorrectly by substituting a *c* for the first *s.*

Conspectus is defined as "a survey, outline or synopsis." To the Romans it meant "a view or range of sight."

Corpus in Latin means "body." Today the *corpus delicti* ("body of the crime") is what the detectives look for in homicide cases. *Habeas corpus* is a legal writ ordering a person to be brought to court. It translates verbatim into "You should have the body."

Most interesting is the fact that this word gives us *corps* ("body of troops"), *corporation, corpse, incorporeal* ("having no material body") and *corpulent.* When a person has lots of body, he's *corpulent.* And when a teacher administers *corporal* punishment, he or she hurts the body.

Does the noncom come from this same root? Probably not. His ancestry is usually traced back to caput ("head").

Crepitus means "crackling," from *crepitare* ("to rattle, creak, rustle, crackle or clatter"). When firecrackers go off on July 4, they *crepitate.* The adjective *decrepit* is one of the relatives. If a building is *decrepit,* it literally is creaking away.

Then again, the structure might be *dilapidated.* That word comes from *lapidare* ("to throw stones"). If we break the word down, it means that the building's stones are thrown apart!

Crocus is a word you really should look up if etymology excites you. The Romans took it from the Greeks, but that lovely spring bloomer also has a Semitic and Assyrian history. It's nice to know that a bloom that pokes up from posthiemal ground today also thrilled the folks who lived more than two thousand years ago.

Discus is a circular object thrown in Olympic games. From that word we have obtained *disc* and *disk.* Did you ever wonder why there is a difference in spelling? Well, the Greek word was *diskos;* hence the confusion. When you refer to a "D.J." (player of recorded music on radio programs), is he a *disc jockey* or a *disk jockey?* The answer is, either. *Disc* is preferred, because of our attachment to the Romans.

From the same root we get *dish.* Actually, this word goes back to *dikein* ("to throw"). Like Maggie in an old comic strip, can you picture Xanthippe throwing plates at Socrates?

Emeritus, as an adjective or noun, conveys the idea that a person (a professor, for example) is an honored retiree. Originally the word meant "one who has served his time; a veteran." *Merit* and *demerit* are in the same family.

Exodus is a Medieval Latin extraction from *exodos,* the Greek word for "a going out." As you probably know, the *Exodus* is the departure of the Israelites, under Moses, from Egypt. The second book of the Bible describes that event and is named for it.

Focus in old Roman days meant "fireplace or hearth." Since it was the spot where the family gathered, it took on the idea of the center of activity. Somewhere along the line other meanings were attached to it, and the noun even acquired a verbal sense. When you *focus* on a problem, you concentrate on it.

———

Fungus originally meant "mushroom" and was probably a Latin modification of *spongos* (the Greek word for "sponge"). Such writers as Plautus added another dimension to the noun. Because of the texture of the top of a mushroom, *fungus* also came to mean "a soft-headed fellow; a dolt." Strangely, considering the human penchant for calling names, that connotation has not survived. But here's a new word for your list: *fungistatic*. It means "preventing the growth of fungi without killing them."

———

Genius started out as a Roman's tutelary spirit. Just as many people today believe that they are watched over and protected by guardian angels, the ancients felt that a particular spirit was assigned to each person at birth. Soon, by metonymy, the sense of the word was extended to mean "wit or talent." Finally, as time went on, the noun was applied to any person with great mental capacity. Incidentally, through the French, we have also received *genie*. To the Arabs that beneficent or malevolent spirit is a *jinn* or *jinni* or *jinnee*.

Someone may ask if *genial* is a member of this family. The answer is yes if you mean "amiable; friendly." But there is another adjective with the same spelling. It means "relating to the chin" and is derived from Greek. So if you said, "That *genial* gentleman has a prominent *genial* feature," your statement would not be tautological.

———

Genus originally meant "birth, origin, race, species, kind." The Romans took it from the Greeks' *genos*. The *gen, gene* root has given us a host of words, among them: *gender, gene, genealogy, general, generation, generic, generosity, genesis, genetics, genocide, genre, genteel, Gentile, gentle, gentleman* and *gentry*.

Also there are *congenital, degenerate, ingenious, ingenuous, progenitor,* and so on.

A favorite of mine is *genethliac* ("relating to birthdays"). And naturally I'm pleased to report that *Eugene* means "well born."

———

Gladius was a Roman soldier's short sword. Today it's a horny part of a squid. But its diminutive relation *gladiolus* is better known. The flower was so called because of its swordlike leaves. And let us not forget *gladiator*—literally, "a swordsman."

———

Hesperus was *Hesperos* to the Greeks. This son of Eos and brother of Atlas became identified with the West. In fact, his name meant "west" to ancient Athenians. Their appellation for Italy was Hesperia ("the western land"). More specifically, the god's name was applied to the evening star, because it sets in the west. Hesperus therefore is a synonym for Venus.

The Romans developed still another synonym as an offshoot of *Hesperus.* They called the evening star *Vesper* and also applied the word to the evening itself. This transition might be called "the wreck of the *Hesperus.*" Seriously, *vespers* are now church songs for the late afternoon or evening.

Hiatus is the past participle of *hiare* ("to gape or yawn"). Today a *hiatus* is a break in a manuscript where a part is missing or lost. It is also any gap or opening and is often used to mean an interruption or lapse in a time period. A typical application of this sense of the word is: "How do teachers spend their time during the *hiatus* between June and September?"

Humerus today is just what it was in Cicero's era—the bone of the upper arm. When this bone is bumped, the nerve often tingles in a strange or funny sort of way. Thus it's appropriate that some humorous person dubbed it "the funny bone," and the name has stuck.

Humus almost means the same to us as it did to the Romans. They used the term for "soil or ground." We regard it as the organic part of soil. I suppose you've heard about the unsuccessful gardener: he lacked a sense of *humus.*

And now to continue our list:

iambus	lotus	nidus	plus
ictus	magus	nimbus	prospectus
ignoramus	mandamus	nucleus	radius
impetus	minus	octopus	ramulus
incubus	mittimus	omnibus	rebus
incus	naevus	onus	
locus	nexus	plexus	

Iambus is just a Latin variation of the Athenians' *iambos*—a metrical foot. 'Tis said that an English poet who was criticized for constantly using that particular beat in his verses defended himself by saying, "*Iamb* what *iamb* what *iamb!*"

Perhaps this inspired the Gertrude Stein line "Rose is a rose is a rose is a rose." Incidentally, you can win bets on that one. There is no "A" before the first word. And nine out of ten people don't know the source. It comes from Gertrude's "Sacred Emily," written in 1913.

Ictus, according to Cicero and Livy, meant "a blow, stroke, stab or thrust." Horace used it to mean "a beat" in his verses. Today it has that same import. To physicians it's a stroke. May your domicile be delivered from nonpoetic *ictuses!*

Ignoramus literally means "We take no notice." It's a former legal term. Circa 1615–22, George Ruggle wrote a play called *Ignoramus.* The stupid lawyer in the drama bore that name. The production was soon forgotten and so was Ruggle, but his character's cognomen became a byword. Today an *ignoramus* is a dunce or know-nothing.

Incubus is discussed in the chapter called "Eyebrow Raisers."

Incus to the Romans was an anvil. Today it is the central one of three small bones in the middle ear. It is shaped somewhat like an anvil.

Lotus is a borrowing from *lotos.* In fact, the Romans often spelled the word with an *os* ending. To them it meant "the water lily of the Nile." In Greek legend it was a fruit supposed to induce dreamy languor and forgetfulness. Have you ever read Tennyson's "The Lotos Eaters"? They're the *Lotophagi* in Homer's ODYSSEY. After eating of the *lotus-tree* they lost all desire to return to their homeland. In current usage a *lotus-eater* is a person who gives himself up to indolence and daydreams. He lives in *lotus land,* and he really ought to see a psychiatrist.

Magus, now and in ancient Rome, is synonymous with the terms "magician" and "wise man." Everybody has a blind spot in his or her education. I must confess that *magus* was one of mine until 1966. Then I read a review of THE MAGUS, by John Fowles. Suddenly it struck me. The word is the singular of *magi!* Of course I had known of the *Magi* since childhood. As a Latin student I should have realized that the title given to the Three Kings of Cologne was the pluralized form of *magus.* Gaspar was a *magus;* so were Melchior and Balthasar.

Mandamus and *mittimus* are legal writs. The former literally means "We command" and the latter "We send." Between the lawyers and the doctors, Latin stays alive!

Minus is the neuter singular form of *minor,* the Latin adjective for "less." In this case the less said the better.

———

Naevus was the Romans' word for "a mole." It means the same today. It also means "a birthmark or tumor." The preferred spelling is *nevus.*

———

Nexus comes down to us unchanged. As of yore, it means "a tie, link, binding." By the way, one of Henry Miller's books bears that title. He also wrote SEXUS and PLEXUS. The man has had a *complexus* ("love; affection") for those *exus* endings. It should also be noted that *annex* is a relative. It's something tied on.

———

Nidus is familiar to veteran crossword puzzle solvers. It was often seen as a definition for "nest" in the thirties and forties. That's what it meant to Nero and what it means today. Any breeding place is a *nidus.* The plural is *nidi* or *niduses.*

———

Nimbus originally meant "a violent rainstorm." Later the Romans associated it with the cloud that brought such a downpour. We accept that meaning today. But Vergil used *nimbus* to mean "a bright cloud or cloud-shaped splendor" (which enveloped the gods when they appeared on earth). Hence the noun has become a synonym for halo or a splendid aura. But the adjective *nimbose* still has only one connotation —cloudy or stormy.

———

Nucleus in ancient Roman times meant "a small nut"; later it stood for the nut tree itself; and finally its meaning became "the kernel or most solid part." That last definition led to our modern conception for the word. To us the *nucleus* means "the core."

Today we talk of *nuclear energy* (a derivative, of course), but it amazes me that few of our highly placed public men, from Eisenhower to Ford and Carter, are able to pronounce the adjective correctly. For years I've heard "nucular." If our leaders continue to say it that way, I suppose such a pronunciation will eventually be accepted, but I hope not.

———

Octopus is one of those New Latin words. It really doesn't belong here, because the ancient Romans did not call the creature by that name. The Greeks, however, had the word *oktopous* ("eight-footed"), and that designation suggested the modern name. The *octopus* does have eight limbs, but they are arms, not feet. To be precise, the mollusk should have been called an *octobrach.*

Be that as it may, it's interesting to note that *octopus* also means an organization that reaches out in every direction. THE OCTOPUS, a novel written in 1901 by Frank Norris, provides a good example of that sense of the word. His *octopus* was the railroad, which strangled the wheat ranchers.

This scary predator has almost half as many plural forms as it has arms: *octopuses, octopi* and *octopodes.*

***

Omnibus literally means "for all." The French had a *voiture omnibus* ("vehicle for all"); the English shortened it to *omnibus;* and Americans settled for *bus.*

The plural of *bus* is *buses* or *busses*—take your choice. I don't like either one. The first looks like an abridgment of *abuse,* and the other can be confused with the plural form of *buss* ("kiss").

In Congress an *omnibus bill* includes a number of miscellaneous provisions or appropriations. In a way it's something for all.

***

Onus is a Latin noun meaning "burden," and to us it carries the same import. It's akin to a Sanskrit word *ánas* ("cart or freight"). The Romans' plural was *onera.* They would be horrified to hear us say *onuses,* but they would applaud our adjective *onerous* ("burdensome").

In law *onus probandi* means "burden of proof."

***

Plexus is a New Latin word taken from the past participle of *plectere* ("to braid"). It means "a network." Some of its relatives are *complex, complexion, duplex* and *perplexed.*

***

Plus literally means "more." *Surplus* is a derivative. And from a form of *plus* we also obtain *plural, plurality* and others.

When I was a boy, golfers and other sportsmen wore *plus fours.* Those knickerbockers were so called because the tailors added four more inches to the ordinary knee-length pants in order to make them loose and comfortable.

Knickerbockers of course were named for the Dutch settlers who favored that type of garb. We often call them knickers. (In England that word now means "panties.")

***

Prospectus to Livy and Cicero meant "a look-out or distant view." The noun was derived from *prospicere* ("to look forward"). Today a *prospectus* is a statement outlining the main features of a new enterprise. It is indeed forward-looking.

***

Radius in Latin means "a ray, rod or spoke." Cicero referred to it as a semidiameter. Thus most of the original uses have remained. We have extended the scope of the word to mean "a range of operation, activity, influence, concern or knowledge."

Our word *ray* comes from *radius*. And, through the French, so does *rayon*.

―――――

Ramulus means "a branchlet" and is the diminutive of *ramus*. Our word *ramification* is from that same root. When a problem contains many *ramifications*, it literally branches out in a great number of directions.

―――――

Rebus is a puzzle made up of pictures or symbols. It is the ablative form of *res* and means "by things." The inspiration for the word probably came from the phrase *nōn verbis sed rebus* ("not by words but by things").

The popular game "Concentration" features *rebuses*. For example, a picture of an eye is shown. This is followed by an L and finally an ampersand. Can you guess the word that is formed?

Here's a *rebus* using symbols: ICURYY4ME. The answers to this and the preceding puzzle appear at the bottom of the next page.

I can't resist the story about a second-year Latin student who was asked to name the founders of Rome. He replied, "Ramulus and Rebus."

―――――

Now let's conclude the list of words ending in *us* that we have taken bodily from Latin:

sinus	strabismus	terminus	versus
solus	stratus	tetanus	virus
status	stylus	tragus	
stimulus	talus	umbilicus	

Sinus in Latin means "a bent surface or curve." Today it is that cavity in our skulls that gives many of us trouble where it connects with the nasal passages. Recently I heard a comedian speak of a convict who suffered from *sinusitis*. It seems that "the fellow *sinus* name to a bad check."

The word also can be used for other bodily cavities. And it still means "a bend or curve."

―――――

Solus means "alone," as it once did in Rome. Now its usage is largely confined to a stage direction. The Italians changed it to *solo*—an alteration that we eagerly accepted, first in its musical sense and then for other purposes. Lindbergh's flight in 1927 popularized the use of the word in aviation.

Status is the past participle of *stare* (pronounced "stah-reh"). That Latin infinitive means "to stand." But the Romans used *status* as a noun having the sense of "position, posture, condition or situation." We have accepted most of those definitions for the word, but in recent years we have added a new dimension. It now also means "high prestige or recognition." In Vance Packard's THE STATUS SEEKERS, written in 1959, he dealt with people who want to keep up with the Joneses and even pass them. This group tries to achieve *status* by buying a new car every year, choosing a Cadillac over a Chevrolet, placing swimming pools in their yards and adorning their women with mink coats.

But that verb *stare* has sired a legion of words. Among them are *statue, obstacle, stance, distant, constant, constancy, instant, instantaneous, stanza, substance, substantiate, static, statistics, state, reinstate, outstanding, stanchion, stature, extant, circumstance, oust* and many more.

Even *rest,* when it means "remainder," is a member of the family, and so is *arrest.*

Printers and crossword puzzle fans will recognize *stet.* Literally, it means "Let it stand!" It is the opposite of *dele* ("Take it out!")

Girls named *Constance* and boys named *Constantine* are listed in books of first names as being firm of purpose. The reason is that, literally, they are standing together. In other words, they don't fall apart when trouble arises.

Stimulus means the same today as it did in Caesar's time—a goad or spur. *Stimulate* is obviously from the same root.

Strabismus is one of those Modern Latin coinages, with a Greek parentage. To the Athenians, *strabizein* meant "to squint." Cross-eyed people have *strabismus.*

Stratus in Latin means "a strewing." *Stratus* clouds do tend to strew themselves in the skies.

Stylus was usually spelled *stilus* by the Romans. At first it meant "a stake." Then it took on the meaning of "a pointed instrument for writing on wax tablets." In modern times *styluses,* or *styli,* are employed for marking mimeographed stencils or for Braille embossing or for cutting the grooves in phonograph records. Thus we see that the usage of the tool has been largely retained.

Answers to rebuses: "Island" and "I see you are too wise for me."

The word *style* comes directly from this source. In its original sense it is a synonym for *stylus*. It's not difficult to see how it developed a new meaning—"manner or mode of expression." That connotation was first applied to writing, but eventually it was extended into other areas, such as the world of fashion. How fascinating it is to follow the vagarious extensions of words! Does a couturier designing a new *style* for women's dresses realize that his art dates back to a stake or a pointed instrument for writing?

It should also be noted that *stiletto* has the same root. This Italian word for "a small dagger" has been adopted by us, and it makes sense when we consider the source.

"Consider the source" reminds me of an anecdote. If you are insulted by an asinine person, remember the story about the Irishman who was kicked by a jackass. He muttered to himself: "Well, I'll consider the source!"

Talus should be familiar to the addicts of the black-and-white squares through its plural form, *tali,* which often appears in crossword puzzles, with "anklebones" as the usual definition.

Terminus in Latin means "limit, boundary or end." To us there is no difference. But I would guess that few readers are aware that Terminus was the ancient Roman god presiding over boundaries and landmarks. I didn't know until I looked this up. Places like New York City really ought to have such a spirit today to protect those landmarks that are constantly being torn down and replaced. Such a practice needs to be *terminated,* and I use the *term* advisedly. (Yes, *term* does stem from the same root, as does *terminology.*)

Tetanus is a Latin borrowing from the Greeks' *tetanos* ("spasm of the muscles"). Our synonym is the word "lockjaw"—one of those words that "tell it like it is."

Tragus has a complex history. In modern usage, especially among otologists, it means "the fleshy protrusion of the front of the external ear." To the Greeks it literally meant "a goat," and eventually, "the hairy part of the ear." Their spelling, transliterated, was *tragos.* To Ovid it was a species of fish, probably with a goatlike appearance.

It may be hard to believe that *tragedy* is linguistically related to a part of the ear, but philologists surmise that it really is. In ancient Greece some performers represented satyrs and were dressed in goatskins.

Umbilicus to a Roman meant "the navel." Modern physicians still use the same word for what is vulgarly called "the belly button." What a vast difference between the language of the street and that of the A.M.A.! At any rate, most of us are familiar with the *umbilical cord,* the structure that connects the fetus to the mother's placenta, and must be severed at birth. Here again we discover new uses for an old phrase. Psychiatrists refer to the *umbilical cord* as an inordinate attachment of the child to the mother. Astronauts describe it as a cable that connects a missile with the launching equipment. This is just one of the many instances of the verbal creativity of mankind. We constantly ascribe new meanings to old words and phrases.

Versus in Latin means "toward or turned in the direction of." Today we define it as "in contest against." The abbreviation is *vs.* "Ali vs. Spinks" was a sports-page headline in 1978.

Virus meant "a slimy liquid" to Vergil, and to Lucretius it meant "an offensive odor; a stench." In English its meaning was originally "venom, as of a snake." Today it's an infective agent that causes various diseases. A modern derivative is the adjective *virulent* ("extremely poisonous or harmful").

Some readers may chide me for having omitted a few of their favorite words with *us* endings. Well, selectivity must be the author's privilege. But let no one take up the cudgels for *bogus, caucus, grampus, ruckus, rumpus* and *syllabus.* Those words do not fit into the category that has been discussed. Let us take a look at them.

Bogus is a slang word meaning "false or spurious." It was originally a machine for making counterfeit money. Lexicographers aren't sure, but they surmise that it might come from *bogle, bogy* or *bogie* ("hobgoblin; bugbear; scary thing").

Caucus does sound like a Latin word, but it's probably of Algonquian origin. The Indians had a similar noun, meaning "adviser." But there is also a Medieval Greek word that must be considered: *kaukos* ("drinking cup"). In the eighteenth century a *Caucus Club* was established. Its purpose was political and social. Perhaps, between the club and the Greeks, the word took hold. At any rate, a *caucus* is a conference of party leaders or members to decide on policies, choices of candidates and other issues. Forgive me if I call it a conventional word.

Grampus brings back personal memories. When I started solving crossword puzzles on the New York City subway, ORC would often appear. Many times it would be defined as "grampus." Not having a dictionary in my lap, I would feel frustrated. Neither word made any sense to me. It's like defining ATLE as "sandarac." What in the world are these puzzle-makers talking about? Is this some kind of foreign language? Those were my thoughts in the thirties. Now, as an editor, I try to define an unfamiliar word with one that is commonly used. For example, the definition for ORC is "a killer whale"* or "a sea animal." Ditto the *grampus*. The derivation of that word, by the way, is too intricate to explain. It eventually can be traced to a Latin accusative, *crassum piscem* ("fat fish").

Ruckus is probably a combination of *ruction* ("riotous outbreak") and *rumpus*. Nobody knows whence we obtained *rumpus,* but in Ireland (1798) a revolt was called the "Ruction." The name, begorra, is a corruption of *insurrection.*

Syllabus does have a Latin background, but the spelling has been changed. In Cicero's time a *sillybus* was not a wayward jitney à la Steinbeck; it meant "a strip of parchment attached to a book-roll, on which was written the title of the work and the author's name." As usual, the Romans had borrowed the word from the Greeks. *Sillybos* was the Athenians' noun for this label. Today a *syllabus* means "a summary or outline containing the main points" and is usually applied to a course of study.

Thus endeth our discussion of words ending in *us*. Now let's consider some of many that end in *a* and have moved over without change from Latin to English. Again we will break them into groups so that we can take a pause now and then.

agenda	caesura	corolla	femora
alga	camera	corona	fibula
angina	catena	costa	flora
antenna	cicada	coxa	formula
arena	circa	dogma	fossa
aura	cithara	et cetera	galena
aurora	cloaca	farina	gemma
bacchanalia	cornea	fascia	

Agenda is the plural of *agendum,* which is also a word in our language but is rarely used. *Agenda* literally means "things to be done." Thus when a chairperson calls the *agenda* to the attention of committee members, he or she is asking them to give heed to the things they must decide upon or accomplish.

* *Orca* is the more popular term for this whale.

The word is a form of *agere* ("to do"), and it has provided us with a lode or load of inheritances. From one principal part or another we have obtained *act, agent, agile, agitate, ambiguous, cogent, exact, exigent, exiguous, fumigate, intransigent, litigate, navigate, prodigal, purge, retroactive, squat, transaction* and numerous others. When we consider that just one Latin verb has sired (directly or indirectly) so many of our commonly used words, we can see what a debt we owe that ancient language.

Alga meant "seaweed" in Horace's works, and it still does.

Angina was used by Plautus as a synonym for quinsy (abscess of the tonsils). *Angina* comes from a Latin verb *angere* ("to strangle or distress"), and both *anger* and *angry* are closely related to it. Today the word still means "an inflammatory disease of the throat." But more and more we have come to associate it with *angina pectoris* ("quinsy of the chest" in ancient days). That condition, by the way, is caused by a sudden decrease in blood supply to the heart.

Antenna in Roman days meant "an extended thing." Ovid used it to mean "a sail." It no longer has anything to do with ships. Today *antennae* are the sense organs on the heads of insects, crabs, lobsters and other arthropods. Sometimes they are called feelers. But it pleases me to note that a TV *antenna* is still an extended thing.

I once wrote a poem about those aerials on our roofs. It was called "Reflections in Suburbia."

> The crooked crosses overhead proclaim
> High homage to the god-of-living rooms;
> As silently as Pharaohs in their tombs
> Men sit before the sacrificial flame.
>
> The incense from the king-size cigarettes
> Is wafted idly toward the altar-box
> Where current ministers harangue their flocks
> With tired wit and lively murder threats.
>
> Tonight I shall not play the pious role
> Nor join the dead who once had been so quick;
> But I shall try to walk, strange heretic,
> Among neglected precincts of my soul.

Arena has been transformed through the ages. Originally it meant "the dried thing" and then it was employed to mean "sand." Since the centers of the Roman amphitheaters were strewn with sand, that place of combat for gladiators soon became known as the *arena.* Today an *arena* is an enclosed place for a boxing match, basketball game or some other sport. Not an iota of sand can be found!

Since the Romans also used the word to mean "the scene of action or contention," it does seem appropriate that we have instituted *arena theaters,* or theaters-in-the-round. In such places the seats for the audience completely encircle the actors.

We still use *arena* in another way that fits its ancestry. It means "the place where the action is." An example is the *arena* of politics.

———

Aura had a dozen meanings in ancient Rome, ranging from "air or gentle breeze" to "sound, tone, echo or odor." In modern times we associate the word largely with atmosphere or aroma. We say, "That girl has an *aura* about her that intrigues me" or "The *aura* of roast turkey permeated the kitchen." Incidentally, the Romans borrowed the noun from the Greeks and changed the spelling considerably.

———

Aurora meant "dawn" to Vergil, and it retains that meaning today, mainly because of the poets. Most people connect it with *aurora borealis* ("northern aurora"). This luminous phenomenon is seen to the best advantage in the Arctic at night. It is supposed to be of electrical origin and is commonly called "northern lights." Herewith a bit of doggerel:

> I must relate without any malice
> That good old *aurora borealis*
> To me does not at all seem pleasing;
> I do not like the thought of freezing
> While watching streamers in the skies:
> I'll leave that thrill to other guys.

Bacchanalia is the neuter plural of *bacchanalis.* Currently it means "an orgy or drunken party." The Romans not only stole hundreds of ordinary words from the Greeks, they also took over their gods. Bacchus (Roman god of wine) and Dionysus (Greek deity) are one and the same.

The name Bacchus is said to be an altered form of *Iacchus,* a Greek epithet for Dionysus indicating that he was a loud roisterer. *Iaché* meant "a shout."

At any rate, the *Bacchanalia* was a Roman festival in honor of that god of wine. Originally only certain priestesses participated. Three days each year these *Bacchae,* or *bacchantes,* practiced secret rites in honor of the god. Later the men got into the act and pandemonium prevailed. The *vinum* ("wine") flowed like water and the festivals turned into drunken orgies. The Roman *Senatus* noted that plots and conspiracies often were hatched during the merrymaking. Hence they banned the festival in 186 B.C.

Today a *bacchant* is a drunken reveler and a *bacchante* is a woman who carouses. A shortened form of the name of the festival is *bacchanal*. It too signifies a party at which everybody becomes besotted. An adjective from the same source is *bacchantic* ("given to carousing").

One might suspect that *bachelor* is a related word, but it isn't. It comes from Medieval Latin *baccalarius* ("dependent farmer, tenant, young clerk or advanced student"). The last of these definitions indicates why some college graduates are granted *Bachelor of Arts* degrees. Incidentally, *bachelor* is related to *bacterium* because both words can be traced back to *baculum,* the ancient Romans' noun for "a stick or staff."

Caesura is a pause or break in a line of verse. Literally it means "a cutting." It's a form of the Latin verb *caedere* ("to cut").

Camera to the Romans meant "a vault." That connotation exists today. The word can be defined as "a chamber, or judge's private office." But the invention of the *camera obscura* (literally, "dark chamber") led to our most common use of the word. We dropped the adjective. Incidentally, there is also a *camera lucida* ("light chamber"). It's an apparatus using a prism or mirrors to reflect an object so that its outline can be traced.

Catena is the Latin word for "chain." In modern usage it means "a connected series of related things." To *catenate* is to link, and a *concatenation* is "a union in a linked series or a chain." Where did "chain" come from? It's a derivative of *catena* via the Medieval French.

Cithara was a Roman instrument resembling a lyre. The word was borrowed from the Greeks' *kithara*. From the same root came another instrument, the *cither*. Nor should we omit the *cittern,* which is a blend of *cither* or *gittern*. The latter was a stringed instrument of the Middle Ages. *Zither,* of course, is a member of this family. But most interesting is the fact that the *guitar* can be traced back linguistically to the *cithara*.

Cloaca in ancient Rome originally meant "the cleanser." Then it came to signify "a sewer or drain"—the definition that applies today. Tarquinius Priscus built an artificial canal to carry the filth from the streets and it was called the *Cloaca*. But the connotation given by Plautus is startling. To him a *cloaca* meant "the stomach of a drunken woman."

To modern herpetologists, ornithologists, ichthyologists and amphibiologists the *cloaca* is a chamber inside reptiles, birds, fish and amphibia.

Cornea is the feminine form of an old Latin adjective meaning "horny." The noun arose in medieval times. This outer coating of the eyeball was probably so named because of its texture. The parent word is *cornu* ("horn"). From it we have inherited *corner, cornet, Capricorn, tricorn, unicorn* and even *horn* itself. You may wish to add *corneous* to your vocabulary. It means "horny."

Corolla is a part of a flower. To the Romans it meant "a garland or small wreath." It was a diminutive of *corona*.

Corona today carries several meanings—crown; halo around the sun or moon; long cigar. The last definition is derived from a trademark, "La Corona." Possibly the manufacturer wanted to convey the idea that it was a kingly cigar. In Latin, *corona* means "crown or garland."

Costa means "rib" in Latin or English. It is not to be confused with the Spanish noun for "coast." Costa Rica, for example, means "rich coast."

Coxa is another anatomical noun akin to a Sanskrit word meaning "the leaper." To the Romans and to our medical profession *coxa* was and is the hip. That part of the body is also called a *huckle*—from an old Norse word *hūka* ("to crouch"). The *hucklebone* is the hipbone. But for some strange reason it is also a synonym for the talus (anklebone).

Fascia was the Romans' word for "a band or bandage." Today it is used in architecture to mean a kind of molding or flat strip. The dashboard of an Englishman's car is called the *fascia board* or *facia board*.

But a relative from Rome, *fasces,* is even more interesting, because it has given us such words as *fascism, fascist* and *fascistic*. It means "a bundle of sticks or rods." The Roman magistrates carried this bundle, with an ax in the middle, its head projecting on top. It was the symbol of authority. When Benito Mussolini came into power in Italy he was head of the *Fascisti,* a group that took over the ancient *fasces* as their symbol.

If a plant grows in bundles or clusters, it is said to be *fasciculate*. And a section of a book that appears prior to the publication of the entire work is called a *fascicle*. Isn't that fascinating?

Does *fascinate* have the same source? No, indeed! It's from *fascinare* ("to bewitch or enchant").

Femora were "thighs" to Tacitus, Tiberius and other Romans. That meaning remains today, although more often the word is applied to the bones themselves. It is the pure plural of *femur;* sometimes the Anglicized form, *femurs,* is used.

Fibula meant "brooch or clasp" in ancient Rome. In modern usage it is the long thin outer bone of the human leg, between the knee and the ankle. It appears to have a clasplike function.

Flora was the Roman goddess of flowers. In the 1700s, Linnaeus popularized the word in his systematic classification of plants. *Flora* are now the plants of a region, and *fauna* are the animals.

Formula is the Latin diminutive for *forma*. Originally it meant "a little shape or figure," and later "a fine form; beauty." So when a modern chemist develops a new *formula* in a laboratory, he can rightfully claim that he's come up with a beauty!

Fossa was a Roman ditch or moat. It came from a participial form of *fodere* ("to dig"). Today the M.D.s partly retain the original idea. To them a *fossa* is a pit or cavity in the human anatomy. But we do have another, very similar word, *fosse,* which means "ditch or moat." It has come to us via Old French and Medieval English.

As you might expect, *fossil* is a relative. It means "something dug up." Now if you call someone *an old fossil,* you may feel a bit ghoulish.

There is another *fossa,* of entirely different origin. It's a lithe and slender mammal of Madagascar.

Galena originally was the dross that remained after melting lead. Today it's the principal ore of lead.

Gemma in Latin is the bud of a plant. Botanists have kept that designation. But *gem* is the more popular word from that root. Like a bud, it's lovely to look at.

Now let us continue with our list of Latin words ending in *a*, keeping in mind that their spellings are the same today as they were years ago.

hernia	lamina	notabilia	quota
idea	macula	opera	regalia
impedimenta	marginalia	orchestra	remora
incunabula	memorabilia	patella	reseda
inertia	militia	pica	rota
insignia	miscellanea	piscina	rotunda
insomnia	nebula	pupa	
lacuna			

Some of the above lend themselves to grouping. *Memorabilia* are things worth remembering or recording. In crossword puzzles the word is often used as a definition for *ana*. Things worthy of notice are called *notabilia,* and marginal notes or extrinsic matters are *marginalia.* Varied collections, especially if works of literature, are *miscellanea.* All these words are neuter plural forms of Latin words.

———

Impedimenta is another neuter plural—and what a delightful word it is! This synonym for encumbrances or things that hinder progress has its roots in *pes, pedis* ("foot, of the foot"). The Latin verb *impedire* means "to entangle or get the feet in something." Thus an *impediment* really trips you up!

———

Still another enchanting neuter plural is *incunabula* (literally, "in the cradle"). Your *incunabula* are your very first stages of infancy. The noun also is used for books published before 1501. These are called "cradle books."

———

Insignia is also a neuter plural in Latin. The original connotation still remains—namely, "badges or emblems or distinctive marks."

———

Opera naturally comes to us from Italy. Verdi and Puccini wouldn't have it any other way. But the word in Latin is another neuter plural and literally means "works." The Italians changed it to a singular noun.

———

The last of those neuter plurals from Latin is *regalia.* We turned the adjective *regalis* into a noun. The singular form today is *regale* (not to be confused with the verb meaning "to entertain lavishly"). In any event, the original adjective conveyed the idea of kingly. In our day that idea remains. *Regalia* are the rights or privileges of kings, hence the ensigns or emblems of royalty. But the more common definition is "splendid clothes; finery." Since the word eventually stems from *rex,* it's easy to see why we associate *regalia* with one's Sunday best.

———

Now let's return, alphabetically, to the latest list of words ending in *a*.

Hernia and *yarn* have the same roots! The reasons are too complicated to relate, but any reader can look this up in an unabridged dictionary. In Latin, *hernia* is a rupture. The protrusion that occasionally occurs in our bodies today is sometimes given the same nomenclature. A related verb is *herniate*.

> Too much too soon poor Bernie ate,
> And then did Bernie *herniate!*

The Romans borrowed *idea* from the Greeks. In Athens, *idein* meant "to see." If you look up *wit* in a good lexicon, you will discover that it can finally be traced back to the same root as *idea*. That does seem appropriate!

Inertia originally came from another Latin word, *iners*. That adjective meant "without *ars*" or "lacking skill." Eventually Cicero and others used *inertia* in the sense of inactivity or idleness. That concept continues in our language. Aside from the definition given to the word by physicists, it means "sluggishness" to most *hoi polloi,* including me.

Insomnia in Latin or English means "the state of sleeplessness." The victim of this condition is an *insomniac.* Some very expressive words have come from the *somn* root. A sleepwalker is a *somnambulist.* He *somnambulates,* and his action is called *somnambulation.*

A *somnifacient* is a sleep-producing drug, and *somniloquy* is the practice of talking in one's sleep. Many a two-timer has gotten into trouble by being *somniloquous.* If you're *somnolent,* you are sleepy, and if you're *somnolescent,* you are beginning to grow drowsy.

Somnipathy is the state into which a hypnotist puts his patient. His art is *somniferous* ("sleep-producing").

The Romans, like the rest of us, had so much interest in sleep that they developed several other synonyms:

sopor—heavy sleep. From this word we get *soporific*—sleep-inducing drug; *soporose*—morbidly sleepy; and *soporiferous*—inducing sleep.

quies—rest. Some members of the family are *quiet, quiescent, quietude, quietus* and even *quit.*

dormire—to sleep. Descendants are *dormant, dormitory* and *dormer* (window originally in bedrooms only). The *dormouse* is a small Old World rodent resembling a squirrel. Because he is nocturnal and becomes torpid in winter, the roots for his name can also be traced to *dormire.*

Lacuna in Latin means "cavity, cavern, pool or pond." The poet Ovid used it to signify a dimple. Today the word means "a blank space, gap, hole, missing part, defect or flaw." In some senses it is a synonym for *hiatus*. What makes the word especially exciting is the fact that it is the parent of *lake* and *lagoon*.

Lamina hasn't changed much in meaning since Caesar's day. It still is defined as "a layer." When rock, wood, a fabric or a plastic is *laminated,* it is composed of thin layers. A *lamina* is also a thin layer of tissue on a horse's hoof. Inflammation of this area is called *laminitis.*

Macula was and is a spot or stain. Our most common derivative is *immaculate* (literally, "not stained"). In a way, an *immaculate* dresser is wearing clean, unspotted clothes. Less familiar descendants are *maculate* and *maculose* ("spotted"), *maculacy* ("smirched, unclean, spotted state") and *macular* ("spotty"). Let us pray that *maculation* does not spoil the products of habilimentation.

Militia in early Rome meant "the serving as a soldier." Finally it denoted "troops," and that definition has survived. The word is derived from *miles* ("a soldier"). A verb from the same root is *militate* ("to have weight or effect"). When a situation *militates* against you, it causes an army of problems to attack you. Note that many people confuse *militate* with *mitigate*. The latter is derived from our old friend *agere* ("to drive"). *Mitis* is a Latin word for "soft or gentle." To *mitigate* means "to make less severe." What a difference from *militate!*

Nebula means "mist, vapor or cloud" in Latin. Today the *nebulae* are immense bodies of highly rarefied gas or dust in the Milky Way and other galaxies. If we say that prospects for success are *nebulous,* we mean that they are not clear. In other words, they are cloudy or misty. *Nebular* is a synonym for cloudy.

Orchestra was originally a Greek word derived from *orcheisthai* ("to dance"). In ancient theaters the *orchestra* was the semicircular space in front of the stage. Anyone who has ever attended an opera or other kinds of musical performances can see why the word has been applied to the group of musicians themselves. It is also no problem to understand why that space directly in front of the stage has been extended to mean the section of seats on the main floor of a theater.

It is interesting to note that the verb *orchestrate* is gradually taking on a nonmusical import. Recently I read this sentence by a well known columnist: "The leaders of the oil powers are *orchestrating* our future."

Patella, as any crossword puzzle fan knows, is the kneecap or knee-pan. In ancient Rome it was a small pan or dish.

Pica in Latin first meant "the painted one," then "the variegated one" and finally "the magpie." Today *pica* means "the genus of magpies." And probably because those birds are omnivorous, the word also means "a craving to eat substances like chalk ashes or bones."

Most people know *pica* as a size of type. In earlier days it was a collection of church rules which, when printed, resembled the colors of a magpie.

Piscina, once a fish pond or swimming pool, is now a basin for the disposal of holy water. It is also called a *sacrarium.* The original meaning of *piscina* has been retained in Italian and Spanish.

Pupa was the Romans' word for "doll or puppet"—and sometimes for "girl." It's easy to see why an insect in its postlarval stage is called *pupa.* Close cousins are *pupil, puppet, pup* and *puppy.*

Quota is the feminine singular of *quotus* ("How many?"). The Latin phrase *quota pars* ("How great a part?") is said to be the reason for our present definition—a proportional share.

An interesting aside: When a Roman asked another about the time of day, he would say, *"Quota?"* It was a shortening of *"Quota hora?"*

It's also fascinating to discover that *quote* and *quotation* are derived from the same root as *quota.* This came about because of the Latin verb *quotare,* used in medieval days. It meant "to divide into chapters by numbers; to mark references by numbers." Even today *quote* may be used to mean "mark; write down; record." In that connection, we use sentences such as: "I asked the used-car dealer to *quote* a price."

Remora is a little fish that takes a free ride on a shark or turtle and even under a passing ship. It can do this because it has an oval sucking disc on its head. The word is made up of the prefix *re* and *mora* ("delay"). Sailors believed that the *remoras* hindered ships when they clung to them.

To lawyers *mora* is a familiar word. It still means "delay." From the same root we have obtained *moratorium, demur* and *demurrage.* Some lexicographers claim that *memory* is also a relative.

A word about *demurrage.* If you have never been in the shipping business, you might assume that the word means "the act of having scruples or objections." It certainly looks like a synonym for *demurrer,* but it isn't. Its definition is: "the delaying of a ship, railroad car, etc. by the freighter's failure to load, unload or sail within the time allowed." It also means "the compensation paid for the delay."

————

Reseda, according to Pliny, was originally the imperative of *resedare* ("to allay"). The plant was used as a kind of amulet to reduce tumors. In modern times the word is a synonym for the garden mignonette. Because the flowers are grayish green, *reseda* is also a definition for that color.

————

Rota in early Rome was "a wheel." Later, by metonymy, it came to mean "a vehicle with wheels; a chariot." It also came to signify "the disk of the sun," and Ovid even called it "the wheel or rack of love."

The *Sacred Roman Rota* is a tribunal of prelates serving as an appeals court. But in a nonecclesiastical sense a *rota* is a roster or list of names. It's also a round of golf tournaments.

Some descendants of that Roman wheel are *rotate, rotameter, rotund, rotunda, round, rote, roll, roulette, rowel, rotogravure, control, rotiform* and *rotor.*

It's easy to see why *rodeo* comes from this same source. In Spanish (and also in one of its English uses) it means "roundup."

In New England a *rotary* is a traffic circle. And the members of *Rotary International* owe their allegiance to *rota* too. The name sprang up because the original members of the club rotated the task of playing host.

————

And now it behooves us to finish our list of Latin-English words ending in *a*.

Sagitta	simia	tibia	umbra
salina	spatula	tinea	ungula
saliva	spica	toga	vertebra
saturnalia	stamina	transenna	via
scintilla	stria	trivia	villa
sedilia	tela	tuba	viola
sepia	tessera	ulna	viscera
serra	testa	ultra	
seta	tiara		

Sagitta literally means "arrow." It is a small northern constellation. Its relative *Sagittarius* ("archer") is a large southern constellation and also a sign of the zodiac.

Some leaves are said to be *sagittate* because they are shaped like arrowheads. *Sagittal* is another adjective in this family.

————

Scintilla meant "a spark" to Vergil. We use it figuratively today to mean "the slightest particle or trace." For example, we might say, "The prosecutor doesn't have a *scintilla* of evidence."

But the verb *scintillate* really keeps the spark alive. It means "to emit sparks; to twinkle or sparkle." Here again we have extended the scope. Sportswriters often report that a certain player *scintillated* in the game.

———

Sedilia is the plural of *sedile,* the Latin word for "seat." Like many other words from ancient Rome, it has been preserved by the church. It is defined as "a set of seats, near the altar, for the officiating clergy."

More interesting is the amazing number of descendants of *sedere* ("to sit"). Here are some of them: *seance, sedentary, sediment, session, siege, assess, assiduous, dissident, obsess, preside, reside, subsidy, saddle* and *supersede.*

By the way, if you remember that *supersede* literally means "sit above," you will never misspell that verb.

———

Sepia in Latin means "the cuttlefish." Because that creature secretes an inky fluid, the word has come to mean "a dark, reddish brown color." It is also a photographer's print in that color and a pigment used by artists.

———

Serra is often defined in crossword puzzles as "saw of a sawfish." To the Romans it was a saw. Our commonly used derivative is *serrated* ("having notches or teeth like a saw").

———

Seta is also familiar to puzzle fans. It was and is a bristle or prickle on a plant. The hairs of caterpillars are *setae* too.

———

Simia means "ape" in Latin. Today it is a Linnaean genus, restricted to the Barbary ape. Its oft-used offshoot is *simian.* Any ape or monkey is a *simian.*

———

Spatula is a Low Latin diminutive of *spatha* ("blade or broad sword"). The Romans borrowed *spatha* from the Greeks. Bakers, plasterers and nurses use *spatulas* today in different ways. They might be surprised to know that the word is related to *spade, spay* and even *epaulet.*

———

Stamina has a fascinating history. In Greek mythology, the Fates spun the thread of human life. This thread, or warp, was called *stēmōn.* The Romans latched onto the three goddesses and changed their names from Clotho, Lachesis and Atropos to Nona, Decuma and Morta. They also transliterated *stēmōn* into *stamen,* and the plural became *stamina.*

Today a stamen is a vital, pollen-bearing organ of a flower. *Stamina* means "endurance." If your corporeal threads are strong and resistant to tugging and pulling, you've got *stamina!*

Stria, tela and *testa* are regular visitors to crossword puzzles. The first means "a narrow groove or channel"; the second, "anatomical tissue"; the third, "a seed covering." From *stria* we have derived "striated" ("striped"). Through the French, *tela* has given us *toile* ("a sheer fabric"). The Romans used *tela* to mean "the warp in a loom." As for *testa,* it originally meant "clay, brick, tile or shell." It was also the plural of *testum,* an earthen vessel in old Rome. Our common word *test* is derived from it, probably because of the use of the cupel, a small container used in assaying metals.

Tiara is thought to be of Oriental origin. It was the headdress of the ancient Persians. The Greeks assimilated the word, and the Romans borrowed it from them. Today it has many meanings. It can be a coronet, or a woman's crownlike headdress or the Pope's triple crown.

Tinea to ancient Romans was "a gnawing worm in books or clothes." We use it as a synonym for ringworm.

Toga came from *tegere* ("to cover"). The *toga virilis* was a robe symbolizing manhood and was draped on Roman boys when they reached the age of fourteen. From then on they wore their *togae* in public. Today the word is used to mean "a professional, official or academic gown." A judge wears a *toga* when he presides at court.

Through its parent verb, *toga* has a fascinating variety of siblings. *Tile, detect, integument, thatch, protect* and *tegular* are some members of the family. A *detective,* by the way, takes away your cover, but a *protector* provides cover for you.

Transenna is a word I learned only recently. To Plautus and Cicero it meant "a rope, noose or springe." It also signified "net or latticework." In modern usage it's "a lattice or screen of stone or metal enclosing a shrine."

Trivia is my personal all-time favorite because it helped to elevate me from the position of teacher to the post of assistant principal in the New York City schools. How? In the forties all candidates for higher licenses in the city were given a grueling battery of tests by the Board of Examiners—a group considered by most of us underlings to be a pedantic and sadistic bunch of bugbears. We studied individually, in groups, or in cram courses for two years before undergoing many trials.

First there was a short-answer test on a broad sweep of subjects ranging from vocabulary and mathematics through literature, grammar, science, social and other studies. Right on its heels came a three-hour essay test on educational areas. Somewhere along the line a thorough physical exam was administered. Then members of the Board of Examiners would visit our schools and give us a field test. Also, our principals were required to fill out an extensive rating sheet. The grand finale was the interview test, in which our speech, our appearance and our ability to present ourselves were assessed. That's where *trivia* comes in.

Chief bugbear of them all, by reputation, was Dr. Levy. His rejection rate was rumored to be 90 percent. Candidates who had faced him in the past described him as mean and sarcastic. "Pray that you don't get Levy," they advised me.

On the fateful day I was ushered into a school hallway. Outside each classroom door was a chair. The proctor, a good-looking woman of my own age, nodded to one of the chairs.

"Sit here. Dr. Levy will be right out."

I blanched. "Dr. Levy! Oh, gosh. Could you do me a favor? Could you seat me someplace else? With some other examiner?"

She smiled. "I hear he's really tough. Okay, follow me."

Just as I had breathed a sigh of relief, out popped Levy!

"Is this the next candidate?"

The proctor winced and I almost fainted. "Yes, sir."

"Well, don't just stand there, young man. Come in." He turned his back and entered the room. As I followed him the proctor shrugged and gave me a weak smile as if to say, "Well, I tried."

Levy sat behind the teacher's desk and ordered me to take a seat exactly five rows back. While he shuffled through my application papers I felt like a drowning man seeing his whole life pass before him. All those years of study—all those tests—and now to be turned down by this grim man! I could feel my legs trembling with fear.

After what seemed like an eternity Levy looked up.

"Well, Maleska, I see you're a Latin scholar."

"Er, not really, sir. I majored in the subject at college and taught it for a few years in New Jersey, but I don't claim to be a scholar."

"Let's find out. Give me the meaning and derivation of *coeval.*"

"It means 'contemporary,' sir. The prefix means 'together' and the root . . ."

"Yes?"

I racked my brain while he drummed his fingers impatiently on the desk. In my nervous state, I just couldn't remember *aevum* ("age").

"Well, let's try another one."

To this day I cannot remember that second word, but I know I flubbed that one too.

Levy tipped his chair back against the blackboard and delivered his satiric *coup de grace*. "You're right, Maleska. You're certainly no Latin scholar."

At that moment terror turned into anger. This S.O.B. was making a mockery of me and the whole interview process. I was sunk anyway, so I might as well go down fighting.

"Excuse me, Dr. Levy. I may not be a scholar, but I don't think two instances prove anything," I blurted out. "Everybody knows that you, sir, are indeed a Latin scholar, but I could probably trip you up—just as you have stumped me."

Levy took a deep breath while I waited for him to eject this upstart unceremoniously. Then came a moment I will always recall with joy.

He leaned forward. "All right, Maleska, try me."

"*Trivia*, sir. What's the derivation?"

"That's easy. In the Middle Ages the *trivium* was a division of the liberal arts."

"Excuse me, sir. You're talking about the singular form in Medieval days. What about the Roman derivation?"

Levy gave me a wan smile. "All right. What's *your* answer?"

I explained that *trivium* was the Roman noun for crossroads and that the place where three *viae* met was a favorite spot for citizens to pass the time of day and talk "trivia."*

"Now, how about *supercilious,* sir?"

Levy waved my new word away. "You've made your point."

Well, I must admit that the ogre turned into a pussycat in the next ten minutes. He chatted with me about my poetry, crossword puzzles and teaching experience. Most amazingly, he put his hand on my shoulder as I was leaving the room and said, "You're a good kid, Maleska."

Needless to say, I passed the test. I even received a congratulatory letter from Dr. Levy a few months later when a poem of mine appeared in the New York HERALD TRIBUNE.

* I should note that some pundits today insist that the true origin of *trivia* is really Dr. Levy's *trivium*. According to them, the seven liberal arts were divided into the *quadrivium* (arithmetic, music, geometry, astronomy) and the *trivium* (grammar, logic, rhetoric). They contend that the former category includes more respectable areas in which truths can be verified, whereas the latter deals with fields in which opinions often outweigh facts. Hence the *trivium* led to our present concept of *trivial*.

As far as I can gather, most etymologists do not buy that theory.

There is also an amusing sequel to that incident. Six years later, while I was studying to become a principal, a colleague told me the "Levy-trivia" story and ended up by saying, "Can you imagine the nerve of that guy—challenging Levy, of all people?"

I must confess to that colleague, if he should be reading this book, that I didn't have the heart to tell him that the nervy guy was his listener!

Tuba, in ancient Rome was a straight war trumpet. Figuratively, it meant "an exciter or instigator." You can see why. If Dr. Levy were alive today he might be pleased to learn that his nonscholar cannot understand why that straight war trumpet has become the conical instrument with an oompah-oompah sound. Incidentally, *tube* is a close relative.

Umbra has many meanings in Latin ("shade, shadow, ghost, faint trace"). It still means a "shade or shadow" and is used by astronomers to mean "the dark cone of shadow projecting from a planet or satellite on the side opposite the sun." It also means "the dark central part of a sunspot."

Obviously, *umbrella* is a derivative through Italian, and lexicographers assume that the pigment *umber* and the fish of the same name owe their heritage to *umbra.* Certainly *umbrage* does: That word has two completely different connotations: 1) "shade-giving foliage," and 2) "offense or resentment."

How did that second definition come into being? Well, the idea of shadow led to feelings of suspicion and doubt. The next step was indignation.

Finally, it should be noted that the lovely word *umbrageous* comes from the *umbra* root. It means "giving shade." Unfortunately it can also be defined as "easily offended."

Ungula was "a hoof" in Cicero's day. To Plautus it meant "the claw of a hen, vulture or eagle"—in other words, "a talon." The poet Horace extended the scope of the noun and used it as a synonym for horse.

Zoologists still use *ungula* to mean "a hoof or claw." They also use *unguis* in the same sense. An *ungulate* is a hoofed animal, such as a horse.

A delightful cousin is *unguiculate*—a mammal having claws or nails.

Does *unguent* come from this source? No, it's from *unguere* ("to anoint").

Villa is one of those rare words that have lived through the centuries with little or no change in meaning. In Caesar's time it was a country house. In Italy, France and all English-speaking countries that definition still exists, although the British have extended it to mean "a suburban, middle-class house."

In Spain, *villa* has become expanded to mean "a town." A *casa de la villa* is a town hall. To the French that public building is an *hôtel de ville*.

Ville as an offshoot is reflected in the names of many towns. There are at least four Bellevilles ("beautiful towns") in the United States and Canada. One is in Illinois and another is in Kansas. A third faces the Passaic River in New Jersey, and the seat of Albert College is Belleville, Canada. Can you think of other towns with "ville" as part of the name? Perhaps you live in one.

It's obvious that *villa* has sired our word *village*. But did you know that *villain* comes from the same source? In Medieval England he was a *villein,* or serf working for a lord who owned a grand estate. The rich looked down on this poor fellow and felt they couldn't trust him. Hence he devolved into a scoundrel. It's mind-boggling to think that *villainy* can be traced back to a lovely Roman estate in the country!

Viscera is the plural of *viscus,* a Latin noun for "inner part of the body." Today we speak of having "a gut feeling" about someone or something. We also talk about *"visceral* sensations," as when we are zoomed down a roller coaster or subjected to a horror film. The adjective *visceral* has come to mean "unreasoning." It also has the connotation of "earthy or raw" and even "intensely emotional."

Incidentally, *viscera* is one of the words that crossword puzzle editors abhor. It fits into the same category as *tumor, cancer, offal* and other such unpleasantly suggestive terms. Most solvers want escape from life's seamier side. When a disgusting word appears, they write letters of protest. Interestingly enough, we have been getting away with *edema, acne* and *gout* for years. Apparently the victims of those ailments suffer in silence.

This section on selected words that end in *a* in Latin and English now comes to an end. The exceptional reader who has been enthralled by such research and who is eager to learn more about words that I don't discuss here is invited to consult his dictionary concerning the following:

azalea	Gloria	propaganda	uvea
cornucopia	intelligentsia	Quadragesima	uvula
diploma	peninsula	tantara	visa

Of course there are many others, but I am not attempting to include every entry in the dictionary. Let us get on to words that ended in *or* in ancient Rome and still do today. I have selected a group of fifty-two. The first half is as follows:

agitator	creator	error	junior
anterior	curator	excelsior	lector
arbor	dictator	exterior	liberator
censor	doctor	fulgor	major
clamor	dolor	imperator	mediator
clangor	donator	inferior	
color	emptor	interior	

Agitator in Vergil's time meant "a driver of cattle." To Cicero he signified "a charioteer or competitor in the games at the Circus Maximus." The noun stems from *agitare* ("to put in motion"). In our century an *agitator* is considered to be a sort of radical. He tries to stir up people concerning social causes. Thus he is quite different from Vergil's cowboy, but if you consider the parent verb, you will see that our current definition is apropos.

Anterior and its kin are a very interesting family. The word is the comparative form of *ante* ("before"). It can be interpreted to mean "a little before." Today it is defined as "situated toward the front," and it's the opposite of *posterior.*

The basic word *ante* is used in card games. People who play penny ante must *ante up* before they receive their cards. Today we employ *ante* as a prefix, just as the Romans did; examples in our language are *antecedent, antedate, antemeridian* (A.M.) and *antenatal.*

Best of all is *antepenultimate* ("third last"). Literally, this word means "before the almost last." The *antepenult* in the word *usufructuary* is the syllable pronounced "choo." What's a *usufructuary*? He's one who enjoys the right of using all the advantages and profits of another person's property. *Fructus* is a Latin word for "fruit, enjoyment or profit." When seeds *fructify,* they bear fruit.

Arbor means "tree" in Latin. That signification is carried forward each year, usually on the last Friday in April, when we plant trees on Arbor Day. Incidentally, the occasion is a legal holiday in Nebraska and Utah.

But we have expanded the original definition. An *arbor* now means "a place shaded by trees, or a bower." A lovely adjective from this source is *arboraceous* ("wooded or treelike"). And when a young tree starts to spread its branches, it is *arborescent*.

Censor was originally a Roman magistrate appointed to take the census. Later his role was extended. He became what he is today—an official supervising public morals. In modern times we also use the word as a verb meaning "to ban completely after examination." A related adjective is *censorious* ("severely critical"). The verb or noun, *censure*, is a member of this judgmental family.

Clamor is a Latin noun meaning "a loud call; a shout." In English it has virtually the same import—a loud outcry; an uproar. The parent verb is *clamare*—to call or cry out. From this source we have obtained *acclaim, declaim, exclaim, proclaim* and *reclaim*. *Claim, claimant* and *clamorous* are other members of the group.

Clangor is also a Latin noun that we have taken over completely. We have also shortened it to *clang* and lengthened it, as an adjective, to *clangorous*—noisy and resounding. This family provides a good example of *onomatopoeia*. The sound of the word suits its sense. Other examples are *bobwhite* (named for the quail's call), *boom, buzz, cuckoo, hiss, murmur, tinkle* and *whir*. Literally, in Greek, *onomatopoeia* means "the making of a name." Its second root has appropriately given us such words as *poem, poet* and *poetry*. The first part of the word has led to *onomasticon*—a wordbook or dictionary or collection of words in a specialized field.

Color comes right down to us from ancient Rome with its original sense practically intact. It means "complexion or hue" in Latin. Vergil and Horace used it to signify "a beautiful complexion." Another Latin extension of the meaning is "artful concealment of a fault." Hence some scholars relate it to *celare*, "to conceal," and even claim that it is a cousin of *hell!*

We, too, have broadened the meaning of the word. For TV broadcasts of football games, for instance, ex-players or ex-coaches, like Don Meredith and Ara Parseghian, are hired to do the *color commentary*. In essence, they try to enhance the broadcast by relating interesting details about the players and surroundings to supplement the play-by-play reporting of the action.

When a person has a distinctive or animated personality we say that he is *colorful*. On the other hand, a bore is *colorless*.

Our use of *color* as a verb does seem to relate to the Romans' idea of artful concealment. People who *color* a story may be lying, offering excuses or glossing over important facts.

In the *color* family, the Latin adjective is *coloratus*. The Italians lengthened the feminine form and used it to apply to ornamental passages in music. *Coloratura* is now a part of our language. One of its meanings is "brilliant runs and trills displaying a singer's skill." Opera lovers revere *coloratura sopranos* like Beverly Sills and Joan Sutherland.

Finally, if you have ever visited the incarnadine* Garden of the Gods, you will agree that *Colorado* is well named. In Spanish that derivative from Latin means "red or ruddy."

Creator, curator and *dictator* all have the same meanings today as they did in ancient Rome.

Of the three, *curator* is probably the most fascinating because of its origin and its cousins. It comes from *cura*, the Latin word for "care." A *curator* at a museum takes care of all the treasures therein. But let's examine the other offshoots.

If a physician finds a *cure* for a patient, he literally took care—or, to paraphrase a commercial phrase, he cared enough to do his very best.

When I grew up in Jersey City under Mayor Hague, one of my many uncles had a *sinecure*. He was paid even though he never appeared on the job. Literally, his post was without care.

Your *manicurist* cares for your hands, and your *pedicurist* cares for your feet. And when you are *secure,* you are, literally, free from care.

When I was head recruiter for New York City schools, I was asked to *procure* teachers. Translated, that means "care in a forward-looking way." Colleagues gave me a ribbing, because a *procurer* is also a pimp. Interestingly enough, studies of prostitutes reveal that many of them attach themselves to pimps because they want someone to care for them.

A sibling of *procurer* is *procurator*. Originally he was a Roman official who managed the affairs of a province. Today he's a sort of agent or person employed to manage another's estate. *Procuration* is synonymous with power of attorney.

Another offshoot is *proctor*. In one sense it's interchangeable with *procurator*. It's also an academic term for an official who maintains order and supervises examinations at a higher institution of learning. But, as I revealed in my "trivia" story earlier in this chapter, a *proctor* also has a lower rank in the examination process.

Amazingly enough, even *proxy* stems from our *cura* root. It's a

---

* *Incarnadine*—red; blood-red, flesh-colored. This word dates back to a Latin root *carn* ("flesh"). *Carnal* and *carnivorous* are two others in the family.

variation of *procuracy,* the office of that Roman above. A *proxy,* too, is an agent. He is a person authorized to act for another. The term is often used in law and in the stock market.

It's not hard to see that *accurate* and *accuracy* come to us from this same exciting source. The words can be traced back to the prefix *ad* (changed to *ac*) and the verb *curare.* Translated, they signify "to take care in relation to."

Are *curious* and *curiosity* descendants also? Yes, indeed! The Romans broadened the original root into *curiose* ("with care") and *curiosus* ("full of care"). The adjectival form eventually came to mean "too eager." Hence, curious!

That *curator* who started all this would naturally be concerned about the precious *curios.* It's intriguing to note that *curio* has two meanings in Latin, neither of which is directly related to modern connotations for the word:

1. a priest associated with the Roman Curia [Senate]
2. a person wasted by sorrow (he cares too much!)

Today a *curio* is an unusual or rare article arousing interest. It's a shortened form of *curiosity.*

Probably the most delightful scion of *cura* and *curare* is that lovely adjective we have stolen from Italy—*pococurante.* Literally and actually, it means "caring little." If you are indifferent or apathetic about a certain issue, you enjoy (or suffer from) *pococuranteism.*

Have you ever heard of a *curet* or *curette?* It's a spoon-shaped instrument for the removal of tissue, used by surgeons who care to cure.

Now get ready for a real surprise! *Sure, assure, ensure* and *insure* can all be traced back to our fabulous Roman root. Your *insurance* agent may be amazed to hear that, as advertised, he really does care.

Doctor merits special attention. In Latin the word means "teacher or instructor." Its parent verb is *docere* ("to teach") and, like *curare,* it has given birth to a slew of English words.

Today most people think of physicians or veterinarians or dentists as *doctors,* but the first meaning of the word in most lexicons is "a person who holds the highest academic degree awarded by a college or university."

One of the words stemming from *docere* is *docile* ("teachable; tractable; obedient"). Another is *docent.* He or she is either a college teacher not on the regular faculty or a tour guide at a museum. The latter definition reminds me of *cicerone,* a word we have taken over from the Italians. Because tour guides are so talkative, they reflect that great Roman orator Cicero!

Doctrine and *document* also come from this prolific source. In ancient Rome, *doctrina* meant "teaching or instruction" and *documentum* meant "lesson or proof."

———

Dogma is listed earlier in this chapter under words ending in *a*. In Latin it means "a philosophic tenet or doctrine," just as it does in English. An adjectival offshoot is *dogmatic*. Because some people have been so firm and unyielding in stating their beliefs, the word has taken on unpleasant connotations—arrogant, opinionated or dictatorial. Those who *dogmatize* are often accused of stating with absolute confidence ideas that are open to question.

It should be pointed out that the foregoing words eventually can be traced back to the Greek verb *dokein* ("to think or seem"). This grandparent is also responsible for the following, among others:

> *doxology*—hymn of praise to God; utterance of thanksgiving
> *doxological*—giving praise to God
> *heterodox*—departing from the usual beliefs; inclining toward heresy
> *orthodox*—conforming to the usual beliefs
> *paradox*—seemingly contradictory statement
> *doxy*—opinion or doctrine

In connection with the above, the story is told that during a debate in the House of Lords, William Warburton (Bishop of Gloucester) whispered to Lord Sandwich, "Orthodoxy is my doxy; heterodoxy is another man's doxy." Actually, Warburton was punning on the word *doxy*. A second word with that spelling means "trollop or prostitute or loose wench." It has come into our language via Medieval Dutch.

That Greek verb *dokein* is also responsible, through the Romans' *decere* ("to be fitting"), for such words as *decent, decency, decor, decorate* and *decorous*.

———

At this point the reader may wonder if the Greeks also borrowed their words. The answer is that they often did. Like Latin, their language is part of the Indo-European family, which includes most of the tongues spoken in Europe and many of those spoken in India and southwestern Asia. As the Greeks conquered other lands, they enriched their own language with words from those countries. For example, when they invaded Persia, they learned words of Aryan or Indo-Iranian origin. Incidentally, it should be stressed that the Greeks were the first to make a scientific study of language in Europe, chiefly because they felt this would enhance their understanding of other fields of knowledge. Appropriately enough, our word *etymology* is of Greek origin.

———

But let us return to our list of words ending in *or*.

Dolor meant "pain, anguish, distress or sorrow" to Cicero and Caesar. The word is in our language today and still carries those definitions. A derivative adjective is *dolorific* ("causing pain or grief"). More commonly used is *dolorous* ("woeful, deplorable, lugubrious"*).

What we need is a *dolorifuge*—something that banishes or mitigates grief.

Dolores is a pretty name. Many a señorita is so called in commemoration of the epithet for the Virgin Mary—*Mater Dolorosa*. Literally, the phrase means "sorrowful mother," referring to Mary's grief at Calvary. Thereafter she became "Our Lady of Sorrows."

Emptor ("buyer") lives in our language mainly as a legal term and especially because of the phrase *Caveat emptor* ("Let the buyer beware").

Excelsior is the comparative form of *excelsus* ("lofty; high"). In that sense it is the motto of New York State and means "Higher!" But a manufacturer who used wood shavings for packing fragile objects or for stuffing furniture seized the word and made it his trademark. Like Kleenex, Silex and other such names, it soon became a noncapitalized English noun.

The reader may have guessed that *excel* and *excellent* come from the same root.

Exterior and *interior* are also comparative Latin forms. One comes from *exter* ("on the outside") and the other from *interus* ("inward"). *Inferior* also fits into this group. It is the comparative of *inferus* ("low or below"). People with an *inferiority complex* feel they are lower than others.

Fulgor unfortunately has become archaic. To the Romans it meant "the flashing thing." Hence it became their word for "lightning." By metonymy it came to mean a "flash, glitter or gleam" or even "splendor, glory or renown."

Our ancestors adopted the word and used it as a synonym for dazzling brightness or splendor, but for some reason it turned out to be a flash in the pan.† However, several of its relatives still sparkle in our dictionaries:

---

* *Lugubrious* (from *lugere,* "to mourn")—very sad, especially in a way that sounds exaggerated or ridiculous

† *Flash in the pan*. This phrase probably dates back to the use of the muskets. When the pan (or hollow part that receives the priming) would emit a flash but would not cause the weapon to discharge, it was a disappointment to the musketeer.

effulgent—shining forth brilliantly; resplendent
fulgence—brilliant luster
fulgent—dazzlingly bright; radiant
fulgurant—flashing like lightning
fulgurate—to emit flashes
fulguration—lightning flash; spiritual revelation or divine manifestation
refulgence—splendor; brilliance

Junior is a contracted comparative form of *juvenis* ("young"). A few of the other words from this source are *juvenile, rejuvenate* and, through the vagaries of crossbreeding, even *young* itself.

Most people who are *senescent* ("growing old") would rather be *juvenescent* ("becoming young or youthful"). Our *salad days* are the period of *juvenescence* ("youthful condition"). By the way, it was no less a master of the English language than Shakespeare who gave us that crisp and succulent phrase. In ANTONY AND CLEOPATRA (Act I, Sc. 5) the queen speaks of "my *salad days,* when I was green in judgment . . ." In other words, she had *sown wild oats.* And whence comes that particular expression? Well, *wild oats* resemble the cereal grain, but they are inferior weeds. Hence a person who sows them is wasting his time on an activity that won't bear fruit. But some young bucks who *sow wild oats* inadvertently cause their female companions to *fructify*—much to the regret of both parties.

———

Lector meant "a reader" in old Rome and especially "a slave reading aloud at an entertainment." Today he is certainly no slave but a professional who gives lectures at colleges and universities. He is also a person who reads the Scriptures aloud at a church service. Finally, he is a member of one of the minor orders of the Roman Catholic Church.

The noun stems from *legere* ("to gather, pick out or read"), and once again we have encountered a fascinating family. Here are some members: *coil, collect, cull, diligent, elect, elegant, intellect, intelligence, lectern, lecture, legend, legion, neglect, negligence* and *select.*

It's delightful and de-lovely to realize that *negligee* came into this family via the bedroom-conscious French. One meaning for that word is "informal, careless or incomplete attire." And, if we analyze the garb's linguistic origin, it really comes out as "not choosy, or unselective." Of course a bride who buys that article today is hardly careless in her choice!

Another remarkable offshoot of our root is *sacrilegious* (a word often misspelled with an *e* as the fifth letter because people confuse it with *religious*). The Romans had a noun *sacrilegus* ("temple robber"). He gathered up sacred objects from a holy place and absconded with them. Thus the first definition for *sacrilege* in modern usage is: "the act of appropriating to oneself or to secular use what is consecrated to God or religion." That crime has been extended to mean any profanation. In other words, a person doesn't have to be a thief to commit a *sacrilege*. He may merely be irreverent about all that is holy and sacred.

One final gem emanates from *legere*. It is *sortilege,* a synonym for black magic or sorcery. The initial root is *sors* ("lot"). In one of its many senses a lot is an object used in deciding a matter by chance. In Rome an augur (or fortune-teller) would often cast out lots and then gather them up or *sort* them. Thus came to us the original meaning of *sortilege*—prophecy by casting lots.

———

Liberator means to us precisely what it meant to the Romans. In Latin and in English it is a deliverer. The Spanish equivalent retains worldwide fame because of Simón Bolívar. In Venezuela he is affectionately called *El Libertador* because of his fight for independence in the revolution against Spain. In Italy, incidentally, a deliverer such as Giuseppe Garibaldi is a *liberatore*.

Naturally, *liberty* is a sibling, as well as *deliver* and *liberal*. Strangely enough, *livery* and *libertine* also belong. They come into the picture because of the parent verb *liberare* ("to set free").

Livery has many meanings today, among them:

1. the costume or insignia worn by retainers of a feudal lord
2. the uniform worn by male servants
3. the boarding and care of horses for a fee
4. a livery stable
5. a place where boats are hired out

The word came to us through the French, who often changed a *b* to a *v*. In Medieval English it was an allowance of food or clothes given free to servants.

A *libertine* in ancient times was a person who had been freed from slavery. In the 1500s a sect of freethinkers arose in Europe. They called themselves the *Libertines*. One of their tenets was that man cannot sin. Hence they indulged in wicked ways. From then on, *libertine* became identified with a dissolute person who acts without moral restraint.

What about the *liberal arts?* In Latin those academic subjects are *artes liberales* ("arts befitting a freeman"), in contrast to *artes serviles*.

Let me add another synonym for tyrant or dictator to your vocabulary. I have just discovered *liberticide* ("a destroyer of liberty"). The word can also serve as an adjective.

———

Liber ("free") and *liber* ("book") are sometimes confused. It's easy to see that *library* and *libretto* are derived from the latter, but *libel* must give us pause. It comes from a diminutive *libellus*, meaning "a little book." Since such a publication often turned out to be a lampoon,* it gave rise to the idea of a false and malicious statement.

Leaf is also an offshoot of the second *liber*, because the Latin word originally meant "the inner bark or rind of a tree, or the pith of papyrus." As is generally known, the leaves of ancient books were made from papyrus.

Another Latin verb that sometimes causes a mix-up is *librare* ("to poise or balance"). From this source we obtain *Libra*, a sign of the zodiac and a southern constellation. A verb that we don't see very often is *librate*. It means "to move back and forth slowly like a pendulum, or to oscillate."

Most interesting is the fact that *deliberate* comes from this source. When you *deliberate* about a problem, you literally weigh it in the scales. Some philologists think that it is eventually related to *liberare*. Thus we come full circle to our *liberator*.

———

Major is the Latin comparative of *magnus* ("great"). A *major* in the army holds a rank greater than that of a captain. In bridge a *major* suit like spades or hearts has greater weight than diamonds or clubs. And then there is the *major domo* (literally, "chief of the house"), who is the top steward in a noble household. Nor must we forget *drum majorettes* or the *major leagues* in baseball.

Majorette is an entrancing word. Literally it means "greater female." The girls who prance in front of the bands are playing a more important role than the boys who blow the horns behind them. Those shapely strutters may be smaller but they are "greater."

Of course *majority* is an esteemed descendant in a democracy. When the *majority* rules, the "greater" number of people have had their say. And if you have reached your *majority* (full legal age), you are "greater" than a juvenile.

———

Mediator is a Low Latin word for an intercessor. Other branches are *mediatrix* and *mediatress*, but feminists will probably cause the demise of those "chauvinistic" designations in the near future.

———

* *Lampoon*—a piece of strongly satirical writing, usually attacking or ridiculing someone. The probable source is the French refrain in a drinking song—"*Lampons!*" It means "Let us drink [or guzzle]!"

Like so many other Latin roots, the verb *mediare* ("to be in the middle") and the adjective *medius* ("middle") have sired a goodly number of our words either in whole or in part. Some examples are the following: *mean* (in its arithmetical sense), *medial, median, medium, mizzenmast, intermediate, medieval, mediocre* and *mediterranean*.

Milieu joined the family in France. The first syllable is a shortening of *mid,* and *lieu* is the Gallic variation of *locus* ("place"). Literally, then, the word means "middle place." We have taken over one of its extended senses—namely, social surroundings; we use the word to mean "environment."

Another French derivative is *moiety,* meaning "half." Sometimes it conveys the idea of an indefinite share or part.

———

And now we come to the last list in this chapter on Latin-English words.

minor	rancor	squalor	torpor
orator	rigor	stridor	tremor
pallor	sapor	stupor	tutor
pastor	senator	superior	ulterior
posterior	senior	tenor	victor
prior	spectator	terror	
procurator	sponsor	testator	

Minor is the comparative of the irregular Latin adjective *parvus* ("small"). The superlative is *minimus,* and its neuter form has given us *minimum*.

Two delicious words from *parvus* are *parvule,* "a small pill," and *parvanimity,* "meanness." Literally, it means "the state of having a small mind," and it is the opposite of *magnanimity*. To the best of my knowledge there is no *parvanimous* to match *magnanimous*. I hereby nominate the adjective for synonymity with ignoble.

———

Orator in Latin and English means "speaker." Would you believe that *adore* is its next of kin? Both words come from *orare,* a Latin verb with many meanings, among them "to speak or pray." *Adore* literally means "to pray to." Its verbatim sense persists in such definitions as "pay divine honors to; revere." But of course the scope of the verb has been broadened. When a swain tells a girl that he *adores* her, he's saying that he loves her very much. And when we say that a child is *adorable,* we don't really have reverence in mind.

Laborare est orare is an old Latin maxim. It means "to labor is to pray."

From the parent verb we have received some other gifts. Among them are *oracle, oration* and *oratory*. The last of that trio has three meanings:

1. skill or eloquence in public speaking
2. a small chapel for prayer
3. a religious society of secular priests, especially the one founded in Rome by Saint Philip Neri in 1564

From Saint Philip Neri's group we have derived the word *oratorio* —a long dramatic musical opus, usually having a religious theme. The reason is that the priests in the *Oratorio* at Rome often performed such compositions. As all music lovers know, in the eighteenth century Handel handled the form very well. His *oratorios* are acclaimed throughout the western world.

From *orare* also come *exorable* and *inexorable*. The former literally means "to be prayed out," and it is easy to gather the literal sense of its antonym. *Exorable* has become obsolescent, but our linguistic inclination toward the negative has allowed *inexorable* to thrive. It means "unrelenting," and is often applied to fate, doom, logic and judges.

Finally, there is *peroration*—the concluding part of a speech. *Perorate* means "to end a speech," but it also carries the notion of declaiming at length, perhaps because so many speakers are long-winded. Some of the Americans on soapboxes also indulge in *spread eagle*. That's a term meaning "high-flown or bombastic speech smacking of *jingoism*." It's derived from the fact that a spread eagle is displayed on the Great Seal of the United States.

As for *jingoism* ("arrogant nationalism"), that word comes from a refrain of a patriotic British musical-hall song (1878), in which the phrase "by jingo" was repeated. Hence a *jingo* came to mean a superpatriot who (like Stephen Decatur) declares, "My country, right or wrong!"

Incidentally, *jingo* is a euphemism for Jesus, just as *bloody* (in vulgar British usage) is possibly a corruption of "by Our Lady." Certainly the Victorians' *Egad* is a minced oath meaning "Oh God" and *Gadzooks* is an old abridgment of "God's hooks" (nails of the Cross).

To return to *orare,* in case some reader wonders whether *oral* is a derivative, the answer is no. That word comes from *os, oris,* which meant "mouth" to a Roman.

Pallor means the same today as it did in Horace's era—wanness. Naturally the adjective *pale* is a descendant, and so is *pallid*. But the most enchanting scion is *appall*. Literally, that verb means "to give wanness to." If something *appalls* you, it makes your face grow suddenly ashen.

Through the Spanish we obtain *palomino*—that cream-colored horse with a silvery-white or ivory mane and tail. As noted in the chapter called "Our Animal Kingdom," the steed's name comes from *paloma,* the Spanish word for dove, because of its grayish color. But *paloma* itself is a daughter of our root *pallere* ("to be pale").

Did you know that *fallow* has two altogether different meanings? Probably the more popular one is "left uncultivated or unplanted." We often say that lands *lie fallow* when they are not tilled. But the other adjective stems from our root and means "pale yellow." Somehow, through the ages, the initial *p* was changed to an *f.* Otherwise the *fallow deer* (which has a yellowish coat spotted with white in the summer) would be called a *pallow deer.*

One would expect *pall* to come from the root being discussed. It seems to have a wan significance. But its parent is *pallium* ("cover"), akin to *palla* ("a woman's mantle"). When a person throws a *pall* on the party, he literally smothers it with a cloak.

By the way, one of the meanings of *pall* in English is "cloak or drape." In that connection, *palliate* can be defined as "cover with excuses." In its most common usage it means "to ease, allay or alleviate."

Those whose interest has been aroused are invited to explore the separate derivations of *pallet, palette, pale* (as a noun meaning "stake") and *paleolithic.*

Pastor has taken on a religious significance. Today he is the priest in charge of a church or congregation. But in ancient Rome he was a shepherd. The transition is simple to fathom. After all, clergymen often refer to their parishioners as "the flock" and worry about the sheep that stray from the fold.

But the adjective *pastoral* still retains its Latin heritage. It means "of shepherds." Consequently its import has become expanded to signify "rural." As a noun it means "a piece of literature dealing with the country."

Of course *pasture* belongs to this family, all of which can be traced to *pascere* ("to feed"). Hence *repast* ("meal") joins the clan.

A fascinating offshoot is *pastern*—that part of a horse's foot that lies between the fetlock and the hoof. And an unpleasant cousin is *pester,* which is derived from an Old French word meaning "to hobble a horse at pasture; to entangle."

The Italians' *antipasto* can be translated into "before the food." (They changed the last letter of *ante.*) This delicious appetizer owes its heritage to *pascere.*

Strangely enough, *pasta* is not directly related. If you enjoy macaroni, linguine, ziti or other forms of such Italian fare, you can thank the Greeks for the source—*passein* ("to sprinkle"). And if you have ever made dough for bread and cakes, you can understand the aptness of the verbal source.

It must be noted that *paste* comes from that same Greek parent.

Prior means "previous" in modern times, and it meant the same to Pompey. Since it also carried the idea of superior, it's not difficult to see why a *prior* is an official at a monastery. But even though he is a superior, he's not supreme. That adjective applies to his boss, the *abbot* —an Aramaic word meaning "father."

As expected, *priority* belongs in this group, and so does *a priori,* a phrase that sometimes means "presumptive." Thus *a priori* acceptance of a new work of art by a master is based on former experience. The critic presumes that the creator will not disappoint him.

Rigor means "stiffness or severity" in Latin and English. Coroners talk of *rigor mortis* ("stiffness of death"). Of course *rigid* and *rigorous* are part of this group, and *frigid* is a distant relative.

From the French we have received *de rigueur,* a phrase meaning "prescribed by etiquette, fashion or custom; proper." In other words, in society an action that is required by stiff and severe rules is *de rigueur.* For example, at some formal gatherings it's *de rigueur* for men to wear a white tie.

Sapor is another of those words that have survived in meaning and spelling without change. It has always meant "flavor." Incidentally, the British spelling is *sapour.* Some other words in the same category are *colour, odour, honour, flavour* and *rigour.* The reason is the influence of the French as a result of the Norman Conquest.

I like *saporous* even though it's not often seen. It's a mellisonant synonym for tasty.

In old French, *sapor* suffered a change in its middle. The *p* changed to a *v,* and we inherited *savor* (or as the British spell it, *savour*). Our adjective is *savory.*

Well, now, here's another surprise. The parent verb is *sapere* ("to taste; to have discernment; to be sensible;" and finally, "to know or understand"). Therefore, through those French of long ago we find *savant* in the family. He's a learned person or eminent scholar. He has taken a taste of knowledge and he finds it sweet. In other words, he has *savvy,* a slangy derivative via the Spanish. Or to mention still another kinsman, he is *sapient* ("wise"). He certainly is no *sap!*

Sponsor in Latin means "one who promises solemnly for another; hence, a bondsman or surety." That seems to be a far cry from the manufacturer who puts up the money for a TV program. But a *sponsor* in a baptismal ceremony is a godfather or godmother, and those people do solemnly promise to look after the infant whenever needed.

From the parent verb, *spondere* ("to pledge or promise sacredly"), we have been given *respond, responsible, response, spouse, espouse, despondent* and *correspond*. When two people are *correspondents*, they literally make pledges back and forth together. That does sound as if love letters are being written.

———

Squalor meant "stiffness or roughness" to Lucretius, but the word took on another meaning—the very one we use today—"filthiness." We also use the word as a synonym for wretchedness, and our adjective *squalid* has come to mean "miserable or sordid" as well as "foul and unclean."

———

Stridor is derived from *stridere* ("to make a harsh sound"). In Latin and English the noun means "a harsh, shrill or creaking noise." Our most common acquaintance with this root is the adjective *strident*. But here are some other relatives, which we appear to be neglecting:

> *stridulation*—a high-pitched musical sound made by insects, as katydids or crickets, by rubbing together certain parts of the body
> *stridulous*—squeaky
> *stridulatory*—able to stridulate; stridulous
> *stridulent*—loud; blatant

Stupor originally meant "amazement" in Latin. It came from the verb *stupere* ("to be astonished; to be struck senseless"). That latter connotation led to the idea of dullness or *stupidity*.

Today we use *stupor* as a synonym for numbness or lethargy. A drug addict or alcoholic has had his senses numbed so extremely that he falls into a state of *stupefaction*.

Our verb *stupefy* carries two meanings: "to astonish, stun and bewilder" and "to make dull." Incidentally, the way to remember how to spell that word is to recall the original Latin verb.

Probably the most interesting derivative is *stupendous,* which certainly has no dull significance. If a play is a *stupendous* success, it's an astonishing or stunning hit.

A little-known relative is *stupefacient*. It can be used as an adjective ("having a stupefying effect") or as a noun ("a drug; a narcotic").

The Greek word for numbness or *stupor* was *narke*. From it we obtained the noun or the adjective *narcotic*. A slangy shortening is *narc* or *nark*—a government agent investigating drug violations. But in England a *nark* is an informer or stool pigeon (dating back to a Sanskrit word for "nose"), and in Australia a *nark* is a killjoy or wet blanket.

———

Tenor comes from *tenere* ("to hold")—a verb that has sired scores of English words. It will be discussed later in this book. To the Romans, *tenor* was "a holding on or holding out; hence, an uninterrupted course or career."

When we speak of "the *tenor* of events," we use the word to mean "course." Other synonyms are, for example: intent, purport, tendency, and general meaning.

What about *tenor,* the male voice or the singer? The noun may seem to have no relationship to *tenere,* but it does, because the *tenor* voice was originally the one that held the melody in the singing or chanting of hymns.

Terror meant "great fear" in ancient Rome, just as it does today. Our adjective *terrible* is an offshoot, but its import has been extended along with that of its synonyms, frightful and awful.

Consider these two sentences:

> I am in *terrible* trouble.
> That singer has a *terrible* voice.

In the first statement the adjective retains the sense of its Latin root. In the second it means "very inferior."

Now, suppose that your friend has just seen a horror film and he reports, "That movie was terrible!" You couldn't be sure whether he thought it was gruesome or very disappointing.

A more astonishing change has occurred in the case of *terrific*. It still means "causing terror" but is more commonly used to express just the opposite. Your friend reports, "That horror film was *terrific!*" It would be a safe bet to assume that he enjoyed it immensely.

It may surprise you to learn that *deter* and *deterrent* belong to this fearsome family. Literally, *deter* means "frighten away." When a person is *undeterred* by difficulties or setbacks, he's not to be scared away.

Torpor is another of those ancient nouns that have survived the centuries without change in spelling or meaning. Like *stupor,* it means "lethargy or apathy." Its adjective is *torpid,* and the verb *torpify* means "to benumb."

And there's *torporific*—stupefying.

Best of all, we have *torpedo*. That was a Latin noun meaning "numbness." But it was also the name given to the crampfish or electric ray because of that creature's benumbing sting. Considering the effect of a direct hit by a modern *torpedo,* the person who named that projectile was right on the mark.

Tremor meant all the things to the Romans that it means to us—a shaking, quaking or quivering. Lucretius used it as a term for "earthquake." We do not, but we often associate *tremors* with that kind of shifting of the ground.

Naturally *tremble* is in this family and also *tremulous*—quivering, palpitating; hence, fearful or timid. Through Italian we get *tremolo*— a quavering effect produced by rapid reiteration of the same tone.

Additionally, we have inherited *tremendous*. Just as with *terrific*, this adjective represents one of the rare instances in which we turn a negative idea into a positive one. *Tremendous* still means "dreadful," but in popular usage it's a synonym for the words "enormous" and— amazingly—"delightful." You hear people say, "We had a *tremendous* time at the party," and you know they don't mean that it was a terrifying experience.

The same phenomenon has occurred with regard to *wonderful* and *marvelous*. Originally both adjectives were used in the sense of awe-inspiring or astonishing. Although these definitions persist, most of us have forgotten them. Instead we use either of the two words as a substitute for "excellent."

Finally, there is *delirium tremens*. That skid-row condition is *tremendous* and *terrific* in the original sense of those adjectives.

———

Tutor to Horace and his contemporaries meant "a watcher, protector, defender or guardian." Today those connotations are present in the definition "the guardian of a child below the age of puberty or majority." But more often we consider a *tutor* to be a private instructor.

In that connection, Carolyn Wells's famous limerick deserves to be quoted:

> "A Tutor who tooted the flute
> Tried to teach two young tooters to toot.
> Said the two to the Tutor,
> 'Is it harder to toot, or
> To tutor two tooters to toot?' "

As I have stated elsewhere in this book, the Romans had *tutelary* gods who watched over them benevolently. The adjective still means "serving as a guardian."

Other descendants are *tuition*, *tutelage* ("protection or instruction"), *intuitive* and *intuition*. The last duo are in the family because of the parent verb *tueri* ("to watch with care").

Alexander Pope said of Shakespeare: "He seems to have known the world by *intuition*, to have looked through nature at one glance." In other words, the Bard had direct knowledge without the conscious use of reasoning. He literally looked inside himself.

———

Ulterior is the comparative of *ulter, ultra, ultrum* ("beyond"). It means "further or more remote" in Latin and English. Thus it has come to connote "beyond what is expressed." We suspect *ulterior motives*—those that are hidden or undisclosed deliberately.

Note that *ultra* is in this group. It has become a prefix meaning "beyond, excessive, to an extreme degree." We use it in such words as *ultrasonic* and *ultraviolet*. It is also an adjective meaning "extreme" or a noun for "extremist." A synonym for the latter is *ultraist*.

Victor completes our discussion of certain words in the list. As in Caesar's day, it means "the winner or conqueror." Boys named *Victor* are not meant to be losers, nor are those named *Vincent*. The parent verb is *vincere* ("to conquer or prevail"). Empress *Victoria* seemed to live up to that linguistic heritage. *Vicky* or *Vickie* of course is a shortened form of *Victoria*.

Remember Caesar's "Veni, vidi, vici"? He came, he saw, he conquered. He *vanquished* his foes (a derivative from Old French). They were *vincible*, but he seemed to be *invincible*.

Other kinsmen of *victor* include *convict, conviction, convince* and *evict. Victim* is a distant cousin, but *vicious* is not related at all. It can be traced back to *vitium* ("a fault or defeat").

To conclude, a favorite poem of the boys whom I once taught at Frederick Douglass Junior High School was INVICTUS, by William Ernest Henley. The last lines are:

> "I am the master of my fate;
> I am the captain of my soul."

Those ancient Romans were *victors* in more ways than one. They not only conquered other people but they became the masters of the western linguistic world. Think about it! The long chapter that you have just read is devoted to only a small sampling of the words that we have inherited *in toto* from them.

CHAPTER 4

The Wild and the Tame

This chapter has nothing to do with animals. That section will come later. The intent here is to discuss two types of words in our language —those that seem to have no relation to their sources and are therefore "wild," and the "tame" words that adhere to their ancestry closely but are nevertheless exciting and fascinating. Most entries in both categories will find their eventual home in Caesar's empire only because that ancient realm has bestowed so many gifts upon us.

Let's begin with some of the mavericks that have strayed far from the fold through semantic changes.

Would you believe that *salary* and *salt* are related? *Sal* is the Latin word for "salt," and money given to the Roman soldiers for that commodity was called *salarium*. Later that word was applied to any stipend, allowance or pension.

I was once told that *sincere* came from *sine cera* ("without wax")— a plausible idea, but untrue. It's a derivative of *sincerus* ("clean, pure") and can be eventually traced back to the verb *creare* ("to create"). *Procreate* and *crescent* are two of its many cousins.

Vaccination and *pecuniary* have really gone astray. They both relate to cattle. The Latin word for "cow" is *vacca*. Hence *vaccine* came into our language as an adjective meaning "relating to cowpox." When a preparation was found to fight the disease, the adjective also became a noun. The verb *vaccinate* naturally followed.

Incidentally, *vaccary* is a "tame" word compared with its sisters. It's a cow pasture or even a dairy farm.

As for *pecuniary,* that adjective relating to money comes to us from *pecus* ("cattle"). When a Roman farmer achieved "wealth in cattle" his status was called *pecunia.*

Peculate ("to steal money or to embezzle") comes from the same bovine root. If we took a *peculator* back to his true origin, we'd have to say he's a cattle thief rather than just any swindler. Similarly, if we wanted to be technical, we'd be forced to conclude that *impecunious* people don't own many steers. But of course the adjective means "poor or penniless."

Peculiar also dates back to those cattle. The Romans developed the word *peculium*. In Latin, and in legal English today, the word means "private property." Now, if some object or trait belongs to you exclusively, it is *peculiar* to you. The American jurist R. B. Taney spoke of "the *peculiar* character of the Government of the U.S."—meaning its distinctiveness.

But, as often happens, the meaning of the adjective has devolved. A person who has *peculiar* habits (in the original sense of the word) or who enjoys his privacy is considered to be odd or strange.

The synonym *eccentric* has suffered the same fate. This Greek derivative literally means "out of the center of the circle" and is used in that sense by astronomers and mathematicians. But people who are not in the center of things, or who are off-center, are regarded as strange. They're *peculiar,* whether they own cattle or not!

———

At the beginning of the chapter I mentioned *vaccination.* That reminds me of another word, one which is often misspelled. When a physician *inoculates* a child against smallpox, he literally puts an "eye" into the tot's skin. If you remember that *oculist* and *monocle* are related to *inoculation,* your orthography will be correct.

The problem seems to arise because of the spelling of *innocuous* ("harmless"). That word is also easy to handle if you keep the derivation in mind. It stems from *nocere* ("to harm"); the prefix means "not." By the way, *innocent* comes from the same source, and so does *noxious* ("harmful").

An evil cousin is the adjective *pernicious* ("deadly"). It stems from *necere* ("to kill"). Both *nocere* and *necere* owe their origin to the Greeks. In Athens, *nekros* meant "dead body."

There are several rather scary words from this root. Here is a selection:

> *necrology*—obituary; list of recently deceased people
> *necromancy*—black magic
> *necrophilia*—erotic attraction to corpses
> *necrophobia*—morbid fear of dead bodies
> *necropolis*—cemetery
> *necropsy*—postmortem

The Romans' equivalent, *corpus,* has been discussed in a previous chapter. Somewhat allied in meaning is *caro, carnis* ("flesh or piece of flesh"). In English, *carnal* means "bodily or in the flesh." Because of its nonspiritual import it has come to mean "sensual or sexual." *Carnal knowledge* is sexual intercourse.

Some obvious words from the *carn* root are:

> *carnage*—bloody slaughter
> *carnelian*—red variety of quartz; flesh-red color

carnivorous—flesh-eating

carrion—decaying flesh of a dead body

charnel—(through Old French) a building or place where corpses or bones are deposited; usually called a *charnel house*

chile con carne—("hot pepper with meat") spicy Spanish stew

incarnate—in the flesh (as in the saying "the Devil *incarnate*"); personified

But there are some "wild" words in this group too. Because of its color the lovely *carnation* has joined the family. And then there is *caruncle* ("a naked, fleshy outgrowth—as a bird's wattle"). What'll they think of next?

Carnival is probably the most enchanting descendant. Its original English meaning is still in use; it's a synonym for Shrovetide, the period before Lent. The second part of the word comes from *levare* ("to raise or remove"). In old Italian, *carnelevare* meant "the putting away of flesh." Well, that's what happens in many households when the fasting period called Lent rolls around.

Since there was much merrymaking just before Lent, *carnival* took on a festive sense, and soon it was applied to any traveling amusement show that appeared at a feast. A slangy noun for a person who works in one of those attractions is *carny*. Wouldn't it be ironic if such a person were a vegetarian!

Some lexicographers, however, suggest that the ending of *carnival* is a shortened form of *vale* ("farewell"). In that case the word would literally mean "farewell to meat!"

Not to be confused with our fleshy Latin root is *Carna* ("The Swinger"). She was a goddess who guarded the door hinges. *Crone,* on the other hand, is related to *carrion;* hence that withered old hag can truly be said to have decaying flesh. No wonder the woman is shunned by the "madding crowd."

The Romans, by the way, had a word for a *meat rack.** It was called a *carnarium.* Considering the fact that we have retained their *cinerarium, auditorium* and other such words, I wonder why our butchers didn't hold onto a useful, expressive noun.

———

Among my favorite "wild" words are *sinister* and *dexterous* (sometimes spelled *dextrous*).

The popular meaning of *sinister* today is "wicked, evil" or "most unfavorable." The original Latin adjective meant "left, on the left hand or side." But, like many people in our time, the Romans also had their superstitions and prejudices. Since left-handed people were in the minority, they had to be "awkward or perverse." Gradually the connota-

* *Meat rack* in some parts of the U.S. is now a slangy synonym for a singles bar. That tells us something about the candor of young people today!

tions grew worse. *Sinister* came to mean "unlucky" and finally "evil" —a sense that we have retained.

However, I should note that I have found a few authorities who ascribe no bias to the Romans in the debasement of *sinister*. They point out that when Roman augurs began to emulate their Greek predecessors and face north on auspicious occasions, the East (or lucky side) was on their right. Hence the opposite side—or *sinister*—had to be unlucky or evil.

Dexter, in Latin, means "right, to the right side." The word remains as an adjective in our modern English dictionaries and retains the same sense. But it also means "auspicious or fortunate." Considering the above story about the augurs, you can see why *dexter* continues to have a lucky significance. And if you buy the idea of bias in favor of right-handed people, you can see why *dexterity* came to mean "skill in using one's hands" and then "mental skill or cleverness." The Romans' word for a person's right hand was *dextra*.

I happen to have an acquaintance named *Dexter*. The trouble is that he's left-handed. In a way he's a living *anomaly* ("departure from the general rule or arrangement").

There is also a breed of short-legged, hardy cattle called *Dexter*. They have no direct relation to our Latin word but are named for the Irishman who originally developed the stock in the nineteenth century.

As a boy I was an avid reader of the books about the Merriwell brothers. Frank Merriwell was my superhero, but I also admired Dick. If I remember correctly, he was *ambidextrous*. While pitching in an important baseball game he felt his right arm begin to tire. So he switched to the left arm, and struck out the "bad guys" on the other team.

Incidentally, did you ever wonder why a left-handed pitcher is called a *southpaw?* According to some authorities, the term was invented by a writer in Chicago (c. 1885). The ballpark in that city was so located that the pitcher's left arm faced toward the south. But if we look back at those late Roman augurs, a leftie should really be called a *westpaw*.

Twice in the above paragraphs the word *auspicious* has been mentioned. It deserves to be classified as "wild" because we no longer think of birds when we use the adjective, yet it has its roots in *avis-spicere* ("to see a bird").

In ancient Rome an *auspex* was an augur, or seer, who watched for omens in the flights of birds. Apparently those diviners found good signs more often than bad ones. In any case, *auspicious* has come to mean "favorable, boding well for the future, propitious." For example, when a peace treaty is signed or a new canal is opened, some politician is bound to get up and state: "Ladies and gentlemen, this is an *auspicious* occasion." And a dissenter in the back, with a background in Latin, may be heard to whisper, "He's for the birds!"

Auspices of course comes from the same source. It means "patronage." If a program on TV were to be shown under the *auspices* of the Audubon Society, that would be a perfect match!

Mention has been made above of *omen, diviners* and *propitious.* Let's take a look at that futuristic trio.

Omen is a Latin word meaning "prognostic sign." In English an *omen* is a thing or happening that's supposed to predict what is to come—good or bad. But its adjective, *ominous* (from the genitive case of the Latin noun), leaves out the good and clings to the bad. It means "threatening," and it's even a synonym for our friend *sinister.*

Diviners are perforce a revered group. Their root is *divus,* the Latin noun for "a god." Well, if they are really able to predict coming events, they must be godlike or have God-given talents.

Those soothsayers should not be mixed up with *divines* ("clergymen, theologians, priests"), nor should they be equated with *divas*—from the same root.

But it's fascinating to note that certain farewells—the French *adieu* and the Spanish *adios*—are members of this family. When you bid farewell to your friends in Paris or Madrid, you commend them to God.

Propitious literally means "seeking forward." Its parent verb is *petere* ("to seek"). If you examine the word you will see that hope really does spring eternal within the human breast, because it means "favorable." After all, pessimists and prophets of doom also seek forward for what is unpleasant or direful.

Some "tame" words from the *petere* root are *petition, compete* and *competitor.* It's easy to discern the seeking quality of that trio.

Because *petere* also means "to rush at," *impetus* presents no problem, nor does the adjectival offshoot, *impetuous.* But *petulant* ("peevish") requires a bit more cogitation, and so do its relatives *perpetual* and *repeat.*

The most appetizing member of this Latin family is *appetite* (literally, "a seeking toward or rushing toward"). As soon as "Come and get it!" resounds through the boarding house, the rush is on.

When *competitor* was mentioned above, I immediately thought of *rival*—and what a "wild" word it is! The fact that it comes from *rivalis* ("of a brook") seems incredible. Actually, *rivalis* soon became a noun in ancient Rome. It meant "one living near or using the same stream as another."* Then it came to mean "a neighbor" and eventually "one who has the same mistress as another." When Sheridan wrote the famous play THE RIVALS he was echoing that Roman interpretation, whether he knew it or not.

A relation of *rivus* ("brook") is *ripa* ("bank"). From these consanguineous roots we get a strange variety of English words. For example, *arrive* literally meant "to come to the bank"—hence, "to reach the shore." *Derive* carried the idea of diverting a stream from its channel. *River* of course belongs in this immense family. Strangely enough, so does *rive,* and we can even trace the *Rhine* back to these roots. *Rivulet* is a tiny relation. But the most interesting of all is *riparian* ("of, adjacent to, or living on river banks").

Cousins of this tribe, by the way, are *ripe, rip* and *row* (the last meaning "a line of adjacent seats"). Some words certainly do go astray as time moves on; the relationship to brooks and banks gets lost in the transmittance.

Another "wild" word is *ambulance.* When you think of this vehicle speeding toward a hospital with its siren blasting and its sick or injured patient tucked inside, it's hard to imagine that the word comes from *ambulare* ("to walk"). We owe the word to the French medicos of Napoleon's era. They developed the *hôpital ambulant* (literally, "walking hospital"), which traveled from place to place on the battlefield to help the wounded. The British, and then the Americans, took over the idea and called the vehicle an *ambulance.*

But the original sense of *ambulare* persists in *ambulatory* and *ambulant.* Those adjectives both mean "able to walk, itinerant, peripatetic." Today most postoperative patients are encouraged by their surgeons to be *ambulatory* as quickly as possible. They are urged into *ambulation* ("walking").

Amble ("saunter") and *perambulate* ("walk about") are derivatives. In England a baby carriage is called a *perambulator* because the infant's nana strolls around with it. The shortened form, well known to crossword puzzle fans, is *pram.*

Itinerant and *peripatetic* appeared a few paragraphs ago. These are interesting words.

Iter ("road") is the Latin root for the first of the duo. *Itinerant* can be used as an adjective or noun, meaning "traveling from place to place, or traveler." A travel agent may prepare an *itinerary* for one who is about to *itinerate.*

Peripatetic means "walking about from place to place or traveling on foot."

In his poem "The Bear" Robert Frost wrote:

> "A baggy figure equally pathetic
> When sedentary and when peripatetic."

As a noun the word means an *itinerant*. When capitalized, *Peripatetic* pertains to the philosophy or methods of Aristotle, who conducted discussions while walking about in the Lyceum of ancient Athens. He obviously loved to use shank's mare ("walk"), but his teachings were not *pedestrian.*

My pun on *pedestrian* illustrates the fact that a "tame" word can sometimes have a "wild" connotation. Since the Latin root *ped* means "foot," it's easy to understand why a *pedestrian* is a person who walks. But because walking is considered to be less exciting and exotic than speeding around in a vehicle, the adjective *pedestrian* has come to mean "prosaic, commonplace, undistinguished, ordinary."

Exotic itself is another example of how usage adds to the meaning of a word or changes it radically. The adjective has a Grecian heritage. In Athens *exo* meant "outside," so the Greeks developed the word *exotikos,* and the Romans transliterated it into *exoticus.* In either case it meant "foreign."

We still retain "foreign or strange" as the definition for *exotic,* but because the unfamiliar excites our curiosity, we have extended the sense of the adjective. It's probable that the vast majority of Americans don't realize that *exotic* means "foreign," but they do know that it has the following connotations.

1. strikingly and intriguingly unusual or beautiful
2. mysterious, romantic, picturesque, glamorous
3. strangely lovely, enticing, exciting

The popularity of *exotic dancers* (Turkish belly dancers) may have helped to bring the above meanings into the foreground. We pushed aside the idea that those entertainers were so called because they were foreign and we placed the emphasis on their enticing beauty. Thus any stripteaser, no matter what her origin, became an *exotic dancer.*

Advertisements about *exotic* ("foreign") islands such as Bali and Tahiti strengthened definitions using the terms "romantic" and "picturesque." We even have a noun *exotica.* It means "foreign or unfamiliar things, such as curios or rare art objects, strange customs, plants of other lands, etc."

In a way, *exotic* and *pedestrian* have become antithetical (more about that word later), although they didn't start out as opposites. The *ped* root has many descendants. Some are easy to recognize—for example, *pedal* and *pedestal*. The *centipede* and the *millipede* are instances of exaggeration; one does not have a hundred feet, nor does the other have a thousand. But the Latin source is simple to discern.

Expedite doesn't cause a problem either when you dig into its literal meaning—to free one caught by the feet. The definitions "to hasten or speed up or facilitate" fit the roots perfectly. The same is true of *impede* and *impediment*.

Relatives of *expedite,* by the way, are *expediency, expedience, expedition* and *expeditious*.

A fascinating descendant is *pedigree*. This synonym for family tree came to us via Medieval French. *Pié de grue* means "crane's foot." Because of the resemblance of the lines in a genealogical drawing to the feet of cranes, the French designation certainly seems apt.

Pawn, meaning "chessman," is one of the "wilder" words in this family. *Pedo, pedonis* meant "foot soldier" in the Middle Ages. Later it was used as a term for "one who has flat or broad feet." Through Medieval French and English the word was changed to *poon* and then *pown;* finally it found its way to the chessboard as *pawn*. Since the piece can move only one space at a time, its medieval senses are appropriate.

Would it astonish you to learn that a *peon* and a *pawn* are close relatives? The Portuguese changed *pedo* to *peao,* and our Hispanic-English word for "a laborer" evolved subsequently. It's also worth noting that *peon* in India or Ceylon signifies "a foot soldier, constable, office attendant or messenger."

It may also surprise you to hear that *pioneer* is next of kin to *pawn* and *peon*—again through the Latin word for "foot soldier." In Medieval France another alteration of *pedo* was *pionier*.

How did our idea that a *pioneer* is an early settler come about? Well, originally he was a soldier who constructed or demolished bridges or built roads for the army to use. Since he went ahead of the rest of the troops, a *pioneer* soon became identified as one who prepared the way for others.

Through the Italians we have obtained *piedmont*. As an adjective it means "lying along or near the foot of a mountain range." As a noun it's the region fitting that description. *Piedmont* (the natives call it Piemonte) is an appropriately named area in northwestern Italy. It is almost entirely surrounded by mountains, and its terrain slopes down to fertile plains.

Trivet has had its face lifted through the years. It originally combined *tri* ("three") with *ped*. Its Greek cousin is *tripod*.

Another Greek-rooted word that was mentioned earlier is *antithetical,* the adjectival form of *antithesis,* "exact opposite." Love is the *antithesis* of hate.

This is one of our "tame" words because it reflects its source rather neatly: *anti* ("against") and *tithenai* ("to set or place"). Because of the vagaries of linguistic history, it's astonishing to note that our verb "do" is related to the verbal root of *antithesis.*

Some other words in this Attic family are *thesis, hypothesis* and *parenthesis.*

Epithet is an interesting derivative. It literally means "something put on or added." When we use a word or phrase to describe a person, place or thing, we are employing an *epithet.* Examples are: Richard the Lionhearted; Rome, the Eternal City; and the "ox-eyed one" (Homer's term for Hera).

Because the use of *epithets* is really name-calling, we have allowed the word to take on a disparaging or abusive sense, as when we call an intellectual an egghead. In the opening scene of *Julius Caesar,* the tribune Marullus hurls *epithets* at the people celebrating Caesar's recent victories:

> "You blocks, you stones, you worse than senseless things!
> O you hard hearts, you cruel men of Rome,
> Knew you not Pompey?"

Apothecary is another offshoot of *tithenai.* The Romans borrowed the Greek word *apothēkē* and came up with *apotheca* ("storehouse"). In the early days, therefore, an *apothecary* was a fellow working in a warehouse. He was literally "a person who put things away." Later, people began to employ his appellation as a synonym for shopkeeper. In Shakespeare's day he was a druggist or chemist. As Romeo drinks the poisonous potion he cries: "O true *apothecary!*/Thy drugs are quick. Thus with a kiss I die."

In England and Ireland a licensed pharmacist is still called an *apothecary,** but in America the term has died out. Perhaps it should be revived. Our drugstores have expanded so much that they do look like cluttered warehouses!

While checking on *apothecary* I have discovered that *boutique* is in this family. Now, that's really a "wild" one, but not so hard to fathom if you remember the French penchant for changing some letters into other letters. Go back two paragraphs and gaze on that Greek storehouse. Drop the initial letter and change the second letter from *p* to *b.* It begins to make sense, especially when the idea that an *apothecary*

---

* *Chemist* is also commonly used in England as a synonym for a druggist.

was once a shopkeeper is kept in mind. And so, if we carry the thought to a ridiculous conclusion, we can imagine that a fashionable woman patronizing her *boutique* is very close to visiting her *apothecary*.

Also in the family of our druggist is *bodega*. In Spanish that's a wine cellar, but through American-Spanish usage the word has evolved into "a small grocery store or wine shop"—not exactly a chichi *boutique*.

But in this instance we are again treated to the skill of scholarly philologists who have assiduously tracked down words to their sources. In a way they remind me of bloodhounds or topflight detectives. They should be good at solving mazes.

In case you have lost track, this section of the chapter began with *antithesis* and *antithetical*. Last but not least of the relations that I have chosen to include is *bibliotheca* ("a library or collection of books").

The first root of that word has given us a cluster of delectable entries in our dictionaries. Aside from *bibliomania, bibliophile* and *bibliophobe* (covered in other chapters), here are some other gems to add to your treasury:

> *Biblicist*—scholar specializing in the Scriptures
> *biblioclast*—destroyer or mutilator of books
> *bibliofilm*—microfilm for photographing pages of books
> *bibliognost*—person having thorough knowledge of books
> *bibliogony*—production of books
> *biblioklept*—one who steals books
> *bibliolater*—a book worshiper
> *bibliolatry*—worship of the Bible; extravagant devotion to books
> *bibliomancy*—divination by books, especially the Bible
> *bibliopegist*—bookbinder
> *bibliopole*—bookseller
> *bibliotaph*—person hiding or hoarding books
> *bibliotherapy*—guidance in psychiatry through selected reading
> *bibliotist*—expert in handwriting and in determining authenticity of
>   authorship

If you really examine the above list and then refer to your lexicons for words related to the second roots, you will find a host of other words that we have inherited from the Greeks. For instance, I can think of *iconoclast, agnostic, idolater, epitaph* and *psychotherapy*. The *mancy* source alone has given us scores of words like *chiromancy, hydromancy, pyromancy,* and so on. The diviners do seem to be multifarious and multitudinous.

But let us return to our Latin extractions. *Companion* captivates me. Literally, it means "bread fellow" or "one who breaks bread with another." *Panis* ("bread") is the basic root. I am reminded of a refrain in a well known song: "Let us break bread together." Truly, people who perform that act are *companions*.

Some *companions*, however, are not necessarily buddy-buddy. They have been *incarcerated* in the same cell block. That verb comes from the Romans' *carcer* ("prison or jail").

The British spelling is *gaol*. Why? They adopted the Norman French *gaole*, while we Americans preferred to accept a variation of the Middle English *jaiole*.

Incidentally, as you follow the discourse in this book, notice how often our immediate ancestors have tended to shorten words as much as possible. In the above instances a final vowel has been dropped, and in one case (*jaiole*) another vowel has been eliminated.

This is the age of speed and directness, and language seems to follow that trend. It is especially evident in our penchant for adopting slang words. For example, in connection with *incarcerate*, more and more people today refer to a *convict* as a *con*.

Would you suspect that *cancel* bears any relationship to *incarcerate*? Indeed it does! The Latin word *cancer* means "lattice," and it's an alteration of *carcer*. Then came the diminutive *cancelli* ("screens usually made of latticework")—a word that has found a niche in our language.

When writers, editors, musicians et al decided to omit a passage, they drew horizontal and vertical lines over it, thus forming a pattern that looked like a lattice. In other words, they *canceled* the passage. Interestingly enough, the post office partially uses that method today in order to *cancel* a stamp.

Lifers who are *incarcerated* may well feel that they have been *canceled* by society.

Before proceeding I should point out that another Latin *cancer* means "crab." As a sign of the zodiac it retains that sense. The Romans borrowed it from the Greek noun *karkinos*, the source of our word *carcinoma* ("cancerous growth").

Additionally, *candidate* deserves attention because it has such an astonishing background. It comes from *candidatus* ("clothed in white"). Apparently the Romans who sought public office wanted people to picture them as pure as the driven snow.

Candid comes from the same root. The parent verb is *candēre* ("to shine"). In English the adjective is still sometimes used as a synonym for white, but because that so-called color is associated with purity and clarity, *candid* is commonly employed to mean "frank, very honest, forthright or even blunt." Would that all our *candidates* spoke with *candor!*

Candle and *incandescent* are members of this radiant clan. *Incense* and *incendiary* are cousins through a related verb, *cendere* ("to burn").

———

At this point let me comment on the fact that color bias seems to be built into our language. The following anecdote partly illustrates what I mean.

Years ago, when I was a principal in Harlem, I observed two dark-skinned tots of prekindergarten age. The girl was teasing the boy. Lithe and quick, she would give him a slap and skip away. She knew he was too plump and clumsy to catch her. After a few futile attempts he resorted to name-calling.

"You dope!" he screamed, but she only laughed. He tried a few other epithets, which disturbed her not one whit. Then, in complete frustration, he brought out his ultimate verbal missile. "You—you black!" he yelled.

That did it. In a burst of fury the little girl leaped on him like a tigress and wrestled him to the floor. As I separated the pair I could not help but feel deep sorrow. Why, I asked myself, would two black children of such a tender age be ashamed of their complexion? Who had taught them? How had they acquired this awful self-image?

That happened in the days before Stokeley Carmichael popularized "Black is beautiful!" and prior to the era when heroes like Muhammad Ali openly began to express pride in their color. It was a time when everybody used "Negro" as an acceptable term. Then, led by people from the West Indies, the American Negro gradually came to think of the designation as opprobrious. In a P.T.A. meeting that I attended in the 1960s one woman expounded as follows: "*Ne* means 'no,' and *gro* means 'grow'! The white men who call us Negroes don't want us to grow!"

At any rate, if those two tots were transplanted a few decades forward, I wonder whether the little boy would have used that name, and, if so, whether the girl would have laughed it off. She might even have felt flattered—but perhaps not, because our language evokes bad and evil connotations for *black* and (in many cases) just the opposite for *white*.

Consider the following words and definitions extracted from various reputable dictionaries:

> *black*—soiled; dirty; evil; wicked; harmful; disgraceful; sorrowful; dismal; gloomy; disastrous; sullen; angry (as black looks); deep-dyed (as a black villain)
> *blackball*—exclude socially; ostracize
> *Black Death*—deadly disease in the fourteenth century
> *black dog*—dejection; blues; melancholy; despondency
> *blacken*—speak evil of; defame; slander

> *black eye*—bad reputation
> *blackguard*—contemptible scoundrel; villain
> *Black Hand*—lawless Sicilian secret society
> *Black-Hander*—extortioner
> *blackheart*—disease of potato tubers
> *blacklist*—list of persons who are disapproved of or who are to be punished or discriminated against
> *blackmail*—practice extortion
> *Black Maria*—patrol wagon
> *black mark*—unfavorable mark on one's record
> *black market*—place or system for selling goods illegally
> *Black Mass*—requiem Mass or blasphemous parody of the Mass by Satan's worshipers
> *black rot*—plant disease caused by fungi or bacteria
> *black sheep*—person regarded as less respectable or successful than the rest of his group or family

There ought to be a way to eliminate some of the above. Maybe we should boycott them. Someone has suggested a better way—change the first syllable in all of them to *white,* or if that's too drastic, use a variety of hues. Thus a villain would become a *blueguard,* or an extortionist would be a *purplemailer.* It certainly would be colorful!

Some readers may regard the foregoing paragraphs as *supererogatory*—a high-sounding adjective if I ever saw one. It means "going beyond what is needed or expected." The related verb is *supererogate* ("to do more than duty requires"). It can be analyzed as follows: *super* ("above"), *e* ("out"), *rog* ("ask"), *ate* (common suffix for English verbs). Now, I suggest that you put the parts together in terms of the meaning. You will see that it is one of our "tame" words.

Subpoena is a conformist too. Literally, it means "under penalty." Anyone *subpoenaed* to appear in court must do so or pay the penalty.

What's most interesting about that word is that it has not been changed to *suppoena.* The retention of the *b* is rare; the change to *p* in other cases is common—for example:

> *supplicate*—to petition earnestly; from *sub-plicare* ("to fold"). When you *supplicate* you "fold under" or bow.
> *supplant*—to take the place of; from *sub-planta* ("sole of the foot"). The Romans developed the verb *supplantare* ("to put under the sole of the foot; to trip up").
> *support*—to carry the weight of; from *sub-portare* ("to carry")

In fact, one might even expect *subpoena* to have been changed to *suppena,* because diphthongs are usually shortened to one vowel in the transition to English. *Penal, penalize* and *penalty* are examples. They all come from the same source as *subpoena.*

Other words in this group include *pain, impunity, penologist* ("specialist in criminal reform or jail management") and *punish*. The root has also influenced the development of such nouns as *penance* and *penitentiary*.

─────

But *pen* and *pencil* have no relation to the above or to each other. Early writing instruments, such as quills, were made from feathers. The Latin word for feather was *pinna* (an alteration of *penna*). It's fascinating to contrast that root with modern fountain pens and ball-points.

Pencil comes from *penis,* the Latin word for "tail." The diminutive of that word is *pencillus*. The artist's brush that was used in early days resembled a little tail. Later the shape and use of the implement were changed and the word was shortened to its present form.

─────

Before we leave words that start with *pen,* a few more deserve mention. In Latin, *paene* means "almost," and *insula* means "island." I live on a *peninsula* in Massachusetts. It's not quite an island because of a little piece of ground, no wider than ten feet, that serves as a road to my home. In winter, whenever the fury of the storms and the height of the tides combine, my wife and I become *isolated*. That's a verb derived from *isola,* the Italian noun for "island."

I was about to say "We become *insulated,*" and I would have been correct, because that word may be used as a synonym for *isolated*. But in modern times we tend to think of *insulation* as material that retards the passage of heat out of a house or deters the cold blasts from entering. It forms an *insular* or *islandish* barrier. That second adjective may sound outlandish, but it can be found in an unabridged lexicon.

Penultimate is another delightful word from our *paene* root. It means "next to the last." If you reach the *penultimate* chapter of this book, you will have almost completed your perusal. And if you come to the *antepenultimate* section, you will have two chapters to go.

─────

The geographical significance of *peninsula* reminds me of *Orient* and *Occident*. One comes from *oriri* ("to rise") and the other from *occidere* ("to fall down, or set"). Since the sun rises in the East and sets in the West, it is no accident that *Orient* and *Occident* are proper nouns today.

Let me make a short digression in connection with the above. In the 1940s, John Dewey's democratic educational philosophy was carried to an extreme in some New York City schools. An assistant superintendent was sitting in on a lesson in which the teacher had just taught the position of the earth in relation to Old Sol. At the end, according to his story, the teacher called for a vote on whether the sun sets in the East or the West. The assistant superintendent blessed the

Lord, thanked his lucky stars and breathed a sigh of relief when West won by a narrow margin.

Bless is one of our "wild" words. It falls into the same family as *blood* because of the sanguinary aspects of ancient sacrifices and consecrations. Through the centuries the spelling became so altered that it is difficult to see the connection today.

One word leads to another. *Sanguinary* means "bloody, bloodthirsty, murderous," but *sanguine* has come to mean "confident or optimistic." Why has the latter become one of our "wild" words? Well, a ruddy complexion, in medieval physiology, suggested a warm, passionate or cheerful temperament. The idea has persisted to this day. If you are *sanguine* about the future, you have high hopes; but if you think that *sanguinary* events await us, you foresee bloodshed.

Consanguinity ("blood relationship") belongs in this group, as does its adjectival form. Cousins, for instance, are *consanguineous*.

This leads us to *primogeniture* ("the condition or fact of being the first to be born of the same parents"). The roots are *primus* ("first") and *gignere* ("to beget"). In law this word has much importance. It applies to the exclusive right of the eldest son to inherit his father's estate. Note the emphasis on the male; one can understand why some feminists have resorted to contumely in their fight against chauvinism.

Contumely has a very interesting background. Lexicographers assume that it is rooted in *tumere* ("to swell") and in earlier years meant "puffed-up, arrogant speech."

At any rate, Hamlet's "To be or not to be" soliloquy introduced the word to most of us. He said:

> "For who would bear the whips and scorns of time,
> The oppressor's wrong, the proud man's *contumely* . . ."

Today the word means "insult or humiliation." It is not to be confused with its relative *contumacy,* defined as "stubborn rebelliousness, disobedience or insubordination." *Contumelious* people are insulting, but *contumacious* ones resist authority.

Let's look at some of the kin:

> *tumescent*—swelling up
> *tumid*—swollen, bulging; hence, pompous or bombastic
> *tumor*—bodily swelling
> *tumefacient*—causing swelling
> *tumefaction*—a swollen part
> *detumescence*—a lessening of a swelling

But here are some of the "wilder" relatives:

tuber—fleshy part of an underground stem, as a potato
tuberculosis—infectious disease
protuberate—to bulge
truffle—fleshy fungus regarded as a delicacy

As you can see, linguistic nuances and variations have caused us to rove around in this chapter. I once used "spatiate" as a clue for *rove* in a crossword puzzle and received a letter from a rather obtuse solver who asked me why I was trying to show off. I replied that I was merely attempting to let the fans ramble or stroll among new pastures.

Rove is related to archery. In Medieval English, *roven* meant "to shoot at random." The expression *at rovers* signified "haphazardly," and *rover* itself meant "a random mark at an uncertain distance used as an archer's target."

In 1845, Longfellow wrote these famous lines:

> "I shot an arrow into the air,
> It fell to earth I knew not where."

Our American poet was indeed *at rovers*. Incidentally, some philologists point out that *rover* is a Middle Dutch synonym for robber. That makes sense, because one of the definitions for *rover* is "pirate." I would guess that those buccaneers often shot at random.

———

The mention of pirates somehow calls up the adjective *despicable,* and the discussion on roving suggests *peregrine* to me. Let's take them in order.

Despicable means "contemptible or vile." For years purists have been trying to get people to use the first pronunciation, with the accent on the initial syllable, but it's apparently too difficult for Americans to accept. Most announcers and all of my friends place the emphasis on *spic,* just as they stress the *quiz* in "exquisite."

Be that as it may, the root of the adjective is *despicere* ("to look down upon").

Peregrine is from *peregrinari* ("to travel"). As an adjective it means "roving or alien." There is also a *peregrine* falcon, which is famous for its swiftness and its migratory habits. The basic root of this word is *ager* ("field"). Literally, it can be taken to mean "beyond the borders of the field (or home)."

Now let me cite some of the members of this widely distributed unit. Through Old French we get *pilgrim.* Then of course there are *agriculture* and *agrarian.* The wild ass called the *onager* belongs, as does *acre.*

But I like *peregrinate* and *peregrination* best of all. They remind me of an activity that has always entranced me and millions of others —travel.

Because of this book I have been *procrastinating* my proclivity toward *peregrinism*. In other words, I have been putting off the pleasure until the future. The Latin word for "tomorrow" is *cras.*

I don't mean to be *maudlin* about the matter, but the *crux* of the situation is that I would *decline* abroad and would be unable to withstand the *vicissitudes* if I did not have the *dinero* to afford the *expenses.* I'd be in such a *dither* that the *stewardess* on the plane would probably advise that I turn back as soon as I deplaned.

Admittedly, that's a devious way to introduce eight words into this chapter, but it does permit me to elucidate concerning a fascinating octad. Now let us pursue them seriatim.

Maudlin means "weakly emotional or tearfully sentimental, especially from too much liquor." The word dates back eventually to Mary Magdalene, from the practice of representing her in paintings as a weeping penitent, with eyes swollen and red. The connection in the spelling comes from *Maudelyne* in Medieval English.

Crux now means "a puzzling problem or pivotal point." In Caesar's day it signified "a cross used for torture." Crossword puzzle addicts can readily see how its first modern definition came into existence. The French changed it to *croix.* Thus the *Croix de Guerre* ("Cross of War") became a military decoration for bravery in battle.

Decline has several meanings today. One of them is "to refuse an invitation." In that sense it seems faithful to its original Latin sources: *de* ("away") and *clinare* ("to incline"). But it also means "to deteriorate," because of a semantic change that occurred years ago when the French developed *decliner* ("to sink") from the Latin root.

Vicissitudes are shifting circumstances; ups and downs. The word is derived from the Romans' *vicis* ("turn or change"). At first it may seem incredible that *vicar* is a relative. But the first meaning of that word is "a person who acts in place of another; a deputy." This definition does fit in with the idea of change.

Today in various religions a *vicar* is a minister, parish priest or church officer. The Pope is called the *Vicar of Christ* because Roman Catholics believe he is God's earthly representative.

A kindred adjective is *vicarious* ("performed, received, enjoyed or suffered in place of another"). Sports fans who watch athletes receive *vicarious* thrills as they imagine themselves participating in place of their heroes.

Our *Vice-Presidents* fall into this same category. They are, in truth, deputies for the elected chiefs. *Viceroy* ("deputy for a sovereign") is another member of the family. The last syllable is an alteration of *roi,* the French word for "king."

Finally, *vice versa* ("conversely") belongs in this group. In Latin that phrase signifies "the position being changed."

Dinero is the Spanish word for "money." It is derived from *denarius,* a Roman silver coin originally equivalent to ten asses. Via the Southwest it has become a slang word in our language.

Expenses are familiar to all of us who must pay those monthly bills. The word comes from the past participle of *expendere,* the Latin verb meaning "to pay out." This is definitely one of our "tame" words.

Dither is a variation of *didder,* a dialectic British word meaning "quiver, shake, or tremble." We now use it to signify "a state of strong excitement or agitation." In the popular "Blondie" comic strip featuring Dagwood Bumstead, the nervous boss is well named. He is *Mr. Dithers.*

It should be noted that *dither* may also be used as a verb meaning "to shake, waver or vacillate."

Stewardess is the last and most interesting word in my paragraph about the need for money in order to enjoy traveling abroad. This is one of our many nouns containing a feminine suffix. Among these endings are *ess, ette* and *trix.* Feminists are endeavoring to strike these words out of our dictionaries. Recently I was chauvinistic enough to define Edna St. Vincent Millay in a crossword puzzle as "a poetess." An angry letter chided me for using that suffix. Strangely enough, I received no criticisms when I used the word *stewardess* and called her a "707 attendant."

At any rate, *steward* and *stewardess* have been ameliorated by the passage of time. A *steward* originally meant a "sty ward" or "keeper of the pigs." Later he elevated himself to become the person in charge of the affairs of a large household or estate. He then got into the restaurant business as the man in charge of food and drink. Subsequently he expanded his scope to become a sports official. At sea he assumed a dual role: he became an attendant looking after passengers' comfort and an officer in charge of stores or culinary arrangements. Finally he underwent a sex change and took to the air, and lately (because of lawsuits) he is seen on the jets along with his female counterparts.

On the whole, I am in favor of the feminist movement. Just as our language discriminates against blacks, it may be subtly violating women's rights. But I am not sure how far we should go. Should we call Jane Fonda an *actor* rather than an *actress?* What about *waitress, seductress, temptress, countess, hostess, priestess, mistress, seamstress,* and so on? Where do we draw the line?

In the *ette* category, must *majorettes* and *suffragettes* suffer extinction?

As for *trix,* I can see my way clear. Amelia Earhart was just as fine an aviator as any man of her time. *Aviatrix* seems unnecessary, and so do *janitrix, spectatrix* (and its companion *spectatress),* *inheritrix, exec-*

utrix, proprietrix (and *proprietress), rectrix, curatrix,* and *administratrix.*

In that connection, I have often sat through many meetings at which the person in charge has been a woman. It has intrigued me to note the changes in her title that time has wrought. In the forties the head of our school P.T.A. was the *chairman* (a term that gave me a twinge). Then she became a *chairwoman* and *chairlady,* and now we hear of the sexless *chairperson.*

There were once *anchormen,* who coordinated radio and TV news programs. Now they are *anchorpersons.* I am not sure whether that term should be spelled as one word or two, since it has not made its debut in any lexicon at my disposal. Suffice it to say that the feminist movement is only one of many cataclysms in society that have given rise to changes in our language. The dictionaries of 2080 will make our present lexicons look strange indeed.

Whether or not *suffragettes* become just plain *suffragists* in the near or distant future, their heritage is fascinating but puzzling. Some authorities surmise that the word goes back to *suffragari* ("to use a broken piece of tile as a ballot"). That sounds correct, because *fra(n)gere* meant "to break into pieces" in ancient Rome. However, other philologers opt for *sub* plus *fragor* ("loud noise or applause"), because of the early practice of voting by acclamation. Perhaps both sets of scholars are right.

Finally, have you ever seen a *saxifrage?* It's a perennial plant that grows in the crevices of rocks: *saxi* ("rock") and *frage* ("break"). Literally, this lovely flower is a "rock breaker." Therefore it's not surprising that it's also called a *breakstone.*

This chapter has provided only a taste of the words that we have inherited from the ancients and have either changed drastically or have adhered to as much as possible in the original spellings and meanings. As I have stated earlier, tomes could be written about the thousands of words that have come down to us from the Romans alone. It is my hope that the sampling I have given will inspire some readers to delve into other derivations. A fascinating experience awaits those who do.

CHAPTER 5

Roots, Branches and Twigs

Let me begin this chapter with another story about my experiences while toiling in Frederick Douglass Junior High School in New York City. As an English teacher I was expected to build the vocabulary of the young Harlemites in my classes. Many of my colleagues simply handed out a mimeographed list of words and definitions to the boys to memorize for examinations. Instinctively I realized that such a rote-learning process was a waste of effort and time. But I had no idea as to what method I should use instead.

Then, on a blue Monday, one of the four assistants to the principal arrived at my classroom door with about forty abridged dictionaries. He was a stern, humorless and forbidding man with only one interest —to display his authority.

"Mr. Maleska," he said, "these dictionaries are to be used in all of your ninth-grade classes. You will store them in your closet, and you will not allow them to be taken home. However, once a week you are ordered to distribute them and base a lesson upon them. I shall be inspecting your plan book to see what procedures you employ to build the vocabulary of your students."

Well, the immediate reaction of the boys was negative. The dictionary to them was the dullest of all books, and they told me so. What to do? Should I follow the example of more experienced colleagues and write a list of words on the board for them to copy, look up, and then use in a sentence? I tried this but soon realized that I was only intensifying their hatred of the dictionaries.

Finally I hit upon a solution, which I never revealed in my plan book because it was too bizarre. I invented a game called "Stick the Teacher." After passing out the lexicons I asked the boys to scour the dictionary for unusual words and then call them out. If I could not give a satisfactory definition, then the class scored a point. If I knew the word, a point was recorded in my favor.

The smarter students turned immediately to the back of the book and gave me toughies like *xebec, xyloid* and *zygote*. Others settled for words like *prolix, comestibles* and *funicular*. The scores were always close. I learned a lot, and (I hope) they did, too. At any rate, the interest was high. Only last year I received a long letter from a former student who remembered that game and said that it had given him his initial interest in exploring dictionaries. He is now a successful playwright.

One thing leads to another when you are trying to maintain motivation as a teacher in a depressed area. You can't keep plucking at the same strings. When the tide of interest in "Stick the Teacher" was ebbing, I realized that I had to come up with something new. That's when I hit upon the Latin-English tree!

I sprang the idea on my best class one Friday afternoon. On the blackboard I drew a tree. At the bottom I placed the root *port* (from *portare,* "to carry"). I explained to the class that this Latin root had blossomed through the centuries and had endowed us with many English words. These, I went on, were leaves on the tree.

For example, a *porter* is one who carries. A *report card* is something to be carried back to parents. A *portable* typewriter is capable of being carried and *transport* means "to carry across."

As I spoke I drew the leaves on the tree. Then the boys began to add their own foliage, and something like the sketch below emerged.

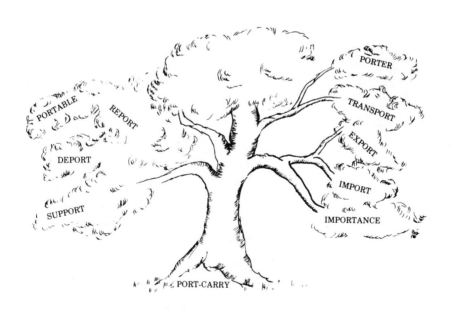

The visual approach fascinated the boys in that class, but the idea might have died on the vine had it not been for Leroy Davis, a student who had never before shown much interest. Over the weekend he fashioned a small, flat block of wood, drilled a hole in it and marked the block *PORT*. Then he fixed a tall branch into the opening and attached little tabs to the twigs. On each tab he had carefully lettered one of the words from the root. Finally he sprayed his creation with the silvery material that often decorates Christmas cards.

On Monday, when Leroy presented this work of art to me, I almost fell over. I could have kissed him right then and there. Collecting my wits, I let the class decide where we should display our beautiful tree. On the radiator? On the bookshelf? On my desk? On a little table in a corner near the blackboard? They finally chose the table.

Then one of the boys asked, "Could I make a tree too?"

"Certainly!" I replied, "But you don't want to use Leroy's root, do you? How about *vide, vise?*"

"What does that mean?"

I explained that it meant "to see," and soon another tree appeared, this time drawn on the blackboard. It sprouted with such words as *vision, visible, visual, provide, revise, advise, vista, supervise, visage* and *providence*.

After that the idea caught fire. Almost every boy in the group wanted his very own root. The class president volunteered to ask their woodshop teacher if they could make the root blocks in his room. As for the branches—no problem! Trees do grow in Harlem, just as they do in Brooklyn. Naturally, however, I cautioned them to take only dead branches.

Here are some of the roots that were doled out and then explored during the next few weeks:

ROOTS	SOME BRANCHES
duc, duct ("to lead")	Duce, reduce, product, induction, deduce, duct, conductor, abduct, ducal, duchess, duke, introduce, seduce, educe, conducive, educate, viaduct, aqueduct
voc, voke ("to call")	invoke, provoke, revoke, evoke, convoke, vocal, vocation, vocabulary, vocalize, provocative, avocation, advocate, equivocate
dic, dict ("to say")	diction, edict, predict, dictaphone, dictator, addict, indict, indicate, contradict, dictionary, verdict, dictum, benediction, jurisdiction, valedictory
scrib, script ("to write")	scribe, scribble, inscribe, subscribe, prescribe, describe, transcribe, ascribe, script, Scriptures, circumscribe, postscript, inscription, prescription, description, transcript, conscription

ROOTS	SOME BRANCHES
mov, mot ("to move")	move, remove, remote, motion, motor, movement, commotion, emotion, demote, promote, motel, motivate, automotive
ven, vent ("to come")	advent, avenue, adventure, circumvent, convene, convent, convention, event, eventual, intervene, invent, prevent, revenue, supervene, vent, venture
spec, spect ("to look at")	spectacle, spectator, inspection, respect, suspect, prospect, speculate, introspection, retrospect, aspect, spectrum, circumspect, expect, perspective
vert, verse ("to turn")	verse, version, revert, reverse, convert, converse, invert, inversion, subvert, supervision, introvert, extrovert, pervert, perversion, contravert, divert, diversion, versus, vertigo, transverse, universe, avert, anniversary, controversy, adverse, adversary
tend, tent ("to stretch or strive")	contend, tend, tendon, tent, attend, attendant, attention, tense, distend, extend, intend, pretend, pretense, ostensible, extensive, intention, portend, portent
pon, pose ("to place")	component, compose, composition, composure, composite, depose, repose, suppose, supposition, impose, purpose, proposal, dispose, disposition, expose, exposition, exponent, postpone, transpose, interpose, position, preposition, positively, proposition

Trees began to burgeon all over my room. My other classes became envious and asked if they could have the same project. Why not? I scurried to my Latin and English dictionaries to find new roots. When I ran out of Roman sources I turned to the Greeks (see the end of Chapter 1). Luckily the shop teacher was my good friend. He kept altering his lesson plans to meet the needs of my "nutty" unit. To save the trees in Harlem from total destruction he even devised a way to use pieces and splinters of wood he had on hand as branches and twigs.

Soon my room looked like a jungle! Trees lined the open closets and stood on the radiators, my desk and the table where Leroy's original product still gleamed up front.

One day our new principal was walking down the hall during a change of classes. As he passed my room he did a double take and stopped dead in his tracks.

"Maleska," he said, "aren't you an English teacher?"

"Yes, Dr. Zuckerman."

"Well, your room—it looks like a science lab."

"Oh, you mean the trees. They're from my vocabulary-building unit."

"Vocabulary? Where do trees fit in?"

"Let me show you, sir."

He walked all around the room admiring the various creations. "Terrific!" he exclaimed. "What an idea! May I have one?"

Then I told him about Leroy and said that the boy might be pleased to present his *objet d'art* to his principal. Dr. Zuckerman inspected Leroy's work and nodded. "Fine! Send him to my office."

While signing out that day, I peeked into the inner sanctum. There, on the principal's desk, Leroy's tree shone in new glory!

One thing leads to another when a classroom project really makes a hit. The next step was to show the importance and meanings of the prefixes and suffixes. I called them "our twigs."

Conductor and *composer* provided the initial impetus. I explained that the prefixes meant "together" and that *con* always changes to *com* before the letters *b, f, m* and *p*. The "one who" idea carried by *or* and *er* was easy for the boys to see. They already had been exposed to Leroy's *porter.*

Here are some of the prefixes we discussed:

PREFIX	MEANING
con, com, co, cog, etc.	together, with, jointly
re	back, again
mis	badly, mistakenly, wrongly, incorrect
a, ab	not, away
de	down, do the opposite of
dis, di, dif, etc.	away, not, apart
in, ig, im, etc.	very, into, not, without
per	through, throughout
pro	before, forward, on behalf of, in place of
sub, suf, sup, sur	under, beneath, below, somewhat
ad, ac, ag, ap, etc. *ob, oc, op,* etc.	against, toward, to
e, ef, ex	out of, away from, outside
trans	across
ante	before
post	after
retro	backward
inter	between, among
intra, intro	within
super, sur	above, over and above, higher, extra

Sometimes prefixes can fool us. Note that *sur* (last on the above list) is an alteration of *sub* ("under") and a shortening of *super* ("above, over"). In such words as *surrogate* and *surreptitious* the prefix means "under." But in *surmount, surrealism, survey, surname, surplice,* and *surplus,* for example, it's an abridgment of *super.*

Probably the most interesting word in this group is *surplice.* Today it's a loose, white, wide-sleeved outer vestment worn by the clergy and choir in some churches. But originally it was worn by clergymen of northern countries over their fur coats. In Medieval Latin it was called *superpellicum* ("over a fur coat").

And here are several of the suffixes:

SUFFIX	MEANING
tion, sion, ment, ness *tude, ation, ition*	the act of or the state of
ive, al, ic	pertaining to
ous	full of; having
ate	to make or cause
ant, ent	one who; doing
ance, ancy, ence, ency	the quality or state of

Here are a number of words that emerge, using the root *grad, gress* ("to step, walk, go") and combining it with some of the above prefixes and suffixes:

WORD	LITERAL MEANING
aggressor	one who steps against
congressional	pertaining to the act of walking together
degradation	the act of stepping down
digression	the act of stepping away
graduation	the act of going
ingress	a walking in
progress	step forward
regress	step back
retrograde } *retrogress* }	step backward
transgression	the act of stepping across

That last word merits attention. When we commit a *transgression,* we sin. Literally, we have stepped across the boundaries between right and wrong.

I have deliberately omitted *egress* from the above list because of a story connected with it. As I recall the tale, P. T. Barnum had erected a large tent in a small town and had filled it with strange animals. The local people were enchanted. However, they hung around inside so long that there was little room for new customers to join the throng. So Barnum took down the *Exit* sign and replaced it with *To the Egress.* Thinking that some exotic bird lay behind that flap in the tent, the crowd swarmed forward—and found themselves stepping outside.

I hope that readers will notice the irony in the literal meaning of

Congress (see congressional above). Our representatives may walk together up the steps at Capitol Hill, but usually that's as far as it goes between Democrats and Republicans.

Now let's take another root, give it the same treatment, and see what happens. *Fund, fuse* come from *fondere, fusus.* That Latin verb means "to pour or pour out."

Here are a few words that have come down to us:

WORD	LITERAL MEANING
confusion	the state of being poured together
diffuse	to pour apart or in different directions
effusive	pertaining to a pouring out
infusion	the act of pouring in
profusion	the act of pouring forward
refund *refuse*	to pour back
suffusive	pertaining to a pouring from underneath
transfusion	the act of pouring across

That last word on the list certainly has adhered faithfully to its Latin origin, especially when we connect it with blood donors.

Through Old French an extra vowel was added to the root. Consequently, we find words like *confound* and *profound* in this family.

———

Now let's try one more. The root is *nomen, nomin,* from *nominare* ("to name").

WORD	LITERAL MEANING
agnomen	a name added to
cognomen	a name going along with
denomination	the act of putting a name down
ignominious	having no name
misnomer	incorrect name
nomination	the act of naming

Some of the above words may need further explanation. An *agnomen* is a nickname, and a *cognomen* is a family name or surname, such as Kelly or Cohen. In ancient Rome it was the third word in a person's name. For example, Cicero was the *cognomen* of Marcus Tullius *Cicero.* Incidentally, the accent for both of the above words falls on the second syllable.

Denomination has undergone a semantic change. It has taken on a religious significance in popular usage and is synonymous with sect.

Ignominious and *ignominy* are very interesting words. If a person has no name (perhaps he's illegitimate), he sometimes suffers from public shame and dishonor. Hence the adjective has come to mean "disgraceful or despicable." And a word synonymous with the noun is "infamy." Aren't you glad you have a *cognomen?*

———

Now let's see how well *you* can do with some other Latin roots. Like my boys at Frederick Douglass Junior High School, you will have some assignments. (But please don't send me trees!)

Here are some basic Roman underground growths that need "branches" and "twigs" to fill them out in our language. If you will consult the Appendix (pp. 434–35), you will find my own orchards.

ROOT	MEANING
ag, act	do, drive, impel
cad, cas	fall
cap, capt, cept	take, seize
clud, clus	close, shut
cur, curr, curs	run
fac, fact, fect	do, make
frag, fract	break
leg, lig, lect	choose, read
mit, miss	send
pend, pens	hang, weigh, lay
plic, pli	fold
sed, sid, sess	sit, seat
sent, sens	feel
solv, solu	loosen, free
ten, tin, tent	hold, contain
volv, volu	roll, turn

The above, of course, is only a sampling of the many Latin roots that have gained strength through the centuries and have flowered in our language. Some of them have departed a bit, through usage, from their original intent. Those are like sprouts that form new and different buds from the main source, but it is amazing how many have blossomed without much change. It cannot be said too often that our linguistic debt to the Romans is beyond comprehension. Every letter we write, every contract we sign, every story we read is likely to contain words that date back to the days of Caesar and Cicero or their immediate descendants.

This is the last chapter on our direct Latin heritage. The next chapters move on to French and other Romance languages that have indirectly supplied us with a fund of Latin words.

CHAPTER 6

The French Connection

In 1066, at sunset on Senlac Hill, an errant arrow struck King Harold II in the eye, and he succumbed to the wound. His Anglo-Saxon soldiers, already losing to the forces of the Duke of Normandy, became completely disheartened by the loss of their leader and fled from the field. Thus William the Conqueror won the Battle of Hastings—the only one, by the way, in his invasion—and marched on London.

William brought not only troops with him; he brought thousands of words. The domination of the Normans was thorough and ruthless. French became the language of the nobility and was used by the military. Soon lawyers, rich merchants and leaders in the fields of fashion and the arts were brought into the Normans' linguistic fold. Although English remained the language of the peasants, the influence of the conquerors over a period of almost three centuries soon seeped through; willy-nilly the common people began to Gallicize their language. French phrases passed *tout à fait* into English, and semantic changes in everyday vocabulary were accelerated even before the Renaissance. That period, of course, brought its own linguistic transformations.

And so today French leads all the Romance languages in affecting English speech and writing. Some philologers estimate that almost one-third of our words come from French.

Now let us review the historical events above, with stress on the French phrases and words that have permeated our language. The following paragraphs may be exaggerated and may contain an anachronism* or two, but they are apropos (French-English for "relevant").

When Harold was rendered *hors de combat*, the event proved to be the *coup de grâce* for his weary troops. Earlier that day they had been led into a *cul-de-sac* by the clever Norman soldiers. And so William's *coup d'état* became a *fait accompli* all because of a little arrow. The

---

* *Anachronism*—a chronological error in which a person, custom, object or event is assigned a date or period other than the correct one. To picture Daniel Boone wearing a Colt revolver would be an *anachronism*.

Duke, a *bête noire* to all Anglo-Saxons, now had *carte blanche* in England. The previous ruling class became, in truth, an *ancien régime.* *C'est la guerre! C'est la vie!*

But soon the *crème de la crème* of English society felt that they would be *au courant* if they spoke French. Not to do so would be a *faux pas.* Indeed, it might be deemed *lèse majesté!* "*Noblesse oblige,*" they told themselves.

Did the *nouveau riche* or the *chevaliers d'industrie* object? *Au contraire!* If French was the *dernier cri* in speech, they would go along. Why make a *cause célèbre* out of this matter? It was *comme il faut* to follow the leaders. *Savoir-vivre* required that one should cultivate *savoir-faire* and *sang-froid.* How else could one maintain one's *amour-propre?*

Tout de suite the upper-class English took up such gambling games as *rouge et noir* (or *trente et quarante*) and *chemin de fer.* They conceded that the Norman *bons vivants* knew how to live *sans souci.*

The dictates of the *beau monde* affected them too. At *boutiques* they bought *crepe de Chine* and carefully chose their *robes de chambre* and *robes de nuit.* (Naturally, they were always on the lookout for a *bon marché.*) Their *raison d'être* seemed to be tied up with the desire to emulate the fashions of their Gallic conquerors. To be *a la mode* or *bon ton* was to achieve the *beau ideal.*

And at dinner they sampled the *hors d'oeuvres* and sipped the *soupe du jour.* Then they devoured *pommes de terre* (often *au gratin*) along with the *pièce de résistance,* prepared by the *cordon bleu.* After that, they tasted various *bonnes bouches* including *crêpes suzette.*

Usually they topped off the meal with *demitasses* served in *clair de lune* cups. Sometimes they decanted a little *crème de menthe* or *crème de cacao* or maybe some *pousse-café.* On such occasions they raised their glasses and cried, "*A votre santé!*"

In the *beaux-arts* they tried to keep up with the *avant-garde* and cooed over each new *chef-d'oeuvre* or *objet d'art.* A few *vers-libristes* published their *belles-lettres* (sometimes using *noms de plume*), discussed current *tours de force* or *romans à clef* and enjoyed one another's *bons mots* during their *tête-à-têtes.*

And, of course, attendance at a *ballet blanc* or *ballet bouffe* was *de rigueur.* In that *milieu* they stared through *pince-nez* at the *mise en scène* and applauded each *pas de deux.*

In the area of *amour,* the *boulevardiers* ogled the *jeunes filles,* especially those who possessed a certain *je ne sais quoi.* More often they formed liaisons at their *pieds-à-terre* with *demimondaines.* Unfortunately, now and then a *femme fatale* would crop up, and the poor suitors would cry, "*La belle dame sans merci!*"

Many a *ménage à trois* was formed. Were such arrangements conducive to *joie de vivre?* Probably not. In fact, these *affaires de coeur* sometimes resulted in *affaires d'honneur.* The *gendarmes* who discovered the losers of such duels would then cry, *"Cherchez la femme!"*

Many of the Gallic phrases in the above paragraphs can be guessed from the context. However, some deserve special attention, especially for those readers who have never studied French.

Hors is the French preposition for "out of or outside of." Therefore it's easy to see that when Harold became *hors de combat,* he was disabled. But what about *hors d'oeuvres?* Well, the literal meaning is "outside of the works." When cooks prepared the main meal, they thought of the appetizers or side dishes as things outside of the principal task.

A *chef-d'oeuvre* means a "chief work." Translate that into "masterpiece." Our word *chief* comes from the same source. Strangely enough, the root is *caput,* the Latin noun for "head." Through the Old French and Medieval English many changes took place in the spelling.

A reader may ask, "Why is *chef* now related only to cooking?" The reason is that the French developed a term, *chef de cuisine* ("head of the kitchen"). As often happens, the phrase was abridged to a single word. And isn't it interesting that *cuisine* originally meant "kitchen" in French? It still retains that meaning, but Parisians have extended its sense to mean "cookery"—and so have we.

The root for *cuisine* can be found in *coquere,* the Latin verb meaning "to cook." It's astounding to discover the relations that have suffered alterations in spelling through the ages. Consider the following: *cook, kiln, kitchen, apricot, biscuit, concoct, decoct, precocious,* and that famous Italian cheese *ricotta* (literally, "cook again").

To get back to our story, *coup de grâce* means literally "stroke of mercy." Hence it's a death blow or something that puts a person out of his misery.

Cul-de-sac means "the bottom of the sack." In other words, that area is definitely not the way out. Today it's a synonym for a blind alley or dead-end street. It's also a situation from which there is no escape. In our story, the center of the Norman line pretended to retreat at Hastings; when the Anglo-Saxons rushed into the vacuum, the French flanks closed in on them. They found themselves in a *cul-de-sac.*

Bête noire literally means "black beast" (reading backward, of course). This indicates to me that the French are as guilty as we are of using language that is inadvertently prejudicial to one of the human races. The phrase has come to mean "a person or thing strongly detested, feared and avoided." Why didn't the French call this bugbear a *bête blanc?*

Ancien régime usually refers to the political and social system prior to the French Revolution, but it can also be defined as "an outmoded system or government."

Most of us know that a *faux pas* is a social blunder, but I wonder how many readers are aware that it really means "a false step."

Lèse majesté (which we have altered to "lese majesty") can be translated word for word into "injured sovereign." Incidentally, the first word in that phrase is monosyllabic. It's pronounced *lēz*. The accent in the second word falls on the first syllable. Taken together, the term means "treason." If you have ascertained that *lesion* and *majestic* are English siblings, you are right.

Chevaliers d'industrie are not really tycoons. They are swindlers! They ride in with a flourish, bilk you cleverly and then depart in a hurry. As an addendum, it's almost obvious that the first word in that phrase is a cousin of *cavalier* and *cavalry*. The memorable actor-singer who was entranced by Gigi was Maurice Horseman or Maurice Knight.

Tout de suite translates as "all in succession." The phrase has gradually come to mean "immediately." One of its kinsmen is *tout le monde,* a phrase now used in our upper classes to signify "everyone." The next time you attend an elite cocktail party and a debutante says to you, *"Tout le monde* is so distingué!" just swallow your olive and reply, *"Très bien, mon amie!"*

Rouge et noir, as card players know, means "red and black." Because of the importance of thirty and forty in that game, it is also called *trente et quarante*. In French, *rouge* means "red." The famous Parisian nightclub *Moulin Rouge,* frequented by Toulouse-Lautrec, really means "Red Mill." Needless to say, *rouge* has become a fixture in our language, designating a cosmetic. When a woman applies *rouge* to her cheeks, she reddens them.

Roulette is a French diminutive of *rota* (the Latin word for "wheel," which has been discussed previously). It's a little wheel of fortune that goes spinning around. While playing this game, some bettors at Monte Carlo prefer *rouge;* others select *noir*.

Chemin de fer literally means "road of iron." Hence, in France, it's a railroad. How did it become the title of a card game similar to "Twenty-One"? The answer is that it's a speedy game, just like a locomotive.

Sans souci means "without care." In 1745–47 Frederick the Great built a palace at Potsdam and named it *Sans Souci*. Four decades later (1786) he died there. Incidentally, I find it fascinating that a Prussian gave his retreat a Gallic name.

Bon marché ("good market") is the French expression for a bargain. In Paris there is a large department store called the *Bon Marché*. I can't attest to whether it lives up to its name.

A *bonne bouche* (literally, "good mouth") is any choice morsel or delicacy. A *bonbon* would fit into that category. In a manner of speaking, it's a good goodie.

Pommes de terre ("earth apples") are potatoes, and *crêpes suzette* are French pancakes. Suzette is a pet name for Suzanne. Possibly the first chef to make the concoction named his creation after his *amie*.

Au gratin literally means "with the scraping or burned particles left at the bottom of the pan." But in common usage it means "with bread crumbs and grated cheese, browned in an oven."

A *roman à clef* is a novel in which real persons appear under fictitious names. Literally, it's "a novel with a key."

Je ne sais quoi translates into "I know not what." It signifies "something elusive or hard to describe" and usually relates to charm or charisma.

A *pied-à-terre* is a lodging or dwelling, especially one used temporarily. The literal meaning is "foot to the ground." The expression is used more extensively in England than in America.

Demimondaines are kept women or courtesans. The *demimonde* is a class of women on the fringes of respectable society; hence the significance of the literal meaning, "half world."

A *ménage à trois,* if taken literally, is "a household of three." That sounds tame enough, but the phrase has become associated with *amour*. It is an arrangement by which a married couple and the lover of one of them live together. And if the other spouse takes a lover, I assume it would become a *ménage à quatre*.

While examining French words and phrases that we have assimilated, I began to notice that they fell mainly into eight categories:

Clothing and Fashion	War and Diplomacy
Food and Drink	Gambling
The Arts	L'Amour
Shelter and Furniture	Miscellaneous

Now let's take a look at a sampling of words in each group. In the list below and those to follow, words marked with a check will be discussed.

CLOTHING AND FASHION

appliqué	boutonnière	casaque	chine
bandeau	✓brassiere	cerise	✓cloche
barrette	bretelle	chapeau	cloqué
beige	broché	chic	coiffeur
bon ton	burnoose	chichi	coiffure
bouclé	camisole	✓chiffon	coque
bouffant	cap-a-pie	chignon	corsetiere

costumier	ecru	moiré	sabot
couturier, -iere	√froufrou	nacré	sachet
√cravat	√guimpe	negligee	samite
crepe	lamé	panache	soutache
cretonne	lapin	passé	soutane
√crinoline	lingerie	peignoir	svelte
crochet	mannequin	picot	toque
√culotte	marquisette	plissé	√trousseau
décolleté	modiste	rabat	√voile
dishabille			

Brassiere comes from *bras* ("arm"). Actually, in French it means "an infant's undergarment or child's bodice or shoulder strap." The noun dates back to the Old French word *braciere* "armor for the arm; an arm guard").

Our word *bracer* is from the same root. In archery that's a leather guard worn on the arm holding the bow. Of course there's another kind of *bracer*—the one lifted by patrons at taverns.

Chiffon is the French diminutive of *chiffe* ("an old rag"). I have not been able to discover how the "little old rag" has undergone such amelioration. As every woman knows, it's now a lovely sheer, lightweight fabric often used for lawn-party dresses or for evening gowns.

It's also intriguing to note that *chiffon* has another meaning to chefs. It denotes "light and porous, as by the addition of stiffly beaten egg whites." If you have ever tasted *lemon chiffon pie,* you will attest that it bears no resemblance to tiny dirty tatters.

I think you will be surprised to learn that the chest of drawers called a *chiffonier* (or *chiffonnier*) was originally the French word for "ragpicker." I can picture Parisians stuffing old clothes in those compartments!

Cloche literally means "bell or bell jar." It's a bell-shaped glass vessel used for covering plants or food. But it's also a woman's hat shaped like a bell. Incidentally, the word is related to *clock*. Would it be fair to say that when mademoiselle wears a *cloche,* she's out for a good time?

Cravats have an interesting history. They were originally scarves worn by Croatian mercenaries in the French army. Since *Cravate* meant "Croatian" to the French, the name was applied to the distinctive neckwear. In fact, in the seventeenth century the French decided to imitate the Croatians. They dressed a regiment of the cavalry in *cravats*. The idea then took hold in Paris, whence it spread throughout the world. As its popularity extended, somewhere along the line *cravat* became a synonym for necktie.

———

Crinoline, like many other words, came to the French via their Italian neighbors. In Milano the word was *crinolino* and literally meant "horsehair flax." Interestingly enough, the material is still sometimes partly made of horsehair, though cotton is sometimes substituted. It's a coarse, stiff cloth used for hoopskirts. When petticoats were in vogue, the fabric was a best seller.

———

Culottes are trousers for females, made full in the legs to resemble skirts. Actually, *culotte* in French means "a little backside." In English it can also be defined as "hair on the thighs of an animal, such as a Pomeranian dog."

But the derivative word that is most fascinating is *sansculotte* (literally, "without breeches"). This is a term of contempt applied by the aristocrats to the republicans in the poorly clad French Revolutionary Army, who rejected knee breeches in favor of pantaloons because they wanted to be different from the elite.

We have gained several expressive terms from that Gallic upheaval. One is *sansculottism* ("radicalism") and another is *sansculottize* ("to cause to be radical"). When Patty Hearst was kidnapped by the Symbionese Liberation Army, was she *sansculottized?*

———

Froufrou is the kind of word I love. It has a French flavor, something like that of "Fifi" and "chichi." Its definition is also enchanting: "a rustling or swishing, as of a silk skirt when the wearer moves." Can you imagine the *froufrou* that emanated toward all those swains when Scarlett O'Hara entered the ballroom?

The word has taken on other meanings in our modern world. It can be defined as "frilly trimmings in women's clothing, such as ruffles, beads, flowers, veils." It also can mean "fussy details and amenities in a social setting." Thank heaven, I'm not eligible to participate in the *froufrou* of the smart set, the jet set, the wet set, the dry set or any other coterie.*

Guimpe and *wimple* are related words. The latter is the head covering worn by nuns who haven't kicked the habit. The former (pronounced *gamp*) is a blouse worn under a jumper, or a yoke insert for a low-necked dress. A trimming for upholstery is called *gimp;* it has the same ancestry. *Gimp* is also a thread or yarn used for embroidery. It

———

* *Coterie*—a clique; an intimate and often exclusive group of people having a common interest or purpose. Originally and ironically, the word meant "an organization of peasants." *Cot, cottage* and *cote* come from the same root.

has no relationship to the noun meaning "a cripple" or the verb meaning "to limp or hobble."

———

Every bride knows that a *trousseau* is the special wardrobe that she assembles for her marriage. But I wonder if she knows that it really means "a little bundle." Worse yet, the word is a cousin of *truss* —a supportive device used to prevent enlargement of a hernia. The eventual Latin root is *torquere* ("to twist"). A bride would be horrified to know that her lovely collection of clothes, linens and accessories is related to *torment, distort, torture, extort* and *contortion.*

Voile is the French noun for "veil." In English it has assumed the meaning of "a sheer fabric." The transition is not difficult to fathom.

———

And now let us consider some of the words that have filtered into our language because the French are so adept in the culinary art and in preparing beverages that please the palate. (Wine lovers will please excuse the omissions. They are covered in the chapter called "The Place Is Familiar.")

FOOD AND DRINK

à la carte	casserole	√croissant	madeleine
apéritif	√chowder	croquette	menu
au jus	√cocotte	√crouton	meringue
√au naturel	compote	daube	moule
√baba au rhum	consommé	√demitasse	√mousse
bisque	√convive	filet	mouton
blancmange	coq au vin	flan	muscat
blanquette	coquille	√fondue	√parfait
bombe	côtelette	√frangipane	potage
√bonne femme	coupette	frappe	purée
boudin	crème d'ananas	gateau	ragout
bouillabaise	crème de bananes	√gigot	rechauffé
bouillon	crème de café	glacé	rissole
brioche	crème de cassis	√gourmand	rotisserie
√brochette	crème de moka	√gourmet	sauce
brut	crème de noyau	grille	sauté
√café	crème de violette	jujube	vermouth
canapé	crémerie	macédoine	vichysoisse

Au naturel means "in a natural condition—hence, naked or nude." To a French chef it signifies "cooked plainly, or without dressing."

———

Baba au rhum is a fruity cake. This popular pastry literally means "little old woman with rum." *Baba* is a borrowing from the Poles. A related word is *babushka* (a Russian grandmother). The term is kind of a pet name for "granny" in English. But because so many *babushkas* in eastern Europe wear kerchiefs or scarves around their heads, their name has been applied to the head covering itself.

Bonne femme ("good housewife") is a term used for home-style cooking. If you see *filet de sole bonne femme* on the menu in a French restaurant, it might be a good idea to try the fish.

Brochette means " little pointed tool or little spit." We use the word to mean "skewer," but we also apply it to the meat that is broiled on a skewer. *Broach,* by the way, is a related word.

Café ("coffee or coffeehouse") was borrowed from the Turks. Their word was *kahve.* The broadening of the meaning of *café* is remarkable. First, the beverage itself; next, the little lunchroom where it was served; then a barroom; and finally a nightclub. When we speak of *café society* we don't mean that the group is just sitting around sipping demitasse.

Incidentally, let's not forget that *cafeteria* belongs in this family. In Mexico it's a coffee shop or place to buy refreshments. Again, note the expansion of the sense of the word. Any *cafeteria* in one of our big cities is a far cry from a little snack bar.

Chowder comes to us via *chaudière,* the French word for "pot or the contents of a pot." The word can be traced back to *caldus* or *calidus,* the Romans' adjectives for "hot." *Cauldron* is a cousin.

One might think that *chow,* our slangy synonym for food, is a member of the *chowder* family, but the experts guess that it has a Chinese origin. It's possibly related to *chow mein* ("to fry flour").

Cocotte was originally baby talk for *coq* ("hen"). It's an alteration of *cocasse* ("a kind of pot"). The word means "a small shallow baking dish." More commonly, however, it is a term for a prostitute. Can you guess why?

Convive means "guest" to the French. They inherited the word from the Latin *convivia* ("one who lives with another and eats with another"). The parent verb is *vivere* ("to live").

In English, *convives* are fellow banqueters, or comrades at the table. You can spring that one on your friends the next time you attend a formal dinner.

Of course *convivial* and *conviviality* are next of kin. But did you know that a *convivium* is a banquet?

Other descendants of *vivere* are *viva, vivacious, vivid, revive* and *survive.*

Victuals is in the family too, by way of the past participle, *victus.* The idea is that one needs food to live.

Finally, through a complicated series of semantic changes, *quick* turns out to be the oldest relative of them all.

―――――

Croissants are well named. They are rich, flaky rolls formed in the shape of a crescent. *Croissant* is the French word for "crescent."

The rolls originated in Vienna. Chefs created them to celebrate the defeat of the Turks in 1689. The Turkish emblem is a crescent. Hence the Viennese were symbolically devouring their enemies.

―――――

Croutons are those small, crisp pieces of toast or fried bread that are often served with soup or salads. In French, *croûton* means "crust or hunk." It's an alteration of *crusta,* a Latin noun for "the skin, rind, shell, crust or bark."

In our slang we have extended *crust* to mean "gall, insolence, nerve or audacity." People who have *crust* are thick-skinned.

―――――

Demitasse is a small cup of coffee, usually taken black. This post-prandial beverage is well named. Literally, it means "half a cup."

―――――

Fondue (sometimes spelled *fondu*) is a treat that grows ever more popular in America with each passing year. Primarily, it is a dish made by melting cheese in wine, with a little brandy and seasoning added. Then cubes of bread are dipped into the mixture. So far, so good. The word is derived from the past participle of the French verb *fondre* ("to melt").

However, some intrepid and carnivorous soul asked himself or herself, "Why not try it with meat?" And so cubes of beef, veal and other meats were soon dipped into simmering oil and then garnished with a variety of sauces. Vegetables, mushrooms and other goodies were added to the dipping process, and this too became a *fondue.* Then someone else developed another approach, reverting partly to the original: a cheese souffle with bread crumbs was concocted and was called a *fondue.*

My advice is to question the waiter carefully before you order this dish in a restaurant. There are *fondues* upon *fondues* that confuse, and you should ask "Whose?" What have you got to lose?

―――――

Frangipane is another word that the French borrowed from the Italians. A nobleman named Marquis Frangipani invented a perfume that became popular from the sixteenth century on. His *frangipani* imitated the lovely odor of red jasmine. The Parisian women originally dabbed it on their gloves and enjoyed its effects on each amoureaux.

Then a clever chef came up with a great idea. He created a dessert of almond cream flavored with *frangipani,* or jasmine perfume. The dish was called *frangipane.* After that a new concoction evolved. The creamy delicacy was inserted into pastries as a filling. In America today that is the popular conception of the word.

When you order a *frangipane* you are asking the waiter to bring you a tart—a small open pie with a sweet filling. The British slangsters got hold of the word "tart" and cunningly changed it to mean "a loose woman or prostitute." In the London argot, *tarting up* is furnishing or attiring or decorating in a cheap and showy way.

Gigot is a leg of lamb or mutton. It's the diminutive of *gigue* ("a fiddle") and was named for its shape. Incidentally, a *gigue* is also a jig or lively dance movement.

An interesting offshoot is the *gigot sleeve* on a woman's garment. Its shape resembles a leg of mutton.

Gourmand and *gourmet* are often confused. The former is a glutton, and the latter is discriminating about what he eats or drinks. Synonyms for *gourmet* are epicure and connoisseur. In Old French the spelling was *groumet.* In those days he was a vintner's young assistant or wine taster.

Mousse literally means "froth" in French. It is derived from the Latin adjective *mulsus* ("mixed with honey or sweet as honey"). The word has at least three definitions in English:

1. frothy dessert
2. purée of fish or meat lightened with gelatin or whipped cream or both
3. light, spongy, creamy food, usually containing gelatin, cream or whites of eggs. (In this sense it is often spelled *mousseline.*)

It grieves me to report that *mildew* is a relative of this delicious dish.

Parfait to a Frenchman means "something perfect." The popularity of this flavored custard or cold dessert with layers of fruit syrup and ice cream seems to indicate that it is living up to its name.

Next, let us turn to the Gallic influence on English words that pertain to such arts as the theater, music, dance, painting, literature and connected fields. Again, only a sampling is listed below.

THE ARTS

allemande	chansonnier	coupé	√gouache
apache dance	√chassé	courante	√harlequin
√aperçu	clarinet	cramignon	√ingénue
arabesque	clavecin	craquelure	motif
artiste	√clavicor	crèche	ormolu
√atelier	√clavier	critique	pastiche
√ballet	√collage	danse macabre	polonaise
bal masqué	comedienne	danseuse	√potpourri
√bas bleu	concert	debut	précis
√bassoon	√connoisseur	denouement	première
beguine	conservatoire	dilettante	√protégé
√bibelot	√conte	eloge	revue
√bijou	contredanse	encore	roulade
brisé	corps de ballet	√étoile	salon
√burlesque	coryphée	√étude	tableau
cabriole	côtelé	√farceur	taupe
√cénacle	cotillion	√fugue	√timbre
√chanson	√couac	genre	valse

Aperçu is an outline or brief sketch. A relative is *perceive*. The eventual Latin root is *capere* ("to hold").

———

Atelier has an unbelievable history. The grandparent of this artist's studio meant "a shaving or splinter." Thereupon *astelier* emerged. That noun was originally a woodpile, then it became a construction yard, and finally a workshop. The second letter was dropped as time went by, and the word became associated with painters and architects. Note the latter; they do deal with wood.

———

Ballet is a diminutive of *bal* ("dance"). When you waltz in a *ballroom,* you are in the same league, but not when you watch a *ball game.* That's from an entirely different root. Incidentally, if you are a *balletomane* or afflicted with *balletomania,* you are a devotee of SWAN LAKE, LES SYLPHIDES and LE SPECTRE DE LA ROSE.

———

Bas bleu literally means "blue stocking." In the eighteenth century the Bluestocking society was formed. Its members were women, some of whom wore unconventional attire, including the color of their hosiery. Their discussions centered around literary matters. Hence a *bas bleu* came to mean two things, depending on the extent of one's male chauvinism: "a female pedant" and "a learned woman."

I prefer the latter.

———

Bassoon is a woodwind instrument with a deep tone. The French took *basson* from the Italians' *bassone* and we added an extra vowel. The word is related, of course, to *basso*.

Bibelot means "a trinket" in French and in English. We also use the word to signify "a miniature book especially of elegant design or format." *Bible* and *bibliography* are among its kinsmen.

Bijou is a Parisian's jewel. We have taken over that meaning completely. In my youth I was sure that the word meant "theater" because so many owners of movie houses gave that glittering title to their buildings.

Have you ever heard of *bijouterie?* That's a synonym for trinkets or jewelry. I would like to think that it's one of the gems in this book.

Burlesque today is associated with striptease acts, but 'twas not always so. We took the word from the French, who had borrowed it from *burlesco,* the Italian adjective for "comical." Originally such shows featured comics in baggy pants who performed low comedy.

It is sometimes forgotten that a *burlesque* is also a literary or dramatic opus that ridicules what is usually considered serious and dignified. For example, Samuel Butler's HUDIBRAS falls into this category. Other compositions make fun of the trivial. Alexander Pope's THE RAPE OF THE LOCK is a mock-heroic poem that deals with an actual incident. (In a rash moment Lord Petre clipped a bit of Arabella Fermor's crowning glory.) Pope's lampoon can be truly classified as a *burlesque*.

A *cénacle* is a coterie of writers or other artistic people. Literally, it is the scene of the Last Supper. The word can be traced back to the Romans' *cena* ("dinner").

Cenacle (without an accent) is a retreat house, named for the Society of Our Lady of the Cenacle, a congregation of nuns founded in France in 1826 to direct retreats for women.

Chansons are songs. The parent verb is the Romans' *cantare* ("to sing"). Note again how the French liked to change *c* to *ch*. Naturally, *chant* comes from the same root. Other directly related words include *chansonnier* ("cabaret singer"), *chansonette* ("little song"), *chanteuse, chanticleer, chantey* ("song originally sung by sailors in rhythm with their work") and *chanteyman*.

Some relatives, via Italy, are *cantabile, cantata, canto* and *canzone*.

Among the other members of this prolific family, we find *accent, canorous* ("musical"), *cant* ("whining or singing speech used by beggars, etc.—hence argot, jargon, secret slang"), *canticle, cantor, descant, enchant, incantation, incentive* and *precentor* ("director of a church choir").

Oddly enough, *canary* does not belong in this group. Its Latin root is *canis* ("dog")! The Canary Islands, to which the bird is native, were called *Canariae Insulae* ("Dog Islands") because large dogs were once bred there.

Chassé is a rapid, gliding dance step forward or sideways. In French it is literally defined as "a chasing." Callers at square dances altered it to *sashay:* "Everybody *sashay* around the hall." Then *sashay* came to mean "to strut or flounce or walk casually." As a noun it now means "a trip, excursion or venture."

Sashay always reminds me of *traipse*—a word once favored by cartoonist Al Capp's group in Dogpatch. It means "to gad about or walk aimlessly." Lexicographers suppose that it might be a variation of *tramp,* but they are not sure whence it sprang up. My guess is, in the Ozarks or Appalachia.

Clavicors are bass horns. The French derived the name from two Latin roots—*clavis* ("key") and *cornū* ("horn").

Claviers are the keyboards of pianos, harpsichords and organs. By metonymy a *clavier* has also become any instrument having a keyboard. Finally, it can mean " a dummy keyboard for silent practice."

By the way, the word originally meant "a key holder."

Collage literally means "a pasting." It's an artistic composition made with bits and pieces of materials pasted together in seemingly haphazard fashion. Newspaper clippings, pressed flowers, ticket stubs, etc. are often used in this medium.

Today we have extended the meaning. A *collage* can be any collection of miscellaneous items.

Collage is not to be confused with *montage.* The latter is a photographic process for making composite pictures. Its source is the French verb *monter* ("to mount"). When a number of separate exposures are made on the same negative, that art is called *photomontage.*

Connoisseurs are people with expert knowledge and discrimination in particular fields, especially the arts. They are, in truth, aesthetes.

The word dates back eventually to *cognoscere,* the Latin verb meaning "to know thoroughly." Some relatives are *acquaint, cognition, notice, notify, notion, notorious, quaint* and *recognize.*

You may ask how *quaint* got into this family. After all, in spelling and meaning, it seems to be a total stranger. Well, in Old French it was spelled *cointe* and meant "expert or elegant." Medieval Englishmen changed it to *queinte.*

In Elizabethan times the word meant "skilled in the use of language." A line from Shakespeare reads: "How *quaint* an orator." Gradually the idea of skill came to be associated with uniqueness. By the nineteenth century such writers as Sir Walter Scott were using the adjective to mean "odd or strange." Some other definitions for it today are "picturesque, old-fashioned, singular, naïve, illogical, artificially unfamiliar and different in a pleasing way." Obviously we have really made a versatile workhorse out of poor old *quaint.*

Conte is another excellent example of how semantic changes through the centuries seem to make strange bedfellows. Who would believe that this short adventure tale has any relationship to *pavement* or *amputate?*

Conter ("to relate") is the French parent of *conte.* But the grandparent is *computare,* the Latin verb meaning "to reckon with." Other kinfolk are *account, computer, count* (as a verb), *counterman, deputy, disputation, impute, putative* and *repute.*

The Latin verb *putare* had a variety of meanings. One of them was "to strike, strike off, prune or trim." Another was "to reckon, think or count." Hence it's easy to see how *amputate* and *compute* are descendants of the same root.

Pave and *pavement* come in via a Latin alteration of the parent verb. To the Romans, *pavire* meant "to ram down, beat or strike."

Couac is a strange word of French origin. It was formed in imitation of the strident sound made by a reed instrument that is out of order or blown incorrectly. I am reminded of a popular gag: "An oboe is a wind that nobody blows good."

Incidentally, *couac* is pronounced exactly like *quack.*

Étoile is the French word for "star." The motto of Minnesota, the North Star State, is: L'Étoile du Nord. In English an étoile is a prima ballerina.

Étude means "study" in French and in English. To musicians it's a practice piece or exercise. However, it also contains the idea of dwelling on a special point of technique and being performed for artistic value, as the *études* of Chopin and Schumann. Incidentally, when new crossword puzzle constructors submit atrocious 23x23 puzzles, I sometimes inform them that they should try to compose an *étude* (15x15 daily puzzle) before they attempt a symphony.

Farceurs are jokers or wags. They are also actors in or writers of *farces*. A woman who is skilled in that theatrical art is called a *farceuse*. (I wonder if French feminists object to the term.)

The parent Latin verb is *farcire* ("to stuff"). Consequently, one can readily understand why *farce* means "forcemeat or stuffing." But why is it also defined as "a light, satirical or humorous drama"? The answer is that in medieval days the traveling troupes stuffed a boisterous, comical diversion between the acts of the principal presentation in order to give themselves a breather, change scenery and perform other chores.

Today any ridiculous situation or display is called a *farce*. People who have not enjoyed a party, for instance, will say to each other, "The evening turned out to be a *farce*, didn't it?"

Fugues are complicated polyphonic musical compositions. Literally, they are "flights" of music. *Fuga*, the Latin noun meaning "fleeing," is the source. Its other scions include *centrifugal, fugitive* and *refuge*.

A most interesting cousin is *subterfuge* (literally, "a fleeing below"). When you use deceptive artifices, you retreat into underhanded tricks. Some of the Watergaters were masters of *subterfuge*.

The adjective *febrifuge* means "serving to reduce a fever." A perennial European herb called the *feverfew* was reputed by old wives to have that power. Does the plant come from the same root? Yes! *Febris* ("fever") is the first source, changed through the Anglo-French. *Fuga* is the second source. The Anglo-French loved their *v*'s and *w*'s!

My favorite member of the tribe is *fugacious*, meaning "lasting for a short time; of unsubstantial nature; evanescent; wandering."

But all "acious" words entrance me. They have a delightful ring to them. When I hear *perspicacious* used in place of shrewd, a thrill goes through my spine. And how about *audacious, capacious, fallacious, loquacious, sagacious, tenacious, vivacious* and *voracious?* Aren't they all as delicious as a piece of French pastry?

Take *salacious*, for example. The very sound is exciting, unlike its synonym, pornographic. That adjective has a harsh, unmusical tone.

Then there are *pertinacious, pervicacious* and *contumacious*. How nice they sound compared with stubborn and insubordinate!

I would rather call a glutton *edacious* than say that he is greedy. And I prefer to believe that the aspirins I swallow are *efficacious* instead of effective. When somebody appeals to me as an honest person, I like to think of him as *veracious* or *unmendacious*—not just truthful. The bullies in my life are *menacious* and *pugnacious*, and those who exploit me will be pleased to know that my bent for musical words makes me think of them as *predacious* and *rapacious.* Any sarcastic critics of this book should be told in advance that I will regard them as *mordacious* and will not bow down to them in a *sequacious* way. If they are insolent upstarts, I will think of them as merely *procacious* and not lose a wink of sleep. Certainly they will not cause me to be a bibulous or *bibacious* barfly, although their slings and arrows may send me further into the arms of Lady Nicotine. Yes, I do tend to be *fumacious,* and often wish I could resist the temptation to light up that next cigar.

Dear reader, pardon my verbal *fugue!*

Gouache (pronounced "gwash") is a method of painting with opaque watercolors. The French borrowed the word from the Italians' *guazzo* (literally, "a puddle"). Readers who have followed this text thus far may not be surprised to learn that the term is descended from Caesar's *aqua* ("water"). What amazes me as I write this book is the fact that thousands upon thousands of words from the ancients have undergone tremendous structural changes as different nationalities and cultures have adapted them to their own languages and purposes.

Harlequin, if capitalized, means "a conventional buffoon of the commedia dell'arte traditionally presented in a mask and parti-colored tights." However, as a common noun the word has taken on a few other colorations:

1. any clown
2. a small duck with distinctively patterned plumage
3. a variegated textile pattern

As an adjective *harlequin* can be defined as follows:

1. bright, parti-colored; spangled like the dress of Harlequin
2. like spectacles with frames that flare in an upward slant like the slits of Harlequin's mask
3. comic, ludicrous, colorful

This word, like so many others, has gone through a multitude of aberrations. It can be traced to a Medieval Latin term, *Herla rex*—a mythical king identified with Woden.

A derivative is *harlequinade,* which has come to mean "a farce or fantastic procedure."

Ingénues are ingenuous. They are artless, innocent young women. Hence they are actresses who play such roles. If one takes their roots literally, these girls must be very, very young. The parent verb in Latin is *gignere* ("to beget") and the prefix means "not." Therefore, *ingénues* are so immature that they can't have children.

Potpourri (pronounced "pō-pŏo-rē") is a combination of miscellaneous, and often incongruous, elements (originally, a stew). An anthologist who has compiled literature from various sources can be said to have published a *potpourri*. Additionally, the word has a basic meaning that is not familiar to me: "a mixture of dried flower petals and spices that have been kept in a jar and used to scent the air." Also, it is a "medley of songs."

For a change, the French borrowed this word from the Spanish. In Madrid an *olla podrida* is literally "a rotten pot," but it has come to mean "a stew" and, by extension, "an assortment, medley, olio, or miscellany."

Some unpleasant cousins of *potpourri* are *porulent, pus, putrefy, putrid* and *suppurate*. That last word, I am sorry to tell you, means "to fester, as a wound."

Protégé goes back to the Latin verb *protegere* ("to protect"). A *protégé* is a man under the care and protection of an influential person, such as a sponsor, teacher or patron. The female form is *protégée;* it may soon become obsolescent, along with its counterpart *protectress*.

Timbre is a distinctive quality of tone or sound. In Medieval French it meant "a bell struck by a hammer," and in Old French it was a drum. The root is the Greek word *tympanon,* from which we also get *tympanum* ("ear drum") and *tympany* ("resonance on percussion— hence, bombast"). A *tympanist* in an orchestra is the person who plays the kettledrums.

Timbre can also be spelled *timber,* but it has no relationship to trees or wood. The source of its look-alike can be traced to Sanskrit and Greek words meaning "to build."

The fact that *timber* ("lumber") and *domicile* are related linguistically seems appropriate. But it may strike you as a bit odd that *dame, domino, madame* and *madonna* can claim the same ancient ancestors as the *timber* wolf.

And now let us take up another grouping of French words that have seeped into the English language. The list that follows is by no means a complete one, but it should serve to indicate that we have indeed brought the French into our homes.

SHELTER AND FURNITURE

√armoire	√chauffer	Limoges
auberge	chauffeuse	maître d'hôtel
√boudoir	chiffonier	marquetry
√cabriole	√concierge	√oriel
√chaise longue	√console	√pension
chalet	étagère	√portiere
√chandelier	√hospice	potiche
√château	√jalousie	√taboret
	√kiosk	

Armoire is a warlike word that has been tamed. Although it's a large ornate cupboard or wardrobe, its eventual Latin source is *arma* ("weapons"). Can you picture Caesar taking off his armor at home and placing it in his *armarium* ("closet")?

Boudoir comes from the French verb *bouder* ("to pout or be sulky"). Originally it was a room to which a person could go if he or she felt sullen, depressed or unsociable. In a way, it was a kind of den. Today it's a bedroom or a woman's private dressing room. Of course she can pout there too as she puts on her lipstick.

Cabriole is a style of furniture leg that curves outward at the top and then descends in a tapering reverse curve that ends with an ornamental foot. It literally means "leap or caper" and was named for its resemblance to the foreleg of a capering animal.

Chaise longue is literally a "long chair." A fascinating thing happened to this French import. Americans who relaxed in it naturally compared it to a couch or sofa. Either inadvertently or deliberately, they changed the spelling to *chaise lounge*. Lexicographers had to give in. Both entries appear in most modern dictionaries. This is an up-to-date example of how folk usage can alter a word.

Chandeliers ornamented French homes long before Edison came on the scene. Hence it's understandable that those lighting fixtures are literally candlesticks. Their close kin are *candelabra* ("decorative candlesticks having several arms or branches").

There are three interesting aspects to *candelabrum*. First of all, it's a word taken wholly in spelling and meaning from the ancient Romans. Secondly, it's a hard word for most of us to spell; we tend to reverse the *e* and the *l*. Finally, its plural has been used as a singular form by so many people that *candelabras* has been accepted by those same lexicographers who are still holding out on *chaise lounge*.

Two other members of this family are *chandler* and *chandlery*. The former is a maker or seller of candles; the latter is his storehouse.

The most common definition for *château* is "a country house, especially one resembling a castle." Appropriately, *castle* is a related word. In Old French it was spelled *chastel*. The Latin root is *castellum* ("a castle, fort or citadel"), from the verb *castrare*.

It will probably shock you to learn that *castrate* is linguistically akin to *castle* and *château*. In ancient Rome, *castrare* meant "to emasculate—hence, to deprive of strength; to restrain or check." The latter definitions fit nicely with *castle*. It's a fortified place built to check the forces of the enemy.

A *chauffer* is a portable stove, not to be confused with *chauffeur*. Originally the latter was a stoker employed to keep the heat going. Many of the early French cars ran on steam; therefore the *chauffeur*'s new job was to heat up the engines. It's ironic to think that today many a *chauffeur* drives an air-conditioned limousine. Heat is the least of his problems!

A *chauffeuse*, by the way, is not only a female employed to drive but also a low-seated French chair near the hearth. Parisians can sit there comfortably and throw another log on the fire.

Concierges are doorkeepers; they are also custodians or head porters at apartment houses and hotels. Would they be pleased or disappointed to learn that their heritage is *conservus?* It's the Latin noun for "fellow slave."

Most of us know that the verb *console* means "to comfort." Does the noun from the French have any relationship? Indeed it does! *Consoles* were originally *consolateurs* in France; these were carved human figures used to support cornices. They were also rails used in choir stalls. When the singers stood up to perform, they had a place to lean for support. Note the similarity between *support* and *console*.

Today *console* as a noun has many meanings.

1. a decorative bracket for supporting a shelf, cornice bust or other object
2. the desklike part of an organ that contains the keyboard
3. a small table designed to be set against a wall
4. a cabinet for a radio or TV set or a phonograph
5. a panel housing the controls for electrical or mechanical equipment

As you read the above paragraphs you were probably aware that the accent for the verb *console* falls on the second syllable, whereas the stress for the noun is placed on the first syllable. This stress pattern is common practice in English. Here are just a few examples:

VERB	NOUN	VERB	NOUN
attribute′	at′tribute	discourse′	dis′course
combat′	com′bat	perfume′	per′fume
compound′	com′pound	refund′	re′fund
discount′	dis′count	refuse′	ref′use

The change of accents also applies to adjectives vis-à-vis verbs. Consider the following:

VERB	ADJECTIVE
absent′	ab′sent
frequent′	fre′quent
present′	pres′ent

Hospices are shelters or lodgings for travelers, students or the destitute; they are often maintained by monastics. They are similar in meaning and derivation to *hostels* and *hotels.*

The source, as usual, is a Latin word. *Hospes* meant "guest or host"; the Romans couldn't make up their minds, probably because they thought that *hospitality* ("friendliness") was a reciprocal duty.

At any rate, it's fascinating to note that *hospital* belongs in this family. It was originally a kind of *hospice,* or place for travelers to rest. But in 1048 the shelter provided by monks for pilgrims in the Crusades was filled with so many people who had fallen ill on the journey that *hospital* came to mean "a place to care for the sick and injured."

The fact that the Romans had the same name for guest and host reminds me of comedian George Carlin's routine in which he talks about obvious contradictions in terms, such as being a "guest host" on the Carson show or buying "jumbo shrimp." Whether Carlin knows it or not, these expressions are examples of the use of an *oxymoron*—a figure of speech of Greek origin meaning "the combination of opposite or contradictory ideas or terms."

Oxymora fascinated Shakespeare. In Act I, Scene 1, of ROMEO AND JULIET he makes Romeo spew out a whole slew of them in connection with his passion for Rosaline, the girl of his dreams before his meeting with Juliet. Here's what this lovesick swain says:

> "Why, then, O brawling love! O loving hate!
> O any thing! of nothing first create.
> O heavy lightness! serious vanity!
> Mis-shapen chaos of well-seeming forms!
> Feather of lead, bright smoke, cold fire, sick health!
> Still-waking sleep, that is not what it is!
> This love feel I, that feel no love in this."

Oxymoron meant "astute silliness" to the Greeks. How apt! There are many examples in our language. Stephen Douglas was called the Little Giant. Custer's demise took place at Little Big Horn. Bert Lahr portrayed the Cowardly Lion in a movie. In one of his odes Thomas Gray said, " 'Tis folly to be wise," and in *Twelfth Night* one of the characters quotes Quinapalus: "Better a witty fool than a foolish wit."

My favorite *oxymora* are "thundering silence," "make haste slowly" and Noel Coward's play *Bitter Sweet.*

Jalousie and *jealousy* are consanguineous. There is a secret or hidden connotation to both words. For example, Othello was blinded by unwarranted *jealousy* but kept it concealed from Desdemona until it was too late. People who hide behind *jalousies* ("blinds") are able to see out, but usually no one can see them inside. They guard their privacy *jealously.*

Kiosk, or *kiosque,* is a word that the French borrowed from the Turks. In its original sense it was a summer house or open pavilion. The French thought of it as a bandstand. We use it today to mean "an outdoor newsstand, a structure at the entrance to a subway" or even "a telephone booth." To the British it is a stand where merchandise is sold or information is provided. There seems to be no end to the versatility of this word. Though once a summer structure only, it is now a stand for all seasons.

Oriel is familiar to crossword puzzle fans through the clue "a bay window." In the Middle Ages it was a porch or gallery. Philologers surmise that it is related to *aula,* the Latin word for "a court" and that its immediate ancestor is *auleolum,* the Medieval Latin word for "a niche or small chapel." Whatever its roots, it certainly is a pretty sight.

The story is told that an American in Paris saw the sign *Pension* on one building after another. Told that they were boardinghouses, he commented, "I didn't know there were so many retired Frenchmen."

The French and other Europeans developed their meaning for the word from the fact that a *pension* ("fee") had to be paid for their children who boarded away from home as students.

The Latin root is *pendere, pensus* ("to weigh or pay or hang").

Portieres are heavy curtains usually hung in doorways. The French word *portier* means "doorkeeper," and *portiere* is its feminine form. Literally, these curtains are feminine doorkeepers.

Taboret actually means "a small drum." In common usage, it is a cylindrical stool or seat without arms or a back—obviously named for its resemblance to a little drum. But commercial artists have their own definition for the word. To them, it's a small cabinet for supplies. Incidentally, an alternate spelling is *tabouret*.

Next let us turn to those French-English words that deal with international relations, whether evil or beneficent. In this category the French have given us scores of words. A few are listed below.

WAR AND DIPLOMACY

aide-de-camp	caisson	cuirassier	oubliette
ambuscade	√camouflage	√debacle	paladin
arrière-ban	cartel	√détente	perdu
attaché	casque	√entente	√poilu
avant-courier	chargé d'affaires	espionage	politesse
√banquette	congé	esprit de corps	rapport
barrage	√cordon sanitaire	étape	rapprochement
bayonet	corps	√grenadier	reconnaissance
beau sabreur	corps d'elite	kepi	√sabotage
bivouac	corps diplomatique	√laissez-faire	√saboteur
√boche	√corvette	matériel	sortie
√cadet			

Of the forty-five words in the above grouping about one-fourth relate to diplomacy, and the rest are directly or indirectly military. Does this indicate the state of man's inhumanity to man versus his ability to get along with others?

Banquette may sound like a feast, but it isn't. Instead it's a platform for gunners. It has also come to mean "a built-in upholstered bench along a wall in a restaurant." In the South it's a synonym for sidewalk.

Some related words are *bank, bench* and *bunco*—all eventually having a Germanic source.

Boche is French slang for a German soldier. This derogatory term arose in World War I. It is a contraction of *tête de caboche* ("head of cabbage"—hence, "hard head"). Later the G.I.s used a different disparaging term for the German troops. Their word was *Krauts,* an abridgment of *sauerkraut* ("chopped cabbage fermented in a brine of its own juice").

Most of us think of *cadets* as West Pointers or other students training to be officers. Actually, the first meaning of *cadet* is "a younger son." But in former times such a scion had no chance to inherit his father's estate. The rule of primogeniture dictated that the eldest son would receive the property, money and other resources. Therefore it became customary for the younger sons to make a living by joining the army.

The word is derived from *capitellum* ("little head" in Latin). The Gascons, in southwestern France, developed *capdet,* and thence it was shortened to *cadet.* The grandparent is *caput* ("head")—and what a large family that word sired! Here are some of its members: *cap, cape, capital, capitol, capitulate, caporal, caprice, captain, cattle, chapter, chief, decapitate, kepi, kerchief, mischief, precipitate* and *recapitulate.*

Caddies are also members of the group, via *cadet.* They were originally errand boys in Scotland. And from *caddie* the British developed *cad.* This ungentlemanly fellow was a menial helper centuries ago. Then he became associated with rowdyish town boys, as distinguished from the hardworking students at local institutions. The transition to his present status is simple to comprehend.

Camouflage is a derivative of *camouflet* ("a puff of smoke; a smoke bomb"). In French, *moufler* means "to muffle or cover up." And so when soldiers use *camouflage* to conceal themselves, they are really blowing out a screen of smoke and covering up.

Cordon sanitaire reminds me of a book of cartoons that gave me many a chuckle years ago. I think it was called FRACTURED FRENCH. In any case, it depicted various Gallic phrases ridiculously. For example, *carte blanche* was one of the headings, and the sketch showed two men carrying an obviously inebriated girl out of a wild party.

You can guess what the cartoonist did with *hors d'oeuvres.* Anyway, I'm not sure if *cordon sanitaire* showed a group of garbage collectors on strike, but it would have fitted into that context.

In truth, the phrase has two meanings:

1. a barrier restraining free movement of people or goods so as to keep a disease from spreading
2. a belt of countries isolating another nation in order to check its aggressiveness or lessen its influence

---

Corvettes are fast warships. The word is probably derived from Middle Dutch *corf* ("a basket or small ship"). I refuse to say that if you drive a certain popular car, you are liable to become a basket case.

Debacle means "the breaking up of ice" in a river. As a result, the second definition is "a violent flood." Finally our most common association with the word evolved. Today a debacle means "a calamitous failure or collapse, or an overwhelming defeat." A flood of waters or opposing forces causes a disaster or a *debacle*.

Détente literally means "an easing." It has taken on an international significance and now refers to a relaxation of tension between nations. Its cousin *entente* means "understanding" in French. This word also has acquired a diplomatic connotation. It has come to mean "an understanding or agreement between or among nations." In 1904 the *Entente Cordiale* was signed and it developed into the *Triple Entente,* involving Great Britain, France and Russia. That noble effort came to an end in 1917 when the Bolshevist revolution occurred.

Grenadiers were initially soldiers who carried and threw *grenades.* The British liked the word and changed it to apply to a special regiment or corps attached to the royal household. The noun now also refers to deep-sea fishes of the cod family. These fish have long tapering tails and are sometimes called *rattails*.

Of greatest interest is the fact that the French named the *grenade* for the pomegranate because of its original shape. In fact, *grenade* is an obsolete synonym for pomegranate. Our G.I.s later noticed the resemblance of the U.S. missile to a tropical American fruit and called it a pineapple.

Laissez-faire means "let (people) do (as they please)." It is the policy or practice of noninterference and is used by governments that allow industrialists to fix the rules of competition without regulations. Naturally, labor unions are opposed to this approach.

I have included the phrase in this category because it is also used in the sense that one nation should not meddle with the affairs of another.

Less known, but perhaps more apt, is *laissez-passer,* a permit or pass allowing officials of one country to travel in another.

An *oubliette* is a dungeon with a trapdoor in the ceiling as its only opening. Via Latin ancestors, *oblivion* fittingly is in the same family.

Poilu actually means "hairy or virile" in French. The term was applied to any French soldier in World War I. He was the counterpart of one of General Pershing's *doughboys.* And whence did that particular nickname arise? Lexicographers assume that it refers to the large brass buttons on the uniforms of soldiers dating as far back as the Civil War. In those days a *doughboy* was also a little doughnut.

Sabotage and *saboteur* have fascinating histories. In French a *sabot* means "a wooden shoe." This footwear was commonly worn by peasants. Since the upper classes considered such lowly persons to be awkward and slipshod, the verb *saboter* was created. It meant "to botch the job, to be clumsy and careless."

Some philologers think that *sabotage* arose from the fact that the peasants threw their wooden shoes into the machinery at factories. My own opinion is that the first *saboteurs* were peasants who rebelled against the oppressions of their masters. They didn't necessarily have to throw their shoes; the fact that they wore them was enough to cause the landowners to label them as deliberate damagers of property.

———

Next, let us proceed to one of the favorite pastimes of the French, the English and most other groups. Here is a small selection of words, some of which have been transferred from Paris and Monte Carlo to London, Las Vegas, Reno and Atlantic City, among other places. All the words in this win-or-lose category will be discussed.

GAMBLING

baccarat	craps	parimutuel
bagatelle	croupier	roulette
boule	écarté	vingt-et-un
brelain		

Baccarat is a card game similar to chemin de fer and twenty-one. The origin of the word is not certain. Possibly it came from a town of the same name in eastern France. However, the French call the game *baccara.*

———

Bagatelle means "a trifle." The French borrowed it from the Italian noun *bagatella,* which has the same meaning.

The game *bagatelle* is played on an oblong table with a cue and usually nine balls. In recent years it has been associated with pinball.

Finally, the word signifies "a short piece of light verse or music for the piano."

The Latin root is *baca* ("berry"). That seems to fit, because a tiny berry is a mere nothing.

———

Boule literally means "ball" in French. It's a game similar to roulette. The word also is used as a synonym for a pear-shaped synthetic sapphire.

———

Brelan is an old French gambling game somewhat like poker. Its immediate ancestor is *berlenc* ("gaming table or gambling house"). *Brelan carré* is a similar game, sometimes called "four of a kind."

———

Craps comes to us via the Creoles in Louisiana. They borrowed the name from an obsolete English slang word, *crabs,* which meant the lowest throw in an old dice game called "hazard." It's interesting to note that today a player who throws two aces "craps out."

Why the plural of a certain crustacean was used is apparently impossible to determine. But dice players who make such a losing throw have been known to act crabby.

Croupier displays the Gallic sense of humor. Its French root is *croupe* ("rump") and it originally meant "rider on the rump behind another rider." Drolly, the French applied it to the original *croupiers* who were advisers, standing (or maybe sitting) behind the players at the gaming tables. This practice still exists in baccarat and chemin de fer, but today a *croupier* is usually an attendant who collects the losers' bets and pays the winners.

Finally, at a public dinner party the person who sits at the lower end of the table and acts as an assistant chairman is called a *croupier.* That's most appropriate; he's sitting on the rump!

Écarté is a game for two, played with thirty-two cards—sevens up through aces. The word is the past participle of *écarter* ("to discard"). The game is well named, because all the cards dealt may be discarded and replaced from the pack.

Parimutuel literally means "a mutual stake." It's a system of betting (as at a horse race) in which the winners share the total stakes minus a small percentage for the management. All racetracks are now equipped with *parimutuel machines* that register and indicate the number and nature of the bets and then compute the payoffs. They are sometimes called totalizers.

Roulette owes its origin to *rota* ("wheel" in ancient Rome). The Late Latin diminutive *rotella* is the immediate ancestor.

Aside from being a casino game, with a lively little ball bouncing around inside a spinning bowl, *roulette* is a small toothed wheel attached to a handle. This implement is used to make the perforations in a row of postage stamps so that they can be easily separated. By metonymy the incisions themselves have come to be known as *roulettes.*

As a verb the word means "to make dots, marks or incisions."

Vingt-et-un is the game of "twenty-one." Literally, it means "twenty and one."

Leaving the casinos, we now turn to the boudoirs. Here is a small list of words on the tender passion, French style.

L-AMOUR

√accouchement	√billet-doux	√débauchée	√oeillade
affaire d-amour	coquetry	√divorcée	√paramour
√amourette	√coquette	√fiancé	√rendezvous
beau	√courtesan	√odalisque	√roué

Accouchement comes from the verb *accoucher,* which first meant "to put to bed" and soon acquired an association with childbirth. In that sense it means "to deliver a child." *Accouchement,* therefore, is confinement for giving birth to a baby. A synonym is parturition.

An *accoucheur* is a male attendant at childbirth or an obstetrician. An *accoucheuse* is a midwife.

Our word *couch* comes from the same root, *collocare* ("to place together or lay together"). Apparently, if you wish to compose yourself when you feel dislocated, you should lay your weary bones on a *couch.*

Amourette is a trifling or short-lived love affair. The woman involved in such a brief encounter is also an *amourette.*

Billets-doux are literally sweet short notes—hence, love letters. In FRACTURED FRENCH they are little bills due to be paid. That joke is ironic in a way, because *bill* and *billet*—and also *bullet*—are relations.

Doux has some sweet cousins. Among them are *dulcet* and *dulcimer.* The former means "melodious" and the latter is a musical instrument that looks somewhat like a xylophone.

Do you remember *Dulciana,* the heroine of THE MAN OF LA MANCHA? As a common noun she's an organ stop with a sweet tone. Speaking of the theater, let's not forget LA DOLCE VITA, the Italian phrase for "the sweet life."

Coquette has an entertaining background. It's the diminutive of *coq* ("cock"). The noun *coquet* has become obsolete in English. Too bad! It meant "a little cock—hence, a flirtatious man." But *coquet* has survived as a verb meaning "to flirt, trifle or dally," and *coquetry* means "dalliance or flirtation."

Coq itself entered the English language meaning "a trimming of cock feathers on a woman's hat." Sometimes it is spelled *coque.* Then of course there is *coq au vin,* a dish of chicken in red wine with lots of other ingredients.

Opera lovers will recall LE COQ D'OR (THE GOLDEN COCKEREL) by Rimsky-Korsakov.

Courtesans are ladies of the court, but not straitlaced ones. In truth, they are high-class prostitutes or kept women. Their ancestry can be traced back to *cohors,* the Latin noun for "an enclosure or court, a fenced-in multitude—hence, a company of soldiers."

Relations include *cohort, cortege, court, courteous, courtesy, courtier, curtain* and *curtsy*.

Debauchees are dissipated persons, libertines or people given to sensual excesses. *Debauch,* if followed to its source, means "to separate branches from a trunk." Thus the word has taken on evil connotations, such as "to lead astray, corrupt, seduce, deprave, debase." *Debaucheries* are orgies.

Divorcée and *divorce* come into our language, via Medieval French, from *divortere* and *divertere*. Those Latin infinitives mean "to turn oneself in a different direction, or to go different ways."

It's strange to think that *divertissement* ("amusement") and the dissolution of a marriage should be closely related.

Incidentally, a *divorcée* is a woman. Her erstwhile partner is a *divorcé*.

Fiancés must be trusted by their *fiancées*. Their titles stem from the French verb *fier* ("to trust"). The eventual root is *fidere*—the Romans' verb meaning "to trust or confide in."

Some of the many members of this trusting tribe are *affiance, affidavit, confederate, confidence, defy, diffident, faith, fealty, federal, fidelity, fiduciary, infidel, infidelity, perfidious, perfidy* and good old *Fido* (a dog I trust).

Odalisques are concubines or female slaves in harems. The French developed the word from their association with the Turks. As every crossword puzzle fan knows, an *oda* is defined as "a room in a harem."

Matisse and other artists loved to depict reclining harem maidens. Consequently such paintings are called *odalisques*.

Oeillade is the kind of word that might eliminate all the contestants in a spelling bee, unless any of them happened to be versed in French. The immediate parent is *oeil* ("eye"). The definition of the verb is "to eye amorously; to ogle."

The Roman ancestor is *oculus* ("eye"). As you can see, it has suffered quite a Gallic face-lift.

An *oeil-de-boeuf* is a round or oval window—literally, "the eye of an ox."

Best of all is the *trompe l'oeil* ("trick the eye"). It's a painting or other representation that creates such a strong illusion of reality that the viewer at first thinks it's three-dimensional.

Paramour, when analyzed, means "by way of love." In Middle English it was an adverb. Today it's a noun with some sexy meanings:

1. a lover or mistress
2. the illicit partner of a married man or woman
3. one participating in an adulterous relationship

Rendezvous should probably have been placed in the category containing military words because one of its primary meanings is "an assembly of troops, ships or planes." However, since *coquettes, courtesans, debauchees, paramours* and *roués* do arrange *rendezvous,* it seems appropriate to include it here.

The word literally means "present yourself or yourselves." This translation certainly sounds like the order from a general or an admiral.

The American poet Alan Seeger, killed in action at the age of twenty-eight in World War I, prophetically wrote "I Have a *Rendezvous* with Death." As a teenager, my late friend Countée Cullen won a prize for "I Have a *Rendezvous* with Life." He went on to become one of the greatest black poets in America, but his career was cut short when he died suddenly in his early forties.

Just in case some reader is wondering, *rendezvous* means "a meeting or the place where the meeting occurs."

Roués are lecherous, dissipated men. In French the literal translation for these profligates is "broken on the wheel." That is a reference to the use of a certain torture in which the victim was strapped to a revolving wheel and stretched to the breaking point.

What's the connection? Well, in 1720 or thereabouts the Duc d'Orleans (regent of France) had a group of dissolute companions who so scandalized the country that folks thought they ought to be *roué*—in other words, given the treatment on the wheel of misfortune.

Incidentally, one version of the origin of the word takes into account that a man who has been broken on the wheel is all tuckered out. That idea may have some validity. Roués who flit from one woman to another sooner or later must get fatigued.

By the way, the Latin root is our old friend *rota* ("wheel"). See *roulette* in the previous category of this chapter.

Finally, we come to an olio of French words that have found their way into our everyday speech and our prose and poetry. Naturally, this mixture is the longest list of all, but it must be emphasized that it only scratches the surface. Keep in mind that almost one-third of the entries in our dictionaries have a French connection. That adds up to over 100,000 in an unabridged lexicon.

156

MISCELLANEOUS (*a* through *c*)

abattoir	√bonhomie	√caporal	contour
abbé	bouquet	capsule	√contretemps
√accolade	bourgeois	carillon	cortege
adieu	bourse	carrousel	coterie
aplomb	briquette	cassette	cougar
apropos	√brochure	√causerie	coulee
√argot	√brouhaha	chagrin	√couvade
√au revoir	bruit	chevrotain	Creole
automobile	brunette	chicanery	cretin
avocet	√buccaneer	civet	crevasse
badinage	√cabal	√cliché	critique
bastille	√cabotage	clientele	croquet
baton	cache	√clique	crosier
beau geste	cachet	cloture	crotchet
√bizarre	√cajole	commune	cupel
blasé	camaraderie	concessionaire	curé
bloc	√canard	confidante	cuvette
√boîte			

WORD	DEFINITION	DERIVATION
accolade	1. ceremonial embrace 2. ceremony for conferring knighthood 3. award; bestowal of praise	*accoler* ("to embrace"); from Lat. *ad collum* ("to the neck")
argot	1. secret jargon of criminals 2. slang	*argoter* ("to beg"); probably from *ergot* ("claw")—hence, "to get one's claws into"
au revoir	goodbye (temporarily)	*au* ("to the"), *revoir* ("seeing again"); from Lat. *revidere* ("to see again")
bizarre	odd; queer; grotesque; fantastic; unexpected and unbelievable	It. *bizarro* ("angry, fierce, strange"), Sp. *bizarro* ("bold, knightly"), Basque *bizar* ("beard")
boîte	small nightclub or cabaret	*boîte* ("box")
bonhomie	good nature; amiability	*bon* ("good"), *homme* ("man")
brochure	pamphlet; booklet	*brocher* ("to stitch")
brouhaha	hubbub; commotion	probably imitative; possibly from Heb.
buccaneer	pirate	*boucanier* ("user of a *boucan*—a Brazilian roasting grill"); originally applied to French hunters of wild oxen in Haiti

WORD	DEFINITION	DERIVATION
cabal	1. small group engaged in intrigue 2. junta 3. intrigue; plot	*cabale* ("club of plotters"). The word *cabal* was popularized in England because of the initials of the ministers of Charles II —Clifford, Arlington, Buckingham, Ashley and Lauderdale.
cabotage	1. coastal navigation and trade 2. air transport within a country 3. the right to engage in navigation near a foreign coast	*caboter* ("to sail along the coast"); from Sp. *cabo* ("cape")
cajole	1. coax with flattery 2. wheedle	*cajoler* ("to chatter like a jay in a cage—hence, to wheedle or coax"); blend of *cavus,* the root for "cage" and *gaiole* ("birdcage"). *Jail* is a relation.
canard	1. fabricated, malicious report 2. groundless rumor 3. airplane with a horizontal stabilizer forward of the wings	*canard* ("a duck"). In Med. Fr., *vendre des canards à moitié* meant "to sell half ducks—hence, to deceive or cheat."
caporal	a kind of tobacco	*tabac du caporal* ("corporal's tobacco"), considered better than *tabac du soldat* ("soldier's tobacco")
causerie	1. informal discussion; chat 2. short, conversational piece of writing	*causer* ("to chat"); from Vulg. Lat. *causare* ("to complain")
cliché	1. stereotype printing plate 2. trite expression; platitude	*clicher* ("to stereotype"); from Ger. *klitsch* ("clump; claylike mass"). Original meaning of *clicher* was "to pattern in clay."
clique	1. small exclusive circle of people 2. snobbish group	*cliquer* ("to click"). In Med. Fr., *clique* meant "a clicking sound." Later sense may have come from secrecy of exclusive groups; also possibly an alteration of *claque* ("group of frowning followers").

WORD	DEFINITION	DERIVATION
contretemps	1. awkward mishap 2. embarrassing occurrence 3. syncopation	*contre* ("opposite"), *temps* ("time")
couvade	custom among primitive peoples in which the father takes to bed when a baby is born as if he himself had suffered the pains of childbirth	*couver* ("to cover or sit on, as a bird on eggs; to hatch"). *Covey* is a related word.

And now here is our second group of miscellaneous English words borrowed from the French. This list will start with words that begin with *d* and will continue through those that begin with *n*.

√debris	√elegant	√gauche	mal de mer
debutante	elite	gaucherie	matinee
√déclassé	enfant terrible	gout	mélange
derange	essence	guillemot	métier
detour	√fainéant	habitué	milieu
√de trop	fete	hauteur	moraine
diligence	fiacre	idée fixe	√morgue
distrait	√fleur-de-lis	impasse	mot juste
√dossier	flux	√jardiniere	√naïve
√doyen	fringe	√lagniappe	naïveté
√éclat	gaffe	levee	noel
élan	gasconade	√malaise	√nuance

WORD	DEFINITION	DERIVATION
debris	1. rubble; litter; ruins 2. heap of rock fragments deposited by a glacier	Old Fr. *debriser* ("to break apart")
déclassé	1. lowered in rank or social position 2. of inferior status	*dé* ("down"), *classé* ("class")
de trop	1. superfluous; unwanted 2. too much; too many	*de* plus *trop* ("overmuch")
dossier	1. collection of documents, records, and reports on a single subject 2. file	*dossier* ("bundle of documents with a label on the back"); from *dos* ("back")
doyen	1. senior member of a group 2. person uniquely skilled by experience	*doyen* ("dean"); from Late Lat. *decamus* ("chief of ten")
éclat	1. brilliant success 2. dazzling display 3. approval; acclaim; fame	*éclat* ("splinter, fragment; explosion; ostentation")

WORD	DEFINITION	DERIVATION
elegant	1. characterized by dignified richness and grace 2. tastefully luxurious 3. refined 4. impressively fastidious in manner and taste	*elegant* ("tasteful; stylish"); from Latin *e* ("out") and *legere* ("to choose")
fainéant	lazy, idle person; do-nothing	present participle of *faindre* ("to feign or shirk"); literally "(he) does nothing"
fleur-de-lis	1. iris 2. coat of arms of former French royal family (Charles V et al)	"flower of the lily"
gauche*	1. lacking social grace 2. awkward; tactless	literally, "left" in Fr.— hence, "gawky, ungainly"; from Fr. *gauchir* ("to become crooked or warped")
jardiniere	1. ornamental bowl, pot or stand for flowers or plants 2. garnish for meat consisting of several vegetables	*jardinière* ("female gardener")
lagniappe	1. something given or obtained gratuitously, as a bonus 2. a tip or gratuity	from Creole Fr. and Am. Sp. *la ñapa* ("the addition"); derived from practice of giving a small present to a customer
malaise	1. vague feeling of physical discomfort or uneasiness 2. vague awareness of moral or social decline	*mal* ("bad"), *aise* ("ease")
morgue	1. place where bodies of unidentified persons are kept 2. newspaper's reference library containing back numbers, photographs, clippings, miscellaneous information	*morgue* ("haughtiness, stolidity, impassivity")
naïve	1. unaffectedly or sometimes foolishly simple 2. childlike; artless, unsophisticated 3. not suspicious	fem. of *naïf;* from Lat. *nativus* ("natural")

* *Gauche.* Compare this with "sinister" in Chapter 4; note the same prejudice against left-handers.

WORD	DEFINITION	DERIVATION
nuance	1. slight or delicate variation in tone, color 2. shade of difference	*nuer* ("to shade"); from Lat. *nubes* ("cloud")

Herewith is the last group of words borrowed from the French.

√outrageous	√portmanteau	savant	triste
parvenu	poseur	√Scaramouch	verjuice
√pastille	√pourboire	seneschal	vis-à-vis
√patois	puissant	√sobriquet	visa
√penchant	raconteur	√soi-disant	voyageur
√persiflage	√réclame	soiree	√voyeur
pique	√riant	√soupçon	√vrille
piton	√risqué	√toupee	√wagon-lit
plaque			

WORD	DEFINITION	DERIVATION
outrageous	1. exceeding limits of decency or reasonableness 2. very offensive or shocking 3. violent; unrestrained 4. extravagent; fantastic	*outre* ("beyond"); from Lat. *ultra;* derivation not related to "rage"
pastille	1. aromatic or medicated lozenge 2. small cone used for fumigating or scenting the air 3. paper tube causing fireworks to explode	*pastille* ("lozenge"); from Lat. *pastillus* ("little roll or lozenge"), via *pascere* ("to feed")
patois	1. provincial or local dialect 2. specialized vocabulary of a group; jargon	Old Fr. *patois* ("uncultivated speech"); akin to *patoier* ("to shake paws; behave crudely")
penchant	1. strong liking or fondness 2. inclination; taste	*pencher* ("to incline"); from Lat. *pendere* ("to hang")
persiflage	1. light, frivolous or flippant style of speaking or writing 2. such talk or writing; banter	*persifler* ("to banter"), via *per* ("through") and *siffler* ("to whistle, hiss, boo")
portmanteau	traveling bag	*porter* ("to carry") and *manteau* ("cloak, coat")
pourboire	tip; gratuity	*pour* ("for"), *boire* ("to drink")

WORD	DEFINITION	DERIVATION
réclame	1. publicity; vogue; notoriety 2. showmanship; gift for publicity 3. acclaim not necessarily earned	*réclamer* ("to appeal or call back")
riant	laughing; gay; smiling; cheerful	pres. part. of *ridere* ("to laugh"). *Ridicule* is related.
risqué	1. very close to being indecent or improper 2. daring; suggestive	past part. of *risquer* ("to risk")
Scaramouch	1. stock character in old Italian comedy, depicted as a braggart and poltroon 2. boastful coward; scamp; rascal	from *Scaramouche,* via It. *Scaramuccia* (literally, "a skirmish")
sobriquet	1. nickname 2. assumed name	from Med. Fr. *sourbriquet* ("tap under the chin; nickname")
soi-disant	self-styled	*soi* ("self"), *disant* ("saying")
soupçon	1. slight trace, as of a flavor 2. hint; suggestion 3. tiny amount; bit 4. literally (from Fr.), "suspicion"	from Med. Fr. *sospeçon,* via Lat. *suspicio* ("suspicion")
toupee	hairpiece; a man's wig	*toupet* ("tuft of hair; forelock")
voyeur	Peeping Tom	from *voir* ("to see"), via Lat. *videre* ("to see")
vrille	spinning nose dive executed by an airplane pilot as a maneuver	literally, "tendril" in Fr., via Lat. *vitis* ("vine")
wagon-lit	1. European railroad sleeping car 2. compartment in such a car	*wagon* ("railway coach"); from Dutch *wagen* ("cart"); Fr. *lit* ("bed")

Almost every English word and phrase listed or discussed in this chapter is spelled exactly the same in French, except that accents may have been dropped occasionally in Anglicization, thus altering pronunciation slightly. In many cases we have also borrowed the meanings of the words in this section from the Parisians. And remember that my presentation of such words represents only a mere sampling.

Reviewing those English words that have a French connection but have changed in spelling and meaning would have required an entire book. Lafayette, you are indeed here!

CHAPTER 7

Imports from Spain and Italy

If Hitler had conquered the western world, as he obviously hoped to do, our language today would probably be flooded with words and phrases of German origin. Powerful, aggressive nations leave their marks upon the speech of the countries that they invade and defeat. Alexander the Great, Darius I, Hannibal, Flaminius and Julius Caesar willy-nilly changed the speech of the people they had subdued in ancient times.

Just as William the Conqueror's men had spread French throughout England after their victory at Hastings in 1066, so the armies of the Spanish *conquistadores* (Coronado, Pizarro et al) brought their language to our hemisphere. Subsequent Spanish settlements in the Southwest, West and South—as well as in countries below the border—have caused thousands of their words to seep into our everyday expressions and our writing.

The Italians, on the other hand, were too busy fighting one another; therefore they made few conquests outside their own country. The result is that our language reflects Italianate words and phrases less than any other Romance language. (The single exception is in the field of music; more about that later.) But it does seem ironic that the Romans' direct descendants should be the least of our linguistic benefactors. As the Spanish say, they should be *numero uno*.

Aside from wars and invasions, there are two other factors that must be considered when we contemplate effects on what H. L. Mencken called "the American language." The Renaissance is one; immigration is the other.

In the great European revival of art, literature and learning that took place between the fourteenth and sixteenth centuries, Italy was the initiator. Consequently a goodly number of the words and phrases of that great land were absorbed by the British. But the movement also stirred up an interest in Spanish literature and painting, thus paving the way for many Hispanic transferences to English.

In immigration the Italians got the jump on Spanish-speaking people decades ago. But in recent years the influx of Puerto Ricans, Cubans, Mexicans, Dominicans and other people of Hispanic background has been tremendous. As a result, during the last three decades many of their words have crept into our speech, and the number will probably increase by leaps and bounds in the future.

As an aside, let me point out that a melting pot such as the United States, with a relatively short history, is far more likely to accept and absorb the expressions of foreigners than a land with a more ancient background. This is the difference between us and the French. Recently a Parisian statesman tried to ban the importation of English words into France; he deplored the adulteration of his native language. In contrast, Americans and their leaders openly welcome all comers from various sources whether they be Hindu, Russian, Oriental or of any other background. The upshot of this phenomenon is that English has gradually supplanted French as the "universal language."

At any rate, we do have some very interesting entries from both Spanish and Italian. Let us take a sampling of the former first.

As in the case of the French imports, our Hispanic borrowings can be divided into various categories:

Geographical Terms and Outdoor Places
Mammals, Fish, Birds and Insects
Bullfighting
Food and Drink
Clothing and Shelter
Dances
Miscellaneous

Please note the difference between the above groupings and those related to the French. The world of fashion is missing, as are the areas of war and diplomacy. In the arts, except for the dance, the pickings are meager. The same can be said for furniture and relations between the sexes. On the contrary, sports and geographical entries, as well as bestial words, far outnumber the contributions of the French. Does this disparity reflect the difference between the two cultures or does it relate to the caprices and accidents of historical events and geographic locations? Probably a little of both.

Let us begin with a sampling of words that fall into the first category. In the list below and those to follow, words marked with a check will be discussed.

GEOGRAPHICAL TERMS AND OUTDOOR PLACES

abra	√boca	√canoe	gaucho
agostadero	bosque	√canyon	√lasso
√alamo	buckaroo	coquito	llano
arado	√cajón	cuesta	loma
arroyo	√cañada	√estancia	√machete

√marijuana	nutria	saguaro	solano
mesa	√palmetto	sapodilla	√tornado
√mescal	pampas	savanna	vaquero
√mesquite	patio	√sierra	√vega
√montaña	√pelota	silo	yucca
noria	√playa		

Most of us know about the *Alamo,* a Franciscan mission built circa 1722 at the present site of San Antonio, Texas. And some of us are aware that Davy Crockett and Jim Bowie died there when Santa Anna's forces finally stormed into the building. But I wonder how many people know that an *alamo* is a poplar or cottonwood. Apparently the mission was located in an area where those trees abounded.

Boca means "mouth" in Spanish. We apply the word to the mouth of a river. *Boca Chica* is one of the islands in the Florida Keys. Its literal meaning is "tiny mouth." Then there is *Boca Raton,* a town in southeastern Florida. In Spanish, *ratón* means "mouse." Mickey Mouse is Miguel Ratón. By the way, a bookworm is a *ratón de bibliotheca.* The Spanish changed the worm into a mouse.

In the Southwest a narrow gorge with steep sides is called a *cajón* (the plural is *cajónes*). Sometimes this phenomenon of nature is referred to as a box canyon. That designation is appropriate not only because of the shape of the gorge but also because *cajón* means "a large box."

Cajun should not be confused with the Spanish box. The word designates a native of Louisiana originally descended from Acadian French immigrants. It is an alteration of the noun Acadian, and some of Evangeline's people take umbrage at the nickname.

To a westerner a *cañada* is a little canyon or creek. The word is an extension of *caña,* meaning "cane; small hollow object."

Canada, the country, has an altogether different background. It's from a French-Huron word, *kanáda,* meaning "village or settlement."

Canoe has a Spanish-Carib background. To a South American the boat is a *canoa.* Columbus recorded the word *canoa* in his log in 1493. Incidentally, the first pun I remember hearing came from a waggish uncle of mine when I was a tot. He asked me, "Eugene, *canoe* row a boat?" I've been hooked on puns ever since.

Canyon is derived from an American Spanish noun *cañon* (pronounced "canyon"), meaning "a long tube or hollow." The ultimate ancestor is the Romans' *canna* ("reed"). You might even say that a *canyon* is a gorge-ous spectacle.

To Hispanic Americans an *estancia* is a ranch or farm. To a Madrileño the word means:

1. room; stopping place; habitation
2. day in a hospital or fee paid for it
3. stanza

The noun is related to *stanchion* ("an upright bar, beam or post used as a support"). Some experts trace *estancia* and *stanchion* back to the Latin verb *stare* meaning "to stand."

Lasso is an alteration of *lazo* ("a loop, noose or snare"). It's fascinating to note that *lace* is in the same family.

A *machete* is a large heavy-bladed knife used to cut down sugarcane or dense underbrush. It's the diminutive of *macho*—a word that has recently come into common usage.

What's a *macho?* Well, the word has many meanings. Of course it means "male." It's also a screw, hook, bolt, tap, spur, buttress, abutment or sledge hammer. That last definition probably gave rise to *machete*.

Interestingly enough, in colloquial Spanish a *macho* is a blockhead. In English he's a strong, virile fellow who has lots of *machismo*. As an adjective in our language *macho* means "virile or courageous."

Marijuana (often spelled *marihuana*) is a native American Spanish word blended with a personal name, *Maria Juana.* So that's why it's called "Mary Jane!"

The plant is a wild tobacco or type of hemp. The dried leaves and flowers are used for smoking, especially when formed into a kind of cigarette.

The butts of those cigarettes are called "roaches" (short for *cockroaches,* probably because of their size).

"Pot" is the common slangy word for this *cannabis sativa* plant. Other terms include "weed," "tea," "gage," "reefer" and "grass."

In a recent crossword puzzle for THE NEW YORK TIMES I defined *oro* as "Acapulco gold." Several solvers sent in complaints. They had written in *pot!*

Mescal and *mesquite* are alterations of words in the Nahuatl language. The Nahuatls were various people of ancient origin ranging from southeastern Mexico to parts of Central America. Among them were the Aztecs, whose proud empire was destroyed by the Spanish conquest. Again, it is fascinating to note that the victors not only foist words from their language onto the victims but are also the beneficiaries of the vocabulary of their captives.

At any rate, *mescal* is a cactus, a drug that is also called peyote, and a Mexican liquor distilled from the fermented juice of certain agaves. That other intoxicant, tequila, is also a product of the century plants.

In Spanish, *mesquite* is spelled *mezquite*. It's a shrub or small tree. Its pods are used as fodder. Vast pastures in the Southwest and Mexico are covered with *mesquite grass*.

And did you know that a suburb of Dallas is named *Mesquite?* It was so called because of the trees growing there.

Every native of Butte or Helena probably knows that *montaña* means "mountain" in Spanish. In American Spanish, and in English, it's a forested region on the slopes of the Andes.

Montana Number One is a breed of productive hogs developed in the state.

By the way, let me share with you a bit of history I recently discovered: Helena was once called Last Chance! That name really has a Wild West flavor.

Palmettos are palms with fan-shaped leaves; they are native to southeastern United States. In fact, South Carolina's nickname is the *Palmetto State*. The word is a diminutive of *palma*.

Pelota in Spanish means "ball or ball game." It is also the Spaniards' name for *jai alai*. That sport can be literally translated from the Basques into "festival merry." The players have *cestas* ("baskets") strapped to their forearms; they use the devices to catch the ball and hurl it against the *frontón* (originally, "wall of a handball court").

The development of *frontón* is exciting to follow. As *jai alai* became ever more popular in America, the game moved indoors, and the structures that housed it were called *frontons*. (We Americans don't particularly like accent marks, although out of deference to the French we have kept many of their acutes and graves.) To add to the confusion, *pelota,* or *jai alai,* is called *frontón* by the Mexicans.

Playa has undergone a startling transformation. In Spanish it's a beach; in English it's a desert basin that temporarily becomes a shallow lake after heavy rains.

Sierra has two basic meanings in Spanish. It's either a saw or a mountain range. We combined the two. Our definition is "a mountain range having a saw-toothed appearance, such as the Sierra Nevadas."

Incidentally, *nevada* means "snow-covered" in Spanish.

The eventual root for *sierra* is *serra,* the Latin noun meaning "a saw."

———

Tornado is the past participle of *tornar,* the Spanish verb meaning "to turn or return." A related Hispanic noun, which got twisted up, is *tronada* ("thunderstorm"). A parent Latin root is *tonare* ("to thunder").

In the Midwest this violent, whirling column of air is called a twister. That's most appropriate!

———

In Spanish a *vega* is a lowland or plain. Hence Las Vegas would have been called Des Plaines if the French had beaten the Spanish to the punch. Incidentally, did you know that the original name of Las Vegas was Nuestra Señora de los Dolores de Las Vegas? Translated, that means "Our Lady of the Sorrows of the Plains." How fitting for those millions of losing bettors!

It's amazing to observe how many cities and towns in the United States bear Spanish names. Let's take a sampling merely from California and Texas, and let's skip the many places that were named for saints (for example, San Francisco, Santa Clara, San Antonio).

Here's another matching test for you. The answers appear on p. 436, in the Appendix. Even if you never studied Spanish, you should be able to guess at least half of the items.

CITIES OR TOWNS	LITERAL MEANINGS
1. Palo Alto, Cal.	a. salt pits
2. Zapata, Tex.	b. wood; timber
3. Salinas, Cal.	c. butterfly; night-light
4. Mariposa, Cal.	d. plain
5. Cuero, Tex.	e. ash tree or ash wood
6. Madera, Cal.	f. high pole or stick or mast
7. Llano, Tex.	g. the golden one
8. Modesto, Cal.	h. leather; rawhide; pelt; wine skin
9. Fresno, Cal.	i. unassuming
10. El Dorado, Tex.	j. shoe of an anchor; buskin; half-boot

It should be added that the legendary city of El Dorado has inspired citizens of states other than Texas to name their home towns optimistically. There's an El Dorado in Arkansas and another in Kansas. In Illinois the city combines the words into Eldorado; and in Missouri we find Eldorado Springs, near Joplin. Finally, El Dorado is an occasional nickname for California itself.

Before leaving this topic I should mention Corpus Christi, Texas. In Latin it's the "body of Christ." Spaniards, among others in the Roman Catholic Church, have a fiesta in honor of the Eucharist. It's called Corpus Christi and it occurs on the Thursday after Trinity Sunday, which comes sometime after Easter.

And now let us turn to our Spanish legacy in the area of the second category. The following is only a small sample of our inheritances.

MAMMALS, FISH, BIRDS AND INSECTS

alpaca	√guacharo	merino	√puma
barracuda	guanaco	√mosquito	√rodeo
bonito	guano	palomino	tapir
√chinchilla	√iguana	pinto	√tuna
√cockroach	junco	√pompano	vicuña
condor	√llama	porgy	

Lexicographers are puzzled about the origin of the name of that tiny rodent called the *chinchilla*. Some guess that the Spanish borrowed it from the Aymara, an Indian people of Bolivia and Peru. But my favorite explanation is that the word is a diminutive of *chinche* ("bedbug"). If so, it would be a good illustration of South-of-the-Border humor.

In our language the *chinch bug* is an insect that damages grain plants by sucking out the juices. *Chinche,* by the way, has other meanings in Spanish: "a pest; finicky person; nagger." In American Spanish it means "thumbtack."

Chinchilla also has other connotations. Aside from being the costly fur of the rodent, it's a breed of domestic cat with long, soft, silver-gray hair. Finally, it's a heavy cloth used for overcoats. In this sense it is probably named for *Chinchilla,* the Spanish town in which it was first made.

Some readers may recall the 1934 hit song "La Cucaracha." Translated, that's "The Cockroach." English-speaking folks anglicized *cucaracha* rather wittily.

In Spanish the adjective *guácharo* means "sickly." As a noun it is the oilbird. The fledglings of this nocturnal flier secrete an oil which South Americans extract and use as a substitute for butter.

But the most interesting fact about the *guacharo* (no accent in our language) is that it is probably named for its sickly cry.

Guano is not a mammal, fish, bird or insect, but it seems to fit under this heading. It's the manure of sea birds found especially on islands off the coast of Peru. Because it is valuable as a fertilizer, it has become synonymous with that word.

The Arawakan Indians of South America and the West Indies had a word, *iwana,* which the Spanish changed into *iguana* and passed on to us. The lizard received its best publicity in Tennessee Williams' play *The Night of the Iguana.*

Hillaire Belloc once wrote the following delightful lines:

> "The *Llama* is a woolly sort of fleecy hairy goat,
> With an indolent expression and an undulating throat
> Like an unsuccessful literary man."

And in a Puns & Anagrams crossword puzzle, the clue for the animal was: "Does the young of this animal call for its Mmama?"

Seriously, this cousin of the *alpaca, guanaco* and *vicuña* was first named by the Quechua, a group of Indian tribes dominant in the former Inca empire. Again, the captors borrow from the captives!

Mosquito is a Spanish and Portuguese diminutive of *mosca* ("fly"). The Latin ancestor, with the same meaning, is *musca.*

In Spanish a *mosquito* can be defined as a "tippler." Will someone tell me why?

We make some crazy changes in words. *Skeeter* is a colloquial alteration of the name for the pest. And has anyone ever told you that the female of the family is the one that stings or bites? Somehow I take comfort from that. Macho mosquito, you're bonito! Since misery loves company, I am also pleased to learn that those females attack fish, frogs, turtles and even other insects. Great Scott, what a lot!

Pompano is an English variation of pámpano ("a vine or tendril or kind of fish"). The fish is so popular in Florida that a city was named for it. *Pompano Beach* is a fast-growing resort north of Miami.

Puma is another word that the conquering Spaniards took from the Quechua people. A *puma* is a cougar, is a catamount, is a mountain lion, is an American lion, is a panther. Move over, Gertrude!

Rodeo is included in this list because one of its meanings in Spanish is "cattle ring." As in English, it also means "roundup." Other Hispanic definitions are "detour and subterfuge." In Madrid, "to beat about the bush" is *andarse con rodeos.* What a difference between that phrase and our western jamboree!

Tuna is a strange anagram for *atún,* the Spanish word for the fish that's also called *tunny.*

Here's a new one for you. A *tuna* is also a prickly pear. The origin is also Spanish.

In our next category, "Bullfighting," all the following words will be discussed: *matador, picador, toreador, torero* and *veronica.*

Chess players may be astounded to hear that *mate* and *checkmate* are related to *matador.* The latter means "killer" in Spanish. Incidentally, a *matador* is also the principal trump in certain card games, such as *ombre.* In other words, it's "the killer." Finally, the word can be defined as "a variation of the game of dominoes."

Picador comes from the Spanish verb *picar* ("to prick"). That derivation fits to a tee, because the *picador* is a horseman who uses a lance to prick the neck muscles of a weakened bull.

The Latin ancestor of *toreador* is *taurus* ("bull"). The Spanish noun is derived from *torear* ("to fight bulls").

Torero also comes from *taurus.* It's a generic term referring to any bullfighter, but often is used as a synonym for *matador.*

Some bullfighter must have had a girlfriend named *Veronica.* In any case, this move, in which the matador holds his cape out and pivots slowly as the bull charges past him, is probably named for some woman.

Here is an abbreviated list in an area in which we have gained a great number of words from our friends in Spain and Mexico.

FOOD AND DRINK

abalone	cassava	√frijol	√sarsaparilla
atole	chicle	guava	√taco
banana	chili con carne	maize	tamale
√barbecue	√coconut	√olio	tapioca
bodega	√coquina	panada	tequila
√cacao	√cuba libre	√pimiento	√tomato
√cantina	√enchilada	√potato	√tortilla

The Taino, an extinct Indian people of the West Indies, have given us a word that delights every picnicker. *Barbecue* is literally "a framework of sticks." If any of those Indians were alive today, they would be amazed to see the use of charcoal. The Spanish word for our outdoor party is *barbacoa.*

Cacao is still another word that the *conquistadores* appropriated from the Nahuatl. *Cocoa* is our modification of this beverage-producing bean, although we have accepted *cacao* too.

The French borrowed the Italian word *cantina* ("wine cellar") and changed it to *cantine,* and we promptly altered the French spelling into *canteen.* As time went on we developed many meanings for that noun:

1. post exchange (or PX)
2. place where refreshments and entertainment are provided for soldiers
3. recreation center, as for teenagers
4. place where food is served to people in distress in a disaster area
5. small flask for drinking water

But the Spanish also borrowed *cantina* from the Italians. They kept the original meaning but also extended its usage. In Spain today a *cantina* is what we call a *canteen.*

Then along came the American Spanish with their own ideas. To them a *cantina* means "a saloon or barroom."

Incidentally, this word is a good example of the importance of the diacritical mark called a tilde. *Cantiña* is the colloquial Spanish synonym for a popular song.

Coconut (sometimes spelled *cocoanut*) has an interesting history. It's derived from the Spanish-Portuguese word *coco.* In Lisbon a *coco* is a bogeyman. Hence philologers assume that the resemblance of the *coconut* to a grotesque head gave rise to its name.

Unless you collect seashells or you're a clammer or a southern builder, you probably never heard of *coquina.* In our language the word has two basic meanings:

1. a small marine clam
2. a whitish limestone formed of broken shells and corals, used for buildings or roadbeds in the South

The noun is probably a dialectic form of the Latin *concha,* from which we also get *conch.* By the way, that mollusk with a spiral shell is pronounced the same as *conk.* It must be unpleasant to be *conked* on the head with *conchs!*

A *Cuba libre* is a tall rum-and-cola drink mixed with lime juice. Literally, it means "free Cuba," and originally it was a drink of water and sugar quaffed by the rebels during the Cuban war of independence. I wonder what intrepid bartender was the first to lace the beverage.

Enchiladas are tortillas rolled with meat inside and served with chili sauce. The derivation is from *enchilado,* the past participle of the American Spanish verb *enchilar* ("to season with chili").

Frijoles (pronounced "frē-hō-lēs") are southwestern kidney beans or cowpeas. The eventual ancestor is the Greek word *phasēlos* ("kind of bean").

_____

Olio means "oil" in Spanish. But the English word with the same spelling is a modification of *olla* ("pot"). The Spanish developed a stew called *olla podrida* ("rotten pot"). All kinds of meats and vegetables were tossed into the pot. Hence our variation, *olio,* came to mean "a miscellaneous mixture; hodgepodge; potpourri." Another connotation is "a musical medley."

_____

At least two groups of lexicographers state that there is no difference between *pimiento* and *pimento*. They are realistic, because most people use the two interchangeably. But a purist would say that a *pimiento* is a garden pepper used as a garnish or a stuffing for olives, while *pimento* is allspice or a vivid shade of red.

_____

Those Taino Indians of the West Indies (see *barbecue,* above) are also responsible for *potato*. Their word was *batata;* the Spanish changed it to *patata,* and we gave it the *o* sounds.

Batata has survived in English. It's the *sweet potato*.

_____

Why do the experts accept "sass-pa-ril-a" as the first pronunciation for *sarsaparilla?* Well, they had to yield to popular usage. Folks just refused to say "sarsa." And now when a person orders the drink at a fountain, he merely asks for a "sass."

Its Spanish ancestors are *zarza* ("bramble") and *parrilla* ("little vine"). It's really a tropical American spiny, woody vine of the lily family. The dried roots were formerly used in medicine. Then an extract led to the popular carbonated drink.

_____

My Spanish dictionary lists the following definitions for *taco:* "wad; plug; stopper; rammer; billiard cue; writing pad; popgun; snack; swig; draught; swear-word; muddle; mess."

Yes, what a mess! Can you imagine a newcomer to Madrid asking for a *taco* and being handed a billiard cue? But notice that "snack" is somewhere in the middle of that muddled list. That's the one that has been adopted by English-speaking people. A *taco* is a Mexican food consisting of a fried, folded tortilla stuffed with chopped meat, shredded lettuce and other fillings alone or in combination. That's quite a "wad" to put into your mouth. But when in Taxco, don't knocko *el taco* —or socko!

_____

Tomato is another of those words that were originated by the Nahuatl. Their word was *tomatl*. The Spanish changed it to *tomate*.

In colloquial Spanish, *tomate* also means "a hole in the stockings." I wish I knew why.

Tortilla is the Spanish diminutive of *torta* ("a cake"), which goes back to Late Latin: *torta* ("twisted loaf").

Throughout Mexico, *tortillas* are a staple food; they are thin, flat, round cakes of unleavened cornmeal or flour, baked on a griddle.

Someone may ask why *heros* are not on my list. The answer is that the popular *hero sandwich* has no linguistic relation to Spain or Mexico. It was named for its heroic size.

And now we come to some items relating to clothing and shelter.

CLOTHING	SHELTER
√chaps	adobe
√mantilla	cabana
poncho	√fonda
√rebozo	√hacienda
serape	√posada
√sombrero	√presidio
	√pueblo
	√ramada

Chaps are those extra leather trousers, without a seat, worn by cowboys. The word is a shortening of the Mexican noun *chaparejos* or *chaparajos,* so named because the trousers offer protection from *chaparro.*

What's *chaparro?* In Spain it's an evergreen oak, but in the Southwest it's *chaparral*—a dense thicket of shrubs and thorny bushes. Hope you chaps understand.

Mantilla is the diminutive of *manta*—a shawl or cape made of coarse cotton; also, a horse blanket. The *mantilla* is a woman's lacy scarf worn over the hair and shoulders.

The *rebozo* is a relative of the *mantilla*. It's a long stole worn by women around the head and shoulders. It comes from the verb *rebozar* ("to muffle").

Sombreros are well named, because these broad-brimmed hats provide shade for their wearers. The root word is *sombra* ("shade"), and that noun is a neat combination of the Latin words *sub umbra* ("under the shade").

One would suppose that Henry, Peter and Jane know that a *fonda* is a boardinghouse or inn in the Southwest. A related word is *fonduk*, which has two meanings:

1. a business establishment or commercial warehouse in northern Africa
2. an inn or hotel in northern Africa

Hacienda suffered an initial change from the original somewhere along the line. In Old Spanish it was spelled *facienda* ("employment or estate"). The Latin ancestor is the same word, but to the Romans it meant "things to be done." Isn't it interesting to discover that Cicero's agenda has been transformed into a modern ranch, plantation or large estate?

I wonder if anybody in Hacienda Heights, near Los Angeles, is reading this paragraph. If so, I'll wager he's a bit surprised.

A related word from the same root is *fazenda,* a Brazilian coffee plantation. It's a Portuguese variant of Cicero's *facienda.*

Posada comes from *posar* ("to lodge"). The Late Latin grandparent is *pausare* ("to stop"). A *posada* is an inn. It's also a Christmas festival marked by a candlelight procession.

In the Southwest a *presidio* is a military post or fortified place. The eventual Latin ancestor is *praesidium* ("defense"). From this same root we get *preside* and *president.*

The Spanish not only introduced the horse to the Indians but also gave at least one large group a name that has stuck. The *Pueblos* are American aborigines of New Mexico and Arizona; they include the Hopi and the Zuñi. Today we even call the dwellings and villages of these Indians *pueblos*—such is the weight of the Spanish influence.

In Spain a *pueblo* is a town, village, settlement, people or nation. The first two definitions are commonly used in the Southwest and West. In fact, a city in Colorado bears the name.

Because a chain of motels has latched onto the word *ramada,* one would think that it is a synonym for an inn. But no. It's an arbor or open porch in English. In Spanish it's also an arbor, but another meaning is "mass of branches." That definition fits nicely, because the root word is *rama* ("branch"). Of course the eventual source is the Romans' *ramus.*

Our penultimate category is "Dances." Here are a half dozen to be discussed: *cha-cha, conga, fandango, rumba, seguidilla* and *tango*.

The *cha-cha* is a dance of Cuban origin. Some dictionaries now give *cha-cha-cha* as an alternate. Having attended a few weddings lately, I predict that the triple *cha* will eventually win out. All the dancers at those feasts kept chanting "cha-cha-cha."

You may be interested to learn that the *Cha-Cha* are also a group of poor whites of French ancestry living in the Virgin Islands. The origin of the term is unknown.

Have you ever danced in a *conga* line? I used to get a kick out of it. Although we have inherited the dance from the Cubans, it really has an African origin. *Conga* is the Spanish feminine of *Congo*.

The drum employed to accompany the dance is also called a *conga*.

Fandango may be a Spanish derivative of *fado*, the Portuguese folk song. At any rate, it's a lively dance performed by a man and a woman with castanets, in triple time.

Interestingly enough, the word has taken on several other connotations:

1. tomfoolery, especially in public affairs or other matters of serious import
2. a southwestern ball or party featuring dancing

The noun has even become a verb. WEBSTER'S THIRD quotes "fighter planes *fandangoing* in the skies."

A related English word is *fandangle*, meaning "an ornate or fantastic ornament" or "nonsense; tomfoolery."

Now, will someone please enlighten me as to why the dance has become equated with silliness? It doesn't seem foolish to me.

The name Xavier Cugat and *rumba* seem to be wedded like man and wife. Blacks from Africa brought the dance to Cuba, and Mr. Cugat helped to import it into the U.S. The word is derived from *rumbo* ("carousal; spree; ostentation").

Seguidilla is another fast Spanish dance accompanied by castanets. Aside from also being music for that dance, the word means "a stanza of four or seven short lines, sung to *seguidilla* music."

The root verb is *sequir* ("to follow"), from the Latin *sequi*.

Tango means "I touch" in Latin, but the dance for two does not date back to the Romans. Instead it's an American Spanish alteration of the African word *tamgu* ("to dance"). I have also recently learned that *tango* is a variety of bingo, which is a variety of lotto, which is a variety of keno.

Finally, here is a small collection of words from various sources which we have borrowed from the Spanish.

MISCELLANEOUS

√bastinado	√comrade	√guitar	peon
√bonanza	dinero	√mestizo	√picaroon
√cigar	√gringo	√peccadillo	

Bastinado (sometimes spelled *bastinade*) comes from *bastón* ("stick"). It's a blow with a stick or a form of corporal punishment once practiced in Asia; the victim was placed face down and his ankles were tied between two poles. Then the soles of his feet were cudgeled.

The word can also be applied to the stick or rod that is used for the thrashing.

One would think that *baste,* when it means "beat soundly," belongs in the same family, but the resemblance is only coincidental. The verb stems from *beysta,* an Old Norse word.

In Spanish, *bonanza* means "fair weather," and its figurative connotation is "prosperity or success." The latter idea caught on in the U.S.A., especially among western miners. A *bonanza* is a very rich vein or picket of ore or the mine in which such a strike is made. Finally, it has come to mean "any source of wealth or profits."

The Mayans had the noun *sīk* ("tobacco") and the verb *sikar* ("to smoke"). The Spanish conquerors did some borrowing again and developed *cigarro*. We dropped the last two letters to form *cigar*. And of course the diminutive became *cigarette*.

It may seem strange, but *comrade* and *camera* are relations. Their ultimate common ancestor is the Greek noun *kamara* ("vaulted chamber").

Centuries ago the Spanish created *camarada* ("chamber mate"), and the French changed it to *camarade*.

Originally, in English, *comrades* were men who shared the same sleeping quarters. Soon that sense was extended—*comrades* became men who shared the same fortunes and experiences. As soldiers, they were *comrades-in-arms*.

Today our usual synonym is companion or associate. And since

English-speaking Communists use the term when addressing one another, a *comrade* is also a Communist.

Finally, there is *comradery,* an Anglicized form of *camaraderie.*

Gringo is often used disparagingly by Spaniards and Latin Americans to indicate a white foreigner, especially an Englishman or person from the United States. The word is an alteration of *griego* ("Greek"). You know the expression "It's Greek to me," meaning "It's very strange [or incomprehensible]." Well, the Spanish had the same kind of idea. The *griegos* became any strangers, whether Greek or not.

The female foreigner in Spain, Mexico and other Hispanic lands is a *gringa.*

Actually, the Spanish cannot claim that *guitar* is their legacy to us. The French, Arabs and ancient Greeks had a hand in the evolution of the word. Here's the history: French—*guitare;* Old Spanish—*guitarra;* Arabic—*gītār;* Greek—*kithara.*

At any rate, the instrument and its close relations have enjoyed worldwide popularity for many centuries.

A *mestizo* is a man of mixed parentage; in western United States and in Latin American lands he's the offspring of a Spaniard or Portuguese and an American Indian. The female of this species is a *mestiza.*

The Latin ancestor is *miscere* ("to mix").

Peccadillo comes from the Spanish diminutive of *pecada* ("sin"). Literally, it means "a little sin." Hence it denotes any slight offense or petty fault.

A taradiddle ("fib") is a *peccadillo.*

Picaroon has a great sound. In fact, many "oon" words delight me. Consider such mellisonant nouns as *poltroon, doubloon, bassoon, macaroon, pantaloon* and *honeymoon.* Then there is *rigadoon*—a once popular lively dance for two.

But the *picaroon* isn't really a sweet fellow at all. He's a pirate, rogue or tramp. His root is *picaro,* the Spanish word for "scamp or knave." That noun, by the way, has also been transferred bodily into our language.

Picaroon has two other meanings: "a pirate ship" or "to act as a pirate."

We have invented an equally pleasant-sounding adjective—*picaresque* (from *picaresco*). The word is often applied to a certain kind of fiction featuring roguish, witty heroes. Some examples of *picaresque* novels are: Defoe's MOLL FLANDERS, Smollett's THE ADVENTURES OF PEREGRINE PICKLE and Fielding's TOM JONES.

Before we leave our amigos, let us not forget such expressions as *castles in Spain, Mexican jumping bean, Spanish omelet.*

Finally, there is *Mexican stud.* If you're thinking of a Don Juan, you're wrong. It's a variety of poker.

Let us now turn our attention to Italian imports. From the beginning it must be emphasized that the French borrowed extensively from the Italians and then passed their adoptions along to us. Thus some of our Gallic linguistic heritage rightfully belongs to the people of such Italian cities as Roma, Firenze and Milano. For example, take *peruke* ("wig"). We extracted the word from the Medieval French noun *perrugue.* But the Parisians had already appropriated it from *perruca* or *parruca,* which meant "head of hair or wig" in Old Italian.

As I noted earlier in this chapter, the Italians monopolize the area of musical directions. Here is a sampling of words and phrases that anyone who plays an instrument must learn.

MUSICAL TERMS

alla breve	con abbandono	con maesta	larghetto
allegretto	con affetto	con moto	largo
allegro	con agilita	con ottava	legato
amoroso	con alcuna licenza	con sordino	lentamente
andante	con amore	con spirito	lento
andantino	con anima	diminuendo	moderato
animato	con bravura	doloroso	pianissimo
arioso	con brio	forte	presto
assai	concitato	fortissimo	soave
brillante	con espressione	gentile	soavemente
cantabile	con forza	giocondo	spirituoso
cantando	con fuoco	giocoso	staccato
capriccioso	con grazia	grandioso	subito
col legano	con gusto	impetuoso	tristezza
coll'ottava			

Even if you have never tinkled a piano, blown a horn or plucked a cello, you can discover a number of our own words hidden in the above list if you peruse it carefully.

Italian phrases have become familiar to us via music, literature, sculpture and other sources. Here are just a few instances:

Arrivederci	This Italian farewell was popularized by the song "Arrivederci, Roma."
A vostra salute	A toast, "To your health!"
Benvenuto	In Napoli, "Welcome!" Note that Cellini's parents saluted his entrance into this world when they named him Benvenuto.
Che sarà sarà	Compare this phrase with the Spaniards' "Que será será." Both mean "What will be, will be." The Spanish version became a popular song in 1956.
Così fan tutte	This is the title of a famous opera by Mozart. Its literal translation is "So do they all" (referring to women). Freely interpreted, the meaning is "Women are like that."
Divina Commedia	Dante's great poem
Il Penseroso	Rodin statue. The French call it "Le Penseur"; to us it's "The Thinker."
La donna è mobile	Celebrated tenor aria from Verdi's RIGOLETTO. It means "The lady is fickle."
L'Allegro	Famous poem by Milton ("THE CHEERFUL ONE"). Its counterpart is "IL PENSEROSO" (see above).
sotto voce	Literally, "under the voice." This phrase has come to mean "aside; privately."

Besides musical directions, the Italians have endowed us with scores of other words in the area presided over by Euterpe.* Some of them are listed below. Checks here and in lists to follow indicate words that will be discussed.

MORE MUSICAL TERMS

√a cappella	√cantabile	√contratempo	√prima donna
allegretto	cantata	√crescendo	ritornello
√alto	√canzone	√diva	romanza
aria	capriccio	√fagotto	scena
arietta	√cavatina	falsetto	√scherzo
arioso	cello	fantasia	segno
√arpeggio	√coda	√maestro	√segue
basso	coloratura	mezzo-soprano	√sonata
√basso profundo	√concertino	obbligato	√stanza
√bel canto	√concerto	√ocarina	tempo
√bravura	contrabass	√pastorale	√toccata
√buffa	√contralto	√piano	tremolo
√buffo	contrapuntal	√piccolo	vibrato
caccia	contrapuntist	√pizzicato	viola
cadenza	contrapunto	√ponticello	violoncello

* *Euterpe* is the Greek Muse of music.

A cappella (sometimes spelled *a capella*) literally means "according to the chapel" or "in chapel style." Translated, that comes out as "unaccompanied by musical instruments," because it has been the custom of priests in the chapel and many choirs to go it alone, as it were.

————

In Italian, *alto* literally means "high." In English it's the part sung by the highest male voices. As a boy I had such a role in a church choir. When I became a teenager I, of course, had to quit. I wasn't sure if I'd become a baritone or a tenor. When I tried out for the college glee club the director said to me, "Maleska, you have nice timbre in your voice, but you switch from one key to another in the middle of a song. I suggest you take up football."

————

In Italian, *arpeggiare* means "to play on a harp." As a result, *arpeggio* means "the playing of the notes of a chord in quick succession." The chord that is so played is also a synonym.

————

Basso profundo means "low, deep." A man with such a voice can really stir you, especially when he sings a song like Kern's "Ol' Man River."

————

Bel canto literally means "beautiful song." In our language it's a style of singing characterized by brilliant vocal display and purity of tone.

————

In Italian, *bravura* means "bravery." In music it's a brilliant passage or piece that displays the performer's skill and technique. In other words, he or she must be really courageous to try it at all!

A related word is *bravo*. You hear it shouted at operas, concerts and plays when the performer has pleased the audience immensely. Some purists yell *brava* if the performer is a female.

Strangely enough, a *bravo* is also a hired killer, an assassin or desperado!

————

Buffo means "comic" in Italian. Most opera fans know that the *buffo* is the singer, usually a bass, who plays a comic role. If the comic is a woman, she's a *buffa*. You can guess what *opera buffa* is.

Buffoon and *buffoonery* are members of this family.

————

Cantabile comes from the Late Latin word *cantabilis* ("worthy to be sung"). As an adjective *cantabile* means "melodious, flowing, songlike." As a noun it's the music composed in that easy style.

The word has no relation to a *Cantabrigian*—a native of Cambridge, England, or Cambridge, Massachusetts—hence a student at

Cambridge or Harvard. The popular short form is *Cantab*. In New England the annual football contest between the *Cantabs* and the *Elis* (Yale students) is respectfully and excitedly called "The Game."

But *cantabile* is definitely related to *cantabank*. The last syllable of that word comes from *banco* ("bench"). A *cantabank* was originally a singer who stood on a bench or platform. Today the fellow is generally considered to be a singer of ballads.

A *canzone* is a lyric poem of Provençal or early Italian troubadours. It's also an ode suited to a musical setting. Finally, it's the setting itself, resembling that of a madrigal.

Derivatives are *canzonets* ("short, light, graceful, sprightly songs").

Cavatina has a fascinating background. Its Latin ancestor is *cavare* ("to extract or dig out"). In Italian it means "a little separate song." To English-speaking music lovers it's an operatic solo that is simpler and briefer than an aria, or a solo song that is part of a larger composition. In other words, true to its Roman heritage, it's an extract.

A *coda* is a musical passage formally ending a composition or section of one. Appropriately enough, it stems from *cauda,* the Latin noun for "tail."

If the finale is a brief one, it's called a *codetta*.

The musical composition called the *concerto* is characteristic of the sixteenth and seventeenth centuries. Typically it has three movements. A short one is a *concertino*. Of course *concert* is a relative. The eventual Latin root is *con-certare* ("to strive together"). That certainly fits when you consider the struggles of the orchestra players and their conductor, all trying to keep the same beat and hit the same notes.

In the nineteenth century an English physicist named Sir Charles Wheatstone invented the *concertina*—an instrument that looks like a small accordion.

Contralto literally means "against high." The word has come to mean "the lowest female voice or a singer possessing such a voice." Marian Anderson is one of the great *contraltos*.

Contratempo ("against the time or beat") is syncopation, or the shifting of accents in a musical composition.

Crescendo comes from *crescere,* the Latin verb meaning "to grow." When the music grows in volume, it reaches a *crescendo*.

Considering the Italians' great love for music, especially opera, it seems fitting that a prima donna or leading female singer should be called a *diva*. In Italy that word means "goddess." (See *prima donna,* below.)

A *fagotto* is a bassoon or organ stop. Anglicized, it's a *fagott,* and the player is a *fagottist*. And then there's the *fagottino,* which is a tenor bassoon or tenoron.

The word is related to *fagot* ("a bundle of sticks"). I don't know why —or maybe I should just say I forgotto. But let me not forget the *contrafagotto,* which is the largest member of the oboe family. Its synonym is contrabassoon.

Maestro comes from *magister,* the ancient Romans' word for "master." In the world of music a *maestro* is a great composer, conductor or teacher.

A *maestro di cappella* is a choirmaster.

An *ocarina* is a small simple wind instrument or toy of the flute class. It looks like a sweet potato and therefore has been given that nickname. Its originators apparently thought it resembled a little goose, because that is what the word literally means in Italian.

> Dear reader, send Eugene a
> Little ocarina;
> He's been to Pasadena,
> And even Catalina,
> But nowhere has he seen a
> Little ocarina.

Pastorales can be musical or literary. They are operas or cantatas with rural themes, or pieces of prose on the same subject.

What an interesting background the *piano* has! Its name is a short form of *pianoforte,* which literally means "soft or smooth and loud or strong"). When we consider the versatility of the instrument, we must admit that the Italians knew how to choose the perfect name.

The *piccolo* is also well named. The word for that tiny flute literally means "small" in Italian.

Pizzicato means "plucked." A note or passage played by plucking the strings of instruments is called a *pizzicato*. The word is also a musical direction.

The bridge of a stringed instrument, such as the violin, is called the *ponticello*. The first part of the word dates back to the Latin *pons, pontis* ("bridge"), and the ending is a diminutive.

Most exciting is the fact that *ponticello* also means "the change in an adolescent boy's voice." In truth, he has formed a little bridge between puberty and manhood.

Prima donna literally means "first lady." (See *diva,* above.)

In Italian a *scherzo* is a jest or sport. Hence the word aptly describes the third part of a sonata or symphony, in which the music is lively and playful in three-four time.

When defining *segue* for a crossword puzzle, I like to use the clue "musician's transition," because that's exactly what it is. The idea is to continue playing without a break from one part of the composition into the next. The Latin root is *sequi* ("to follow"). *Sequential* is a close relative. You can see how that adjective belongs with *segue.*

Sonata literally means "sounding." The composition is for only one or two instruments and has from two to five movements. Beethoven loved this musical form. His "Spring" and "Moonlight Sonata" are good examples.

Cesar Franck composed a famous *sonata* for the piano and violin. Some wag has called it "The Franck Sonata."

"Old Blue Eyes" doesn't know it, but I was among the first to discover him. In the 1930s my future wife and I helped a college friend and her fiancé celebrate her birthday at the Rustic Cabin, a cabaret in Bergen County, New Jersey. The skinny singing waiter was a fellow named Frank Sinatra. His voice enchanted us, and we kept giving him requests for songs. I can still remember him at the microphone announcing, "This one's for Floss" (the birthday girl). You can imagine how thrilled I was when that emaciated young man with the unusual voice became a superstar.

My other great piece of clairvoyance in those days occurred in the literary field. A college professor named Lawrence Conrad gave his class a challenging assignment in English composition. He asked us to pick out an obscure writer and justify our claims that the author would become famous. I had just read a tale in STORY magazine called "Ten Thousand Armenians." It delighted me, and so I chose William Saroyan!

Now I hear some reader crying, "That's so-not-a proper digression!"

Stanza in Italian means "a stopping place." The Latin source is our old friend *stare* ("to stand"). In English a *stanza* is a group of lines of verse forming one of the divisions of a poem or song. Note that word "divisions." It really is a stopping place.

––––––––

Toccata comes from the past participle of the Vulgar Latin verb *toccare* ("to touch"). It's a composition in free style usually for the piano, organ or harpsichord, often employed as the prelude to a fugue. The form was originally designed to show off the technique of the artist. He was invited to show his "touch."

––––––––

Another area in which the Italians have bestowed a great number of words and phrases upon us is that of eating and drinking. The following is a partial list.

FOOD AND DRINK

√artichoke	√fra diavolo	polenta	√spaghetti
√broccoli	√gnocchi	√prosciutto	√tortoni
√cacciatore	√linguine	provolone	√trattoria
√cauliflower	√macaroni	√ravioli	√tutti-frutti
cioppino	√maraschino	√ricotta	√veal scallopini
√coffee	√minestrone	√rigatoni	√vermicelli
√cannelloni	√mozzarella	√risotto	zabaglione
√chicken tetrazzini	√pasta	√salami	ziti
√espresso	pistachio	√scampi	√zucchini
√fettuccine	√pizza	√semolina	

Artichoke doesn't sound Italian at all, but we derived the word from the people in Lombardy. They called the plant *articiocco* (pronounced "ar-tee-chó-ko"). We brutalized that lovely word to make it seem as if we're telling little Arthur that he can't swallow the vegetable.

It should be added that the Italians borrowed the word from the Arabians.

––––––––

Broccoli literally means "a little sprout." The plant is a relative of the cauliflower.

There's also a color called *broccoli brown* and a *broccoli rab* is an Italian turnip. The term is a modification of *broccoli di rapa* ("flowering tops of the turnips").

––––––––

Cacciatore in Italian means "hunter." Because the hunters flavored their meat with herbs and spices, their name was adopted for that style of cooking. So the next time you enjoy *chicken cacciatore,* think of yourself in a campfire setting.

––––––––

Cauliflower is *cavolfiore* in Italian (literally, "cabbage flower.") The Latin root *caulis* means "cabbage." The plant *cole* is a linguistic cousin of *cauliflower.*

In Italian, coffee is *caffè.* And in French of course it's *café.* The word can be traced back to the Turks and Arabs.

Cannelloni is an Italian dish of large-sized macaroni stuffed with forcemeat or a cheese mixture. The name was chosen because the casings for the dough are tubular. Literally, *cannelloni* means "small tube."

We have developed another dish called *cannelon,* which is an offshoot of the one from Italy. It is a hollow roll of puff paste stuffed with finely chopped meat or, as a dessert, with cream.

Related words are *cane, canal, canyon, canister, channel* and even *kennel.*

One of my wife's specialties is *chicken tetrazzini,* and what a delicious dish it is! The meat is cut into small pieces and minced in a cream sauce with spaghetti and Parmesan cheese and served as a casserole.

The dish was invented by a chef who was so enraptured by the performances of opera star Luisa Tetrazzini that he named his concoction for her. Judging from the taste, he was really inspired!

Espresso is a shortened form of *caffè espresso* ("pressed-out coffee"). It's prepared in a special machine that grinds the beans into powdered form; steam under high pressure is then forced through. Connoisseurs often add a few drops of anisette to the brew plus a piece of lemon rind.

By metonymy, *espresso* has also come to mean the shop that serves this full-bodied beverage.

Fettuccine are literally "little ribbons." They are broad, flat noodles served with sauce or butter. A Roman chef has gained fame because of his special way of preparing the noodles with a creamy sauce. He named the dish after himself: *fettuccine alfredo.* Too bad he wasn't the chef who idolized the opera star—*fettuccine tetrazzini* has a nice ring to it.

If you order an Italian dish that's labeled *fra diavolo,* you can be sure that the sauce will be as hot as Hell. The phrase means "within the Devil." Now, how can I convince anyone that *lobster fra diavolo* is a dish for the gods?

By now you must realize how metaphoric yet realistically expressive and humorous the Italians are, especially in their nomenclature. Take *gnocchi,* for instance. They are small dumplings of a pasta often made with cheese or riced potato and served with a sauce. They actually look like knots in wood, and the word is an alteration of *nocchio.* What does it mean? A knot in wood, of course!

Here are some other Italian expressions that should not only give you a chuckle but should also provide you with an insight into the delightful character of the people from Merano in the north to Palermo in the south. The literal meanings are in parentheses.

> *essere una buona forchetta*—to be a hearty eater ("to be a good fork")
> *essere in forse*—to be of two minds ("to be in maybe")
> *quattro gatti*—scanty attendance ("four cats")
> *fare l'indiano*—to turn a deaf ear ("to do the Indian")
> *parlare grasso*—to use gross language; to tell off-color jokes ("to talk fat")
> *asino calzato e vestito*—a perfect ass ("an ass with shoes and clothes on")
> *come il cacio sui maccheroni*—just about perfect ("like cheese on macaroni")
> *avere un diavolo per capello*—to be extremely irritated; to be in a hell of a bad mood ("to have a devil for each hair")

Typical of the drollery I have been referring to is the word *linguine.* Literally, they are "little tongues"—and that's what they look like to anyone who has a poet's imagination. The singular is *linguina,* but it's hardly ever used. Who would want only one of those delectable bits of pasta? No, a heaping plateful is better—preferably *con vongoli* ("with clams").

Probably the most interesting word in this list is *macaroni.* It's a form of pasta having a diameter of .11 to .27 inches and is not to be confused with *spaghetti, linguine* or *vermicelli,* which are thinner.

The immediate source of the word is *maccarone,* a Neapolitan term for "dumpling or small cake." Some lexicographers claim that it can be traced back to the ancient Greek word *makar* ("blessed"). In later Greek texts (200–600 A.D.) *makaria* was literally a "blessed cake."

Well, bless the Greeks and Italians for passing along this tasty item to us. One of my own favorites is *elbow macaroni*—the bent type.

In the eighteenth century, *macaroni* took on another connotation in England—a dandy who adopted foreign mannerisms. The affectations of those fops must have been more Italianate than Gallic; otherwise one would expect them to have been called *macaroons.* Yes, those cookies are a French borrowing from *macaroni.*

Incidentally, when Yankee Doodle "stuck a feather in his hat and called it *macaroni,*" he became a fop wearing a plume. If the meter had allowed, the word "himself" would probably have replaced "it."

An adjective derived from the Italian dish is *macaronic*. It means "mixed or jumbled," possibly because of the way the dish was served (with sauces, meats, spices, etc.) or, as one philologer says, because *macaroni* was regarded as coarse peasant fare. At any rate, the adjective was specifically applied to the mixture of vernacular words with Latin or with non-Latin words having endings in the Roman style. This kind of writing is also called Dog Latin.

Macaronic verses are burlesque compositions having an incongruous and ludicrous mixture of various languages.

––––––

The Italians took the adjective *amarus* ("bitter") from the ancient Romans and changed it to *amaro*. Then they dropped the initial letter and developed *marasca* ("wild cherry"). The diminutive became *maraschino*, that special kind of cherry that is usually added to a Manhattan cocktail. *Maraschino* is also a strong, sweet liqueur made from the fermented juice of the *marasca*.

––––––

If you have never tasted *minestrone*, you're in the minority. This rich, thick Italian vegetable soup has been gaining popularity in America for many decades. The word is an augmentation of *minestra* ("any thick soup").

But the derivation is most interesting! The parent verb is *minestrare* ("to dish up"), and the Latin ancestor is *minestrare* ("to serve or dish up").

It's fascinating to realize that *minestrone* and *minister* are close relatives.

Incidentally, the Italians have another word in this family: *ministrina* ("thin or clear soup").

––––––

Italians love diminutives, and I think it says something about their character. Such words as *falsetto, operetta* and *bambino* abound in their language. *Mozzarella* is a good example. It's the diminutive of *mozza* ("a kind of cheese"). The verb in question is *mozzare* ("to cut off").

The cheese is moist and rubbery, but it's an important ingredient of such popular dishes as *lasagna* (literally, "the noodle") and *manicotti* (literally, "muffs or sleeves"). It's also used in the preparation of pizza and ravioli.

Incidentally, *mozzarella* seems to be one of the few cheeses not named for the area in which it originated. Consider Cheddar, Edam, Parmesan and scores of others. This subject will be taken up in the chapter called "The Place Is Familiar."

––––––

Pasta is the flour paste or dough used in making *macaroni, spaghetti, ravioli* and other such foods. Hence it is the generic term for any of those dishes. Without any alteration in meaning or spelling, the word was taken from a Late Latin noun. The ultimate root is the Greek verb *passein* ("to sprinkle").

One of my favorite dishes is *pasta fagioli,* a soupy mixture containing lots of *fagioli* (beans) mixed with several other vegetables. The pasta for this Neapolitan dish is usually *ditalini,* a dialectal word meaning "little thimbles." Italian Americans from Naples often pronounce the dish "pasta-fazool." Don't ask me how they spell it!

Strangely enough, *pasta fagioli* is not in any of my unabridged dictionaries, although all the other dishes that I am discussing can be found in most of them. I predict that it will appear in some future lexicon, or else the authors ought to be beaned by the Neapolitan Americans.

Finally, here's another Italian idiom for you to smile over: *pasta di figliolo.* Literally, that translates into "dough or paste of a son." But in Italy the phrase has come to mean "a good-natured sort of fellow." I think I know how the new connotation evolved, but I'll leave it to the readers to use their own imaginations, Italian-style.

———

In the 1930s few people of non-Italian ancestry knew what a *pizza* was. Now it is one of America's favorite snacks. *Pizza parlors* and *pizzerias* have mushroomed. That verb reminds me that the original dish featured cheese and tomatoes baked on a thin layer of dough. Now there are dozens of varieties of *pizze* or *pizza pies;* anchovies, sausages, mushrooms, pepperoni and other garnishes have been added. There seems to be no end to the creativity of chefs in this culinary area.

The etymology of the word is in doubt. Some experts believe that it comes from Old Italian *pizza* ("a point"). Others trace it to Medieval Greek *pitta* ("cake or pie"). Whatever its origin, the dish is certainly delicious.

———

Prosciutto is the Italian word for "ham." It presumably was so named because it is dry-cured. The Late Latin root is *perexsucare* ("to suck out").

———

The Italians' penchant for naming items according to their resemblance to other objects is revealed once again in *ravioli.* To the originators of the dish the small casings of pasta filled with chopped meat or cheese looked like little turnips. *Rava* means "turnip" in Italian dialect and the diminutive is *raviola.* The Latin ancestor is *rapum* ("turnip or beet"). Another derivative is the plant called *rape*—not to be confused linguistically with the sexual crime. That word dates back to the Romans' *rapere* ("to seize").

———

Ricotta is also well named. This cheese is made from the whey of other cheeses. Appropriately, its literal meaning is "cooked or boiled again." The Latin verb *recoquere* is the immediate ancestor.

———

Another perfect designation is revealed in the derivation of *rigatoni*. These large casings of *pasta* bear ridges. *Rigato* is the past participle of *rigare* ("to mark with lines"). Again, note the use of the ending. In this case the size is exaggerated.

———

Risotto is rice sauteed in oil with a mixture of finely chopped onions and garlic with seasonings. It is then diluted gradually with broth until it is tender and moist. It is often served with Parmesan cheese.

———

Salami is the Italian plural of *salame* ("preserved meat or salt pork"). This highly spiced sausage can be traced back to *sal,* the Roman noun for "salt."

———

Scampi are Italian prawns, or large shrimp. Thus the dish *shrimp scampi* is an instance of tautology.

———

Semolina is a granular milled product of durum wheat and is used chiefly in the making of macaroni and other forms of pasta. It is the diminutive of *semola* ("bran") and can be traced back to the Latin *simila* ("finest wheat flour"). Probably the Romans borrowed their word from the Assyrian *samīdū* ("fine meal").

The wheat of southern Europe is known to produce the best *semolina,* and since that product is the basis of pasta, you can understand why the spaghetti served in Italy is so superior to our own. Finally, you might be interested to learn that *semolina* is used for certain French breads. No wonder the *pain* in Paree is such a pleasure!

———

Spaghetti, the most popular form of pasta, is another of those diminutive nouns that express so much so well. *Spago* is a cord in Italian. Hence *spaghetti* are literally "small cords."

Somewhat derisively, the slangsters have come up with a phrase for a U.S. cowboy film that has been made in Italy; they call it a *spaghetti western.* But the electricians do not mean to be derogatory when they refer to certain insulating tubing as *spaghetti.* The name was chosen because of the remarkable resemblance to those little cords.

———

Tortoni is an ice cream made with heavy cream, sometimes with maraschino cherries, almonds and other flavoring ingredients. The root word is *torta* ("tart"), according to some philologists, but others claim that it was probably named after an Italian restaurateur in Paris. Signor Tortoni, I am told, lived in the nineteenth century.

Biscuit tortoni is an individual portion of the ice cream, frozen and served in a small paper cup.

The above desserts should not be confused with *spumone,* which is another form of Italian ice cream, containing fruits, nuts or candies. Its origin is *spuma* ("foam"), an Italian and Latin noun.

———

A *trattoria* is a small, inexpensive Italian or Italian-American restaurant. Here are its roots:

> *trattore* ("innkeeper")
> *trattare* ("to handle or manage")
> *tractare* ("to treat"—Latin)

So the next time you trot over to a *trattoria* you can expect a treat.

———

Tutti-frutti has a nice ring to it, and the ice cream has a nice taste. It means "all fruits."

———

Veal scallopini is a popular dish we have imported from Italy and still another instance of Italian chefs' delight in diminutives. *Scallapo* means ("thin slice"). The dish does feature very thin slices of meat, sautéed slowly with herbs and wine. *Veal Parmesan,* on the other hand, is made with cheese.

———

Perhaps you won't want to eat *vermicelli* when you hear that this pasta literally means "little worms." Not to worry; the imaginative Italians chose that name because the strings of pasta are so thin.

———

Zucchini is an Italian variety of summer squash that has grown popular in America. The word is a diminutive plural of *zucca* ("gourd").

———

I realize that the above list gives short shrift to beverages. The reason is that most of our linguistic imports from Italy in that category are wines named after towns or regions. They will be mentioned in "The Place Is Familiar."

———

Now let us turn our attention to the contributions to our language from the Italians in all of the arts besides music—an area previously covered. Below are some of the many words in that category.

THE ARTS

√amoretto	√gesso	√patina	√sestina
√amorino	impasto	√Pietà	√stanza
√ballerina	√impresario	√Punchinello	√stucco
canto	√intaglio	√putti	studio
√caricature	√libretto	relievo	√tempera
√cartoon	literati	√replica	√terra cotta
√chiaroscuro	majolica	√saltarello	√terrazzo
extravaganza	√novella	scena	√terza rima
√fantasia	√ottava rima	√scenario	√tondo
√fresco	√ovolo	√sepia	torso
√gala			

An *amoretto* is an infant cupid, such as those found in Italian art of the sixteenth century. The noun is a diminutive of *amore* ("love"), which comes of course from the Latin word *amor*.

Amorino is still another diminutive. It has come to mean "cherub."

Ballerina could well have been placed in the musical category, but since dancing is her specialty, it fits here. This danseuse owes her etymological origin to *ballare,* the Italian verb meaning "to dance." *Ball,* as a dance, is a related word.

The Italian verb *caricare,* derived from Vulgar Latin, means "to overload." That's just what a *caricature* does, whether it's an artist's exaggerated drawing or a writer's satirical piece about a person.

When I was growing up I loved *cartoons* and always thought they were simply synonymous with caricatures and comic strips. Then I read a story about Michelangelo and discovered that *cartoon* has another meaning. It can be an artist's full-size preliminary sketch of a design or picture to be copied, for example, in a fresco, mosaic, or tapestry.

The word comes from *cartone* ("a pasteboard") and is an augmentation of *carta* ("card"). The Latin root is *charta* ("leaf of papyrus"). If you have always wondered why the *Magna Charta* could also be spelled *Magna Carta,* now you know.

Chiaroscuro has been taken over in English without the slightest change. Literally, it means "light and shade." It's a style of painting using those two opposites to produce a dramatic effect and the illusion of depth.

Fantasia literally means "fancy" in Italian. In addition to its musical uses, it can be a poem or play in which the author's fancy roves without restriction. It's also an Arab performance featuring dancing and various kinds of shenanigans on horseback, including rapid-rhythm gunshots and shouts.

Walt Disney's FANTASIA helped to popularize the word. Do you remember Dumbo, propelled by his huge ears, flying around, and those big elephants dancing to a Tchaikovsky air? *Fantastic!* And by the way, do you know what a *fantast* is? He's a visionary or dreamer.

Fresco is the art of painting with water-based pigments on wet plaster. "Wet" is significant because one definition for *fresco* is "fresh." If you have never seen Giotto's *frescoes* at the basilica in Assisi, I recommend that you hop the next plane and do so. Thrilling!

A reader who knows *gala* only as an adjective meaning "merry" may ask why I have included it among the arts. Well, it's also a noun meaning "an entertainment for a special occasion." In Italian, *gala* means "festivity, show, pomp."

Gesso is the Italian word meaning "gypsum or plaster of Paris prepared for use in painting, sculpture or bas-reliefs." Our painters and sculptors have embraced the word in its entirety.

Another Italian word that we have adopted without change in sense or spelling is *impresario*—a manager or conductor of an opera or concert company. We have extended the use a bit to mean the director of TV shows, art exhibitions and even sports contests. A modern synonym is producer. The late Sol Hurok comes to mind as one of the great *impresari*.

The Italian root is *impresa* ("enterprise"), and the Vulgar Latin grandparent is *imprendere* ("to undertake"). Incidentally, let's not look down our noses at Vulgar Latin. Actually, the Romance languages developed mostly from that colloquial form of the parent tongue. I keep reminding myself that today's colloquialisms are tomorrow's accepted, dignified words. And if it had not been for Vulgar Latin, our language would be less endowed with such beauties as *impresario*.

The chief meaning of *intaglio* is "an engraving or incised figure in stone or other hard material." The Italian verb is *intagliare* ("to engrave, carve, cut"), an offshoot of a Late Latin verb *taliare* ("to cut").

You can see why *tailor* is a relative.

Libretto is the diminutive of *libro*, which evolved from *liber*, the

Latin word for "book." Today the "little book" is the text for an opera, oratorio or other long choral work.

Most composers of operas are not *librettists.* Notable exceptions are Wagner, Leoncavallo and Menotti. Two of Verdi's *librettists* were Piave and Boito.

It's interesting to note that the text of a musical comedy is also called "the book," as differentiated from the music itself, which is "the score." You may have heard of the bookie who attended MY FAIR LADY. He had no trouble with the plot, but he didn't know the score.

Novella and *novel* are cousins. Both are derived from *novus,* the Latin adjective for "new." *Novelty* of course is in the same family.

A *novella* is a short story with a moral. The tales in Boccaccio's DECAMERON are satiric *novelle.*

Ottava rima (literally, "eighth rhyme") is a stanza of eight lines. The rhyme scheme is *abababcc.* The English form has ten or eleven syllables in each line.

Sometimes *octave* and *ottava rima* are used as synonyms.

Ovolo, a convex molding known to all crossword puzzle fans, dates back to the Romans' *ovum* ("egg"), because of its elliptical shape.

Patina originally meant "tarnish" in Italian, and in Medieval Latin it was a shallow dish or pan. In English it is defined as "the green film that forms on copper or bronze by long exposure to a moist atmosphere." Because it is valued aesthetically, it is often produced artificially, as by treatment with acids.

We have extended the use of the word; it now applies to the thin coating or color change resulting from age. Antique collectors delight in the *patina* on wood or silver. And the connection with aging has prompted writers to apply *patina* to people. It can mean "the look a person has acquired from long custom or settled use." In that sense it seems to me like a colorful aura.

An accepted variation is *patine.* I first met that word when I read THE MERCHANT OF VENICE. Lorenzo says:

> "Sit, Jessica. Look how the floor of heaven
> Is thick inlaid with *patines* of bright gold."

The passage in which those lines appear is one of the most beautiful and thought-provoking in all of English literature. If your curiosity is excited see Act V, Scene 1.

A *Pietà* is a representation of the Virgin Mary mourning over the body of Christ after the Crucifixion. In Italian the word means "pity." The Latin root is *pietas* ("piety").

The *Pietàs* of Michelangelo are some of the greatest pieces of sculpture in the world. The one at St. Peter's in Rome has received the greatest publicity, but my favorite is in the Duomo at Florence. Although I gazed on it almost a decade ago, the eyes of Nicodemus still haunt me, and not just because Michelangelo used his own likeness, at the approximate age of seventy, for that forlorn figure.

Punchinello has a fascinating history. This buffoon in puppet shows got his name from Neapolitan dialect. His eventual ancestors are *pulcino* ("chicken") and the Latin noun *pullus* ("pullet").

The British adopted him; he became the quarrelsome, hook-nosed husband in the Punch and Judy shows. But sometimes that grotesque character put one over on his wife. At that point he was pleased as Punch.

Putti are cherubic little angels or cupids often used in painting and sculpture, especially during the Renaissance. If you visit St. Peter's Cathedral in Rome, you will see many a *putto* on the gigantic columns.

In Italian, *replica* originally meant "reply." Then it developed into "repetition." Today we use it in two ways:

1. a copy or reproduction of an original work of art
2. any copy or close reproduction

The Late Latin root is *replicare* ("to repeat"), which is a combination of the Roman prefix *re* ("back") and the noun *plica* ("fold"). *Replicate, replication* and *reply* are all of the same clan.

Saltarello (sometimes spelled *saltarella*) sounds salty, and in a way it is—but not because of its linguistic background. It's a lively Italian dance featuring hops and skips, and it's also the music for that ballroom exercise.

The Latin root, fittingly, is *saltare* ("to jump or leap").
Related words include:

saltant—jumping; dancing
saltation—the act of jumping or dancing
saltatory
   a. of or adapted to leaping or dancing
   b. proceeding by leaps, hops or sudden movements
   c. discontinuous

Scenario is an Italian adaptation of the Late Latin adjective *scae-*

narius ("of the stage"). It has evolved into a synonym for screenplay, or outline of the plot of a play or film. Naturally, the people who write such material had to have a name, so we dubbed them *scenarists*.

As I have explained in another chapter, the origin of *scene* can be traced back to the Greek word *skēnē,* which originally meant "tent." Homer described Achilles sulking in his *skēnē.* Today, when hipsters talk about "making the scene," I can't help but think of them as constructors of tents, like Omar Khayyám.

Sepia has several meanings, the first rather disgusting and the others artistic:

1. a dark-brown ink or pigment originally prepared from the fluid secreted by the cuttlefish.
2. a sketch or picture using the above pigment
3. a dark reddish brown color
4. a photographic print in the above color

The Italian noun is *seppia* (they love to add extra consonants!), but the Latin root is *sepia* ("cuttlefish").

The Italian word *sesto* ("sixth") has given us *sestina,* a form of poem having six six-line stanzas and a tercet. What's a tercet? It's a group of three lines that rhyme. Here's my tercet; you can curse it.

> In the creative, poetic arena
> I confess I have never seen a
> Completely delightful *sestina.*

Stanza literally means "a stopping place" in Italy. Hence, if you're a touring poet in Roma looking for a *stanza,* you're not in quest of some divisions for your verses; you merely want to rent a room. I can understand the switch from habitation to the specific area overlooked by Erato, but I have not been able to uncover how, when, where and by whom the decision was made to zero in on poetry. Apparently it just "evolutionized" (a word I've just concocted in frustration).

Incidentally, the Latin progenitor is *stans* (the present participle of good old *stare,* "to stand").

In defining the word "plaster" for a crossword puzzle, I was once tempted to write, "Don't get *stucco* on this one!" Sober judgment prevailed and I refrained.

This word that we borrowed from the Italians originally comes from an Old High German noun, *stukki,* or *stucki* ("crust, covering, fragment"). At any rate, the material is used to decorate walls, whether interior or exterior. Even the Romans used it; their word was *tectorium*.

Also, may I point out that *stucco* fits admirably in the category of the arts. Sculptural and architectural ornaments are made of this mixture of pulverized white marble and plaster of lime, with water added. Some of the artistic creations take the form of flowers, garlands and fruits.

Relatives of *stucco* include *stock* and *stoker*.

Tempera is a medium used by painters, consisting of pigment usually mixed with egg yolk to produce a dull, opaque finish. This Italian import can be traced to *temperare,* the Latin verb meaning "to mix in true proportion." Most lexicographers assume that the ultimate root is tempus ("time").

Of special interest is the fact that *temper, temperament, temperance, temperate* and *temperature* all belong in this Roman tribe.

In Italian, *terra cotta* literally means "cooked earth." This hard, waterproof clay is a standby for potters and builders. The word also means "a shade of orange."

Terrazzo is a flooring material of marble or other stone chips set in cement or marble and polished when dry. Literally, this mosaic form means "terrace" in Italian. Apparently the new connotation caught on because so many terraces of villas had such artistic surfaces.

Terza rima was the verse form used by Dante in his DIVINA COMMEDIA. The rhyme scheme is rather complicated: *aba-bcb-cdc,* etc. There are other variations.

Sir Thomas Wyatt introduced the form into England in the sixteenth century. Shelley and Byron were among the great poets who tried it. Literally, the phrase means "third rhyme."

Finally, I should call your attention to the fact that *aba-bcb-cdc,* etc. are forms of tercets. (See *sestina,* above.)

A *tondo* is a round painting or sculptured medallion. The word is a derivative of the Latin adjective *rotundus* ("round"). Guess what English word is a relative!

Strangely enough, in the areas of clothing and shelter we have only a small inheritance from Italy. Most of the imports in the first category have been transmitted to us by Roman Catholic officials.

CLOTHING

biretta—a square cap with three or four projections and a tassel on top

mozzetta—a prelate's short cape having a small hood

zucchetto—an ecclesiastic's skullcap

SHELTER

bagnio—brothel; house of prostitution

This word once meant "a bathhouse," and in the Orient it was a synonym for a prison.

campanile—a bell tower

casino

    a. a place for gambling, dancing, entertainment

    b. a card game (also spelled *cassino*)

In Italy a *casino* is a small country house; it's the diminutive of *casa*.

cupola

    a. a rounded roof or ceiling

    b. a small dome on a roof

    c. a dome-shaped structure

The word is derived from *cupola* ("a little tub").

loggia—a roofed open arcade or gallery on the side of a building and usually facing an open court

The *loggia* at the Piazza della Signoria in Florence is famous for its group of statues.

pergola—an arbor, usually with an open roof and often featuring latticework

seraglio

    a. harem

    b. palace of a sultan

The Italian word is *serraglio,* meaning "an enclosure or paddock." It can be traced back to the Latin noun *sera* ("a bolt or lock").

Finally, we come to an interesting conglomerate group of words and phrases borrowed from Italy.

MISCELLANEOUS

agio	√camorra	fascist	inamorata
√alfresco	caprice	√fata morgana	inamorato
amore	carnival	felucca	√inferno
autostrada	√carton	√fiasco	√influenza
bambino	√catafalque	generalissimo	lava
banco	√cavalier	√ghetto	√lira
√belladonna	√ciao	√gondola	√madonna
√braggadocio	√cognoscenti	√graffito	√mafia
buffalo	√credenza	grotto	√major-domo
√cameo	√ditto	√imbroglio	√malaria

manifesto	pellagra	scarp	vista
mohair	piazza	sequin	viva
√motto	√pococurante	sirocco	volcano
√nuncio	√punctilio	√stiletto	√zero
√padrone	√regatta	umbrella	√zingana
√paparazzo	√salvo	√vendetta	√zingaro

Alfresco (sometimes spelled as two words) literally means "in the cool." In Italian or English the adjective now carries the idea of being outdoors or in the open air.

Belladonna is a poisonous plant of Europe or the United States. Another term for it is "deadly nightshade." Why, then, should it carry such a lovely name (literally, "beautiful lady")? The reason is that it has been used as a cosmetic for dilating the eyes. Isn't that an eye-opener?

Braggadocio is really not an Italian import. The word was coined by Edmund Spenser. In THE FAERIE QUEENE the fellow is the personification of boastfulness. But since the British poet chose to put an Italian ending on the word, some credit must go to the language that inspired him.

Braggadocian is the adjective derived from Spenser's noun.

Because *cameo* is a finely carved gem, the word has recently acquired two other definitions:

1. a minor but well defined role, usually played by a noted actor
2. a fine bit of descriptive writing

A *camorra* is any group of persons united for dishonest purposes. Around 1820 some Neapolitan criminals formed a secret society that became notorious for violence, blackmail and terrorism. Borrowing the Spanish word for "quarrel," they called themselves the *Camorra*.

Carton, like *cartoon,* is from *cartone,* the Italian word for "card or pasteboard."

What a strange history *catafalque* has! First of all, the word can be defined in several ways:

1. an ornamental, rather elaborate structure for solemn funeral rites in churches
2. a pall-covered empty coffin used at Roman Catholic requiem Masses after the burial
3. a hearse

The Italian source is *catafalco* ("funeral canopy"); the French borrowed the word and Gallicized the spelling. But the ultimate ancestors are a mixed breed: *kata,* from Greek, "down," and *fala,* from Latin, "a wooden tower."

Cavalier is directly from the French, but the Italians deserve more credit, because their word *cavaliere* was transported to Paris centuries ago. The ancient Roman root is *caballus* ("horse"). Via the same routes, *cavalry* and *cavalcade** have come into our language.

There are so many meanings for *cavalier* that I cannot give them all. Chiefly, the chap is a man-of-arms on horseback, or a knight. Hence he's also a gallant or a lady's dancing partner. In British history he became a supporter of Charles I against Parliament.

Possibly because he was a Royalist or aristocrat, the fellow took on a pejorative sense when he was turned into an adjective. Such definitions as "haughty, arrogant, carefree or offhand" evolved. If someone gives you *cavalier* treatment, you're getting what is known in the streets as "a fast brush-off."

Finally, as one who loves lyrics, I am compelled to mention the *Cavalier* poets: Herrick, Carew, Suckling, Lovelace et al. They were so named because of their association with the court of Charles I. You may be fascinated to learn that they called themselves "sons of Ben." They met with Jonson regularly in the Apollo Room of London's Devil Tavern, and they called him their "literary father" because he taught them to emulate the easy style of Latin poets such as Ovid.

Ciao, the Italians' informal greeting or farewell, has become popular with the jet set and others. The word is pronounced like a G.I.'s meal—"chow."

I am reminded of an Italian custom. Just like the Spaniards, they have the word *pronto,* which we have taken over. It means "quick or ready." When I visited Italy I was amazed to hear the natives' answer to the ringing of the phone. "Pronto!" they shouted. I soon learned that it was their idiom for "Hello!"

The *cognoscenti* are the experts or people in the know, especially in the fine arts. A *cognoscente* can presumably distinguish an original Cézanne from a fine copy. The Latin root is *cognoscere* ("to know"). Relatives include *incognito* (from Italian, too), *cognizant, recognize, connoisseur, notion, acquaint* and *quaint.*

---

* *Cavalcade* originally meant only "a procession of horsemen or carriages." Then it became any kind of procession. Finally it evolved into a synonym for any sequence of events.

> Just like *tutta la gente,**
> I'm no *cognoscente,*
> But I think I know plenty!

Credenza has a delightful etymology. This buffet, sideboard or bookcase without legs originally meant "belief or confidence" in Italian and goes all the way back to the Romans' *credere* ("to believe"). The word is derived from the practice of placing a nobleman's meal on a buffet or sideboard to be tasted first by a servant. If the poor fellow didn't die on the spot, the lord of the manor believed it was safe to take a bite.

Some words in this Latin family are *credo, credulous, credence, credit, credible, miscreant, recreant* and a host of others.

In the Tuscan dialect *ditto* means "said." It's from *dictus,* the past participle of *dicere* ("to say") in Latin. Thus the first meaning of the word is "the aforesaid." But it should be noted that we often use it as an interjection, and it has recently come into usage as a verb.

Morgan le Fay, in Arthurian legend, was a malicious fairy and half sister of the king. In Italian, *Fata Morgana* actually means "Morgan le Fay." How did this phrase come to be synonymous in English with any mirage or distortion? Well, the Sicilians often saw such phenomena near the Strait of Messina. Objects seemed to be reflected in the sea and sometimes appeared to rise on a sort of aerial screen high above the waves. Since Morgan le Fay was fabled to be a native of Calabria, just across the waters, the Sicilians shrugged and called each optical illusion a work of that sorceress—in other words, a *fata morgana.*

Fiasco has an interesting history. This ambitious project that turns out to be a complete failure literally means "bottle" in Italian, and in fact it can also be used in English to mean "a bottle of wine."

No expert is sure how this container for Chianti took on the connotation of "a complete failure." I wonder if it is possible that Italian glassblowers coined that definition when they were unsuccessful in their attempts to form a bottle of a certain ornamental shape. It sounds like a good story, but it's probably far off the mark.

In any case, our word *flask* is directly related to *fiasco.*

Ghetto, according to one group of philologers, originally meant

---

* *Tutta la gente*—all the people, or common folk

"foundry" in Italian. The section occupied by Jews in Venice had once been the site of a cannon foundry.

Jews were *ghettoized* in many European cities. In other words, they were forced to live in one area only. Today a *ghetto* is any section occupied by a minority group. Because such people are usually forced (by economic pressures or social discrimination) to live apart from other groups, the word is often used pejoratively. In its worst sense a *ghetto* is a slum.

Naturally, *gondola* has a Venetian origin. The name of that long, narrow flat-bottomed boat so beloved by tourists is considered by some lexicographers to be an alteration of *dondolare* ("to rock and roll")! Others conjecture that it can be etymologically traced back to the Greek word *kondy* ("drinking vessel").

Aside from being a canalboat, a *gondola* is also a flat-bottomed river barge, a topless freight car, a chair or couch with the back sweeping up like the end of the Venetian boat, and, finally, the car attached to a dirigible or balloon.

Loving diminutives as they do, the Italian *gondoliers* also invented the *gondoletta*.

Graffito literally means "a scribbling," from *graffio* ("a scratch"). The ancient Greek ancestor is *graphein* ("to write"). Hence you can readily see that *graffito* has scores of kin.

But the closest relative is *sgraffito,* a method of making designs, as on murals and ceramics. It is also the decoration or pottery produced by this method.

The plural of *graffito* is commonly used to mean "scrawled pictures or words written in public places such as sidewalks, walls, phone booths and lavatories."

The archaeologists who uncovered Pompeii were amazed to find *graffiti* on the walls. Visitors to New York City are also astonished to see the exteriors (and interiors) of most subway cars covered with gaily colored designs, apparently executed surreptitiously while the cars are parked in the railroad yards.

Verbal *graffiti* can range from religious messages such as "Repent!" or "Jesus loves you" to the scatological creations in men's rooms. I remember seeing the following command over a urinal in a rest room on a turnpike: "Bulls with short horns stand close!"

Thus far I have never seen the word *graffitist,* but I'm sure someone will coin it soon. Perhaps I've just done so.

Imbroglio originally meant "a confused heap." Thus one might say, "An *imbroglio* of manuscripts and letters lay on the editor's desk." But it's more often used today to mean "a confused and violent altercation." *Embroil* is one of its relations.

———

Dante's INFERNO deals with Hell. An *inferno* is any hellish place; it's also a conflagration. The Latin root is *infernus* ("situated beneath; lower"). Since Pluto ruled the lower world, called Dis by the Romans and Hades by the Greeks, and since our flaming hell is also reputed to be down under the earth, you can see how such a tepid word as *infernus* gave rise to a hot one—*inferno*.

The adjective *infernal* not only means "hellish, fiendish or diabolical" but has developed into a synonym for damnable or outrageous. We say, "He's an *infernal* nuisance" or "Stop that *infernal* racket!"

———

The Italian astrologers gave us *influenza*. Literally, it means "influence," but the notion arose that the cause of the disease was influenced by the stars.

———

Many a *lira* glistens under the waters of the Fountain of Trevi in Rome. The plural of this Italian coin is *lire*. However, only the smaller denominations of *lire* are made of metal; like our dollar bills, the larger denominations are paper. Incidentally, when an American visits Italy, he is suddenly plunged into higher math, because the Italian monetary unit is worth so much less than ours. A pair of shoes costs thousands of *lire*.

The word comes from *libra* ("balance or pound"). If horoscopes interest you, then you probably know that *Libra* ("The Balance") is a zodiacal constellation between Virgo and Scorpio. Anyone born between September 23 and October 22 is a *Libra*.

———

Madonna literally means "my lady." The title is usually applied to the Virgin Mary. Thousands of artists have painted *Madonnas* through the centuries.

———

In Sicilian dialect, *mafia* means "boldness, bluster, swagger." Thus arose the name *Mafia* (or *Maffia*) for that notorious secret society of terrorists and racketeers. The members are called *Mafiosi*.

———

Major-domo in Medieval Latin was *major-domus* ("elder of the house"). The Italians changed it to *maggiordomo,* and the Spanish alteration was *mayordomo*. Both groups can claim credit for transmitting the word to us.

The fellow is a chief steward. In colloquial usage, he's any butler or steward.

———

Malaria is literally bad air. The name originated because people once believed that the miasma from swamps was responsible for the disease. They overlooked the mosquitoes that bred in those fens!

———

In Italian, *motto* means "word." In French, *mot* has the same meaning, and *bon mot* ("good word") is a witticism. The common ancestor is the Latin *muttum* ("a grunt or muttering").

———

A *nuncio* is a permanent official representative of the Vatican to a foreign government. *Nuncio,* or *nunzio,* means "messenger," from the Latin *nuntius.*

———

Padrone means "patron," from the Latin *patronus.* When Italian immigrants poured into America early in this century, they often put themselves in the hands of *padroni* who promised them jobs and other aid. But too many of those men exploited the newcomers shamelessly.

Today *padrone* has several other meanings:

1. boss or chief
2. landlord or innkeeper
3. master of a Mediterranean trading ship

The word should not be confused with *padre,* which means "priest" in Italian or Spanish. To a G.I. he's the chaplain.

The Spanish equivalent of *padrone* is *padrino* ("godfather, dueler's second, protector or best man").

All of the above words ultimately owe their heritage to *pater,* the Latin noun for "father."

———

Paparazzo is such a recent borrowing from Italy that you probably won't find it in your dictionary. But it's bound to appear in future lexicons, partly because of the publicity given to the *paparazzi* in connection with their harassment of Jackie Onassis.

In Italian dialect, *paparazzo* literally means "a buzzing insect." But the word has taken on another connotation. It's applied specifically to a free-lance photographer who uses any means—fair or foul—to take candid shots of celebrities.

Now, picture a male movie star leaving a nightclub with a new girlfriend at his side. With cameras clicking, a dozen *paparazzi* immediately swarm around the couple. "Buzzing insects" they are indeed!

———

As I have mentioned briefly in a previous chapter, *pococurante* is a delightful word to add to your vocabulary. In literal translation it means "little caring" or, by reading backward, "caring little." Hence a person who is *pococurante* is indifferent or apathetic. *Pococurantism* is a synonym for nonchalance.

———

Even though *punctilio* means "an instant of time" or a "small detail," in common usage it refers to a point of etiquette or conduct in a ceremony, or the observance of petty formalities.

The adjective *punctilious* is a derivative. People who merit that description are scrupulously exact or very fussy about details.

> Persons *punctilious*
> And supercilious
> Make me bilious

(Another of my cursed tercets.)

The Italians and Spanish share the honors for *punctilio*. The former evolved *puntiglio,* and the latter *puntillo*. Both mean "a little point." The Latin ancestor is *punctum* ("point").

———

The Henley, on the Thames, and all those other *regattas,* on the Charles River or at Newport, Rhode Island, have attracted worldwide interest, but few of us know that the first *regatta* was the *regata* at Venice, in which gondoliers raced. This dialectal word came from *regalar* ("to compete") and literally meant "a striving for mastery."

In modern usage a *regatta* is any race involving various kinds of vessels—for example, sculls, yachts, speedboats.

Finally, *regatta* has taken on two new connotations, the first presumably with reference to the garb of yachtsmen and the second possibly in connection with the color of the sea:

1. a strong twilled English cotton fabric for clothing, usually with colored stripes or checks
2. a strong shade of blue

———

Salvo is a modification of the Italian *salve* ("Be safe!"). The Latin grandparents are *salve* ("Hail!"), *salvus* ("safe") and *salvére* ("to be in good health").

In a way *salvo* can be compared with *goodbye* ("God be with you"), because the original meanings of both words have been generally forgotten through usage.

When a hero or top official is greeted, he's given a twenty-one-gun salute. That's a *salvo*—or a way to say "Hail!" When a hitter such as Mickey Mantle stroked a home run, the Yankee fans gave him a *salvo,* whether they knew it or not.

Members of the United States Navy and the United States Air Force know that we have evolved an ironically opposite meaning for *salvo.* It's no salute or cheer when a warship fires a *salvo* at the enemy or when a bomber releases a load of explosives.

The ancient Romans used a needlelike device for writing on wax tablets. The instrument was a *stilus.* Today we call it a *stylus* or *style.*

Who would think that a tool used for peaceful, creative ends could become such a dangerous weapon as a *stiletto?* This "little dagger" has a French-derived cousin, *stylet*—equally ominous.

However, *stiletto* and *stylet* do have their more constructive aspects. The former can be a sharp instrument for making holes in cloth; in England it's a woman's spike heel. *Stylet* to a surgeon is a slender probe.

The above reminds me of experiences that other crossword puzzle editors and I continually undergo. Solvers who are accustomed to only one way to use a word often fail to look before they leap. For example, I once defined *stylet* as "a small dagger" and immediately received a nasty letter from an M.D., who informed me irately that the word in question was a wire inserted into a soft tube (called a catheter) for passing fluids from the body. His was a third meaning for the word; mine was the first. Of course I sent him a polite reply; editors are not expected to return insult for insult. They just acquire ulcers and get frayed away.

Vendetta is the Italian alteration of the Latin *vindicta* ("vengeance"). This blood feud is typified in ROMEO AND JULIET. Some of the many relations include *vindicate* and *vindictive.*

It must be admitted that the Arabs deserve the basic credit for *zero.* Just as they have given us our numerals, they sent *sifr* ("cipher") to Italy. There it was changed to *zero.* Then the French got into the act. (How they loved Italian words!) We adopted their *zéro* and dropped the accent, as we usually do.

It is always exciting to observe the expansion of the use of words. *Zero* is just one of many examples. Once it meant "nothing" and nothing more. Now it has a dozen connotations. One of the latest is *zero hour,* the time set for the start of an assault. It is also called *H hour*—which is similar to *D day.* I look forward to *M minute* and *S second!*

Zero hour has been taken over by civilians. A deadline or any crucial time is called by that name.

Then of course there is that final moment in a countdown when the announcer proclaims, "Zero!" Who could ever predict that "naught" could mean so much to so many!

I had always thought that *zero in* ("focus on a target") was definitely derived from those World War II Japanese Zeros that attacked our warships. No! The dictionaries tell me that the phrase has its origin in the calibrated adjustments of the sight settings on a firearm, such as a rifle.

Incidentally, do you know what *zero-zero* means? If you hear your pilot tell the tower that conditions are *zero-zero*, you are in trouble. His ceiling (height at which he can fly) and his visibility are double-nil and double-zilch.

Zingana means "zebrawood." That's a tropical tree or shrub with a striped appearance. It is used in cabinetwork. A *zingana* in Italy is a female Gypsy. Her garb is far from drab.

Zingaro (or *zingano*) is a male Gypsy in Italy. The country seems to have many *zingari*. When I visited Rome a *zingaro* importuned me from the Via Archimede almost to the Villa Borghese. It was a bit frightening, but I was determined not to be gypped* by a Gypsy. At last I turned on him and recited the Lord's Prayer in Latin, delivering it in a mad, pompous voice. I proceeded only as far as "Pater noster, qui est in coelis, sanctificatur nomen tuum," and then the fellow bolted. "Pazzo Americano," I heard him exclaim. *Pazzo* is the Italian adjective for "crazy as a loon."

If you have guessed by now that Italians are high on my list of favorite people, you are *corretto*. After all, I married a *bella signorina* whose father was born near Napoli and whose mother came from Sorrento. Beyond that, she makes a great dish of *manicotti,* and her *bistecca alla pizzaiola* is out of this world!

---

* *Gyp* is a colloquial word meaning "to cheat or swindle." The origin is unknown, but most lexicographers surmise that it is a shortening of *Gypsy.* As a noun *gyp* is also used by the British to mean a male servant, as at Cambridge University. Could that institution be called a *gyp joint?*

Gyp reminds me of *cozen,* another verb for "defraud." Its old Italian ancestor is *cozzonare,* "to act like a horse trader."

CHAPTER 8

Words from Everywhere

As I have said previously, America is not only the melting pot of the world, but we have gladly accepted the words and phrases of other peoples around the globe and have assimilated them into our language. As a result, English is not just a linguistic mixture of the Romance languages and Anglo-Saxon; it contains a mélange of the vocabulary of scores of groups from every continent on our planet. Openheartedly, and almost naïvely, we have become the most avid adopters of foreignisms in the history of civilization.

This phenomenon has occurred for a number of reasons. Aside from the chief factors—wars, conquests and immigration—we must take into account the results of tourism. Until recently we had a virtual monopoly in that area; our travelers absorbed and brought back myriads of new words. Earlier, British colonialism and tourism had added much to the stock of words in the English language.

Of course our basic concerns for food and drink, shelter and clothing—as noted in preceding chapters—have caused us to embrace thousands of foreign words in those categories. And all of the arts have contributed immensely, as well as games and sports. Various religions, too, have had their share in enlarging our vocabulary.

Finally, the Industrial Revolution and the great advances in science and technology have made our dictionaries blossom with neologisms. As man invented and manufactured new products, names had to be coined for them. In recent decades the explorations in space and the forward thrusts in such fields as engineering and electronics seem to have given rise to a brand-new word almost every day of the week. And it must be remembered that a goodly number of those words come from scientists in Germany, Russia and Japan.

But let us now consider some of the nonscientific words we have obtained from each of those three countries, beginning with Germany.

The fact that we engaged in two great wars with the Germans during the first half of this century caused a great number of their military words to enter our lexicons. Here is a sampling. All the words in this list will be discussed.

Anschluss	flak	panzer
Big Bertha	Gestapo	putsch
blitz	Junker	rucksack
blitzkrieg	Luftwaffe	stalag

Anschluss ("union") isn't really a military word, but it became associated with war in Hitler's day. In 1934 he tried unsuccessfully to force an *Anschluss* with Austria; it culminated in the assassination of Engelbert Dollfuss, the Austrian chancellor. Then in 1938 he marched his troops into Austria and achieved an *Anschluss*.

Big Bertha was a large German gun used in World War I. It's an alteration of *dicke Bertha* ("fat Bertha") and was named for Bertha Krupp. The Krupp Works at Essen supplied the Germans with military equipment in both wars.

Any large, cumbersome machine or tool can be called a *Big Bertha*. Certain cameras and lenses that are excellent for long-range photography also bear the frau's name.

Blitz is a short form of *Blitzkrieg,* which literally means "lightning war." Any sudden overwhelming attack is a *blitzkrieg* or *blitz*.

Football players have adopted the word. When the defense *blitzes* the opposing quarterback or puts the *blitz* on, they are rushing forward in great numbers.

Flak (sometimes spelled *flack*) is an abridgment of *Fliegerabwehr-kanone,* which is a combination of three words meaning "aviator-defense-cannon." The first word begins with *Fl,* the second with *A,* and the third with *K.*

Actually, the original meaning of *flak* was "antiaircraft gun." But the shells ejected from those guns soon superseded the first meaning in the transfer to English.

Today *flak* means "strong, abusive criticism." Some lexicographers label that definition as slang, but it's predictable that it will be legitimized in the future.

Gestapo is another of those acronymic names. The German parent is *Geheime Staatspolizei* ("secret state police"). If you examine that word carefully, you will find *Ge-Sta-Po* in neat sequence.

We have not only taken over the word as a noun with evil connotations but have also used it attributively. Sometimes our police are accused of employing *Gestapo* tactics.

Junker comes from *junc herre* ("young nobleman"). Today he's a Prussian aristocrat or German military officer, especially one who is autocratic and antidemocratic.

The word is pronounced *yoon-ker*. Its Dutch cousin is *younker* ("young man or youngster"). Our word *young* stems from the same family.

The *Luftwaffe* was Hitler's air forces. The first syllable means "air" and the second means "weapon."

When I played football at Montclair State College, our archrival was an institution named *Panzer*. No wonder they gave us such trouble! The word means "armor." The German *panzer* divisions in World War II were armored forces organized for quick attacks. As a noun in English, *panzer* has come to mean "tank." Incidentally, the original German word is *Panzerkampfwagen* ("armored battle-wagon").

That combination of Teutonic nouns is typical of the Germans' penchant for polysyllabic words and their reluctance to use Greek or Latin roots for new objects or concepts. I am reminded of their reputed reaction to the tanks that the British introduced in World War I. Rumor hath it that they coined a new word for the monstrous vehicle: *Schützengrabenfürchtennichtsautomobil,* which translates into "protection-ditch-fearing-nothing-automobile."

Putsch means "a sudden rebellion." The Germans borrowed it from Swiss dialect, where it means "a push or blow or thrust." *Putschists* are advocates of sudden attempts to overthrow a government. You might call them putschy people.

The resemblance of *putsch* and *push* is only a coincidence. The latter can be traced to *pulsus,* the past participle of the Latin verb *pellere* ("to beat"). *Pulse, pulsation, repulsive* and *compulsion* are a few of the next of kin.

A *rucksack* is a form of knapsack—a bag for carrying supplies while on a march. The first syllable of *rucksack* is a dialectal form of *Rücken* ("back").

Stalag is another of those abridgments. The origin is *Stammlager* ("base camp").

Again a coincidence arises. The German prison camp has no relation to *stalagmite,* which dates back to the Greeks' *stalagmos* ("a dropping").

Have you ever had trouble distinguishing a *stalagmite* from a *stalactite?* Both are deposits of carbonite of lime in caves. The first builds up from the floor, and the second hangs from the ceiling. A good mnemonic is *g* for ground and *c* for ceiling.

Next, let's look at just a few delicious imports from Germany related to food and drink and kindred areas:

kaffeeklatsch	lager	rathskeller	schnitzel
kirsch	marzipan	sauerbraten	strudel
kohlrabi	pretzel	sauerkraut	wurst
kümmel	prosit	schnapps	zwieback

Kaffeeklatsch (sometimes Anglicized into *coffee klatch*) is an informal get-together for a chat. *Klatsch* means "gossip."

Kirsch is the short form of *Kirschwasser* (literally "cherry water"). It's a dry, colorless brandy distilled from the fermented juice of morello cherries.

The Germans borrowed *Kohlrabi* (we lowercase it) from the Italian plural *cavoli rape* ("cole rape"). This garden vegetable is related to cabbage.

Kümmel means "caraway seed." It's a colorless liqueur flavored with caraway seeds and such aromatics as anise and cumin.

Lager (or *lager beer*) comes from *Lagerbier* ("beer made for storage"). In German, *Lager* means "storehouse." True to its name, the beer is aged in refrigerated storehouses or cellars for several months.

Marzipan is another Teutonic borrowing from Italy. *Marzapane* had been a Venetian coin in the Middle Ages and also a small weight. Then it became a little box for a certain almond-flavored confection, and finally it was the sweet itself.

But the Italians can't complain that the Germans pilfered their word. They acquired the word from the Arabians.

Pretzel is from *Brezel*. But that German noun finds its ultimate source in the Romans' *brachium* ("arm"). The original *pretzels*—and those today that are still shaped like the letter B—resembled a pair of folded arms.

Prosit is also from Latin. Literally, it means "may it be good." For some reason the Germans took a fancy to the word. When they raise their steins and shout *"Prosit!"* their toast conveys "To your health!"

By the way, *stein* should probably have been included in my list.

It's an abridgment of *Steingut* ("stoneware"). *Stein* means "stone" and *gut* means "goods."

(Devotees of two famous Rubinsteins, Anton and Artur, may be interested to know that the surname of each means "ruby stone.")

Rathskellers are places below street level where Berliners tip their steins and cheerfully bellow "Prosit!" Originally they were located in the cellars of town halls: *Rat* ("council or town hall"), *Keller* ("cellar of a town hall") Question: Do German *Ratskellers* keep feline rat killers?

Sauerbraten and *sauerkraut* may be taken up together because they both begin with a German word meaning "sour." *Braten* means "roast," and this meat dish is a standby in German homes and restaurants. *Kraut* means "cabbage."

Schnapps (or *schnaps*) is a strong Holland gin. It is also any of various distilled liquors. In German, *Schnaps* means "a dram or nip." Our verb *snap* is a relation.

Schnitzels are veal cutlets, German style. The parent is *Schnitz* ("a piece cut off"). *Schnitzel* is the diminutive form. If it comes from Vienna, it's a *Wiener Schnitzel*. *Wien* is the German name for Vienna and is pronounced "Vēn." *Wiener* is an abridged form of *Wienerwurst* ("Vienna sausage"). To Americans it's a frankfurter, a frank or even a hot dog.

Many of our snack-bar owners misspell the word and advertise *weiners*. This reversal of the first two vowels has become so prevalent that WEBSTER'S THIRD lists it as an acceptable variant. Moreover, *weinies* and *weenies* are often employed colloquially. The same nonstandard spelling appears in *ice tea* and *ice coffee*. Purists shake their heads in disgust, but those alterations are good examples of how folk usage often prevails.

Strudel has a fascinating background. Literally, this pastry means "whirlpool." The name was chosen because of its spiral cross section. Our word *stream* is a relation. You probably won't remember that etymological tidbit the next time you consume some apple *strudel*.

Wurst is the best for many lovers of sausages. *Bratwurst* is a highly seasoned sausage made of veal or pork. *Brato* means "lean meat." *Knackwurst* is also very spicy. The initial syllable stems from *knacken* ("to crack or split or make a crackling noise"). Sometimes the word is spelled *knockwurst*.

Zwieback literally means "twice baked"—and that's almost exact. This baked biscuit is then sliced and toasted. Sometimes *rusk* and *zwieback* are equated. The former is from *rosca,* a Spanish twisted roll of bread. Literally, it means "a coil or screw."

———

And now let us review a few of the German phrases and words that are familiar to many of us:

Achtung!	"Attention!"
Auf Weidersehen	"Till we meet again" or "Goodbye"
Ausländer	Foreigner; outsider
Danke schön	"Thank you very much." (The words were popularized by Wayne Newton in 1963 when he sang "Danke Schoen.")
Der Alte	"The old one"—nickname for former West German Chancellor Konrad Adenauer
Donner und Blitz!	"Thunder and lightning!" (The expression is used as an expletive.)
Gesundheit!	"To your health!" (This can be a toast or consoling word to a sneezer.)
Unter den Linden	Main street in Berlin (literally, "under the limes")
Wie geht's?	"How goes it?" "How do you do?"
Wunderbar!	"Wonderful!" (A song hit several decades ago featured the word.)

German and Austrian psychologists and psychiatrists have made many contributions to our language. Here are just a few:

> Angst
> Anschauung
> Gestalt
> Weltschmerz

Of the four, *Angst* seems to have become the most commonly used in America, perhaps because of such problems as inflation, the energy crisis and the hustle and bustle of our cities. Or maybe we have adopted the word because it sounds so much like *anxious, anger, anguish.* At any rate, *Angst* is a feeling of anxiety or a gloomy, often neurotic, state of depression or fear.

The Danes can claim partial credit for the word. Incidentally, the plural is *Ängste,* and in English the singular and plural are sometimes spelled with a lowercase *a.*

———

Anschauung is probably the least used of the four. It means "intuition or sense perception."

———

Gestalt psychologists popularized the German word that literally means "shape or form." They studied behavior from the standpoint of response to configurational wholes. Their approach is often called con-figurationism, and their thesis is that we see an object or hear a melody not as a collection of parts or separate notes but as a whole or unit. When you put it all together, as we say colloquially, you've got the *gestalt!*

Weltschmerz literally means "world pain." It's a mood of sentimental sadness or pessimism about the state of the world. If the situation on Mother Earth doesn't improve immensely in the next few years, I'm afraid we're all going to be afflicted with "world pain."

Many German breeds of dogs have become our pets. Among them are the *poodle, schnauzer* and *spitz.*

Poodle comes from *pudeln* ("to splash"). *Puddle* is a related word.

Schnauzers must be growlers or snarlers. In German, *schnauzen* means "to growl or snarl." But if you own a nonsnarling dog of this breed, you might prefer *Schnauze* as the real source; it means "snout."

Spitz means "pointed" in German. The thin, pointed rod that we call a *spit* is a related word. If you've never seen a *spitz,* you might be interested to know that it's a small dog with a sharp-pointed muzzle, or *Schnauze.*

Finally, let's look at a selected olio of words transmitted from German to English. Those with checks will be discussed.

alpenglow	√Frau	√kitsch	√turnverein
alpenhorn	√Fraulein	√lieder	umlaut
alpenstock	√glockenspiel	Lorelei	verboten
autobahn	√kegler	schloss	√verein
bund	√kaput	√schneider	wanderlust
√edelweiss	√kindergarten	√schuss	√Wunderkind
√ersatz			

The Alpine plant called *edelweiss* has petallike leaves that are white and woolly. It was well named: *edel* means "noble or precious" and *weiss* means "white."

As an aside, did you know that Houdini's real name was Erich Weiss? Translated, that's Eric White. And Giuseppe Verdi can be Americanized into Joe Green.

Ersatz comes from the German verb *ersetzen* ("to replace"). In English it means "artificial or synthetic" and conveys the idea of substituting something inferior for the real thing.

Frau means "wife or married woman" and is the German equivalent of Mrs. The word comes from Old High German *frouwa* ("mistress"). From there it can be traced back to a basic Indo-European word *per*, and it is part of an immense family. Among the members are *fore, before, forefathers, far, fare* and *first.*

The plural is *Frauen.* A Franz Lehar operetta is called WIENER FRAUEN (VIENNESE WOMEN).

Fraulein is the diminutive of *Frau.* She's an unmarried woman.

Glockenspiel, when translated backward, means "play bells." This percussion instrument produces a series of bell-like tones when struck with small hammers. *Clock* is a related word; it is so called because the first *clocks* were bell-like in form.

A goner is a person who is *kaput.* He's finished, ruined, done for. The word is sometimes spelled *kaputt,* and that form is the exact duplication of the German adjective meaning "lost or ruined."

The Berliners borrowed the word from the Parisians. *Capot* means "not having made a single trick in the game of piquet." The original meaning of *capot* is "a hooded cloak." You can make your own guess as to how it came to signify being shut out in a card game.

Kegler is a colloquial synonym for a bowler. The word stems from *kegel* ("ninepin or tenpin").

Kindergarten literally means "a garden of children"—a lovely word indeed! What amazes me is that we did not change the *t* to a *d* somewhere along the line. Many people do pronounce it that way.

In German, *Kitsch* is "arty trash"—from *kitschen* ("to smear or slap together, as a work of art"). The original meaning in German dialect was "to scrape up mud from the street."

Hence *kitsch* is shallow, pretentious, inferior artistic or literary material slickly calculated to have popular appeal.

Lieder (pronounced like "leader") is the plural of *lied*—a German folk song or popular song. *Lieder* are also art songs, such as those composed by Schubert.

Schneider is a word familiar to gin rummy players. When you *schneider* your opponent, you prevent him from scoring a point. Curiously enough, the word means "tailor" in German. Perhaps some modern Hoyle can tell me the connection. Is it because the old verbal forms meant "to cut or reap," or was there an expert in gin rummy or skat whose name was *Schneider?*

Schuss is a straight downhill run in skiing. As a verb it means "to ski straight down a hill at full speed." In German, one meaning of the word is "gunshot." When you *schuss,* you literally shoot down the slope —as fast as a bullet.

A *turnverein* is a gymnasts' club. Turners are tumblers—from *turnen* ("to turn") in Old High German. *Verein* means "a union or association."

Wunderkind literally means "wonder child"—hence, a child prodigy. Mozart was indeed a *Wunderkind* in the field of music. At three he had a precocious knowledge of the art, and at the age of five he made his debut in public at the University of Salzburg. His instrument was the harpsichord. Even more amazing, he composed minuets at five, a sonata at seven, and a symphony at the age of eight. *Wunderbar!*

And now let us review some of our words that are of Russian origin. Communism has provided us with such words as *commissar* (since 1946, a minister), *oblast* (U.S.S.R. subdivision), *Presidium* (chief, permanent administrative committee) and *soviet* (council).

From pre-Lenin eras we have obtained *czar* (or *tsar* and *tzar*), *czarina* (or *tsarina* and *tzarina*), *pogrom, ukase* and *cossack,* among others.

A *pogrom* is an organized persecution and massacre of a minority group. The *czars* often prompted such attempts to wipe out the Jews. *Czar,* by the way, can be traced back to *Caesar.*

A *ukase* is an imperial decree or arbitrary proclamation. The Romanovs often issued such fiats, thus paving the way for their own downfall.

Cossack also dates back to the reigns of Ivan the Terrible and his fellow rulers. The word *kazak,* or *kozak,* was of Turkish origin; it conveyed the idea of a free, independent person or vagabond or adventurer. The *Cossacks* were members of a favored military group, especially in the Ukraine. Since these expert horsemen often charged into groups of dissidents, the word became associated first with policemen on horseback. Now it is used as a derogatory term to mean any policemen who work for a company or government to break up riots or demonstrations.

Our culinary heritage from Russia is more pleasant. Four samples are *borsch, kvass, samovar* and *vodka.*
Borsch (or *borscht*) is a beet soup, served hot or cold, often with

sour cream. Because such a dish was very popular among the Jewish clientele in the Catskills and White Mountains, comedians began to refer to the hotels in those summer resorts as the *borscht circuit*.

Kvass (or *kvas*) is Russian beer. This fermented drink is made from a mixture of rye, barley and other cereals.

Samovar literally means "self-boiler." It's a copper urn used in Russia for making tea.

Vodka is the Russian diminutive of *voda* ("water"). I am reminded that the French call brandy *eau de vie* ("water of life"). *Vodka* looks like water and also looks like gin. At any rate, this Russian liquor is distilled from rye or wheat and has a sneaky kick to it. The drink has gained much popularity in America. *Vodka* martinis seem to be crossing the bar just as often as their ginny kin.

Here are three Russian imports of the beastly variety: *beluga, Borzoi* and *corsac*.

A *beluga* is a large white sturgeon or dolphin. Sometimes the latter is called "the white whale." Was Moby Dick really a *beluga?* In any case, the Russian source is *byeluga,* from *byely* ("white").

Borzoi means "swift" in Russian. A dog of this breed is large and long-legged, like a greyhound. The head is narrow and the coat is silky. It's called "Russian wolfhound" because it was trained to pursue wolves.

The *corsac* (or *corsak*) is a bushy-tailed fox of central Asia. Its other name is "Afghan fox."

The Steppes are vast Russian grasslands—from *step* ("lowland"). To the north is the *tundra,* another treeless plain. The Russians borrowed the word from the Lapps' *tundar* ("hill").

Siberia may not have any hepcats, but it can boast of steppe cats. The usual name for such an animal is *manul.* It's a small wildcat that also inhabits parts of Mongolia and Tibet.

The *telega* and the *troika* are two of the vehicles that help the Siberians to get around. The former is a four-wheeled springless wagon, and the latter is a carriage or wagon drawn by a team of three horses running abreast. The source is *troe* ("three").

We have enlarged the connotation for *troika*. It can mean "a triumvirate or group of three people with authority."

Among the words we have absorbed from Moscow's space program are *Sputnik* and *Lunik*. When Sputnik I was launched in October 1957, it caused quite a stir in the United States because the Russians had outdone us. Theirs was the first artificial satellite placed in orbit. *Lunik,* by the way, had a dog as a passenger. I'm not sure if it was a *Borzoi.*

Probably the most popular of Russian-originated musical instruments is the *balalaika.* You may remember seeing it in the movie DR. ZHIVAGO. It looks like a guitar with a triangular body. Etymologically it may be akin to *balabolit'* ("to chatter").

It may surprise you to learn that we borrowed *intelligentsia* ("intellectuals") from the Russians. Of course the word ultimately has a Latin origin. *Intelligere* means "to perceive or understand." The verb is a combination of *inter* ("between") and *legere* ("to choose").

Artel is familiar to crossword puzzle fans. It's an association of people working collectively and sharing the income. Sometimes the word is defined as "Russian craft society."

It's most interesting to note that the word was borrowed from the Italian noun *artieri* ("artisans or workmen").

Kulaks and *artels* don't mix. Any wealthy farmer who exploited the peasants in the pre-Communism years was called a *kulak.* The words means "fist"—hence, "tightwad or pinchpenny." In the 1920s most *kulaks* refused to collectivize their farms, and many of them were liquidated.

Bolshevik almost literally means "the larger majority." The Bolsheviks formed the Social Democratic party, which led to the creation of the Communist party after the power was wrested from the czar in the 1917 Revolution.

We have at least three definitions for the word; choose any one of them according to your sociopolitical convictions:

1. a member of the Communist party
2. an extreme radical; an anarchist
3. a revolutionary

N ow we turn to words we have borrowed from Japan and consider a logical grouping: *judo, karate, jujitsu* and *sumo.* All four can be regarded as means of self-defense, although the last is merely a Japanese form of wrestling.

Judo actually means "soft or gentle art" and is a refinement of *jujitsu,* which has the same literal sense. The practitioners of the art use no weapons; instead they employ the principle of turning the opponent's weight and strength against him. Like engineers, they study leverage and take advantage of their knowledge of it.

Karate literally means "empty or open hand." If you have ever seen a *karate* expert chop a solid block of wood in half with the side of his hand, you'll agree that the art is well named. Sharp, quick blows with the feet are also employed.

In recent years many women have taken up *judo, jujitsu* and *karate* as methods of self-defense against rapists. Schools that teach those arts have sprung up throughout the country.

Incidentally, the Chinese relative of *karate* is *kung fu* (literally, "boxing principles").

––––––––

It's ironic that the Japanese yelled "Banzai!" when they charged against Allied forces in World War II. The cheer means "May you live ten thousand years!" Of course, during a *banzai attack* they were cheering each other rather than their foes, but to the soldiers who faced them the interjection sounded like some ominous threat.

The suicide attacks by Japanese pilots familiarized us with another Japanese word—*kamikaze*. It translates into "divine wind." I wish I could explain the connection. At any rate, we now use the word as a synonym for suicidal.

Hara-kiri (sometimes spelled *hari-kari*) is in a class with the above; it's a ritual suicide by disembowelment. Literally, it means "belly cutting." The practice was formerly employed by the *samurai,* who were the warrior aristocracy of feudal Japan. They performed the act to avoid execution or disgrace. One can't help wondering if they cried "*Sayonara!*" as they bade farewell to the world.

––––––––

The following paragraph is intended to show the use of a number of Japanese words, most of which are familiar to Americans.

We took a *jinrikisha* to the home of the lovely *geisha.* Outside, a *ginkgo* spread its fan-shaped leaves. When we entered, our hostess was playing a *samisen.* She was dressed in a flowery *kimono,* sashed at the waist with an *obi.* A tiny *netsuke* was attached to the sash. Immediately she offered us a drink of *sake;* then she heated up the *hibachi* and prepared a delicious dish garnished with *soy* sauce. While we were eating she took some pieces of paper and formed them into figures of animals. Her skill in *origami* amazed us, but we were even more astonished later when she took us back to her garden and showed us how she had dwarfed and shaped some trees in shallow pots. "*Bonsai,*" she explained.

Some of the above words have very interesting literal meanings:

jin-riki-sha	man–power–carriage
gei-sha	art–person
ginkgo	silver apricot
samisen	three strings
kimono	clothes
sake	from *saka-mizu* (prosperous waters)
hi-bachi	fire–bowl
bonsai	tray arrangement

Mikado, as every Gilbert and Sullivan buff knows, is the former title of the emperor of Japan. The word means "exalted gate"—another example of metonymy, or the use of a name for something associated with it. The "exalted gate" refers to the entrance to the Imperial Palace. A comparable usage today is to speak of the White House when we mean the U.S. President.

I have just learned that *mikado* is a shade of orange, brown or yellow, probably because those colors were the favorites of the emperor.

———

Another leader of Japanese origin is the *honcho*—our slang word for "chief" or "boss." The noun comes from *hancho* ("squad leader").

———

Maru is familiar to navy men and other sailors. It's a Japanese merchant ship. The word is often appended as a suffix to the names of ships, the way we use U.S.S. as a prefix for the name of a warship. *Maru,* by the way, means "circle."

———

Incidentally, have you ever heard of a *tsunami?* It's a tidal wave caused by a volcanic eruption under the ocean. Its Japanese roots are *tsu* ("port") and *nami* ("wave; sea").

Following *tsunami* in your unabridged dictionary you will find *tsutsugamushi disease,* a form of typhoid fever. Too bad that such a delightful word has such a dreadful connotation!

———

Finally, let's review the difference between *issei* and *nisei.* The former means "first generation," and the latter translates into "second generation."

The *issei* surreptitiously entered the United States after the "gentleman's agreement" with Japan that was formed in 1907–1908, during Theodore Roosevelt's administration. Tokyo officials at that time agreed not to issue passports to laborers wishing to emigrate. In 1952 the *issei* were finally made eligible for citizenship in the United States.

The *nisei* are native Americans born of Japanese immigrants and educated in the United States.

If the pronunciations puzzle you, note that *issei* is "ē-say" and *nisei* is "nē-say."

It should be added that there are also *kibei* and *sansei*. The former are Japanese Americans who go back to their ancestors' homeland to be educated. The latter are a third-generation group, born and educated in America.

While we're in the Far East, let's take a look at just a few of the words that we have inherited from China.

Naturally, because of the great popularity of Chinese restaurants, foods with Oriental names have become known to millions of Americans. *Chop suey** (alteration of *tsa-sui*—"various pieces") and *chow mein** (*ch'ao mein*—"to fry flour") are the most familiar. *Won tons* grow more popular each year. They are dumplings filled with minced pork and spices. The derivation is *wan t'an,* a word from Cantonese dialect meaning "pastry." The dumplings are especially delicious as a basis for *won-ton soup.*

While eating Chinese food, many Americans try to master the skill of using *chopsticks.* Those implements are linguistic creations of pidgin† English. In Chinese the original word means "the quick ones."

Another example of pidgin English, as used in China, is *chop-chop* ("quickly; promptly"). Still another is *chowchow*—and what a variety of definitions is attached to that word!

1. spicy relish
2. hodgepodge
3. yellow-billed cuckoo
4. breed of dog

The dog is spelled as two words, and the name is often shortened to *chow.* When used to indicate a miscellany, the spelling of the word is *chow-chow.*

The G.I.s' slang word *chow* may also be of Chinese origin. In Peking, *chiao* means "meat dumpling."

Rice and *tea* are of Oriental origin. The former has a long linguistic history and eventually dates back to Sanskrit, a language that is still

---

* According to no less a culinary expert than Craig Claiborne, *chop suey* and *chow mein* are not authentically Chinese.

† *Pidgin* is a concocted word supposedly based on the Chinese traders' pronunciation of their noun for "business." It's a simplified form of speech, mixing two languages. *Pidgin English* is used as a trade language in Far Eastern and South Pacific ports. The French equivalent is *bêche-de-mer*.

used in the ritual of the Northern Buddhist Church. Tea is derived from *t'e,* a word in the dialect of the Chinese at Amoy. It's a corruption of the Mandarin *ch'a.* *

We often say, "Not for all the *rice* in China," and sometimes *tea* takes the place of the cereal grass. Either expression is apt, because China certainly has an abundance of both products. Here are some varieties of *tea* and their literal Chinese meanings:

> *congou*—"labor"—because processing the product requires work
> *hyson*—"blossoming spring"—hence, "first crop"
> *oolong*—"black dragon"
> *souchong*—"small sort"

Kumquat is a word that has a delicious sound, and it's a luscious orange-colored citrus fruit. The original Chinese word, *chin-chil,* means "golden orange."

Wok is another word associated with food. This bowl-shaped metal cooking pan is often used with a circular stand to hold it steady. Its popularity in America is so recent that the word is not listed in most dictionaries, but you can be sure it will be an entry in future editions.

Mandarin is the chief and official dialect of China and is spoken by most of the people. Oddly enough, the word does not have a Chinese origin. It has come to us via the Portuguese and is related to the Latin verb *mandare* ("to command"). But ultimately its etymological history can be traced back to Sanskrit.

As a common noun *mandarin* has a number of meanings. Among them are:

1. a high public official in the Chinese Empire
2. any person belonging to an elite group, especially one respected by the literati or intellectuals
3. a pompous, pedantic official; a bureaucrat
4. a small, sweet orange (probably from the color of the Chinese official's robe) or the tree that bears the fruit.

There is also a *mandarin duck,* as well as *mandarin oil.* The latter is obtained from the peel of the orange and is used in perfumery.

The versatile Chinese have originated everything from gunpowder to games. *Mah-jongg* and *fan-tan* are two of the pastimes we have imported.

* *Ch'a* is familiar to American crossword puzzle solvers and the British in general. In England, *cha* means "tea" and is usually altered into *char.* "A cuppa *char*" is a slangy expression for "a cup of tea." In America, *cha* means "rolled tea." It is also spelled *chaa, chais* and *tsia.*

In the 1920s *mah-jongg* became a fad throughout the United States. It has since had sporadic revivals in certain locales, but its popularity has greatly diminished.

The name of the game literally means "house sparrow"; it's taken from the figure on one of the tiles.

Fan-tan was originally a Chinese betting game played with small objects such as beans. Then it developed into a card game. Since seven is a key card, the game is also called "sevens."

Finally, here is a small potpourri of words we have inherited from the Chinese:

WORD	DEFINITION	LITERAL MEANING
cumshaw	tip; gratuity	"grateful thanks" (beggars' phrase)
ginseng	plant having thick roots, used medicinally by the Chinese	"man"—because the forked root resembles a man with limbs
kowtow	show submissive respect	"knock head" (on the ground)
pongee	soft, thin light-brown silken fabric	"domestic loom"
sampan	small Chinese boat	"three-plank"
tong	Chinese association, political party or secret society	"hall, meeting-place"

T raveling southwest from China, we come to India. Largely because of the long British occupation of this land, we have been endowed with a rich mine of words, some of Hindu or Hindi origin and others Anglo-Indian.

In the area of clothing and fabric alone we have acquired many words. Some of them are listed below. The literal meanings are indicated only when they are of interest.

WORD	DEFINITION	LITERAL MEANING
bandanna	large, colored handkerchief	"a method of dyeing"
cummerbund	waistband; broad sash	"loins band"; from Pers. *kamar* ("loins")
dhoti	Hindu's loincloth or fabric for it	
khaki	twilled cloth, used for soldiers' uniforms	"dust-colored; dusty"; from Pers. *khāk* ("dust; earth")
puttee	covering for the lower leg	"bandage"
sari	Hindu woman's outer garment	
seersucker	striped, crinkled fabric	"milk and sugar"; from Pers. *shir u shakar*

I have deliberately omitted *chintz* from the above list because it merits special consideration. This glazed cotton fabric, often featuring flowery designs, has acquired a pejorative adjectival significance. Because *chintz* usually has a flamboyant, ornate look, *chintzy* came to mean "gaudy, tawdry, cheap." That last connotation evolved into "stingy" or "mean."

Thus we might refer to a restaurant as *chintzy,* or we might pin that label on a landlord or even a gift. The adjective is a prime example of how the sense of a word can expand and change. Incidentally, *chintz* is not an inexpensive fabric; it doesn't really deserve such denigration.

India has also bestowed upon us a largess of designations for people in various walks of life. Here are some of them:

WORD	DEFINITION	LITERAL MEANING
begum	Moslem queen, princess or high-ranking lady	"lady"; from Turk. word for "princess"
coolie	unskilled laborer receiving little pay	"hired servant"; from *koli* ("caste of Gujarat")
dacoit	robber	"attacker"; from *dakā* ("attack")
guru	religious teacher;	"heavy, weighty"—hence, "venerable"
maharajah	former Indian prince	"great king" and
maharani	and princess	"great queen"; from Sans.
mahout	elephant driver or keeper	"of great measure"; from Sans.
pandit	wise or learned man	"learned person"; from Sans.
pariah	outcast	"drummer"; from Tamil *parai*
pundit	learned man, teacher	variation of *pandit*
rajah	prince or chief	see *maharajah*
rani	princess	see *maharani*
sahib	sir, master (native's title for a European in colonial India)	"master"; from Ar. *sahīb* ("friend")
swami	pundit, seer, master, lord	"lord"; from Sans. *svāmin* ("lord")
yogi	Hindu ascetic; mystical person	"one practicing *yoga*"; from Sans. "union, yoking"

Brahmin deserves special attention. Actually, the word is a variation of *Brahman,* a priestly member of the highest Hindu caste. Hence in our language a *Brahmin* is a cultured intellectual of an established upper-class family. Since such a person is exclusive, the word has come to be equated with snob. Cleveland Amory, a scion of this group, has satirized the Brahmins of New England in his book THE PROPER BOSTONIANS.

What is most fascinating and ironic is that the original word *Brahman* now means "a breed of domestic cattle." If a *Brahmin* is called a *Brahman,* he may have a beef!

In the area of shelter, here are two of the words imported from India.

Bungalow is an Anglo-Indian variation of the Hindus' bānglā. In India it's a low one-storied house usually having a wide porch. In America the house is almost synonymous with a cottage. Along some shorelines a seemingly endless number of bungalows for summer rentals stand side by side.

Veranda (sometimes spelled *verandah*) is another Anglo-Indian word. Its source is the Portuguese *varanda* ("balcony"). The grandparent is the Latin noun *vara,* meaning "a wooden trestle or forked pole for spreading out nets." That's a long way from our present definition of *veranda:* "an open porch or portico; piazza, gallery or balcony."

In the field of food and drink, a sampling from India follows:

Curry is another of those strange etymological coincidences that I have noted before. As a verb the word has nothing to do with India. Its source is Vulgar Latin, whether it means "to groom a horse" or "to flagellate." And when flatterers *curry favor,* their source is Medieval English.

But *curry* as an abridgment of *curry powder* goes back to the Tamils, a people of southern India and Ceylon (now Sri Lanka). Their word for "sauce" was *kari.*

Do you know the story of the bride's first biscuits? Well, my wife and I have a personal joke about *curry.* In one of her first attempts at something different she prepared pork chops with that condiment. But she didn't realize how powerful the stuff was! Neither of us could take a second bite. Since then she has avoided *curry* like the plague and has become a cordon bleu (very skilled cook).

My father always drank a *hot toddy* when he wanted to ward off a cold. To me it seemed incongruous, because *toddy* had a babyish sound. Little did I realize that he was quaffing brandy or whiskey mixed with hot water, sugar and spices.

Toddy is an Anglo-Indian word from the northern part of the country. The Hindi noun was *tāri* ("fermented sap of the palmyra tree"). That juice is still used as a beverage, minus the alcohol.

Two musical instruments of Hindi origin are *sitar* and *tom-tom.* The former, which looks like a lute, has been made famous by Ravi Shankar. As for *tom-tom*—one would think that the American Indians or Africans originated that drum. However, it's a variation of *tam-tam,* a name given to it by the Hindi people because of the sound it makes.

One might also assume that the *topee* (or *topi*) had an African origin, because that helmet worn as a sunshade is so often used on safaris in the Dark Continent. But India also has its share of wild animals, such as Bengal tigers, and hunters there too need protection from the sun. The headgear is another Hindi export.

Speaking of animals, that swiftest of beasts, the cheetah, has a Hindi heritage (*citā*). The ultimate root is *citrakāya,* a Sanskrit noun meaning "tiger." Actually, the *cheetah* looks more like a leopard.

'Tis said that a learned man who understood *Lingua Equina* once interviewed the great race horse Man o' War* and asked him if he had any future goals. The stallion is reputed to have replied:

> "Nothing could be sweetah
> Than to beat a cheetah."

Now, if you believe that story, I recommend Aesop or H. C. Andersen.

Sailors, and even landlubbers, may be astonished to learn that *catamaran* and *dinghy* are words that we have borrowed from India.

Catamarans were originally rafts or floats. Now they have also developed into boats with two hulls. Even more fascinating is the fact that a new definition for the vessel has evolved. A *catamaran* can mean "a quarrelsome woman." Why, I don't know. Is it because of the first syllable or because of the noise that the twin-hulled boats make? I wish some scholar or seaman would clear up the mystery.

At any rate, the Tamil people have the word *kattumaram,* which literally means "tie" plus "log or tree." That fits, because the original rafts were made of two or more logs lashed together.

By the way, in Canada a *catamaran* is a big sled used for hauling wood. As in so many other cases, there seems to be no end to the varied uses of certain words.

Dinghy stems from the Hindi word *dingi* ("little boat"). It was, and is, a rowboat or sailboat for passengers or cargo on sheltered coastal waters of India. But we have given it additional connotations. Observe again the phenomenal process of expansion:

1. any small boat propelled by oars, sails or motors
2. small boat carried on a warship or merchant ship
3. lifeboat on a yacht
4. inflatable rubber raft used by parachutists
5. small, single-masted racing boat

That Hindi *dingi* has been winging it indeed!

* *Man o' War* (1917–47) suffered only one defeat in his illustrious career. As a two-year-old he lost to a horse named Upset!

Finally, here is a miscellany of words from India:

bangle	cushy	purdah
banyan	ditty bag	suttee
cheroot	ghat	tatty
chit	howdah	tonga
chukker	juggernaut	tulwar
cowrie	mugger	tussah

Bangles are bracelets, anklets, armlets or any ornamental circlets of gold, silver, glass, plastic or almost any rigid material. Originally these gewgaws were worn by women in India and Africa, but the fashion was soon adopted in Europe and America. The source is a Hindi word, *bangri* ("glass bracelet").

The *banyan* is a remarkable tree. Its branches send out aerial extensions that grow downward. When they reach the soil they form additional trunks. Thus a *banyan* keeps spreading out in an ever-widening circle. One tree can cover a space large enough to shelter a thousand people.

The English gave the *banyan* its name because Hindu merchants, called *banians,* not only took shelter under the tree but also used that area as a marketplace. They even built a pagoda under the leaves of an immense *banyan* on the southern Iranian coast.

Banian ultimately comes from *vanij,* a Sanskrit word meaning "merchant."

Banyan day is an occasion when no meat is served to the crew of a ship. The name is an allusion to the *banians'* abstinence from flesh. In Australia the term is used for any day on which the food is inferior—such as the last day of a weekly ration.

A *cheroot* is a cigar with both ends cut square. The source is *churuttu,* a Tamil word meaning "roll."

Chit has an interesting history. The Hindu word *citthi* or *cittha* means "a letter or note." At first the English transliterated the noun into *chitty,* but they soon shortened it to *chit*—a memorandum or short note. Then came another example of how the meanings of words expand. Because vouchers for small debts at restaurants or casinos involved the scribbling of a quick note, *chit* came to be synonymous with an I.O.U., a check, a bill or even any receipt.

Once more a linguistic coincidence is in evidence. *Chit* has two other meanings, both from Medieval English and having no relationship to each other or to the Hindu-based word with the same spelling:

1. pert young woman (from *chitte,* "kitten or cub")
2. sprout; shoot (from *chithe,* "sprout")

In polo a period of play is called a *chukker.* Although the game did not originate in India, the name for one of its divisions comes from Hindi (*chakar,* "wheel").

From the same root we get *chukka,* an ankle-high boot or shoe of the type originally worn by polo players.

Cowrie (sometimes spelled *cowry* or *courie*) is an English alteration of the Hindi word *kauri*—a mollusk of warm seas or the beautifully polished and often colorful shell of the gastropod. So highly regarded were these shells that the *money cowrie* was once used as currency in parts of Asia and Africa.

If you happen to have a *cushy* job, it must be an easy, comfortable one. British troops picked up the word from the Hindi-Persian *khush* or *khūsh* ("pleasant"). Originally slang, *cushy* is now considered acceptable by many lexicographers.

One would think that *cushion* might have the same root. However, it has a long, separate history and eventually stems from the Latin noun *coxa* ("hip").

Ditty and *ditty bag* are not related. The song can be traced to *dicere,* the Latin verb meaning "to say," but the sailor's little container for needles, thread, tapes and sundries has an unknown origin. Philologers guess that it comes from an obsolete word, *dutti* ("coarse calico"), and that the loincloth *dhoti* is the ultimate source.

Ghat (or *ghaut*) is a Hindi word meaning "mountain pass." It is also the Indian term for a platform or landing place on the bank of a river. We have accepted the spelling and meanings without change.

Some of the platforms are backed by elaborate structures resembling temples, from which the Hindus descend staircases and go bathing. At the head of such a structure is a space where the Hindus cremate their dead. It's called a *burning ghat.*

Howdah is an Anglo-Indian word (from *hauda*). This canopied seat for riding on the back of an elephant or camel ultimately has an Arabic source.

Juggernaut is a fascinating word with a startling history. Its parent is *Jagannāth* ("lord of the world"), an incarnation of the Hindu god Vishnu. The story goes that when a large vehicle containing a graven image of the deity moved along through the streets, some devotees got so excited that they threw themselves under the wheels.

Thus *juggernaut* has come to mean:

1. any large destructive, overpowering, inexorable force
2. anything requiring blind devotion or cruel self-sacrifice

Mugger is still another instance of the fact that two unrelated English words have exactly the same spelling. The robber gets his name from the slang word for "face." A *mugger* came to mean "one who punches in the mug—or face."

But the *mugger* from India is a harmless crocodile (from Hindi *magar*).

The *purdah* is a kind of curtain used by some Hindus and Moslems to protect their women from the eyes of strangers. It is also the veil used by the females and the practice itself. The source is *pardah,* the Hindi-Persian word for "screen or veil."

The chastity of women is very important in Hindu culture. *Suttee* (or *sati*) comes from Hindi-Sanskrit sources meaning "chaste and virtuous wife." Historically, a *suttee* was a widow who threw herself on her husband's funeral pyre and was cremated along with him. In this day and age "sutteean" suicides are *rarae aves.* Women apparently opine that they need not be erased in order to be chaste. Or would they rather be chased?

Those linguistic coincidences keep cropping up:

1. *tatty* (from Hindi *tatti*)—a moistened mat or screen placed in a door or window to cool and deodorize the room
2. *tatty* (presumably from Old English *taetteca,* "rag")—cheap; inferior

Imagine yourself visiting a Hindu friend at his home. He points to his wet screen and says, "Tatti!" You nod and reply "Yes, it does look cheap, doesn't it?"

Mistaking the identity of words can sometimes be as embarrassing as mixing up one person with another. I am reminded of Carl Sandburg's "Primer Lesson":

"Look out how you use proud words.
When you let proud words go, it is not easy to call them back.
They wear long boots, hard boots; they walk off proud; they
        can't hear you calling—
Look out how you use proud words."

A *tonga* is a light two-wheeled carriage used in India. The source is Hindi, *taṅgā*. To the best of my knowledge, the word has absolutely no consanguinity with the name for the Tonga Islands.

A *tulwar* is a curved scimitar or saber used in northern India and in other Oriental regions. The root of course is Hindi (*talwar*).

Tussah is another word of Hindi-Sanskrit origin. It's a silkworm that is the larva of a moth, and it's often cultivated, especially by the Chinese. Such fabrics as pongee and shantung are sometimes called *tussah* because they are made of this silk.

Alternate spellings are *tussore, tussor* and *tusser.*

Before we leave India, mention should be made of *swaraj* ("self-rule") and *Satyagraha,* which has come to mean "nonviolent agitation or passive resistance," although in Hindi it literally signifies "a grasping for truth." Both words can be found in the latest lexicons, and both were popularized by the great Mohandas Karamchand Gandhi, popularly regarded as the architect of Indian freedom.

Gandhi's spinning wheel, his long fasts, his unselfish desertion of a law practice in order to champion the rights of Indian settlers in South Africa—all these captured the imagination and sympathy of people throughout the world. His assassination in 1948 was universally mourned—but his avatar was Martin Luther King, Jr., who modeled himself after the Mahatma.

Both leaders remind me of an Indian practice called *dharna* (literally, "persistence"). It's a method of seeking justice by sitting peacefully and resolutely at the door of a debtor or wrongdoer and, if necessary, fasting to death!

In the previous section *Sanskrit* sources have been cited so often that the language deserves additional attention. Literally, the word means "well-arranged; put together perfectly; refined." And all those definitions are apt because *Sanskrit* is the classical standard language of India. Around 400 B.C. it was the official tongue of the court and the literary vehicle of Hindu culture. It is among the oldest Indo-European subfamilies; hence its importance is immense.

For our purposes a tiny sampling of words from *Sanskrit* will do:

dharma	mantra	sutra
karma	nirvana	swastika
mahatma	stupa	

Dharma literally means "law or custom." In Buddhism and Hinduism it has become synonymous with dutiful observance of cosmic moral laws—in other words, righteous conduct.

Karma and *kismet* have been loosely connected in our speech as synonyms for fate or destiny. The latter is of Turkish origin and really does mean "one's lot in life." *Karma,* on the other hand, means "deed, act or work." To a Hindu or Buddhist, *karma* is the force generated by his deeds that will determine his fate in his various future lives.

Mahatma stems from a Sanskrit word meaning "great soul." The word is reserved for a revered, wise and selfless person. Naturally, Gandhi earned the epithet.

Mantra was originally a Vedic hymn or prayer. Then it became a mystical incantation or formula for devotion. A person who practices TM (transcendental meditation) has a *mantra* as his special word, syllable or sound. Through the use of it he seeks to release his mind.

Nirvana in Buddhism or Hinduism is a certain state of absolute blessedness. We have adopted the word to mean "bliss, or freedom from care and pain." Because so many dope addicts and alcoholics fall into a deep stupor when they seek *nirvana,* the word has also become a synonym for oblivion.

Stupas are Buddhist shrines that resemble towers.

In Sanskrit, *sutra* means "string or thread"—hence, "a string of rules." The Brahmans of India use the word to signify a precept or aphorism or collection of such maxims as a guide to the conduct of life. In Buddhism, *sutra* is any of Buddha's sermons.

The *Kama Sutra* is a Hindu love manual written in the eighth century. It has recently become popular in America. *Kama,* as you may have guessed, means "love."

Swastika, ironically, means "well-being or benediction" in Sanskrit. It's a good-luck sign that dates back to prehistoric times. Unfortunately, the Nazis adopted this mystic symbol and turned it into an emblem of fascism and anti-Semitism.

Traveling southeast from India, we come to Malaya and Malaysia. The Indonesian language of the Malays has been widely used by merchants in the Far East. Consequently commerce is one of the chief reasons that Malayan words have seeped into our vocabulary. In this sampling the checked words will be briefly discussed.

batik	√cootie	sago
√caddy	kapok	√sarong
cockatoo	paddy	√tuan

A *caddy* is a small container for tea. The Malayan source is *kati,* a unit of weight that became Anglicized into *catty* (1⅓ pounds avoirdupois). At first the container of one *catty* of tea was spelled the same as the weight, but in time the *t*'s became *d*'s. It is also on the verge of losing its tea. A *caddy* may now be a device for holding or storing such items as phonograph records, cookies, plugs of tobacco, clothes, tools and even ice-cube trays.

The word should not be confused with *caddie,* the golfer's helper. Unfortunately, some people spell that attendant's name *caddy.* I'm against the variant. We have enough linguistic coincidences.

Cootie is slang for a body louse or nit. The British soldiers adopted the word from the Malayan-Polynesian *kutu* ("louse"). Soldiers on the front line often get *pediculosis* ("infestation with lice"). At such times they feel *pedicular* ("lousy"). Both of those words come from Latin. *Pedis* means "louse" and *pediculus* is the diminutive.

Nits, by the way, are young lice. The verb *nit-pick* is a derivative. When you nit-pick, you are concerning yourself with small, inconsequential details.

Nitwit is not a relation, but the new slang word *nitty-gritty* ("basic elements or facts") apparently has a lousy ancestry.

Are you beginning to feel itchy? Well, let's move on to something more pleasant.

Sarongs gave many a husband the seven-year itch* when Dorothy Lamour wore them in the thirties and forties. To the Malays the wraparound skirt means "sheath."

Tuan is the Malayan equivalent of sahib.

---

* *Seven-year-itch* was originally a synonym for the disease called scabies. Recently it has been given another connotation. A man who feels the urge to be unfaithful or fly the coop after being married about seven years is said to be stricken with the itch. The term was popularized as the title of a Marilyn Monroe-Tom Ewell film (1955).

Hawaii and other parts of Polynesia have supplied us with their share of interesting words. Here are a few from the fiftieth state:

Aloha is a Hawaiian's greeting or farewell. It literally means "love or kindness."

Hula is the native Hawaiian dance featuring pantomimic gestures.

Lanai is a veranda or porch. It is also the name of one of the Hawaiian Islands. In that sense the original word was *nanai* ("a swelling"), in reference to its topography.

Lei is a chaplet, wreath or garland, and has been the subject of endless vulgar jokes because of its pronunciation.

Luau is a Hawaiian feast, often featuring *poi,* a food that has been a boon to crossword puzzle constructors.

Nene (pronounced "nay-nay") is a nearly extinct Hawaiian goose and the state bird. It too is a standby in crossword puzzles.

Wahine is a word that the Hawaiians borrowed from the Maori. It means "woman, wife, sweetheart or mistress."

———

From Tahiti we have obtained such words as *taro* and *tattoo.*

Taro is a South Pacific staple. This large plant of the Arum genus is cultivated for its underground stems, which are the source of *poi.*

Tattoo ("make designs on the skin") and *tattoo* ("signal summoning soldiers to their quarters") present us with another etymological double take. The first comes from the Tahitians' *tatau.* The other is a Dutch derivative of *taptoe,* "shut the tap"—freely translated as "close the barroom."

———

The Australians are a creative group of word-painters. Their slang alone could be the subject of a treatise or a book. Here are just a few imports from down under.

Boomerang is a native name for a bent club that can be thrown so as to return to or near its starting point. We have developed several other meanings for that curved stick:

1. a statement or action that backfires on its originator
2. a movable platform for supporting painters of theater sets
3. a movable stand for supporting stage lights at different heights

Dingo is a native name for an Australian wild dog.

Kangaroos are leaping marsupial mammals of Australia, New Guinea and adjacent islands. Captain James Cook transmitted the native word to us after visiting the islands.

Another Australian animal is the *wallaby* (from the native name *wolabā*). This medium-sized marsupial is a smaller relation of the *kangaroo*.

One of the most interesting Maori words is *kiwi*. The name echoes the call of the bird. In colloquial speech a *Kiwi* is a New Zealander. The edible egg-sized fruit of a subtropical vine is also called a *kiwi*.

Finally, because the *kiwi* is a flightless bird, an air force member who stays on the ground is called by that name in military slanguage.

Speaking of birds, let us not omit the *kookaburra,* a large Australian kingfisher having a call that sounds like a raucous guffaw. It is called "laughing jackass" by the good-humored Australians.

T he Turks and Persians have endowed us with a fund of words. Let's examine a sampling from Turkey first. Three of their V.I.P.s are *khan*, *pasha* and *vizier*.

Khan means "lord or prince." A man named Temuchin became a Mongol conqueror in the thirteenth century; he took the name Genghis Khan and swept through northern China, central Asia, Russia and Bulgaria. His grandson, Batu, led the Golden Horde, which broke up into separate *khanates* in the Crimea.

Pasha is another title appended to a Turkish chief's name. Ali Pasha ("Lion of Janina") was a famous Turkish governor of Albania, where he was born. He is a legendary hero among Albanian and Greek mountaineers because of his exploits as a brigand in those regions. His brigand court at Janina is described in Byron's CHILDE HAROLD's PILGRIMAGE.

Vizier is the most interesting of the trio because of its derivation. Literally, the title means "bearer of burdens; porter," because this high officer in Moslem lands performs the tasks that should be the responsibility of the ruler.

In the area of clothing, *caftan, caracal* and *fez* are among the Turkish words familiar to us.

Caftans are coatlike robes with long sleeves and sashes. They are worn throughout the Near East. Some lexicographers claim that the word comes from the Russians rather than the Turks. It can be traced back to the Persians' *quaftān*.

Caracal is the fur for coats obtained from the reddish brown lynx of the same name. Literally, the original Turkish word means "black ear." The word was transmitted to us via the French.

Fez also comes to us through the Gallic channel. This red brimless, conical felt hat was once the headdress of Turkish men.

———

Two of the Turkish foods we have been introduced to are *baklava* and *yogurt*. The former is a dessert made of paper-thin layers of pastry, chopped nuts and honey. The main accent is on the last syllable, as when a nondieter exclaims, "Ah! *Baklavá!*"

The popularity of *yogurt* (sometimes spelled *yoghurt*) has increased by leaps and bounds in recent decades because of the growing interest in health foods. This custardlike food, prepared with milk altered by bacteria, is reputed to be the staple of hundreds of people who have attained remarkable longevity.

———

Have you ever seen a *chibouk?* It's a tobacco pipe with a long stem and a clay bowl. The *hookah* (from Arabia) and *nargileh* or *narghile* (from Persia) are also pipes for smoking. The latter literally means "coconut," because the bowls were originally made from that fruit of a palm.

———

Puzzle fans are familiar with *imaret* and *minaret*. The former is a Turkish inn, and the latter is a tall, slender tower on a mosque. The Arabian ancestors meant "lamp or lighthouse" and eventually "candlestick." If you have ever seen a *minaret* or picture of one, you'll agree that it does look like a gigantic candlestick.

———

Finally, there is *dervish,* a word that the Turks borrowed from the Persian *darvēsh* ("beggar"). This member of a Moslem order dedicated to poverty and chastity sometimes practices howling, chanting, dancing or spinning around as religious acts. The spinners are called *whirling dervishes*—a term that has captured the imagination of Americans.

Would a G.I. seeing a *whirling dervish* get nervish in the servish? I wonder if Ogden Nash ever tackled the subject?

———

Turning to the Persians, let us examine a brief selection of our inheritances from that great ancient people. But let me note at this point that Persian, Turkish and Arabian legacies often become mingled, as borrowing among the three groups continued through the ages. Furthermore, we are often indebted to the French, who acted as middlemen in the transition to English.

baksheesh	caravansary	divan
bazaar	cassock	houri

Baksheesh (or *bakshish*) eventually comes to us from Persia, although a number of other countries got into the act. The word means "a gratuity, tip or alms."

Bazaar is derived from the Persians' *bazar* ("market"). In the Orient it still retains that meaning. We have slightly enlarged the connotations. There are church *bazaars* and other sales run by clubs. Also, *bazaars* have become synonymous with department stores and fairs.

Caravansaries are Eastern inns at which companies of travelers stop at night. The word *caravan* of course is related—and the French are the transmitters.

Cassocks are long outer garments worn by clergymen, altar boys and choristers. The ultimate Persian root is *kazh* ("raw silk"). Again the intermediaries are the French; their word is *casaque*.

Divan in its early Persian form signified "an account book." What an amazing metamorphosis in meaning the word has undergone through the centuries! Let's try to trace it via metonymy. First, the office in which the accounts were tabulated became the *divan*. Later the special couch for that agency (or for a council room) was called a *divan*.

Here are some of the meanings for the word:

1. the Turkish privy council that was presided over by the sultan or grand vizier (sometimes spelled *diwan*)
2. any council
3. Muslim court of justice
4. smoking room
5. large, low couch; sofa; davenport
6. collection of Persian or Arabic poems, especially by one author (also spelled *diwan*)

The variety of definitions for *divan* prompts me to mention one of the problems encountered by a crossword puzzle editor. Whenever a clue zeroes in on one of the meanings that are not widely known, angry letters often follow. For example, in every dictionary at my command *alamode* is defined as "a thin, glossy silk." Several fans who were only familiar with pie *a la mode* refused to look up the word when I used the above clue; they insinuated that I had made an error or had attempted to show off. Imagine what would be the reactions to some of the authorized but less well-known definitions of *divan!*

Houri could well be credited to the French or the Arabs. The Persians are in the middle. The original Arabic word (huriyah) meant "black-eyed woman." The Persians liked the term and developed it into *huri,* which the French altered into *houri.* Two definitions are:

1. a beautiful dark-eyed nymph or virgin of the Moslem Paradise. (Good Moslems will be rewarded by the companionship of *houris* when they die.)
2. a voluptuous, seductive pulchritudinous woman

A pious old Moslem named Yuri
Was promised that he'd meet a *houri.*
But after he died
He discovered they'd lied,
And, brother, was he in a fury!

———

Our language owes much to the Arabs too. First, let's consider a small selection of people—some good and some evil:

assassin	fellah
Bedouin	ghoul
emir	sultan
fakir	

Assassin comes from an Arabian word meaning "hashish users." The original *Assassins* were members of a secret, fanatical Moslem order during the Crusades. While reputedly under the influence of hashish, they terrorized and killed Christians.

"Hashish" is the Arabian word for dried hemp. A drug formed from the resin of the plant has an intoxicating or euphoric effect when chewed or smoked.

Today we generally restrict the meaning of *assassin* to "a murderer of a politically important person"; but the word can be applied to any ruthless killer, especially one who strikes suddenly.

———

The *Bedouins* are wandering Arab tribes of Syria, Arabia and North Africa. Hence their name is sometimes used in English as a synonym for *nomads.*

Strangely enough, *nomad* is not of Arabic extraction. Its source is *nomas,* a Greek word meaning "wandering about for pasture"—which is exactly what the *Bedouins* and other *nomads* do.

———

Emir and its variations—*emeer, amir* and *ameer*—eventually stem from *amara,* an Arabian word meaning "to command." These Moslem rulers are favorites of crossword puzzle constructors because the craft often calls for a word to begin with a vowel; also, it is relatively easy to fit the other letters into crossing words. A derivative word, *emirate,* also appears often in puzzles.

———

Fakir comes from *faquir* ("a poor man"). *Fakirs* are ascetic Moslem or Hindu mendicants, often on the move. Since some of them claim to be wonder-workers, naturally folks equate them with *fakers*—a word with a different linguistic history.

The pale orange-yellow color *peachblow* is also called *fakir*. I confess I don't know why.

———

A *fellah* is an Arabian peasant or agricultural laborer. The word comes from a verb meaning "to plow." The Arabian plurals are *fellaheen* or *fellahin*. The Broadway musical THE MOST HAPPY FELLA has nothing to do with these hardworking *fellahs*.

———

Ghoul comes from the Arabian noun *ghūl* ("demon of the mountains"). In Moslem folklore, this evil spirit was reputed to rob graves and feed on corpses. Ugh!

To us *ghoul* is a human grave robber or body snatcher. His purpose is usually to obtain valuables or to remove the corpse for illicit dissection.

Our adjective *ghoulish* is a synonym for revolting.

———

Sultan means "ruler" in Arabian. It was once the title for the ruler of Turkey. A *sultanate* is the office of this chief or the region over which he presides.

A *sultana* is the ruler's wife, mother, daughter or sister. Sometimes she is called *sultaness*.

There is also a *sultana bird* (named for its rich exotic plumage). Finally, a pale yellow seedless grape is called *sultana*. The raisin from the fruit bears the same name.

———

Here is a miniature miscellany of some other Arab exports to English-speaking nations:

hajj	jihad	sofa
harem	jinn	tamarind
hegira	kebab	tambourine
henna	salaam	wadi

Hajj (sometimes spelled *hadj* or *haj*) is the pilgrimage to Mecca that all Moslems are required to take at least once in their lives. Such a pilgrim becomes a *hajji*—a title of honor in Islam.

Hajji brings back some fond memories of my years as a young English teacher in Frederick Douglass Junior High School. During that period I read a book by James Morier called HAJJI BABA OF ISPAHAN. The hero's adventures delighted me so much that I decided to share one of them with the pupils in my seventh-grade homeroom class during the last period on a Friday afternoon. The boys listened raptly as I related a tale of capture by the "bad guys" and the thrilling escape.

A week later, when we assembled in the morning, several members of the class asked to be told another Hajji Baba story. I promised that I would tell them one that afternoon if they behaved themselves all day. Well, they acted like little angels in every room that they visited! The other teachers scrawled nothing but compliments on the "class sheet" that was carried from room to room. And so, from 2:15 to 3:00 P.M., I spun another Hajji Baba yarn.

This practice continued month after month. Soon I ran out of episodes from the book and had to make up my own. It was a fascinating experience in instant creativity. Often I had no idea how a particular tale would unfold. But I developed a "Perils of Pauline" technique. Poor Hajji was always left in a horrendous situation as the bell rang at 3:00 P.M. With all the drama that I could muster in my voice, I would say: "What will happen to Hajji Baba now? Will the snakes in the deep pit sink their poisonous fangs into him as he lies helpless? Listen next week! Class dismissed!"

Grateful for the good conduct of at least one class, my colleagues became curious about the "Friday miracle of 7-5" (the designation of my group). After they heard what I was doing they nicknamed me Hajji.

To this day I still receive occasional letters from some of those former pupils. They never fail to mention "good old Hajji." Thank you, Mr. Morier, wherever you are.

Harem comes from the Arabian noun *harim* ("sacred, forbidden place"). It is a house or section of a house in which the Moslem women live. The word can also be applied to the women themselves. For example, a sultan's wives, concubines and maidservants form a *harem*.

An extended meaning is "a number of female animals that surround and mate with a single male." Bulls among the fur seals, and stallions in a group of mustangs accumulate *harems,* which they protect jealously from other males. The sex drive of the bulls among the fur seals is especially fantastic. They often go without food for as long as six weeks and spend their time chasing off young bulls, returning errant females to the pack, and, of course, mating. One bull may have as many as a hundred females in his *harem,* and his weight is four times as great as that of his average mate.

Incidentally, the sultans did not invent *harems.* The ancient Greeks and Romans had such quarters set apart for females. A place of this kind was called a *gynaeceum.*

The original *Hegira* was the flight of Mohammed from Mecca to Medina in 622 A.D. The ultimate Arabic source is *hajara* ("to depart"). In English we use *hegira* to mean "any flight from danger." By extension it has even become synonymous with an emigration or mass exodus.

An alternate spelling is *hejira*. The alert reader may have observed that such variants have been cited throughout this chapter. The chief problem is transliteration. When another language uses alphabetic characters different from our own, our scholars estimate by the sounds how a word would be spelled if it were transliterated into English. Often the experts or the original transliterators from different disciplines do not see eye to eye. As a result, there are sometimes four or five different spellings vying with one another for acceptance as the best of the lot.

The problem is especially prevalent in our adoption of words from such languages as Greek, Arabic, Hebrew, Russian, Sanskrit, Japanese and Chinese. Newspaper officials are constantly confronted with perplexities involving transliteration. For example, when a new Chinese leader emerges, how should his hieroglyphic name be spelled in English? Is he Dung, Tung or Tong, or would he spell as sweet by any other name? Chinese-American specialists are contacted. Lo and behold, they disagree. One is reminded of the pun "One man's Mede is another man's Persian."

Beauticians and the women who frequent their salons are well acquainted with *henna* as a dye or rinse, but it's a good guess that most of them do not know that the word has an Arabic origin. *Henna* is an Old World tropical shrub or little tree. The leaves yield an auburn dye that converts a gray-haired dowager into a kind of redhead. Can you complete this limerick?

> There was an old henna from Penna
> Who sought to attract many menna . . .

Jihad has come to mean "crusade or bitter strife." The original Arabic word carries the idea of holy war. Recently I read a magazine article that referred to Ralph Nader's *jihad* against General Motors and other corporations. Thus do the senses of words become enlarged. I sometimes wonder how often the show-offs are the pioneers in the expansion of meanings.

Jinn is the plural of *jinni*. One would think that the opposite would be true. What's a *jinni*? In Moslem legend it's a good or evil spirit that can assume the form of an animal or a human and exercise power in one's daily life.

Note that the word can be spelled *djin* or *djinn* (transliteration difficulties again!). Hajji Baba often found *jinn* in his cocktail glasses, and at such times he added a drop of dry vermouth and called them martinis.

Seriously, most Americans don't know a *jinni* from a *hinny* ("mule"), but they do cotton to *genie,* because of Aladdin and his lamp. *Genie* is a corruption of *jinni,* influenced by the French *génie* ("spirit"). However, its ultimate source is the Latin word *genius* ("guardian spirit").

———

Kebab can be *kabob* can be *kabab* can be *kebob* can be *cabob,* according to what transliterator is your favorite. The Arabic ancestor is a skewered preparation containing bits of marinated meat. Prefix the word *shish* (Arabic for "skewer") and you have an entree that is very popular today but was little known in our grandparents' era.

———

Salaam is a relative of *shalom,* the Hebrew word for "peace." Just as the Israelis use their word as a greeting, so do the Syrians, Egyptians et al. Since the Arabs' ritual compliment is often complemented by a low bow, with the palm of the right hand placed on the forehead, we have interpreted *salaam* to mean a sign of obeisance; when you *salaam* someone, you pay homage to him.

There is no truth to the rumor that Babe Ruth was called "the Sultan of Swat" because he greeted many a pitcher with a *grand salaam.*

In case the pronunciation is unfamiliar to you, think of "salami" with the last syllable truncated.

———

Sofa comes from *suffah,* the Arabic word meaning "cushion or long bench." We have gone beyond the divan or settee; now being marketed are *sofa beds* and even *sofa tables.*

In the East a *sofa* is a dais fitted with cushions and carpets for reclining above the main floor.

———

A *tamarind* is a tropical Old World tree yielding an edible fruit. Literally, the Arabic source, *tamr hindi,* means "date of India."

———

Tambourine comes from a French diminutive alteration of the Arabic *tanbūr,* which in turn is borrowed from a Persian word meaning "drum." The *tambourine* is a little hand drum with jingling metal disks, and is often used by exotic dancers.

Relations include the *tambourin* ("long, narrow drum used in Provence") and *tamboura* ("Indian lute with a droning sound").

Most interesting is the *tambour* because of its many meanings. Among them are:

    1. drum or drummer
    2. wall of a circular building surrounded by columns
    3. embroidery frame or the embroidery made on such a frame

4. kind of lace
5. rolling top of a desk

All that, and more, from one little drum!

———

Wadi has two basic and rather contradictory meanings.

1. a dry riverbed, gully or ravine in North Africa or Southeast Asia
2. the stream that flows through such a valley

To complicate the picture further, a *wadi* can also be a synonym for an oasis. I think I hear some reader exclaiming *"Wadi* y'know!"
The Arabic root, *wādī,* means "channel."
In case you're wondering, *wade* is not even distantly related.

———

N ext let's look at a sampling of words of African origin.

banjo	gumbo	tsetse fly
chigger	marimba	voodoo
cola	mumbo jumbo	zombie
gnu	safari	

The *banjo* has spawned some interesting scions. For instance, there's the *banjorine.* It has a short neck and is tuned a fourth higher than its sire. Too bad that no one has composed a song about the instrument. It would be a natural for Helen O'Connell.

Banjo clocks and *banjo ukuleles* were so called because of their shape. There is also a miner's shovel called a *banjo* because of its resemblance to the instrument.

Perhaps some authority on baseball jargon can tell me why a fly ball that falls safely just behind the infield is called a *banjo hit.* I can understand how such synonymous terms as "blooper" and "dying quail" originated, but not *banjo hit.* Perhaps it stems from the trajectory of the fly ball, or maybe from the idea that the batter might just as well have held a *banjo* in his hand when he was lucky enough to get the hit.

———

Chiggers are blood-sucking larval mites. The original African name, which we also use, was *jigger.*

By coincidence, a pestiferous flea of the West Indies was named *chigoe.* Because *chigger* and *chigoe* are so similar in sound and also so small and irritating to the skin, people began to interchange the names. Purists and entomologists* may be aghast, but usage always wins out.

* *Entomologists*—specialists in the study of insects

The *chigger* is also called "harvest mite" and "red bug."

Cola is a Latinized variant of *kola,* an African tree or the nut that grows on it, and is a source of caffeine. Of course the carbonated beverage that is produced from an extract of the nut is known all over the world.

But few people realize that *cola* also means "a queue or line of people"—from the Spanish noun for "tail."

Cola is also the plural of that part of the body called the *colon.* Finally, it is the plural of another *colon*—"rhythmic unit in Latin or Greek verse."

The *gnu* pops up in puns and crossword puzzles now and then. It is one of the relatively few African animals bearing names of native origin. The rhinoceros and hippopotamus are among many with Greek appellations. Giraffes bear a French stamp, and zebras got their name from the Spanish and Portuguese. And Leo the Lion has a Latin-Greek linguistic history, even though the Bantu tribesmen called him *simba.* Of course the natives had their own names for other animals, but the invading foreigners often preferred Indo-European terms.

Not so with the *gnu.* Bushmen called it *ngu*—and you can't blame the English for switching the first two letters.

It may interest you to learn that this large antelope has been nicknamed "the horned horse" because its mane, tail and general appearance have an equine resemblance. And the *brindled gnu* (or *blue wildebeest*) is sometimes called "kokoon"—another native name.

I should also note that two smaller antelopes, the *impala* and the *kudu,* were respectively named by the Zulus and Hottentots; and the *okapi* (cousin of a giraffe) was so called by the natives of Central Africa.

Gumbo (the Bantu name for okra) has many meanings:

1. thick soup made from okra pods
2. thick jam made from one or more fruits
3. fine-grained, silty soil of American prairies
4. heavy, sticky mud
5. patois spoken by Creoles and blacks, especially in Louisiana
6. mixture; olio; mélange

The *marimba* is a percussion instrument resembling a xylophone.

Mumbo jumbo has several meanings:

1. any fetish or idol
2. an object to be dreaded
3. a complicated ritual with many trappings
4. a nonsensical activity intended to confuse
5. senseless language; gibberish

The first definition stems from the fact that *Mumbo Jumbo* was an idol reputed to have been venerated by some African tribes. The Europeans' lack of understanding of the worshipers' language and ceremonies presumably gave rise to the later connotations.

Safari comes to us from the Arabs via Swahili. The Arabic verb *safara* means "to travel." It's interesting to observe the expanded uses of the traditional hunting expedition that delighted Hemingway, among others. Because of rising concern for the conservation of the wild animals, many a *safari* today is enjoyed by tourists with loaded cameras instead of loaded guns.

The *tsetse fly* of crossword puzzle fame received its name from the Bantus. The bite of one species causes *nagana*—a Zulu word for a disease of horses and cattle. The pest can also bring on sleeping sickness.

One would think that *voodoo* had a West Indian origin, because the religion or practice is prevalent in that region. Actually, the Creole French borrowed the word from ancestor-worshiping people of West Africa. The noun *vodu* means "fetish or demon." Today *voodoo* is a synonym for black magic, hex or jinx.

Hoodoo is also a synonym for *voodoo;* and it, too, has African roots. some lexicographers presume that it's merely a variation of *voodoo;* others suspect that it arose from the Hausa people of the Sudan and meant "to arouse resentment against another person." At any rate, the word is commonly associated with bad luck.

Sometimes a *hoodoo* is called a *Jonah.* That's because the Hebrew prophet disobeyed God's command while sailing on a ship and caused a storm to endanger the lives of his fellow travelers. *Jonah,* you will recall, is the fellow who had a whale of a time.

In West Africa the *zombie* was a python deity worshiped by tribes that practiced voodooism. Some Haitians and cults in southern United States have adopted the deity. The believers maintain that a supernatural force can enter a corpse and bring the body back to life in a kind of trance. Like a robot, the person who is reanimated will obey commands automatically.

Thus the name of the deity itself became synonymous with the walking dead. This led to three other connotations:

1. a listless or phlegmatic person, easily maneuvered
2. a "weirdo" or "sap"
3. an ugly or odd person

Some bartender with a strange sense of humor invented a tall iced drink that he called a *zombie*. It contains several kinds of fruit juices, varieties of rum, and apricot brandy. Did he give it the name because *zombies* in movies are usually depicted as gigantic creatures? Then again, the drink could possibly put you into a trance or even immobilize you like a python's fangs.

Afrikaners have also endowed us with some interesting words. Let's start with *Boer* itself. This Dutch noun means "peasant." Because a son of the soil was considered to be rude and clumsy and lacking in social graces, our word *boor* cropped up. No pun intended.

The *Boers* are South Africans whose ancestors were Dutch farmers who settled in the area of the Cape of Good Hope in the seventeenth century. The original colonists ran into lots of trouble and were forced to spread out, but they maintained a stubborn, courageous spirit and never shirked hard work. Their descendants resisted the British with remarkable tenacity during the *Boer War* (1899–1902).

Here is a brief selection of Afrikaner words* that have entered our language:

commandeer	eland	veld
commando	kraal	wildebeest
dorp	trek	

Commandeer stems from *kommandeeren,* a Dutch verb meaning "to command." It has three basic meanings:

1. to compel a person to give military service
2. to appropriate, as property, for military purposes
3. to seize arbitrarily for one's own use

Commando is a word that the Boers borrowed from the Portuguese and Spanish, but they popularized it so much that we took it over. To Afrikaners a *commando* is a raid or expedition; it is also their word for militia service in the army, or a force of troops.

To us a *commando* is a soldier specially trained for hit-and-run tactics in enemy territory.

---

* The official language of the Afrikaners, or Boers, in South Africa is called Afrikaans—a development of seventeenth-century Dutch

Dorp has a Dutch ancestry. In South Africa it's a village or township.

———

An *eland,* as most puzzle fans know, is an oxlike antelope of Africa. To the Boers it looked like an elk, so they gave it the Dutch name for that animal.

The Zulus call it by another name—*impofu.* That appellation has entered our unabridged dictionaries as *impofo,* but it's a sure bet that few people have any acquaintance with the name.

The *eland* has many smaller cousins. Among them are the *dik-dik* (Ethiopian native name), *oryx* (from Greek, "pickax") and the *klip-springer.* You can guess that the Boers originated the name for that agile antelope. Their word *klip* means "rock or cliff."

———

Kraal is another Afrikaner borrowing from the Portuguese, whose *curral* means "pen for cattle." Our word *corral* is a derivative of course.

There are several definitions for *kraal,* and the final one is quite shameful:

1. an enclosure for domestic animals, such as cattle and sheep, in South Africa
2. a pen for elephants in Thailand, Sri Lanka and India
3. an enclosure for keeping lobsters, turtles and sponges alive in shallow water
4. a village of South African blacks usually surrounded by a stockade

I am reminded of another word that the Boers have dropped into our language with a horrendous thud—*apartheid.* This is their word for "apartness," and it stands for strict racial segregation.

———

Trek in South Africa means "to travel by ox wagon." Since this mode is quite different from roaring down Route 66 in a Cadillac, the verb also means "to make a slow, difficult journey." As a noun it signifies the journey itself. The derivation, naturally, is Dutch: *trekken* means "to draw along or travel."

We have not only accepted the Boers' verbal and nominal usages of *trek* but have also enlarged the sense to mean "migrate or migration."

———

Veld (or *veldt*) is the South African grassland where the *eland* and the *dik-dik* roam. In Dutch, *veld* means "field."

———

When I first saw *wildebeest* in print I thought that someone in the composing room was three sheets to the wind. I pronounced the word as "wild beast"; later I discovered that the correct orthoepic sound is "will-da-beest."

This variety of the *gnu* actually means "wild beast" in Dutch. Can you imagine the amazement of those early emigrants from Holland when they first encountered all those strange, nameless African animals thundering forward in immense herds?

And how did they react when they first discovered (and named) the *aardvark* busily burrowing for ants and termites? Did they bring home the mammals and use them as exterminators or did they shrink in repulsion when they saw that long snout, large ears, hairy body and sharp claws?

Picture, too, a Dutch husbandman in South Africa encountering the striped hyenalike, fierce-looking *aardwolf*. I doubt that the poor emigrant would realize that he had little to worry about. How would he know at first that the animal had a taste for termites and insect larvae—and not for men?

For those readers who are devotees of etymology (may your name be legion!), the *aardvark* literally means "earth pig" in Dutch, and the *aardwolf* means "earth wolf." Do I hear someone saying, "What an *aard* name"?

Since we have been talking so much about the Hollanders, let's move over to Europe and take a quick look at a few of their other contributions to the English language:

burgomaster	monsoon
cruller	polder
howitzer	sloop
kermis	

A *burgomaster* is the mayor or chief magistrate of a town or city in the Netherlands, Austria, Germany or Flanders. Our word *borough* is a relation.

Those tasty twisted doughnuts called *crullers* are from the Dutch verb *krullen* ("to curl"). *Curl* is a member of this family.

A *howitzer* is a short cannon for firing shells in a high trajectory. The Dutch borrowed the word from the Germans and Czechs. Originally it meant "a sling."

Kermis (sometimes spelled *kermess*) is a charitable fair or entertainment. The original Dutch word literally means "church Mass." The association with fairs comes about because on the feast day of a patron saint the Dutch would organize a kind of carnival.

Monsoon is a word that Holland borrowed from Portugal long ago. The Portuguese in turn had taken it from the Arabs. When a *monsoon* blows from the southwest during the period between April and October it brings heavy rains to India and its neighbors. Hence *monsoon* has come to mean "rainy season."

Polders are low-lying lands that the Dutch have cleverly reclaimed from the sea, usually through the construction of dikes.

A *sloop* is a fore-and-aft rigged sailing vessel with a mainsail and a jib. It has but one mast. The Dutch source is *sloep.*

Possibly a relation is the little French harbor craft called *chaloupe.*

By coincidence, there is another *sloop,* the origin of which is unknown. It's a logger's dray or sled. To *sloop,* in lumberjack's jargon, is to haul logs down a steep slope on one of those sledlike devices. Could it be possible that this *sloop* is a variation of *slope?* In any case, the boss of the operation is a *sloopman.*

Before we leave the Netherlands, some attention should be paid to such expressions as *that beats the Dutch, get in Dutch, go Dutch* and *Dutch treat.* Why do we pick on the Dutchmen? The answer probably stems from the colonial and commercial competition between England and Holland during the seventeenth century. The British were annoyed by the tenacity, intensity and frugality of their eastern neighbors; but they apparently also had a grudging respect for such qualities. For example, *beating the Dutch* came to mean "performing an extraordinary act," and *in Dutch* took on the meaning "in disfavor or trouble."

Less respectful are *Dutch treat* and *go Dutch;* both phrases snidely suggest that a host in Amsterdam would require his guests to foot the bill with him on an even basis. And *Dutch courage* insinuates that a Hollander needs an intoxicant in order to get up his nerve. *Dutch auction* is also derogatory. It conveys the idea that you set a high price at a sale and gradually lower it until a buyer is found. And then there's the *Dutch concert*—a babel of noises. Let's hope that such aspersions on a fine group of people become obsolete in the near future.

On a more pleasant note, consider *Dutchman's breeches.* This delicate spring wildflower is so called because of the shape of its blossoms.

Heading northeast, we come to the Scandinavians. Here is a salmagundi* of a few of the words given to us by the Swedes, Norwegians
and Danes.

fiord	rutabaga	skoal
narwhal	saga	slalom
ombudsman	ski	

Fiord (or *fjord*) is a narrow inlet between steep cliffs. People who
have visited Norway tell me that a boat trip on such an arm of the sea
is breathtakingly picturesque. In fact, it's "gorge-ous."
Our verb *ford* is a relation.

Narwhal has a Danish-Norwegian ancestry. In old Norse, *nāhvair*
meant "corpse-whale." The name came about because of the arctic
cetacean's habit of floating upside down, thus displaying its white un-
derside and resembling a floating dead body. Whalers hunt it for ivory
and oil.

Ombudsman is delightful and a rather recent import from Sweden,
where *ombud* means "deputy or representative." In Scandinavian
lands this official investigates complaints against the government.
    When I worked for six years at the Board of Education in New
York City, I suggested that an *ombudsman* be appointed in each borough to feed back the feelings of the parents and other citizens concerning the instruction of the children, condition of the schools and
other matters relating to their educational environment. The idea was
turned down. Unfortunately there were no Scandinavians in high
places in the ivory tower.

Rutabagas are turnips with large yellow roots and are often called
"Swedish turnips." The British call them "Swedes." The word stems
from a Swedish dialectal noun, *rotabagge* ("baggy root").
    Carl Sandburg, the great American poet, who was the son of poor
Swedish immigrants in Illinois, wrote ROOTABAGA STORIES (1922). In
these "moral tales" for young children, I'm sure he had his own roots
in mind. Incidentally, he followed up a year later with ROOTABAGA
PIGEONS.

---

* *Salmagundi* is a mixture, or potpourri. In its original sense it's a salad of
chopped meat, anchovies, eggs and onions. We borrowed the noun from the French
salmigondis, and they may have taken their word from the Italian phrase *salame conditi*
("salt-flavored"—hence, "pickled meat").

In Old Norse a *saga* was a story. It still is today. Usually we think of it as a lengthy adventure tale. Galsworthy's THE FORSYTE SAGA consists of a number of books that relate the ups and downs of several generations in the same family.

Icelandic manuscripts of the twelfth and thirteenth centuries are also called *sagas*. Other Icelandic literary works of approximately the same period are called *Eddas*—a word familiar to crossword puzzle fans. An *Edda* is also a collection of Old Norse poetry.

Another Old Norse word, *skith* ("snowshoe"), has given us *ski*. As in many other cases, the noun has also been converted into a verb. Besides *skiers* there are also, for example, *ski poles, ski jumps* and *ski boots* in the popular winter sport called *skiing*. And let us not forget the summery derivative, *water-skiing*.

Skoal, too, has an Old Norse ancestry. *Skal* meant "a drinking cup." The Danes and Swedes also deserve credit somewhere along the line for transmitting the drinking toast to us. Today it means "To your health!" You may have heard about the beer-drinking freshman who dropped out of college; he decided he'd rather go to *skoal*.

In one tale that I've heard about *skoal,* the word is allegedly related to *skull* and stems from the ancient Vikings' practice of drinking mead from their dead enemies' bony toppers. I can't find any proof for that colorful account, but it's true that *scalp* is a linguistic cousin of *skoal*.

Slalom is one of several Norwegian words introduced into English because so many people love to glide down the hills on long, flat runners. To a citizen of Oslo a *slalom* literally means "a sloping path." It has come to signify the act of skiing in a zigzag course. *Slalom races* are exciting events in winter Olympics.

As we have noted previously in this chapter, diverse groups from various European lands have helped immensely in the enrichment of our vocabulary. Preeminent among them are the sailors, settlers, traders and soldiers.

Portuguese people in those four categories present us with excellent examples of how words from one language can seep into another language and spread into many others as time elapses. For instance, let's look at Brazil and ask ourselves two questions:

Why is a modified form of Portuguese the official language of Brazil?

Why are so many Portuguese words emanating from Brazil of Tupi-Guarani origin?

The answer to the first question can be traced back to the Portuguese navigators of the fifteenth and sixteenth centuries. In April 1500, Pedro Alvarez Cabral landed in Brazil and claimed the region for his native land. Colonists and traders from Portugal soon established a footing there.

But the indigenous Tupi tribes resisted the invasion of their land by strange settlers, and many battles ensued. As in the case of the North American Indians, the better equipped foreigners finally prevailed. But association with the Tupis, whether hostile or friendly, eventually caused a number of words from their speech to be embraced by the Portuguese. They in turn disseminated the new vocabulary to other lands and languages. Here are a few examples of Tupi-Portuguese words that we use:

WORD	DEFINITION	ORIGINAL WORD
carioca	1. (capitalized) native or resident of Rio de Janeiro 2. ballroom dance or music for it	*cari* (*"white"*), *oca* ("house")
cashew	tropical evergreen tree yielding edible, kidney-shaped nuts	*acajú*
macaw	brightly colored parrot	*macao*
paca	burrowing rodent of South and Central America	*páca*
piranha	vicious, voracious South American fish (also called *caribe,* "cannibal")	*piranha* ("toothed fish")

It's also interesting to note that in Paraguay, a neighbor of Brazil, about 90 percent of the people speak Guarani. Spanish is the secondary language.

The Portuguese borrowed not only from the Tupi people but also from others around the world. In Africa they found the dance called the *samba* and a lemur called *macaco.* In Malay they discovered the *betel nut,* and in India the *mango* (tree or fruit) and *copra* (dried coconut meat) from which coconut oil is extracted. Persia gave them the *pagoda.*

The Caribs and Tupis taught the foreigners a lethal lesson when they poisoned their arrows with *curare,* a resinous substance obtained from tropical plants. The word is also spelled *curari, curara* or *urari.* In Tupi talk that last spelling means "he to whom it comes falls."

Palanquin (or *palankeen*) is our alteration of the Portuguese noun *palanquim.* This covered litter carried by poles on the shoulders of two or more men was once a favorite vehicle for V.I.P.s in eastern Asia. The source is Javanese, and the word is ultimately *palyañka* in Sanskrit.

Another export from Java to Portugal is the Chinese *junk*. The Javanese word is *joñ;* the Portuguese altered it into *junco,* and we turned the boat back into a monosyllabic noun. Lexicographers disagree on the origin of the other *junk,* meaning "trash."

Finally, here is a small taste of words that have come to us from the ancient Romans via Portuguese:

albino	cobra	pintado
auto-da-fé	lingo	sargasso

Albino means "whitish" in Lisbon. The condition of *albinism* is caused by genetic factors. *Albinos* have white skin and hair and pink eyes. The pigmentation problem also affects animals; for example, there are *albino* elephants, mice and rabbits. Some plants that lack coloration are also *albinos.*

———

Auto-da-fé literally means "act of faith." The leaders of the Inquisition used this expression to indicate that their devotion to their religion was strong enough to warrant the burning of heretics on pyres. Their pronouncements and precombustion ceremonies were called *autos-da-fé.* The execution of a nonbeliever soon came to be called *auto-da-fé.*

The Latin ancestry combines *actus* ("a doing or act") with *fides* ("faith").

———

Cobra is a shortening of *cobra de capello,* which means "snake of the hood" in Portuguese. There is also a *cobra plant* on our Pacific coast. It was so called because its curled hoodlike leaf contains a forked, tonguelike appendage.

———

Lingo is an alteration of *lingoa* ("tongue" in Portuguese). The Latin grandparent is *lingua.* To us a speech that is regarded as strange or unintelligible is a *lingo.* Synonyms are jargon, cant, argot and even dialect.

Coming back to the Latin origin, through the Italians, we have inherited *lingua franca* ("Frankish language"). The expression now describes any hybrid speech used as a form of communication between people with different languages. Pidgin English is an example. In its early usage *lingua franca* was a mixture of French, Arabic, Greek, Turkish, Spanish—and, of course, Italian. Traders in the Levant and other Mediterranean areas learned the *lingo* by hook or by crook. I must say that I admire them. It's difficult enough to acquire facility in only one foreign language. Can you imagine the intellectual acuity needed to understand a salmagundi of words in a half dozen tongues?

> Oh, my golly, what
> Amazement have I got
> For every polyglot—
> Something I am not!

Pintado may be familiar to fishermen, seamstresses and bird watchers. The word literally means "painted" in Portugal. The Latin ancestor is *pingere* ("to paint"). Here are some definitions:

1. a long silvery edible game fish
2. a painted or printed chintz once made in India
3. a Cape pigeon, or black-and-white petrel

As a fish the *pintado* is also called *cero*. Crossword-puzzlers will recognize that word.

———

Sargasso is a seaweed. The Portuguese parent is *sargaço*. A related word, via Modern Latin, is *sargassum*—also a variety of seaweed.

The *Sargasso Sea* is a notoriously calm area northeast of the West Indies. Many ships have been stuck in the *sargasso* or *sargassum* abundantly growing in the water. The plant is also called *gulfweed*.

———

As one of Polish-Lithuanian-Irish ancestry, it grieves me to report that our store of words from my father's side is meager. Of course we enjoy such lively dances as the *mazurka* and the *polka,* and some of us may know that a *britska* (or *britzka*) is a long roomy horse-drawn carriage with a folding top.

Readers may remember my point that conquerors introduce their words into other languages. The Poles and Lithuanians have more often been victims than victors. In such suppressive circumstances their linguistic contributions could hardly be impressive. Additionally, it should be noted that various treaties have mongrelized Poland and Lithuania. For example, after World War I the dignitaries at Versailles arranged boundaries in such a way that 40 percent of the people in Poland were national minorities of German, Ukrainian and other backgrounds.

But the Irish, so close to England and so stubbornly resistant to subjection by their powerful neighbors, have given us an interesting fund of words, many of Gaelic or Celtic origin.

Three of the familiar Irish spirits are the *banshee, leprechaun* and *pooka*. The first means "woman of fairyland" in Old Irish. This female spirit is reputed to wail outside a house where a death is about to occur. The second literally means "a little body." In Irish folklore he is represented as an elf in the shape of a tiny old man, who can uncover a cached crock of gold to anyone who is quick and clever enough to catch him. In contrast, the *pooka* (perhaps related to Shakespeare's Puck) is a rather malignant goblin or specter that takes an equine shape and haunts the marshes and bogs.

The wailer above reminds me of the Irish verb *keen*. When Dubliners *keen* at a wake, they are lamenting rather loudly for the dear departed.

Some Irish-American words relate to love. Consider *cushlamochree* (or *cushlamachree*). The Gaelic parentage literally means "vein of my heart"—therefore, "darling." As another example, we have *mavourneen* (or *mavornin*). It means "my darling."

Brogan and *brogue* are related. The former is a diminutive of *brog*, an Irish-Gaelic noun meaning "shoe." Both words have come to mean "heavy shoe" in our language, but *brogue* has taken on another connotation. Probably because the peasants who used such footwear had a distinctive way of speaking, the word has become associated with an Irish accent. But it must be added that some experts estimate that the source is Irish-Gaelic *barrōg* ("wrestling hold"). Their thesis is that the speakers of *brogue* were believed to be so confined by the "grip" of tradition that they could not adjust their tongues to any other way of talking.

Begorra is an Irish euphemism for "By God!" *Erin go bragh* is a Gaelic expression meaning "Ireland forever."

My favorite Irish word is *bonnyclabber*—thick, curdled milk.

Finally, there are *paddy, paddy wagon* and *paddywhack*.

Paddy is a nickname for Patrick. Since so many Irishmen became policemen, a *paddy* became a synonym for cop. Naturally, the officers' patrol vehicles became *paddy wagons*.

As for *paddywhack,* meaning "to spank or thrash," the verb is derived from a Britishism. Just as they looked down on the Dutch for their obstinacy and frugality, the English regarded the Irish as a people easily aroused to pugnacious anger. Consequently, in London dialect, *paddywhack* was originally a derogatory term for an Irishman.

――――――

Leaping northeast across the sea, we come upon the intrepid Scots, with their own style of life and language. Their children are *bairn;*

their lakes are *lochs;* and their lovely hillsides are *bonny braes.* The shrill sounds from their bagpipes are *skirls,* and at funerals they play dirges called *coronachs.*

The aldermen elected in Scotland are *bailies,* and when Glaswegians get into a squabble, they're having a *collieshangie.* If they're at swords' points, they might wield their *claymores.* And in their lingo, rabble or rubbish is *clamjamfry!*

Golf is associated with the Scots because they popularized the game. In fact, they have enjoyed it ever since the fourteenth century. And in 1774 they established the Royal and Ancient Golf Club of St. Andrews, where the basic rules for the game were officially formulated.

The origin of the word *golf* is a moot question. It probably entered Medieval English via Scottish dialect. But some philologers point to the Dutch noun *kolf* ("club"). In any case, the Scots were the first to make *links* a synonym for a golf course. Originally the word applied to any turf-covered ground or sandy tract along the seashore.

One of the Scotch-derived words familiar to golfers is *baff* ("a stroke in which the sole of the club hits the ground and drives the ball aloft"). *Sclaff* ("to scrape the club along the ground before hitting the ball") is a relation.

Scottish courses feature *bunkers,* which are mounds serving as hazards.

Here are five words that we associate with the Scots. Strangely enough, they are all non-Scottish in origin.

WORD	DEFINITION	SOURCE
clan	social group, as in the Highlands	Lat. *planta* ("sprout")
haggis	Scottish pudding	Med. Eng. *haggen* ("to chop")
kilts	pleated, wraparound skirts worn by Scottish men and boys	Old Norse *kjalta* ("fold made by a gathered skirt")
tartan	plaid cloth worn by clansmen, each clan having its own pattern	Med. Fr. *tiretaine* ("cloth having mixed fibers")
thane	clan chief	Sans. *takman* ("offspring")

Scot itself comes from *Scoti,* a Late Latin word meaning "people of North Britain."

Hebrew, the official tongue of Israel, was spoken by the ancient Israelites and is the language in which most of the Old Testament was written. Like Sanskrit, it has endowed various peoples throughout the world with a wealth of words. Here is a small selection of Hebrew gifts to English:

Bar Mitzvah	kosher	seraph	simhah
cherub	matzo	Shalom	Torah
Gehenna	Messiah	shekel	yeshiva
hallelujah	Pharisee	Sheol	
hosanna	rabbi	shibboleth	

Bar Mitzvah comes from *bar miṣwāh* ("son of the divine law or commandment"). There are two definitions:

1. a Jewish boy who reaches the age of thirteen and must accept religious responsibilities
2. the ceremony at a synagogue inducting the boy into that state

When the teenager is a girl, the term is *Bath Mitzvah* or *Bat Mitzvah*. In Hebrew *bath* or *bat* means "daughter."

Cherubs have evolved into sweet, innocent, chubby apple-cheeked babies or tots. In the original sense they were *cherubim*—winged angelic beings supporting the throne of God. In art they are often depicted as cupids.

Gehenna comes to us via the Greeks. The original Hebrew expression meant "valley of Hinnom." Today the word is a synonym for Hell, because the children at Hinnom were once sacrificed to Moloch. Hence the Israelites called the place *Topheth* ("abomination").

Incidentally, *Topheth* or *Tophet* is another synonym for Hell. Some other names for that infernal region are *Sheol, Pandemonium, Abaddon* and *Tartarus.*

Hallelujah (or *halleluiah*) stems from a Hebrew phrase meaning "Praise (ye) the Lord." The interjection is used as an expression of joy or thanksgiving. It is also a song of praise. Through Greek and Latin, the modification is *alleluia.*

Hosanna is another cry of praise to God. The Hebrew source literally means "Save, we pray!"

Kosher comes from *kāshēr,* the Hebrew word for "proper or correct." With reference to food, it conveys the idea of being prepared according to Jewish dietary laws. As a result, the term *kosher* is applied to many foods, especially meats, and to restaurants and kitchens.

It's fascinating to observe how enthusiastically Christians have embraced the word as a synonym for genuine or legitimate. Recently my son said to me, "The guy tried to sell me a diamond ring, but I had a feeling it wasn't *kosher*."

———————

Matzo (also *matzot, matzoth, matzoh, matzah,* or *matza*) comes from a Hebrew word meaning "unleavened." It is a thin bread containing no yeast or other fermenting agent and is eaten at Passover.

———————

Messiah comes from the Hebrew *māshīah* ("anointed"). In Judaism this blessed one is the promised and anticipated deliverer. To Christians he is Jesus of Nazareth.

———————

The ancient *Pharisees,* who were respected observers of traditional rites and ceremonies, have received a bad press because of pejorative references to them in the New Testament. For example, Jesus drove them from the temple. In Matthew 23:23 we read: "Woe unto you, scribes and Pharisees, hypocrites!" That last epithet has entered our dictionaries. A *pharisee* (note the lowercase first letter) is a sanctimonious, hypocritical person. We have even developed the adjectives *pharisaic* and *pharisaical* for persons who are self-righteous pretenders to piety and virtue (see Luke 18:9–14).

———————

Rabbi literally means "my lord" or "my master" in Hebrew. This scholar and teacher of Jewish law is usually the head of a *synagogue* —a word of Greek origin that means "a bringing together or assembly."

———————

A *seraph* is a step higher than a *cherub* in the celestial hierarchy. *Seraphim* have three pairs of wings. Like the little angels just below them, they surround the throne of God. They are represented as fiery beings, full of sacred ardor. Therefore the probable Hebrew origin *sāraph* ("to burn") seems appropriate.

———————

Shalom is the Israelis' "Aloha!" In Hebrew this greeting or farewell means "peace."

———————

Shekel (from *shāqal,* "to weigh") was an ancient Hebrew unit weighing about a half ounce. It then became a silver coin from 2 B.C. to 2 A.D. In our slanguage, *shekels* are the equivalent of *mazuma* and *gelt,* Yiddish synonyms for money.

———————

Sheol comes from a Hebrew verb meaning "to dig." In the Bible it is a place deep under the earth where departed souls dwell.

———————

Shibboleth means "password." It also connotes a distinctive custom, practice or phrase—hence, a slogan. The history of this word is most exciting. In Hebrew it meant "ear of grain, stream or flood"—but that's not important. In ancient days the Gileadites at the Jordan fords used the word to distinguish their own people from their foes, the Ephramites. The latter group were unable to pronounce the first *h* in *shibboleth* whenever they were challenged by sentries. As soon as they said "sibboleth," they were slain.

Simhah, which has several other transliterated spellings, is a happy occasion such as a wedding or *Bar Mitzvah. Simhat Torah* is a Jewish festival that marks the annual completion of the reading of the first five books of the Old Testament and the start of the new cycle. Alternate spellings for *simhah* or *simhat* are *simhath* and *simcha,* among others.

Torah means "law" in Hebrew. It is the entire range of divine knowledge and law in Jewish Scriptures and tradition. The first five books of the Old Testament are called the *Torah.* A synonym from Greek is *Pentateuch.*

Yeshiva in Hebrew means "a sitting." The word has several definitions:

1. an institution for Talmudic studies
2. a seminary for training rabbis
3. a Jewish school for children who are taught secular knowledge as well as religion

---

Our words from Hebrew display the pious, religious aspects of the Jewish people; our Yiddish-derived vocabulary often reveals their humorous side. It's no wonder that so many great comedians come from Jewish families.

Yiddish literally means "Jewish-German." The language is sometimes called *Judeo-German.* Persecuted people often develop quips and other witticisms as a sort of shield against despair. This seems to be true when we examine *Yiddishisms,* albeit the anger and disgust lurk underneath. Indubitably, the polite and bright look askance at the rude, the crude, the mopes and the dopes. With a wry smile, the Jews have contributed:

kibitzer	nudnik	schlimazel
klutz	schlemiel	schmo
nebbish	schlep	schnook

The *kibitzer* (accent on *kib*) is the fellow who stands behind you while you're playing cards and gives you unwanted advice and criticism. The Yiddish verb *kibitzen* is a variation of the colloquial German word *kiebitzen* ("to look on, as at cards"). The eventual source is *Kiebitz* ("lapwing or plover")—a word that probably stemmed from an imitation of the bird's call. Somehow, perhaps from its jerky method of flying or from its habit of hovering around neighborhoods where food is abundant, the bird became synonymous with a busybody or meddler —and so did any person who *kibitzes*.

Klutz comes from *Klotz,* a German word meaning "clod or block." It's easy to see how a *klutz* became a blockhead or clumsy fellow in Yiddish.

Nebbishes are hopelessly inept, bashful or drab people. The Yiddish source is *nebekh* ("pity").

Nudnik (also *nudnick*) has a Russian-Polish ancestry. Some experts trace it back to *nuda* ("boredom"). That fits. A *nudnik* is a bore; he's also a nuisance.

Schlemiels and *schleps* are people who botch things up. *Schlep* can also be used as a verb meaning "to carry clumsily" or "to drag oneself along."

Schlimazels are unlucky, clumsy people doomed to failure and misfortune. A duffer who makes a terrible shot on the links and hits a golfer on an adjoining fairway might be called a *schlemiel,* and the victim of his ineptitude is a *schlimazel.* In Yiddish, by the way, *shlimazel* means "bad luck." The opposite is *Mazel Tov,* which is an expression of congratulations literally meaning "good luck" in Hebrew.

A *schmo* is another of those dullards, and so is a *schnook.* In Yiddish one certainly has a choice of epithets when confronted by a simpleton. But that's not surprising; in our own American slang we have more than two hundred synonyms for a bonehead or a sap.

Following is a mélange of words with a Yiddish source:

bagel	kibosh	schatchen	shtick
bialy	knish	schlock	shul
chremzel	maven	schmaltz	tsimmes
chutzpah	mensch	schmoose	yarmulke
goy	nosh	schnorrer	yenta
	pastrami	schnozzle	

Bagels and *lox* are a popular culinary combination in many Jewish homes. The snack consists of hard, circular rolls and smoked salmon.

The Yiddish word *beygel* ultimately stems from Middle High German *bouc* ("ring or bracelet"). *Lox* is *laks* in Yiddish. The German ancestor is *lahs* ("salmon").

Unfortunately, another *lox* has slipped into our vocabulary. It's a shortening of liquid oxygen, used in rocket fuel.

Bialy is another type of roll, topped with onion flakes. The name is an abridgment of "Bialystok," a city in Poland where the roll was originally concocted.

Recently a puzzle containing the word *bialys* was submitted to me. I was all set to reject it before I looked up the word. Amazingly, the plural is not *bialies*. I wonder if this is the only exception to the rule.

Chremzel (or *chremsel* or *chrimsel*) is another Jewish treat. It's a flat, fried cake made from matzo meal.

Chutzpah (pronounced "khoot'-spa") has recently become a favorite of American slangsters. It means "unmitigated nerve" or "utter brazenness." A Jewish friend of mine told me that a good example of *chutzpah* occurs in the incident of the young man who shoots his parents and then seeks relief money from the government on the grounds that he has become an orphan.

Goy is the Yiddish word for a Gentile. Actually, it means "people" in Hebrew, and the plural is *goyim*. Some experts state that the word is considered disparaging and is in the same class with WASP ("White Anglo-Saxon Protestant"), but I have never resented being called a *goy*. It's always been said to me with a smile—maybe because of my *non-goyish* ways.

I am reminded of the time I was having lunch with four Jewish friends. They took turns telling Jewish jokes, and each punch line was greeted with guffaws. Finally I chimed in, but my attempt fell flat. Later I asked one of them why. He told me that it's embarrassing to listen to a *goy* telling a joke about Jews. After that I stuck to the Pat-and-Mike stories that my Irish mother had taught me. As for Polish jokes, I detest them.

The origin of *kibosh* is disputed. Some philologers think it comes from Yiddish, but William Morris relates that the Irish poet Padraic Colum makes a good case for its Gaelic ancestry (*cie bais,* "cap of death"). In any case, when you *put the kibosh* on a project, you squelch it.

Jewish cooks seem to be versatile and creative. *Knishes* are pieces of thin rolled dough stuffed with mashed potatoes or chopped meat or other fillings and then baked or fried.

Maven is a rather new Yiddish contribution to our vocabulary. The word means "expert."

A *mensch* is a solid citizen—a person of fortitude and good sense who can be trusted with responsibilities. The Middle High German grandparent means "man."

Luftmensch is a derivative. Since *Luft* means "air," you can see how this word means "an impractical dreamer."

Nosh is a Yiddish derivative of *naschen,* a German verb meaning "to taste or nibble." *Noshers* probably need to go on a diet, because they are constantly raiding the refrigerator for snacks.

Pastrami has a Rumanian-Roman history. In Budapest it's *pastrama,* from a verb meaning "to preserve." The eventual Latin root with the same sense is *parcere.*

This highly seasoned smoked beef has become the chief rival of corned beef in every delicatessen.*

Schatchen is a Jewish marriage broker. Other spellings are *shadehan* and *shadchen.* No matter how you put his name in writing, this fellow's come-on is "Have I got a girl for you!"

Schlock is inferior merchandise, or trash. The word ultimately can be traced to the German noun *Schlacke* ("dregs").

A delightful derivative is *schlockmeister* ("master of trash"). The term is often applied to directors or producers of arty, inferior films.

Schmaltz goes back to *Schmalz,* a German word meaning "melted fat." *Schmaltzy* paintings, novels or musical offerings are full of sentimentality and are awfully trite.

Another meaning for *schmaltz* is "excessive praise." Those in the know are hep to the fact that flatterers are laying on the *schmaltz.* (I use slangy expressions to stress that this word, like many others in the list, is still regarded as a vulgar intruder into our vocabulary.)

---

* *Delicatessen* has a complicated background, but it does come to us via the French *délicatesse* ("delicacy"). The interesting point is that we have also borrowed *délicatesse* and have dropped its accent. In English it means "tact." Have you ever met a diplomatic deli owner?

Schmoose (or *schmooze*) is another instance of slanguage from Yiddish. As a verb or a noun it means "chat"—from *shmuesn* ("to chat"). The Hebrew source (*shĕmuoth*) means "gossip."

Schnorrer probably belongs in the previous list of people, who are light years away from being *menschen*. A *schnorrer* will pretend to be your friend but will take you for everything you've got. He's a parasite who lives by sponging on others. The German verb from which this Yiddish noun comes is *snurren* or *schnurren* ("to purr, whir or hum").

I have a funny story to relate on this subject. A Jewish friend of mine confided in me that his brother-in-law had moved in and he was worried because the fellow was a *schnorrer*. Stupidly, I suggested, "Why not put a clothespin over his nose?"

Speaking of noses, we have *schnozzle* in our argot. This word of Yiddish-German background was extended by Jimmy Durante. In fact, Gene Fowler's 1951 biography of the comedian is entitled SCHNOZZOLA.

The German-bred *Schnauzer* is a relation because of its distinctive snout.

Shtick would stick many a *goy* in a spelling bee. Take a second look at those three initial consonants—especially that *t* after *sh!* At any rate, this Yiddish word literally means "prank" and probably stems from Middle High German *Stich* ("puncture or thrust"). In our current slang it has several meanings:

1. one's special talent or characteristic
2. comedian's act
3. device to get attention

Shul is the Yiddish word for a synagogue and is derived from Middle High German *Schuol* ("school").

When I was a young teacher in New York City I suddenly became a *schlimazel* ("unlucky person"). To decide who would be the chairman of the annual school exhibit, an assistant principal drew a name out of a hat. Mine was the one! A few days later I told my Jewish principal that I wasn't sure I could handle such a complicated task and I didn't want to let him down. He looked up at me with a smile and advised: "There's no need to make a *tsimmes* out of this exhibit, Maleska. Just gather the best material from each department and display it in the gym."

Tsimmes? What in heaven's name was that? I found out later that it meant "much ado." In his opinion, I was finding all kinds of complications in a rather simple enterprise.

I have also just learned that a *tsimmes* is a vegetable stew, usually featuring carrots. My principal was literally telling me in Yiddish to stop stewing!

My supervisor could also have told me that I was making a *megillah* out of something relatively simple. That slangy Yiddish word means:

1. a complicated matter or affair
2. a long, involved story or explanation

The word stems from Hebrew. In non-slanguage it's the Judaic scroll containing the story of the Book of Esther. It is read in synagogues to celebrate the feast of Purim. Obviously the account goes on and on and on, with many convolutions.

Again we encounter a spelling problem. Most lexicographers prefer *yarmulke,* but there are also *yamulka, yamalka, yarmalke* and *yarmalka.* This skullcap worn by male Jews when praying, eating or studying is a Yiddish word derived from Polish-Ukrainian. A possible ancestor is the Turkish noun *yağmurluk* ("raincoat").

Yenta is a Yiddish word that has really caught on in our slang. She's a gossipy woman who snoops into others' affairs. The Yiddish source means "vulgar, sentimental woman." The Romans called her a *quidnunc* (literally, "What now?").

Incidentally, the matchmaker in THE FIDDLER ON THE ROOF was named Yente. I sense a connection.

$\mathbf{F}$inally, let us consider the contributions of the Amerinds (Eskimos and American Indians).

Eskimo literally means "eaters of raw fish or flesh." The name evolved from the Algonquins, French and Danish.

Here are a few words from the language of these arctic people:

anorak	mukluk
igloo	parka
kayak	umiak
Malamute	

The *anorak* and the *parka* are heavy hooded jackets originally worn only in the polar regions but now seen on many Americans in wintertime. *Parka* means "skin," which refers to the pelt of the animal from which it is made. The fleece of sheep is sometimes used as a lining. The fur of dogs or the hides of reindeer are often utilized in making the garment.

Igloo (sometimes spelled *iglu*) comes from an Eskimo word that means "snow house." Actually, most *igloos* are made of sod, wood or stone.

The *kayak* and the *umiak* (or *oomiak*) are two Eskimo vessels. The former is a watertight canoe with a skin cover and is often used for hunting; the latter is an open boat having a wooden frame protected by skins. It is used for transportation of people or merchandise and is traditionally propelled by Eskimo women.

Daredevils who love to shoot the rapids have popularized *kayaks* in the United States.

The *Alaskan Malamute* is a powerful sled dog that was named for the Eskimo tribe that developed the breed.

Mukluks are Eskimo boots made of sealskin or reindeer skin. The source is *muklok* ("large seal"). In America this footwear is made of rubber or canvas or a woven fabric called duck. We have converted *mukluks* into lounging slippers.

From various North American Indian tribes we have received hundreds of interesting words. Here is a sampling:

bayou	cushaw	pemmican	tautog
catalpa	hogan	powwow	tepee
cayuse	menhaden	quahog	tupelo
chinook	moccasin	sachem	wampum
chinquapin	mugwump	tamarack	wigwam
cockarouse			

Bayou comes from the Choctaw noun *bayuk* ("small stream"). The Louisiana French altered the spelling and donated the word to us.

In connection with *bayou,* here's another humorous anecdote. A group of us were playing a quiz game and rotating the role of quizmaster. When it became my son-in-law's turn, the subject was geography. With a straight face he pretended to read the following question: "What Louisiana inlet was named for the inventor of the sewing machine?"

After cogitating for a few moments, I shouted, "Howe's Bayou!"

"I'm fine," he replied. "How's by you too?"

Catalpas are trees with large heart-shaped leaves and clusters of whitish flowers. The source is *kutuhlpa,* a Creek word meaning "head with wings" because of the shape of the flowers.

These trees also have long, slender pods resembling beans. Hence they are sometimes called *Indian beans.*

Cayuse is a horse often referred to as an *Indian pony.* The animal was named for a tribe of Indians dwelling in Oregon.

Chinook was also named for an Indian tribe of the West. It's either a hot, dry wind that comes down the eastern slopes of the Rockies or a warm, moist wind blowing from the Pacific to the northwestern coast in winter or spring.

The king salmon of the Pacific is also called *chinook.*

Chinquapin is of Algonquian origin. The name can be applied to a shrubby chestnut tree or an evergreen of the Pacific coast. The nuts that grow on both trees are also *chinquapins.*

The Algonquians also contributed *cockarouse*—a term for a V.I.P. among the colonists. It is probably a relation of *caucus.*

Cushaw is a variety of squash. Again, the source is Algonquian.

Hogan is an alteration of *qoghan,* the Navaho noun for "house."

Menhaden are the most abundant fish on the Atlantic coast. The source for their name is probably a Narraganset word meaning "he fertilizes." The Indians used this fish (a variety of herring) to enrich the soil, and that practice continues today. *Menhaden* are also used for bait and for making an oil.

I live near a salt marsh in Massachusetts. When the tide flows in, schools of *menhaden* swarm within the banks of the marsh. This invasion has apparently given rise to the synonym *marshbankers.* A variation is *mossbunkers.*

> There once was a pretty young maiden
> Who decided she'd like to go wadin',
> But alas and alack,
> She had to turn back
> When she discovered a school of menhaden!

Which reminds me of an X-rated poetic witticism:

COMEDIAN: There was a young woman from Mass. Who went into the water up to her ankles.

STOOGE: But those lines don't rhyme.

COMEDIAN: Wait till the tide comes in.

———

Moccasin is a word I always have trouble spelling. It, too, has a Narraganset origin. Aside from being a heelless shoe, boot or slipper, it's also a snake.

The *moccasin flower* is one of the lady's slippers, aptly enough. This woodland orchid is also called *nerveroot*.

———

Mugwump is a delightful word with an intriguing sound. The Algonquian root is *mugquomp* ("chief"). Hence *mugwump* came to mean "an important person."

Then, in 1884, a group of Republicans refused to support the party nominee, James G. Blaine. When they bolted, the others pinned the name *mugwumps* on them, meaning that they were filled with their own self-importance. But the dissenters adopted the name and used it to their own advantage. Gradually it took on two new connotations: 1) a political independent, or 2) a person who can't make up his mind on an issue.

In that last sense a joke has been passed around for many years: "A *mugwump* has his mug on one side of the fence and his wump on the other."

———

The Crees gave us the word *pemmican*. In their language it meant "fat meat." They mixed fat and berries with strips of lean, dry meat that had been pounded into a paste. Today adventurers use a similar food for emergency rations. It usually consists of beef, suet and dried fruit. My first experience with the word came long ago when, as a boy, I read Admiral Byrd's story of his polar explorations.

In connection with the above, Harriett Wilson (my aide at THE NEW YORK TIMES) has called my attention to a delicious word. *Rubaboo* (or *rubbaboo*) is *pemmican* made into a soup.

———

Those creative Algonquians are responsible for *powwow*. In their language the word signified "a medicine man or conjurer." Because the head shaman* was the leader of any formal meeting with the colonists, his name came to be associated with the conferences themselves. Then, as often happens, the noun was also used as a verb.

Incidentally, my theory about such words as *powwow, bowwow* and *kowtow* is that they achieve wide usage mainly because human beings have an innate love for rhyme. Don't you love *hubbub, hodge-*

———

* *Shaman* means "medicine man." Although some American Indians and Eskimos practiced *shamanism* ("belief in good and evil spirits who can be influenced by the medicine man"), the word is of German-Russian-Sanskrit origin.

podge, ding-a-ling, Hottentot, rat-a-tat, palsy-walsy, hurdy-gurdy, hoity-toity, tutti frutti, et cetera, et cetera? Words like those seem to have less chance of becoming obsolete than others with drab sounds.

———

In my thirty-seventh year, when we purchased a summer cottage near Cape Cod, I first became acquainted with the *quahog.* One of my neighbors suggested that we dig up "kó-hogs" at low tide. I had no idea what he meant. You can imagine my surprise when I discovered that they were hard-shell clams.

Quahog (or *quahaug*) is derived from a Narraganset word meaning "dark shell." My neighbor's pronunciation, by the way, is given as the second or third one in some dictionaries. The preferred pronunciation has a soft sound for the first syllable. Another Cape-Coddism is "kwó-hog."

A *littleneck* is a young *quahog.* The name stems from Littleneck Bay, an inlet of Long Island Sound where the clams are plentiful. When this tiny clam grows a wee bit, it is called a *cherrystone.*

Quahogs are the basis for an appetizer called *clams casino.* My wife has a delicious recipe that we'll share with you.

> In a shallow, round baking pan arrange:
> *24 cherrystones* on the half shell
> Top with the following *mixture:*
> > 1 cup bread crumbs
> > 5 slices green pepper, finely diced
> > 2 tsp. chopped pimento
> > 1 tsp. Parmesan cheese
> > 1 tsp. oregano
> > 1 clove garlic, minced
> > ½ medium onion, minced
> > 8 sprigs parsley, chopped
> > salt, pepper, Accent
>
> *Sprinkle* clams with:
> > ½ cup clam juice
> > juice of ¼ lemon
> > olive oil
>
> *Last step:*
> > Place small piece of *bacon* on each clam.
> > *Bake* in 550° oven for 15 min. Place pan under broiler for 3 min. to crisp bacon. Serves 4 or 5.

———

Sachem is another Algonquian gift to our vocabulary. Their word *sâchimau* meant "chief." When the Tammany Society was incorporated in 1789, it was named for a friendly Delaware Indian chief. Hence the leaders of the powerful New York City political group were called *sachems.*

Probably because Tammany Hall became a seat of bossism in politics, such derivative words as *sachemdom* and *sachemship* have been used disparagingly by modern writers.

———

Tamaracks are *hackmatacks,* and both of these delightful synonyms for North American larches are probably inheritances from the etymologically prolific Algonquians.

I should explain that Algonquian embraced more than a score of Indian languages. The tribes included such famous ones as the Arapaho, Cheyenne, Chippewa, Cree, Delaware, Fox, Narraganset, Ottawa and Shawnee.

———

Tautog ("blackfish") is another Narraganset word I learned in middle age when I aestivated* near Cape Cod. While fishing for flounder in Buzzards Bay (a great name!) I pulled up an ugly-looking dark fish that resembled a large marine perch. The same neighbor who had taught me *quahog* exclaimed, "You've caught a *tautog!*" He put the accent on the second syllable, and this time he was right on the mark. I found out when I looked it up that night. Secretly I wondered what other "og" words this New Englander would teach me. I began to think of him as "My Wizard of Og."

But it really is amazing how experiences in different places can enhance your vocabulary. Travel is broadening in more ways than one.

———

Tepee has a Siouan origin, for a change. The Dakota Indians' word for "dwelling" is *tipi,* and that spelling is still an accepted variation along with *teepee.*

Contrary to popular opinion, not all the Indians resided in these cone-shaped tents made of skin and bark. The Plains Indians were the dwellers in *tepees.*

———

Tupelo comes from the Creek tribe of Georgia, Alabama and northern Florida. Their *ito opilwa* (reading backward, "swamp tree") got massacred in the translation. Meanwhile Andrew Jackson and his soldiers were massacring the Creeks themselves, under the leadership of the famous Tecumseh.

There's a fascinating story involving Tecumseh. A statue of him at the U.S. Naval Academy in Annapolis is really a representation of Tamenend, the Delaware chief for whom Tammany Hall was named. I have been thwarted in my efforts to find out how this substitution occurred.

———

* *Aestivate* (or *estivate*) means "spend the summer." The Latin root is *aestas* ("summer"). It is the opposite of *hibernate,* from the Romans' word for winter, *hibernus.*

Wampum is one of our many slang words for money. That's because of *wampumpeag*—white shell beads used by Indians in southeastern New England as currency. *Peag* is a less used synonym for *wampum*.

———

Wigwam in Ojibwa is *wigiwam* ("lodge or dwelling"). This domed shelter of the Algonquians has a framework of arched poles which are covered with leaves, bark, branches, rush mats and hides. A portable form of wigwam resembles a *tepee*.

Another similar abode is the *wickiup*. Nomadic Indians of the Southwest built this elliptical hut on a framework covered with grass, reed mats and brushwood. Today a temporary shelter is sometimes called a *wickiup*.

———

This concludes our tour of words we have assimilated from almost every corner of the world. I realize that I have shortchanged the reader on all the languages I have covered and have omitted some. For example, I have neglected the Tibetans, who gave us such words as *lama, panda, polo* and *yak*. Nor have I been fair to the Hungarians, who have supplied us with such gems as *paprika* and *shako*. And then there are the Caribs and other people of the West Indies. Without them we would be missing *papaya, savanna,* a dance called the *limbo* and dozens of other beauties. Moreover, individual readers can probably come up with words from other languages and nationalities that I have not mentioned. But this chapter, like all the others in the book, is intended only as a soupcon and—if you will forgive the pun—not a full-course dinner. I do hope it's been digestible!

CHAPTER 9

Our Anglo-Saxon Heritage

Up until now we have been treated to interesting and exotic English words derived from Greek, Latin, the Romance languages and many others ranging from Asian tongues to African dialects and the languages of aborigines of our own continent. We have discovered that the Romans and their descendants or offshoots have contributed the greatest number of words to our dictionaries. But even more important than multiplicity is frequency of use—and that's where our Anglo-Saxon ancestors rise to the top of the heap, at least in our conversational speech.

Before going any further, let me indicate that Anglo-Saxon and Old English are synonymous. More about that later. Now let me illustrate the point about our debt to the Anglo-Saxons when we use ordinary everyday language. Here is an original story in which *every* word has an Old English background:

> At the stroke of five each morning Mother and Father leaped out of bed. Then they began to do many chores about the house. Before the sun rose Mother took water from the well while Father went out into the fields to feed the cows and look after the horses. In summer or in winter, in good weather or bad, everything had to be cared for.
>
> As a small child I often thought how much they must have hated that daily work. Yet they never showed anything but love and hope in our home. They bore hardship without one word of sorrow, and even found time to teach us children how to swim and ride horseback. In the evenings, at dusk, they also taught us the Gospel and little songs about the goodness of God and the wonderful gift of life. They were so thankful that they could give us food to eat and milk to drink as we grew up. They were kind and lovable indeed! To my brother and sister and me they were not only kinfolk but true friends.

Isn't it fascinating that not a single Latin derivative appears in those two paragraphs? Not a trace of French, Spanish, Italian,—and no Greek either. Just plain Old English!

Only one word can be questioned. Strangely enough, it is *they*. Some lexicographers give sole credit to Old Norse, but others state that the pronoun comes to us partly from Old English (*thā*) and partly from Old Norse (*thei-r*).

Of course the Anglo-Saxons did not invent all the words in that story, nor was their spelling the same. But their basic vocabulary was passed down to Middle English (ca. 1100–1500), and thence to us. As the centuries elapsed, changes in orthography and nuances of meaning often took place. As an example, here is a sort of flow chart on the progress of the words in the first sentence of our story.

MODERN ENGLISH	MIDDLE ENGLISH	OLD ENGLISH
at	at, atte	æt
the	the	thĕ
stroke	stroke, strake	strican
of	of	of
five	fif	fif
each	ech, elc	ælc, æghwile
morning	morweninge	morgen
mother	moder	modor
and	and, an	and, ond
father	fader	faeder
leap	lepen	hleapan
out	out	ūt
bed	bed	bedd

As a general rule, most of the following have come down to us from the Anglo-Saxons:

1. basic words such as *bone, hot, man, meat, wife* and *woman* (also some vulgar and scatological "four-letter" words)
2. irregular verbs
3. pronouns, prepositions and conjunctions
4. names of numbers (but *million, billion,* etc. have a French ancestry)

Some readers may ask: "Who were the Anglo-Saxons? When did they settle in England? Whence did they come? And how did their vocabulary develop?"

Let's try to answer the last question first. To do so we must go back to primeval humans' early attempts to communicate. Did they start by imitating the sounds of the birds, beasts, wind, water, thunder and other natural sources? Nobody knows for sure. Also, no one can say with authority whether language started with one group, and then spread out as members of this group went their separate ways, or whether diverse groups were almost simultaneously trying to express their ideas. Most scholars are inclined to believe that the latter phenomenon occurred aeons ago.

At any rate, several prehistoric languages emerged, and each was different from any other. Among them were Hamito-Semitic, Uralic, Bantu and Sino-Tibetan. But the one that we are indebted to is Indo-European, which can be considered as the great-great-great-grandparent of an amazing family of languages.

Let's picture Indo-European as the roots and trunk of an immense tree with about a dozen limbs, some large and some rather small. One of those limbs is called Italic. Its largest branch is Latin, and the branchlets include Italian, Spanish, French, Portuguese, and Rumanian.

Another limb is Celtic, which branched off into Irish-Gaelic, Scottish-Gaelic, Manx, Welsh, Cornish, Breton, Gaulish and others.

Balto-Slavic produced such offshoots as Russian, Bulgarian, Polish, Czech, Slovak, Latvian and Lithuanian.

On another side of the tree, Indo-Iranian gave rise to Sanskrit, and the scions of that language include Hindi, Urdu, Assamese and Bengali.

But one of the sturdiest growths from Indo-European turned out to be Germanic. Its two main branches were North Germanic and West Germanic. The former developed into Old Norse and finally into such languages as Norwegian, Swedish, Danish and Icelandic.

West Germanic is the branch that burgeoned into Dutch, Frisian, Flemish, Afrikaans, German, Yiddish and—yes!—English.

The original inhabitants of Great Britain were the Britons, or Celtics. They migrated to the islands many centuries before the birth of Christ, and scholars estimate that their original territory embraced southwest Germany, eastern France, northern Italy and Iberia.

Another ancient people, whose continental homeland is in dispute, were the Picts. Somewhere around 1000 B.C. they settled in parts of Scotland and Ireland. Interestingly enough, this name was given to them later by the Romans because they tattooed their skins. The Latin word *pictor* means "painter." Some Roman writers called the group *Picti*. As a separate race they faded out in the eighth and ninth centuries. During the reign of Kenneth I they merged with the Scots.

Caesar's troops invaded Britain in 55 and 54 B.C., but the Romans exercised little influence upon the language of the natives, mainly because there was no mass migration to the storm-tossed islands, so forbidding in contrast to sunny Italy.

True, the Romans established military camps in their new province. One can imagine the loneliness of the soldiers assigned to duty in a grim, alien land. What a thrill it must have been for them when the emperor Hadrian visited circa 120–123 A.D. and built his famous wall! Reputedly, the structure was erected as a protection against the Picts.

But the arrival of the Angles, Jutes and Saxons was a different matter. These three tribes crossed the channel and the North Sea in the fifth century, conquered the inhabitants and settled down in their new surroundings.

The Angles probably came from an area that is modern Angeln, where the borders of northwest Germany and south Denmark meet today. They occupied portions of eastern, central and northern England.

According to disputed tradition, the Jutes (probably Rhinelanders —not Jutlanders) crossed the waters at the invitation of the Britons, who needed help in their battles with the Picts. Under the leadership of Hengist and Horsa, they founded the kingdom of Kent and settled near the present site of London and on the Isle of Wight. As time went by they intermingled with the Saxons and the Angles.

The Saxons were a warlike Teutonic people who originated in the Elbe valley. Charlemagne conquered them and caused them to be Christianized. The Old Saxons remained in Germany, but the group that emigrated to Britain got together with the Angles and held sway until the Norman Conquest.

The above groups brought their different dialects to Britain, and what finally emerged was Old English. It was chiefly a combination of Old High German, Middle Low German, Gothic, Old French, Old Danish, Old Norse and Celtic.

As I have noted before, the West German offshoots have provided us with most of the basic words for our modern language. But the Norman Conquest and the Renaissance were instrumental in weaving a linguistic tapestry, with many threads from Greece and Rome.

Personally, I am grateful for the above events. We have inherited a delicious mixture of such reliable, workaday, monosyllabic Old English words as *bad, light, shake, tree, up* and *down,* along with such fanciful polysyllabic beauties as *anfractuous* ("sinuous, winding"), *usufructuary* ("one enjoying the fruits or profits of an estate"), *eudaemonical* ("producing happiness") and *cymotrichous* ("having wavy hair").

In short, our English language offers something for everybody, far more than any other, whether ancient or modern.

CHAPTER 10

Our Animal Kingdom

When I was a little boy and occasionally acted wild or silly, my mother used to say, "Darwin was right!" Since she never explained her observation, I assumed that Darwin was some distant uncle who had decided at my nativity that I was destined to be a ne'er-do-well. Not until I reached my adolescence did I realize that "Uncle Darwin" had expounded the theory that *Homo sapiens* and the pithecanthropoids were related.

Human affinity with the animal world goes far beyond Mr. Darwin's pronouncements. We have made pets of creatures ranging from dogs and cats, gerbils and hamsters, to lions and dolphins. Fauna have interested us to the point of obsession and have taken up lots of space in our dictionaries, not only in straight definitions (from the aardvark to the zebra) but also in phrases and expressions we use every day. We take catnaps, get tips from the horse's mouth, participate in hen parties, put on the dog, buy a pig in a poke and often make asses of ourselves.

This preoccupation with the world of Animalia* is easy to understand. After all, except for plants, they represent our only moving, living companions on earth. (If you think plants are not vibrant, consider the Venus'-flytrap or watch a willow tree grow from a sapling into a burgeoning beauty!)

Our clichés indicate how we associate our own qualities with those that we ascribe to different beasts. One person is as strong as an ox, another as weak as a kitten.

Consider the following:

cross as a bear	ugly as a toad
meek (or gentle) as a lamb	greedy as a hog
brave (or bold) as a lion	busy as a beaver
fierce as a tiger	mad as a March hare
sly as a fox†	stubborn as a mule
quiet as a mouse	poor as church mice
fat as a pig	scared as a rabbit
sick as a dog	quick as a cat

* For the sake of argument, let's include birds, insects, fish, serpents, etc., in the animal kingdom—and let's leave out mankind.

† Of course we also say "as dumb as a fox," meaning just the opposite!

Winged creatures also come in for their share of hackneyed similes:

busy as a bee	free as a bird
blind as a bat	mad as a wet hen
bald as a coot	loose as a goose
crazy as a loon	proud as a peacock
happy as a lark	plump as a partridge
wise as an owl	

The sounds that animals make have also fascinated mankind and have added hundreds upon hundreds of words to various languages. Here are just a few of the expressions that English-speaking people have used for centuries:

bark like a dog
croak like a frog or a raven
purr or mew like a cat or a kitten
quack like a duck
honk like a goose
coo like a dove or a pigeon
chatter like a magpie or a monkey
cackle like a hen
growl like a bear
crow like a cock or a rooster

And, of course, cows moo; flies and bees buzz or drone; grasshoppers and crickets chirp; pigs grunt and squeal; owls hoot; nightingales warble; mules and asses bray; sheep and calves bleat and baa; and hyenas laugh.

In all ancient civilizations, great interest was taken in animals. Sometimes such creatures as cats, bulls and horses were deified. This engrossment naturally led to additions to the individual languages and generated connotations that have been passed down to us.

Aesop comes to mind immediately. That Greek fabulist was a Phrygian slave (ca. 620–ca. 560 B.C.). His talking beasts depicted human frailties and virtues. A moral was always appended to each tale, and many of those lessons persist in our language today. For instance, "sour grapes" comes from the story of the fox that could not reach a bunch of grapes. He consoled himself by declaring that the fruit was sour.

Some scholars say that Aesop himself was a "fable"—in other words, that he never existed. Certainly many of the tales that he supposedly recited at banquets and festivals are not his original creations. Several have been traced back to the Orient and to Egypt in the fourteenth century B.C.

But no less a personage than Aristophanes, the great Greek dramatist, was an Aesopian devotee. Perhaps this is why he also chose to use creatures in the animal world as vehicles for his satires on the foibles of his era. Witness THE BIRDS, THE FROGS and THE WASPS. In the first of those comedies the birds establish Cloud Cuckoo, or Nephelococcygia, a town existing in midair.

Our feathered friends attracted lots of attention among the ancients. Take the owl, for example. When Athenians ventured out at night, they could hear owls everywhere. This led to many superstitions; for example, an owl perched outside a sick person's chamber was an omen of death. But since Athena bore the same name as the city, the owl became her symbol; and the Romans retained the tradition for Minerva. Wisdom was the special province of both deities; hence today we say that a shrewd person is "as wise as an owl." This comparison makes ornithologists wince, because, in truth, the owl is not a smart bird.

Incidentally, one of the Greek proverbs spoke of "sending owls to Athens," just as today we describe a wholly unnecessary act as "carrying coals to Newcastle" (a Northumberland city famed as a coal-shipping port).

The *phoenix* is a legendary, beautiful bird of Egyptian-Arabian origin. It was reputed to live to a ripe old age (five hundred or six hundred years) in the desert, then burn itself on a pyre, and rise from the ashes as fresh as a daisy. Consequently it has become a symbol of immortality or resurrection. The city fathers who named Phoenix, Arizona, and Phenix City, Alabama, had high hopes!

Today any model of excellence or beauty is called a *phoenix*. Also, the word is applied to one that recovers miraculously after ruin or near destruction. Finally, Phoenix is a southern constellation.

The *roc* is another fabulous bird from the same regions. In THE ARABIAN NIGHTS it was described as so huge that it could carry off elephants as food for its nestlings. The bird is familiar to all crossword fans. Also, a large U.S. aerial bomb was named for it not so long ago.

When a person destroys something that has brought him good fortune or success, we say that he has "killed the goose that laid the golden egg." This expression dates back to an old Greek fable in which a farmer owned such a goose. Greedy for more gold, he slaughtered the goose and opened it up to seek additional precious eggs. His folly netted him zero, or, as we say, a *goose egg*.

Chanticleer comes from two French words: *chanter* ("to sing or crow") and *cler* ("clear"). As in the Middle Ages, it still is a synonym for rooster. *Reynard* continues to be an appellation for a fox. Like *chanticleer,* it has come down to us from the medieval "bestiary" (or "beast epic") ROMAN DE RENART, in which the fox tries to outwit the cock.

Let us now turn to the ancients' obsession with four-legged creatures. Several of these beasts are still over our heads. *Canis Major* and *Canis Minor* (named for their shapes) are constellations near Orion. One is "the larger dog," the other is "the lesser dog." An important part of *Canis Major* is Sirius (from a Greek word meaning "scorching"). It is the brightest star in all the heavens and is called the Dog Star.

Also high in the skies are *Ursa Major* and *Ursa Minor. Ursa* is the Latin word for a female bear. Both constellations were originally named by the Greeks. *Arktos* is the Athenian word for bear. It still remains active for astronomers. Arcturus (literally, "bear keeper") is a first-magnitude star in the constellation Boötes. As usual, the Romans followed the leads of the bright people whom they had enslaved. They even borrowed a legend from the Athenians. The original goes as follows: Callisto, a lovely nymph attendant upon Artemis, had an affair with Zeus. Thereupon the angry goddess changed her into a bear. As a bear, she was about to be slain by Arcas, the young hunter she had spawned with Zeus, when the latter snatched her up and fixed her as a constellation out of reach. So what did the Romans do? They altered the story to cause the nymph to have two children. Juno became the jealous one who changed them into bears. Jupiter then converted them into constellations. Incidentally, Callisto is now a satellite of the planet Jupiter. That fits!

The *horse,* if one believes classical mythology, was created by Poseidon, who was later named Neptune by the Romans. *Hippo* was the Greek word; *equus** was the Latin word for this wonderful animal. From both roots we have mined a bonanza.

hippic—relating to horses or horse racing
hippocampus—legendary sea horse having the tail of a dolphin or fish
hippocentaur—centaur (man having a horse's body)
Hippocrene—poetic inspiration
hippocrepiform—shaped like a horseshoe
hippodrome
> 1. stadium for chariot races
> 2. arena for horsemen to perform in
> 3. sports contest with a predetermined winner
> 4. to fix a sports contest

hippogriff }
hippogriffin } mythical monster: part horse, part eagle and part lion

* Anyone who has seen *Equus,* by Peter Shaffer, will understand why this popular play was so named.

hippology—study of the horse
hippopotamus—aquatic mammal
hippus—spasmodic contraction of the pupil of the eye

equerry—officer of a royal household responsible for the care of horses
eques—Roman knight
equestrian ⎫
equestrienne ⎬ horseman; horsewoman
equestrianism—horsemanship
equid—ungulate mammal (horse, zebra or ass)

The derivation of the word *Hippocrene* merits attention. It was originally an ancient Greek fountain that supposedly spouted when Pegasus struck the ground with his hoof.

In his "Ode to a Nightingale" Keats wrote: "O for a beaker full of the warm South, / Full of the true, the blushful Hippocrene."

What the poet was asking for, deep down, was the inspiration to forget "the weariness, the fever, and the fret" of mundane routines where "men sit and hear each other groan."

———

Monsters such as the *hippogriff,* the *griffin,* the *Harpies* and the *Minotaur* thrilled the Athenians. Lest we sneer at their penchant for unnatural creatures, let us remember that civilized men today are enthralled by Bigfoot in the Northwest, the Abominable Snowman (Yeti) in the Himalayas, the gigantic aquatic beast in Loch Ness and the strange beings that reputedly land here in UFOs.

One of the terrifying animals in Greek mythology is the *Chimaera.* Homer described it as having a lion's head, a goat's body and a dragon's tail. Now, there's a malformation to make your hair stand on end! Well, a Corinthian hero named Bellerophon mounted the winged Pegasus and slew the awful thing.

However, like the *phoenix,* the *Chimaera* has been resurrected. In its original spelling it lives today in the form of an ugly fish, related to the shark. Ichthyologists call it an elasmobranch!

But in modern usage, as in many other cases involving ancient diphthongs, the *Chimaera* has become a *chimera.* Here are some current definitions for that Attic atrocity:

1. any monster, in painting or sculpture, having disparate parts
2. a horrible or unreal creature of the imagination; a fantastic fabrication or illusion
3. a utopian dream or aim
4. an organism that is partly male and partly female, or an artificially produced individual (perhaps a clone?)

A related adjective, *chimerical,* carries the sense of the third definition above. Get-rich-quick projects are usually *chimerical.*

In Paradise Lost, Milton spoke of "Gorgons and Hydras, and Chimaeras dire." The *Gorgons* were three witchy sisters led by Medusa. Instead of hair, serpents crowned their heads. A certain mean-looking jellyfish is called a *medusa.* And one of the edible mushrooms bears the name *medusa's head,* as does a weedy rye grass.

Gorgon today is a synonym for a hag. *Gorgonian* means terrifying. And in O. Henry we find *"gorgonizing* him with her opaque yellow eyes." In other words, she caused the poor fellow to be petrified. This is a reference to the Greeks' belief that Medusa's stare could turn a person to stone. Thank Zeus, she was done in by Perseus!

(In case you're wondering, Gorgonzola cheese has no connection with Medusa or with a French writer. It's named for its source, an Italian town near Milan.)

Hydra was another of those frightful creatures dreamed up by the imaginative Greeks. The serpent had nine heads. Every time one was cut off, two shot up in its place. 'Twas a *herculean* task to put the thing out of its misery.

In this age of big business it is interesting to observe Nader's crusaders doing battle with the *"hydra-headed* conglomerates."

But the animal that delights me most is one that was probably conceived by an anonymous American. The beast's name is *gyascutus.* His legs on one side are longer than those on the other side, thus enabling him to walk around steep hills!

To return to the ancients, so great was their interest in the creatures around them that they named eight of the twelve signs of the zodiac for members of their animal kingdom. Let us take a look at three of them.

Taurus is the Latin noun for "bull." It has sired a delightful stock of English words:

> *taurine*—bovine
> *taurocephalous*—bullheaded
> *tauroesque*—in the style of a bull
> *taurolatry*—worship of bulls
> *tauromachy*—bullfighting or bullfight
> *tauromorphic*—resembling a bull

Modern toreadors would be interested in *taurokathapsia,* an ancient Cretan sport in which the performer grasped the horns of a bull and somersaulted over him.

Pisces is the plural of *piscis,* the Latin noun for fish. It has netted us a nice collection of words:

Pisaster—genus of starfishes
piscan—relating to fishes
piscary—fishing rights; place to fish
piscation—fishing
piscatorial ⎫
piscatory ⎬
        —relating to fishermen
pisciculture—the art of breeding, developing and improving fish
pisciculturist—superintendent of a state-owned fish hatchery
piscifauna—the fishes of a given region
piscina—basin for certain ablutions, usually in a sacristy
piscine—having fishlike characteristics

Best of all is *piscinity*—the quality or state of being a fish. Several years ago, when I showed that word to my class at CCNY, a student cried out, "Holy mackerel!"

Capricorn translates literally into "goat horn." It is tempting to surmise that the isle of Capri was named for a goat. Certainly the steep terrain of that lovely spot is a challenge to the climbing ability of wild goats. Research yields the information that the original name was Capreae, but that's as far as it goes.

Another problem revolves around *capricious.* Some philologists claim that the word goes back to *caput* ("head") and *riccio* ("frizzled"). This idea is enchanting. Is a person with frizzled hair a whimsical character? Equally attractive is the claim that the word is derived from *capra* (a she goat). After all, goats are known to be *capricious.* Consider the frisky god Pan and the lusty satyrs. Both had goats' bodies. And certainly, when you *cut a caper* you spring up and down in an outlandish or goatish fashion. A closely related word is *capriole,* meaning "a caper or leap." In a horse show it's a leap with a backward kick of the hind legs while the animal is in the air.

Goat itself comes to us via an Old English word, *gát.* The *goatee* is aptly named because it so perfectly resembles the beard sported by a male goat.

Scapegoat ("a person bearing the blame for others") has a fascinating Hebraic history. It is really an *escape goat.* During Yom Kippur the high priest would bring two goats forward. Lots were cast to see which of the two would be sacrificed. The priest then symbolically laid the sins of the people on the head of the goat that had been spared. Weighed down with the burden of all those misdeeds, it was taken outside and allowed to escape.

Our expression, *to separate the sheep from the goats,* comes from

Matthew 25:32, 33. The text reads: "And before him shall be gathered all nations; and he shall separate them one from another, as a shepherd divideth his sheep from the goats." Does this passage have significance for a U.N. leader?

To get one's goat is a well known Americanism meaning "to vex or anger." But did you know that the *goatsucker* is a nocturnal bird? Its name stems from an ancient belief that it steals the milk from a she goat.

The *whippoorwill* is a goatsucker. Years ago one of those birds used to perch outside my window at exactly the hour when I retired. His "whip-poor-will," repeated incessantly, got my goat.

The *nightjar* also belongs to that goatsucker family. (In my younger days I assumed that it was a chamber pot!) Why is it called a *nightjar?* Because it makes a harsh, jarring nocturnal noise.

To paraphrase Gelett Burgess' "The Purple Cow," I offer the following lamer verses:

> I never heard a nightjar;
> I hope I never hear one,
> But I can tell you, near and far,
> I'd rather hear than rear one.

By the way, Burgess' jingle became so popular that he was surfeited with the resulting adulation. Five years later (in 1900) he added:

> "Ah, yes, I wrote 'The Purple Cow'—
> I'm sorry now I wrote it!
> But I can tell you anyhow,
> I'll kill you if you quote it."

Speaking of cows, there are some real surprises in words relating to those bovine creatures. It's easy to understand why a *cowboy* is also a *cowpoke* or a *cowpuncher,* because he prods the beasts at roundup time. But *cowlick* is not so obvious. This tuft of hair growing in a different direction from the others is so named because it appears to have been licked askew by a cow!

The *cowslip* is a primrose that grows abundantly in the British Isles. In America it is a synonym for the marsh marigold. Does it mean a flower that makes a cow take a header? Well, not exactly. *Slyppe* or *slype* ("paste, slime or dung") is the derivation. Apparently the blossom thrives on natural fertilizers in the pastures.

The *cowbird* is another feathery fiend that doesn't appeal to me. It never builds its own home, but lays its eggs in the nests of other birds. Its name stems from the fact that it feeds on cattle vermin.

Like the *goatsucker,* there is also a *cowsucker.* It's not a bird but a harmless snake. Again the appellation arose because of a widespread belief: the word got around that the snake slithered up at night and milked cows.

A word I like is *cowcatcher*. Originally it meant a triangular frame in front of the old "iron horses," designed to clear the track of obstructions. In the modern vernacular it is a brief TV or radio commercial placed just before a program. The term reveals the workings of the Madison Avenue minds. To New York admen, *cow* is a synonym for all the hicks outside the Big Apple.

I am reminded of the famous headline in VARIETY. This magazine on the dramatic arts once declared tersely that farmers did not like movies concerned with the boondocks.* The headline read, "HIX NIX STIX PIX."

Cousins of the current *cowcatcher* are *cow college* and *cow town,* both derogatory terms for rural establishments. If I were a Texas Aggie or a native of Prairie View, I would resent these neologisms.

Cow, as a verb meaning to intimidate, is simple to assimilate when one considers how docile beef-on-the-hoof are driven into stockyards. But don't be fooled by *coward*. That word can be traced back to *cauda* (a Latin noun for "tail"). Literally, a *coward* is a person who turns tail.

The Hindus revere steer and are forbidden to eat their flesh. Hence we have coined the term *sacred cow*. By this we mean a person, group or organization that is immune to all criticism, even if justified.

The cow's mate, of course, is a *bull*. He is also the consort of a female alligator, elephant, elk, moose, seal, terrapin or whale. And what a wealth of words we derive from this virile fellow!

Take the *Bulldog,* for instance. He is named not only for his fierce, muscular appearance but also for his early role as a bull baiter. Verbally he has become a synonym for "to throw a steer." As an adjective he is attached to *edition*. The *bulldog edition* is the earliest morning publication of a newspaper. It takes a lot of stubborn tenacity to put out that product.

The origin of the term *cock-and-bull story* is uncertain. It may go back to an Aesopian type of fable, or it may be an offshoot of the French expression *"coq-a-l'âne"* ("cock to donkey"). Some philologists think it is related to the reputed sexual prowess of roosters and bovine males.

That last connotation may also account for *bull session,* an informal discussion in which young males *throw the bull* or *shoot the bull.* However, it is also possible that the phrase is a euphemistic cousin of a vulgar eight-letter word referring to taurine excrement.

Bulldoze was originally *bulldose,* or a "dose for a bull." Thus it

* *Boondocks*—from the Tagalog word *bundok,* meaning "mountain." The G.I.s got hold of the word and transformed it into a synonym for the jungle or the rural hinterlands. This is a good example of how deplorable wars do add to our language.

meant a severe thrashing. Later it came to mean "intimidate" or, if you will, "cow." Today a *bulldozer* is a bully, a type of revolver, a machine for clearing land or the operator of the vehicle.

The origin of *bully* will come as a surprise to most readers. It has nothing to do with the animal. Instead it dates back to Dutch and German words for "sweetheart," "lover" or even "baby talk"! Years ago it meant "a fine fellow." Another meaning was "pimp." Considering the fact that those characters are notorious for beating up the girls in their stables, one can't help but surmise that they had their share in bringing about the present definitions for *bully* as a noun or verb.

In such a chiefly British expression as "*Bully* for you!" the interjection connotes congratulations. That idea certainly seems closer to the sources of the word.

Finally, there is *bully beef,* which has a strictly French background. It's derived from *boeuf bouilli,* and can be traced back to the Gallic verb *bouillir* ("to boil"). Some lexicographers state that *bullion* comes from that same French verb, while others maintain that it is related to *billion* (a small French coin) and dates back to *bille* ("a stick or bar"). At any rate, *bullion* is now used in two principal senses: gold and silver regarded as raw material, or a heavy fringe or lace of twisted gold or silver thread.

To add to the confusion, there is the papal *bull*—a formal, sealed document. It's a shortening of a Latin word *bulla* ("seal"). The Italian offshoot is *bullettino,* from which we get our word *bulletin.*

But *bullet* comes from the French word *boulle* ("ball") and is a cousin of the verb *bowl.* When you bowl someone over, you literally knock him down with a ball. *Bowling,* needless to say, comes from the same source.

Philologists either disagree or have doubts about the origin of Wall Street's *bulls and bears* and baseball's *bull pen,** in which pitchers warm up. But there is no quarrel about such expressions as *bull in a china shop* or *take the bull by the horns.* Nor does anyone challenge the obvious fact that a person who *bulls his way* is acting like *el toro.*

That relative of the canary, the *bullfinch,* was so named because of its thick neck. And the term *bullfrog* was coined because of the amphibian's size and bull-like croak. The immense dimensions of the *bull fiddle* (a double bass) also probably account for its name.

———

Another exemplar of strength and ferocity is the *lion.* It is the symbol of Great Britain and Venice. Ethiopia's Haile Selassie was called the "Lion of Judah," and the epithet for Richard I of England

---

* *Bull pen* (sometimes spelled as one word) has several other current meanings. It's a prison, guardhouse or other place of confinement. It's also a dormitory or bunkhouse. Finally, it's an area in a business office which is not divided into compartments. Many newspaper employees sit in the bull pen.

was "Lion-Hearted." In sports, Detroit football fans root for their Lions, and Columbia students sing "Roar, lion, roar." And a well known service organization is called the International Association of Lions Clubs.

Celebrities are called *lions* because they dominate the social scene. When we make a fuss over such people, we *lionize* them.

The animal is responsible for several common phrases too. Anyone who gets *the lion's share* receives the largest part. And *the lion's mouth* is a place of great peril, while *a lion in the path* indicates a dangerous obstacle.

We also speak of *bearding the lion in his den*—confronting some fearsome person in his own surroundings. *Twisting the Lion's tail* is taxing the patience of Great Britain—a phrase that we hear less and less as the economy and influence of that erstwhile world power continue to decline.

———

It's also dangerous to *have a tiger by the tail.* Like the lion, that jungle beast has been adopted by many groups. Tammany used it as an emblem. Princeton and the University of Missouri are among the many institutions that call their teams the Tigers, as does the Detroit baseball club. Clemenceau, the French statesman, was nicknamed "*Le Tigre*" because of the bold program he launched in an effort to defeat the Germans in World War I.

A *paper tiger,* on the other hand, is a nation or person that appears to be strong or powerful but is actually weak.

In sports or in sexual activities a vigorously aggressive person is called a *tiger,* or, if female, a *tigress.* And a loud yell at the end of a round of cheers is a *tiger.*

But the most interesting development is that the word has been given many appendages to form other nouns. *Tigereye* (the gem) and *tiger lily* (the flower) are prime examples. It also precedes bass, beetle, bittern, fish, frog, mosquito, moth, pear, python, rattlesnake, salamander, shark, weasel, wolf and quite a number of other words. Obviously the beast of Bengal has attracted the rapt attention of the botanists, zoologists and their colleagues.

———

The *wolf* has gained a reputation, whether merited or not, for savagery and cruelty. Starting with our days in the nursery, we are taught to fear and hate this cousin of the dog. "The Three Little Pigs" and "Little Red Riding Hood" make him the villain. And so poverty-stricken people try *to keep the wolf from the door,* and all of us beware of that diabolical deceiver, the *wolf in sheep's clothing.** When we

———

* *Wolf in sheep's clothing* is a phrase derived from Matthew 7:15: "Beware of false prophets, which come to you in sheep's clothing, but inwardly they are ravening wolves."

alarm others unnecessarily, we *cry wolf,* and when people are summarily evicted, they are *thrown to the wolves.*

A masher who comes on too strong or who makes advances to many women is a *wolf.* When we eat ravenously, we *wolf* our food down. And dissonance or discord is a *wolf* to musicians. Altogether, the implications are completely negative. No wonder that lupicide is often committed capriciously. "Who's afraid of the big, bad wolf?" Well, Mr. Disney, we are!

––––––

In our symbolism, the direct opposites of the *wolf* are the *sheep* and the *lamb.* To one we attribute such adjectives as stupid, timid and defenseless. The other is considered to be a Milquetoast, a dear person or a dupe.

Recently, in New York, my taxi driver had to stop suddenly because people were crossing against the light. "Sheep!" he exclaimed out the window. "You're a bunch of sheep!" One of the pedestrians looked over his shoulder and gave the cabbie a sheepish grin. No one made sheep's eyes at him, you can be sure!

Most lexicographers concur that *lamb* and *elk* have the same origin, probably in the Greek word *elaphos* ("deer"). If you find that hard to believe, so do I. We do not have many common phrases that are derived from *lamb,* but there is one notable religious reference. In John 1:29, Jesus is called "the Lamb of God, which taketh away the sin of the world."

The male of the species has given us the verb *ram* ("to strike against with a heavy object") and such a noun as *battering ram.* Also there's a *hydraulic ram* (a pump that forces water to a higher level). Probably the adjective *rambunctious* ("wild or boisterous") comes from the same animal, but it's also possible that the word is related to *rumbustical* (also "wild or boisterous") and is akin to *robust.*

When editing or constructing crossword puzzles, one of my favorite definitions for *ram* is: "He's never out of butts."

––––––

In Old English and other tongues of yore the *buck* was a "male goat." As the years progressed, this animal became a male deer or antelope. However, the term is still applied by some to sires of other mammals, such as the hare, rabbit, guinea pig, rat and—yes—the goat. It is even descriptive of male salmon, shad and other game fish.

We do get some interesting words and phrases from this animal. *Buckskin* is obvious. Our slang word for a dollar also applies; it is a shortened form of *buckskin,* which was an item of trade with the Indians. *Buckshot* fits too, and so does *buck fever,* that delightful relation of stage fright. Ohioans will be pleased to know that their *buckeye* tree was named for the male deer because of its appearance. But people with *buck teeth* will not be happy to learn that the term refers to the denture of the same beast.

And yet we shouldn't be fooled by *buckaroo, buckboard, bucket, buckle, buckthorn* and *buckwheat.* Those words have far different origins, which the reader is invited to look up if he cares to do so.

We all know the phrase *"pass the buck."* President Truman gave it a different tinge when he popularized the slogan "The buck stops here." Both expressions come from an old type of knife called a *buckhorn* because of the shape of its handle. This object was often used as a counter in early poker games to indicate the next dealer. Players would "pass the buckhorn." The noun was soon abridged into *buck.* When you *passed the buck,* you were no longer responsible for the first move in the card game; somebody else had the job of dealing. Anyhow, I'm pleased to report that the phrase eventually can be tracked down to our antlered animal.

Speaking of that quadruped, did you ever wonder if a *reindeer* was so called because it could be harnessed by Santa and others? Forget it! The word *rein* stems back to the Latin *retinere* ("to retain"). But, as might be expected, the first syllable of *reindeer* comes from a Scandinavian combination (*hreinn* plus *dyr*). The first part meant *reindeer* and the second part meant *deer*—a good example of tautology.*

In contrast, the Easter *bunny* has an interesting history. It's a lengthening of *bun,* a term in Scottish dialect that originally referred to the tail of a rabbit or squirrel and then came to mean either of those little creatures. The *bunny hug* is an old-time dance, and a *snow bunny* is a person (especially a girl) who is just learning to ski. Her brand-new relation is the *beach bunny*—a girl who joins the surfers but does not participate in the sport.

TV antennas are called *rabbit ears* because of the way they jut upward in the shape of a V. In sports the term is applied to players who are oversensitive to criticism. Their ears hear too much! In boxing it's illegal to hit one's opponent with a *rabbit punch,* or chopping blow, to the back of the head. The expression is derived from the manner in which a rabbit is stunned prior to being killed and butchered.

When some farmers prepared a rabbit for dinner, they would save the paws for good luck. Why? Well, as the joke goes, rabbits must be excellent arithmeticians because they certainly know how to multiply. Seriously, the cottontails' proclivity for procreation made them symbols of fertility. Naturally, the farmers wanted their lands to be fertile,

---

* *Tautology*—redundancy; needless repetition of an idea. This word comes from two Greek roots: *taut* ("same") and *logos* ("word or speech"). A highfalutin synonym for it is *pleonasm.*

and since the *rabbit's foot* touched the earth, they reasoned that by some magical transference it would bring productivity to the soil if kept as a sort of amulet.

Welsh rabbit is probably of jocular origin, because it has no connection with a cottontail. It's a seasoned dish made of melted cheese and milk or cream. Sometimes ale is added. Sober chefs who don't want to confuse people call the dish *Welsh rarebit.*

Some pitchers still complain that manufacturers are making the baseball too lively and therefore causing cheap home runs. They grouse about the *rabbit ball.*

Because the animal is weak and timid, players who are poor in such games as tennis, golf, cricket, or even poker are called *rabbits.*

Speaking of games, *hare and hounds* is a popular children's sport in which the "hounds" chase the "hares," who are given a head start. From *hare* we also get *harebrained* ("giddy or flighty") and the blue flower called the *harebell.* In Middle English the spelling was *harebelle,* and lexicographers assume that the plant got its name because it grew in places frequented by those little leporids. Incidentally, have you ever heard of *little chief hare?* That's a close relation of the rabbit. Its more common name is *pika.*

Another animal hunted by the hounds is the *fox.* Because of its cunning this mammal has generated the verb *to fox* and the adjective *foxy.* Interestingly enough, *foxy* has recently taken on another meaning, albeit a slangy one. When young men talk about *foxy chicks,* they don't mean that the girls are sly. Rather, they are attractive or sexy. In this sense a sexpot is a *fox.*

The horse's gait called the *fox-trot* probably was so named because it requires short, broken steps, the kind taken by the comparatively short-legged fox. The theory also applies to the dance of the same name.

Fox terriers were once used to drive Reynard from his *foxhole.* With their tails wagging gaily, *foxhounds* still perform that task.

Finally, there is *foxfire*—an eerie phosphorescent light caused by fungi on decaying wood. It's possible that the name originated because of the resemblance of this glow to the silvery quality of certain fox fur.

Mention of the hounds reminds me that those persistent canines also gave us a common verb. When a person is *hounded,* he is pursued relentlessly. That's what the *autograph hounds* do to Hollywood's lions.

Because swift steamers and ocean liners could travel so fast, they were soon called *greyhounds.* A bus company latched onto the term with great success. To any other entrepreneurs with lots of the where-withal I offer this suggestion for a fleet of vehicles that feature sight-seeing. Call them *gazehounds*. They're dogs that hunt by sight rather than by scent.

A *buckhound* is not a pursuer of the almighty dollar but a variety of *deerhound*. Both are Scottish hunting dogs.

It's easy to see why a private eye or detective who never gives up in his pursuit of a missing person or criminal is called a *bloodhound*. But if you were a poor speller, you might misinterpret the *horehound*. It's an aromatic Eurasian plant from which a cough remedy or candy is extracted. It has absolutely no connection with those deep-voiced canines. *Hore* is a variation of *hoar* ("gray"), and the second syllable comes from *hune*, an Anglo-Saxon term for "plant." The *horehound* has many hoary, downy leaves—hence the name.

When Elvis Presley sang, "You ain't nothin' but a hound dog," he was bordering on a common definition for hound—namely, "a mean and despicable person." But I don't think the breed deserves such a pejorative connotation. After all, how could equestrians *ride to hounds* on fox hunts if it were not for their four-legged leaders?

But dogs in general have received a bad press even though they are reputed to be "man's best friends" and are probably the most pop-ular pets. We incorporate them into such demeaning phrases as *go to the dogs, dog in the manger, dog-tired, dog-cheap* and *lead a dog's life*. And when we damage books we *dog-ear* them. We suffer through the *dog days* in July and August, and we define ruthless self-interest as *dog-eat-dog*. Furthermore, a fellow who has fallen out of favor with his boss or wife is said to be *in the doghouse*, and *doggerel* is inferior verse.

Even worse, a mean and despicable person is defined as a *dog* or *cur*, and a jocose word for a dog is *snarleyyow*. Mongrels are any ani-mals of mixed breeding, but we usually attach canine significance to them. Inferior food is called *dogmeat;* the G.I.s resent their *dog tags;* and lowly infantrymen are *dogfaces*. When we're disgusted we say "Doggone!" Actors refer to try-out places as *dog towns*, and sailors are not happy to be assigned to the mealtime *dogwatch* although it lasts only two hours. Finally, we have even named an abominable fungus as the *dog stinkhorn!*

Do cute little dogs fare any better? Well, consider the way we sneer at *puppy love* and the fact that one meaning for *pup* is "an inexperi-enced or objectionably brash person." And of course the female dog gets the same slap in the face. Think of the definition for bitch!

Even the poets, prophets and prosaists have joined the parade and have refused to *let sleeping dogs lie*. In the following quotations *man bites dog:*

"You called me a dog."
(Shylock to Antonio, in THE MERCHANT OF VENICE)

"Am I a dog, that thou comest to me with staves?"
(I Samuel 17:43)

". . . broodin' over bein' a dog."
(Westcott, DAVID HARUM)

" 'Who touches a hair of yon gray head
Dies like a dog! March on!' he said."
(Whittier, "Barbara Frietchie")

"I'd beat him like a dog."
(Sir Andrew, in TWELFTH NIGHT)

"Let slip the dogs of war."
(Marc Antony, in JULIUS CAESAR)

"Doth the moon care for the barking of a dog?"
(Burton, ANATOMY OF MELANCHOLY)

The list could go on and on, but I've probably labored the point already. However, as the saying goes, *every dog has his day.* We do have some expressions that favor our canine companions. *"Hot dog!"* as an expression of delight comes to mind immediately. The term *hot dog,* by the way, is derived from the imagined resemblance of a frankfurter to a dachshund. The cartoonist T. A. Dorgan ("TAD") coined the name.

Hot dog is now spelled as one word in slanguage, and it means an athlete who plays up to the crowd. It can also be used as a verb. During the football game that I attended last year, a player who had just scored a touchdown spiked the ball (threw it violently to the ground) and then performed a triumphant jig. A hipster sitting near me exclaimed: "Man, that cat can sure *hotdog* it!"

Hush puppies, which come from Dixie, are small cakes made of cornmeal and fried in deep fat. The name is derived from the fact that they were frequently fed to the dogs.

Dogged gets mixed reviews. It can mean "obstinate," but it also has acquired a more gratifying connotation to us lovers of the genus Canis. It carries the idea of "unshakable" or "unremitting." That's more like it!

Does *dogma* stem from the same source? Not at all! Its origin is not Old English but Greek. This synonym for doctrine comes from *dokein* ("to seem good"). Its cousin, via Latin, is *decent.*

Well, maybe we've spent too much time on our canine friends—a case of *the tail wagging the dog*—so it's time to move over to those other delightful pets, the *cats*.

In English phraseology our feline companions fare somewhat better than the canines. Something we enjoy might be called *the cat's pajamas, the cat's meow* or *the cat's whiskers*. We pay grudging admiration to agile *cat burglars*, and we state that "a cat has nine lives" because it always seems to land on its feet. We also repeat an old saying when we declare that "a cat may look at a king," meaning "Who's afraid of the V.I.P.?"

Games like *puss in the corner* and *one-old-cat* enhance the image of *Felis catus*. And the fun attached to making a *cat's cradle* from looped strings is also relevant.

Moreover, pleasant associations spring up from such children's stories and rhymes as PUSS IN BOOTS and "The Cat and the Fiddle." As tots, we hated Johnny Green for putting poor pussy in the well, and we liked Johnny Stout for pulling her out. Nor can we forget the grinning Cheshire cat immortalized by Lewis Carroll.

But the cat comes in for some subtle and outright disparagement too. Consider *scaredy cat, catty* remarks, *catcalls* and such expressions as *no room to swing a cat* or *as nervous as a cat on a hot tin roof*. Even *kittenish* has come to mean "affectedly coy."

Another derogatory word, *cat's-paw* ("dupe, tool or puppet"), has a fascinating origin. It can be traced to an old fable in which a monkey who wanted to get some roasted chestnuts out of a fire used the paw of his feline friend.

When we *bell the cat* we take a dare. In this instance, too, a fable is the source. In a conversation among mice, one suggested that they hang a bell on the cat's neck to warn them of their foe's approach. But a wise mouse retorted, in essence, "Fine! But who will bell the cat?"

Letting the cat out of the bag is revealing a secret. This phrase comes from a piece of rural trickery in days gone by. Con men of that time would place a cat in a sack and pretend it was a pig fit for roasting. If they were careless, their deceit was disclosed. A related phrase is "to buy a pig in a poke." The *poke* in this sense is a sack. In "The Shooting of Dan McGrew," Robert W. Service refers to *a poke of dust*, meaning "a bag of gold dust."

At any rate, if any of those swindlers at the market got away with their fraud, they'd be *in the catbird seat*—a phrase from Dixie that baseball announcer Red Barber brought to prominence.

Pussyfoot was the nickname given to W. E. Johnson, a law-enforcement officer and prohibitionist. To *pussyfoot* is to act cautiously or timidly or to be noncommittal on an issue. The derivation is obvious.

Catface has three different meanings, all stemming from an imagined resemblance to the countenance of our bewhiskered companion:

1. partially healed scar on a tree or log
2. deformity of fruit resulting from insects' stings or from disease
3. knob or pit on a coat of plastering

A cougar or lynx is sometimes called a *catamount*. This is a delightful abridgment of *cat-a-mountain* ("leopard"). The original phrase in Medieval English was "cat of the mountaine."

In crossword puzzles the word "ament" often appears. It is usually defined as a *catkin,* which is an inflorescence on a *pussy willow*. (Naturally!) *Catkin* is an alteration of an old Dutch word for "kitten" and is so named because it looks like a cat's tail. And, incidentally, for the same reason a certain marsh plant is called a *cattail.*

Most people, in this era when nothing seems to be hush-hush, know that a *cathouse* is a brothel. But when I was growing up, only the victimized children of the slums were exposed to such words. Boys somehow learned the terms secretly, but it was customary to protect girls from a vulgar, sexual vocabulary.

I am reminded of an incident that occurred when I was a beginning junior high school teacher in mid-Harlem. One day I shared yard duty at noon with a young woman who had also just joined the faculty. Painted or chalked on the walls of the school and the adjoining buildings were "Pussy," "I Love Pussy," "Pussy is Good" and other phrases containing the same word.

My colleague turned to me and said, "These people sure do go for cats, don't they?"

I looked her straight in the face and realized that she was not putting me on. "Yes," I gulped. "Maybe that accounts for all the alley cats around here."

The poor girl resigned a few weeks later. She couldn't handle the discipline problem.

Puss (the slang word for "face") does not have any relation to cats. It comes from a Gaelic alteration of "buss." The word *pus* meant "lip." So when a thug threatens to smack someone in the *puss,* he means that he'll give the fellow a "fat lip." *Sourpuss* ("grouch") is an extension from the same root.

Catnip, catmint, catnap, catboat, and *catwalk* are all related to grown-up kittens, but *catsup* is not. The alternate spelling, *ketchup,* gives it away. It comes from "kĕchap," a spiced fish sauce in Malay.

You may ask, "What about *caterwaul* ('to howl') and that creeping larva called the *caterpillar?*" The answer is that both have a feline origin. The latter is very intriguing. It literally means "hairy female cat."

While checking up on the above I came across *Catorama.* "Ah," methought, "it's an exhibit or display of Maltese, Siamese and other breeds!" But, no! Here's the definition given by WEBSTER'S THIRD NEW INTERNATIONAL DICTIONARY: "A genus of deathwatch beetles (family Anobiidae) including some that are pests of stored grain."

"Deathwatch?" That adjective made me do a double take. Why would a beetle receive such a description? Hastily I flipped the pages forward and discovered: "Any of various small beetles . . . that are common in old houses where they bore in the woodwork and furniture making a clicking noise probably by knocking the head against the wood." Visions of haunted houses and those busy beetles click-clicking away popped into my head. I was satisfied, but I had goose pimples.

Underneath the above entry, WEBSTER'S THIRD referred me to *book louse*. Well, I'd heard of *bookworms*, but never *book lice*! Consumed with curiosity, I flipped forward and read: "An insect of the family Atropidae . . . that is injurious to books and papers." Okay so far. May my house—and especially my library—be protected from *book lice*. But what about that family? "Atropidae" had a strangely familiar ring to it.

Once more my fingers did the walking, with great expectations that were instantly rewarded. The Atropidae were named for *Atropos*, one of the three Fates in Grecian mythology. She was the meanest one, because she finally cut the thread of life. Her sister Clotho did the spinning, and Lachesis determined the length of one's years, but inflexible Atropos scissored you into oblivion.

Now let me quote WEBSTER'S THIRD again concerning the Atropidae: "A widely distributed family of wingless insects . . . that include most book lice and that feed on organic debris and often damage processed foods, book bindings, herbarium specimens and similar stored products."

But the note relating to the derivation is even more interesting: "From the belief that the ticking sound made by some species of book lice forebodes a death."

And so we come full circle, having started with *Catorama*. I cite the above as only one of the many adventures that one can have if he or she really peruses an unabridged lexicon. As someone has said before me, "The more I learn the more ignorant I realize I am."

In connection with the journey from *Catorama* to the Atropidae, I recall being asked the familiar question, "If you were on a desert island, what three books would you prefer to have with you?" Think. What would be your choices? You can guess one of mine. As for the other two—see the footnote at the end of this chapter. But please choose your own favorites before you look at mine.

———

When I became an assistant principal at P.S. 169 in Manhattan, the woman in charge of the school said to me, "Gene, you run the place while I get rid of some *cats and dogs* that have piled up on my desk." It was the first time I'd ever heard that expression, but I guessed correctly that she meant little miscellaneous odds and ends.

———

Well, that's just about enough coverage for *cats and dogs*. Now let's get to our other four-legged associates the equines.

The word *horse* probably has a Germanic and Old Norse background; lexicographers aren't sure. In medieval times it was spelled *hors*. Strangely enough, the American Indians were introduced to the animal by the invading Spanish armies, but they certainly made use of it from then on. The *cayuse* was named for the Oregonian tribe of that name. The *Indian pony* is descended from a Spanish breed, but it received its appellation because the native tribes adopted it.

The *mustang* has a Hispanic origin, from *mesten(g)o*. Literally, it's a stray animal. If you saw THE MISFITS, you may remember how Clark Gable tried to capture these feral beasts while Marilyn Monroe objected hysterically. Some experts state that the name actually dates back to *mixtus,* the Latin past participle for *miscere* ("to mix"). Indeed, the *mustangs* are a mixed breed. The story goes that long ago they mingled with domesticated herds on the prairies and produced hybrids.

Palomino has an interesting history. The name in Spanish America literally means "like a dove," because its color resembles that of the *paloma*.

The *bronco* is also of Spanish descent. Appropriately enough, the word means "rough." The *pinto* is a calico horse or pony. Any Mexican can tell you that the word means "spotted." It's assumed that the Spanish American adjective was derived from the Vulgar Latin. *Pinctus* meant "painted." Today in the West a mottled horse is often called *paint* by cowboys.

But *horse* itself has given rise to an abundance of phrases and expressions. We say, "That's a horse of a different color" when we refer to something entirely different. Why the horse instead of the dog or cat or other animal? Frankly, I don't think anybody knows. Shakespeare did mention metaphorically *a horse of the same color* in TWELFTH NIGHT; hence the saying probably goes back at least to the Elizabethan era.

Not long before the reign of Elizabeth I, Thomas Heywood wrote: "A man may well bring a horse to the water, But he cannot make him drink . . ."

James Polk, our eleventh President, was the first *dark horse* to be elected. His name was not even mentioned at the Democrats' convention in 1844 until the eighth ballot. He came out of nowhere to win the race for candidacy. The term obviously arises from race-track jargon.

An unknown contender is "dark" because the form sheets shed no light on him.

To the sport of kings we also owe such phrases as *back the wrong horse* ("support a loser") and *from the horse's mouth* (meaning that the jockey's mount in the race had actually talked like Mr. Ed of old TV programs and had promised to win).

Locking the barn door after the horse has been stolen is simple to translate into "taking precautionary actions too late." But when Heywood wrote in 1546, "No man ought to looke a gift horse in the mouth," his dictum may not be familiar to many readers. The proverb dates back to Saint Jerome in 400 A.D. It refers to the fact that a horse's worth can be assessed by its age, and the condition of its teeth is an excellent criterion. Thus if you inspect the mouth of a horse that is given to you as a present, you are insulting the donor.

Let me point out, however, that Heywood's words have been turned around. We are now told, "Always look a gift horse in the mouth." In other words, before expressing gratitude, inspect the merchandise to see if there's a hitch. This reversal may have some connection with the *wooden horse* or *Trojan horse*—terms now synonymous with people or things designed to destroy from within.

When I was a tot and wrote to Santa Claus about the wonderful toys I wanted for Christmas, my Irish mother always said, "If wishes were horses, beggars would ride." I couldn't figure out what in tarnation she meant. It was like some sort of riddle. Years later I appreciated the aptness of that saying for a poor boy, and recently I've discovered that it appears in John Ray's ENGLISH PROVERBS (1670).

In contrast, *Hold your horses!* and *Don't get on your high horse!* present no great difficulty in interpreting their intended messages. But why does the Pale Horse signify death? People versed in the New Testament will know immediately. In Revelation 6:8, the text reads: "And I looked, and behold a pale horse; and his name that sat on him was Death, and Hell followed with him." By the way, that quotation is a reminder that our familiar quadruped came into being ages and ages ago.

From the same text we have derived the term, "The Four Horsemen of the Apocalypse." They are Conquest, Slaughter, Famine and Death. In 1922–24, when Notre Dame football teams coached by Knute Rockne were riding roughshod over all opponents, the backfield was nicknamed "The Four Horsemen." Collectors of trivia may be interested to know that their names were Harry Stuhldreher, James Crowley, Don Miller and Elmer Layden. The last member of the quartet later became a famous coach himself.

Whoever came up with *horse feathers* as a synonym for bunk or nonsense had the touch of a poet. Maybe he was referring obliquely to

Pegasus, that winged horse of Greek mythology. In any case, he made a good point. Ordinary horses can't fly; hence *horse feathers* is an apt description of any high-flown statement that deserves to be rated as bombast.*

For some reason, medieval households had *horseshoes* nailed to their doors to drive away witches. Was it because the object would kick them away? I don't know, but it's certain that today a *horseshoe* is one of the many symbols of good luck. When a player on the diamond makes a great catch, the opponents yell "Horseshoes!" to indicate that his feat wasn't really based on his skill.

Speaking of baseball, if a pitcher gives the other team the *horse collar,* he shuts them out. This bit of slang may refer to the shape of the O's on the scoreboard or to the fact that the batters have been limited in effectiveness by his excellent deliveries. It's a good guess that both of the above led to the use of the term either as a noun or a verb. In future years it will be exciting to see if it is applied to other areas of life or eventually becomes accepted as part of our language, like so many other terms of unpromising origin.

Horse opera is a case in point. This colorful synonym for a western film or TV program is now listed as slang by only one of my many dictionaries. I assume that it will soon be universally embraced as a legitimate term.

One-horse is another picturesque word. It means "second-rate, inferior, petty or jerkwater." Though the adjective is often used with *town,* it is sometimes affixed to such other nouns as *theory, lawyer, farm* and *exhibition.*

A closely related term is *horse-and-buggy,* meaning "old-fangled; hopelessly outmoded." Those who cling to passé ideas and attitudes are called "horse-and-buggy thinkers." In that connection, *mumpsimus*—a marvelous noun that unfortunately is seldom used—is a person who doggedly adheres to his errors and prejudices even after they have been pointed out to him.

Sometimes plants, insects or fish that are relatively large or coarse have the word *horse* prefixed to their names. Examples are *horse mint, horse mushroom, horse nettle* and *horse radish.* Among the insects there are the *horse fly* and *horse ant.* At sea we find the *horse mackerel* and *horse mussel.*

Sea horse has many meanings. Among them are:

1. walrus
2. fabulous creature, half horse and half fish

* *Bombast*—pretentious words or speech that has little meaning. This word comes from *bombyx* ("silkworm"). Its silk is used for padding the cocoon. Thus the product, *bombast,* is inflated. Later it came to be applied to grandiose oratory.

3. horsefish
4. large whitecap on a wave
5. short-handled clam rake with long prongs

The king crab is often called *horseshoe crab* because of the shape of its protective shell. The name also fits because of its tremendous size. Actually, it is not a true crab or crustacean but is the sole survivor of an ancient order of arthropods, or animals with jointed limbs. A third name for this unique creature is *horsefoot crab*.

Speaking of throwbacks, I find it fascinating that we still measure the might of an automobile engine in terms of *horsepower*.

If you order a *horse's neck* at a restaurant, you'd better specify exactly what you want. It's a tall drink of ginger ale, with or without alcohol. In either case, a lemon rind, which possibly resembles a horse's neck, is draped over the rim of the glass. The other end of the animal, by the way, has given rise to a vulgar synonym for a fool or a boor.

One of the many meanings of *pony* also relates to drinks. It's half a jigger,* or three-quarters of a fluid ounce. But a *pony* is also a *trot,* or a word-for-word translation of a foreign-language text, used illicitly by students. It's possible that one is an offshoot of the other, because a high-schooler can move through Caesar's COMMENTARIES at a moderately fast gait if he uses a *pony.* However, a few linguists suggest that the word might be related to *pons asinorum* ("bridge of asses"). In geometry this phrase is a Euclidean proposition to the effect that the base angles of an isosceles triangle are equal. It has come to mean "any difficult problem for beginners."

Aside from the obvious *pony express* and a girl's *ponytail,* the word has given us two rather recent derivatives in the area of sports:

> *pony backfield*—a group of small, quick runners on offense in football
> *Pony League*—a group of boys, aged thirteen to fifteen who are too old for baseball's Little League

At the Kentucky Derby, people make wagers on the *ponies,* but they also bet on the *colts.* These are not only young male horses but in common parlance they are novices or rookies, or awkward young fellows. The officials at Baltimore failed to take this definition into account when they named their football team.

Two other uses of *pony* have recently sprung up. The noun is now a synonym for a tiny chorine. And because such compact, high-powered automobiles as the Mustang and Pinto have been named for small horses, sporty little hardtops are called *pony cars.*

---

* *Jigger*—a measure in mixing drinks usually equal to 1½ ounces. In this sense the word probably comes from *chigger,* an African variation of *chigoe* ("flea; mite"). Both the *chigger* and the *jigger* are tiny.

As an adjective, *coltish* means "playful or frisky." The noun *colt-pixie* is next of kin. It means "a mischievous hobgoblin supposed to appear as a colt and mislead men or horses into bogs."

My personal favorite is *colt's tooth*—a synonym for youthful wantonness or lustful desire. This phrase stems from the fact that horses develop colt's teeth at the age of three, when their passions simultaneously begin to seethe. To borrow from another expression, they are eager "to sow wild oats."

The counterpart of a *colt*, of course, is a *filly,* a word related philologically to *foal.* Male chauvinists today refer to high-spirited young girls as *fillies.* It intrigues me to notice that Frenchmen designate a young, unmarried girl as a *jeune fille.* Actually, *fille* comes from the Latin word *filia* ("daughter").

The grown-up *filly* presents us with at least two exhilarating phrases:

> *mare's nest*—a hoax or fraud. Mares don't make nests—hence the phrase.
>
> *shank's mare*—one's own legs. When we ride or go "on shank's mare," we walk. In other words, we use our shanks ("legs") instead of the trusty quadruped.

Why do we call an inferior or aged or unsound horse a *nag?* This word is related to the Dutch noun *negge* ("small horse") and is eventually derived from "neigh." Incidentally, it has no alliance with the verb meaning "to engage in petty faultfinding." That word is probably of Scandinavian origin and once meant "to gnaw." How appropriate!

All experienced crossword puzzle solvers know that *haw* is a command to a horse or other draft animal to turn to the left and *gee* is an order to turn right. Bettors at the "Big A" and Belmont and other tracks often describe a "nag" as a *gee-gee.* This is a slangy duplication of the mandate to the old gray mare.

To conclude this hippological section of "Our Animal Kingdom," here's a little quiz for you. Can you match the following titles with their authors? The answers will appear at the end of the chapter.

TITLES	AUTHORS
1. THREE MEN ON A HORSE	a. Zane Grey
2. BEGGAR ON HORSEBACK	b. Edna Ferber
3. THE HORSE'S MOUTH	c. Katherine Anne Porter
4. MY FRIEND FLICKA	d. Joyce Cary
5. PALE HORSE, PALE RIDER	e. Sherwood Anderson
6. SARATOGA TRUNK	f. Walter Blair
7. THE THUNDERING HERD	g. John C. Holm and George Abbott
8. THE HORSE KNOWS THE WAY	h. Mary O'Hara
9. HORSE SENSE IN AMERICAN HUMOR	i. George S. Kaufman and Marc Connelly
10. HORSES AND MEN	j. John O'Hara

Obviously, in a single chapter it's impossible to cover all the phrases that involve the multitude of creatures on land and sea. Individual readers may want to track down the meanings and derivations of some of the following:

red herring	a bee in one's bonnet	count sheep
rat race	squirrel away	the goose hangs high
skunk cabbage	stool pigeon	loan shark
duck soup	pig Latin	mosquito boat
for the birds	cub reporter	eager beaver
as the crow flies	weasel words	dovetail

You may enjoy a test of your skill in *ferreting out* the items that don't belong in the lists below. Each list contains only one phrase that has no connection whatsoever with the creature mentioned in the expression. The answers appear in the paragraphs that close this chapter.

LIST #1
monkey shines—mischievous pranks
roadhog—selfish driver
play possum—feign; pretend
crow's nest—platform on a mast
snapdragon—garden plant
snake eyes—a throw of "two" at dice
white elephant—useless, expensive possession
kangaroo court—unauthorized or mock court
ride piggyback—ride on another's back or shoulders
chicken feed—trifling sum; small change

LIST #2
spelling bee—classroom contest
stud poker—card game
smell a rat—be suspicious
crowbar—a pry or lever
feed the kitty—ante up in a card game
horse around—play roughly or boisterously
with kid gloves—tactfully or carefully
fly in the ointment—pleasure spoiler
monkey suit—uniform
lame duck—official serving out his term after being defeated for reelection

The opossum (shortened to possum) is reputed to feign death when frightened or threatened. Thus people who *play possum* are dissembling or pretending ignorance.

White elephant has a fascinating history. Long ago the king of Siam was the only person allowed to own an albino elephant, because they were so rare. But, like other pachyderms, they had enormous appetites and were expensive to keep. And so, whenever the king felt dislike for a courtier, he would present the poor fellow with a white elephant and wait for him to be financially ruined.

Kangaroo courts disregard or pervert the law or justice. Sometimes they are set up by prisoners or vagabonds or lynch mobs. They are so named because decisions are reached by leaps and bounds.

The expression *ride piggyback* is an alteration of "pick-a-back" or "pick-a-pack." Today *piggyback* is also used as a verb. When truck trailers loaded with merchandise are placed on freight cars, they "piggyback." (The phrase is the only one in List #1 that has no connection with the animal.)

Because the bee is regarded as a busy little creature, its name has been attached to all kinds of activities, such as *sewing bees, husking bees* and *spelling bees.*

The *crowbar* is so named apparently because the tool originally had a forked end that looked like a crow's foot. Incidentally, wrinkles around the outer corner of the eyes are called *crow's feet* because of their resemblance to the bird's footprints.

Feed the kitty actually means to put money into a jug. *Kitty* dates back to a Medieval Dutch word *kitte* or *kit,* meaning "jug or vessel." (This is the only phrase in List #2 that has no connection with the animal.) It should also be noted that the stakes in a poker game are often called the "pot." The reason is the same as the one for "kitty." Originally the players placed their antes, or bets, in a vessel in the center, which the lucky winner emptied. In some places the practice still continues.

Monkey suit (sometimes called *monkey jacket*) is a slang term for a uniform because of the fact that organ grinders always dressed their simian companions in little coats. It should be noted that the term is now also applied to a tuxedo.

Finally, I am reminded of the well known story about the little schoolgirl who submitted a book report that read somewhat as follows: "This book was all about penguins. It told me where penguins live, what they eat, what they do all year, and lots more. It told me more about penguins than I cared to know."

Well, dear reader, I do hope you cared to know!

My three choices for books that I would prefer to have if stranded on a desert island (see p. 291):
1. The Bible
2. An unabridged Dictionary of the English language
3. The complete works of Shakespeare

Answers to the Titles-Authors quiz (see p. 296):
   1–g, 2–i, 3–d, 4–h, 5–c, 6–b, 7–a, 8–j, 9–f, 10–e

CHAPTER 11

Twice-Told Tales

Y ears ago I took a course in semantics. One day the professor handed us copies of a bombastic piece of prose by an eighteenth-century writer and an obscure modern poem. Our assignment was to translate both pieces into very simple sentences. As I remember, it proved to be a challenging task.

That basic idea is the substance of this chapter. Stories are told in highfalutin language and are repeated in plain English on the facing pages. The reader is invited to cover each right-hand page and try to "translate" the sesquipedalian tale without recourse to a dictionary. Note how the context often provides the key to the meaning of an unfamiliar word.

Incidentally, this chapter exemplifies the fact that most good writers have a style that combines less common words with Anglo-Saxon monosyllables. Although the use of such a word as *circumforaneous* ("going about from market to market") provides economy of expression, overuse of such jawbreakers can cause a failure to communicate with the reader. Also, what is sententious is often pretentious. The word for such grandiose phraseology is *lexiphanicism*.

On the other hand, oversimplified writing is not only replete with roundabout phrases and clauses but also boring and infantile.

The golden mean advocated by the Greeks seems to be good advice for would-be authors.

THE PUGNACIOUS PUNDIT

As a philomathical person I have no inclination to pococurantism when confronted with an opportunity for edification. Ergo, while sojourning in India, I attended a disquisition on ditheism by Mahali Lagore, the reputedly charismatic mahatma.

Lagore's allocution was more didactic than exegetic. It caused an energumen in the amen corner to express his approbation stentoriously. The guru's vexation was manifest as he essayed to continue. But anon the intercurrent encomia generated *lapsus memoriae*. The pandit divagated into extraneous precincts.

These discursions had a soporific effect on me. Oneiric tableaux materialized perforce. In my protracted reverie a rumbustious charivari intermingled with visions of a rowdydow. Suddenly a khansamah awakened me. In flaggergastion, I perceived that the durbar had been evacuated.

"Sahib!" the wallah ejaculated. "Weren't you present when the preceptor smote the zealot?"

THE TOUGH TEACHER

As a person who loves learning I am never indifferent when faced with a chance to be instructed. Therefore, while living temporarily in India, I attended a formal lecture on the theory of the existence of two gods. The address was given by Mahali Lagore, who was said to be a sage possessing divinely granted spiritual gifts.

Lagore's speech was more preachy than explanatory. It caused a fanatical rooter up front to shout approval in a loud voice. The religious teacher's annoyance was obvious as he tried to go on talking. But soon the cries of praise that interrupted him produced a lapse of memory. The learned man strayed into areas that had nothing to do with the subject.

These digressions made me sleepy. Dreamy pictures came into existence willy-nilly. In my long daydream a wild confusion of noises was mixed with images of a riot. Suddenly a house steward awakened me. In surprise, I realized that the auditorium was empty.

"Sir!" the worker cried. "Weren't you here when the teacher hit the fan?"

A SAYONARA TO BAKSHEESH

It was Joseph Smythe's quotidian routine to ruminate peripatetically in the course of his peregrination to the urban educational establishment where he served as a custodial engineer. Every morning a frowzy mendicant importuned him. Preoccupied with cosmotellurian cogitations, Smythe would altruistically deposit currency in the schnorrer's stannic container.

This eleemosynary practice continued perennially until the involuntary almoner's wherewithal was grievously depleted. Nevertheless, diurnally he bestowed his lagniappe upon the sycophant.

And then, one morning as Smythe proceeded along his customary itinerary, a gentleman in opulent raiment accosted him. "Your benefactions, sir, have been sagaciously invested. Consequently I am now a plutocrat and find myself in a position to indulge in philanthropy." He directed Smythe's attention to a Rolls Royce situated nearby and placed the keys in the bedazzled eleemosynar's hands.

"Because of your largesse," he ejaculated, "I can now bid a sayonara to baksheesh!"

A FAREWELL TO ALMS

It was Joe Smith's daily routine to ponder while walking on his journey to the city school where he served as a janitor. Every morning a shabby beggar would approach him abruptly and ask for a handout. Lost in thoughts about heaven and earth, Smith would unselfishly drop some coins into the beggar's tin cup.

This charitable practice continued year after year until the automatic donor had little money left. And yet each day he gave coins to the parasite.

And then, one morning as Smith followed his usual route, a richly dressed gentleman stopped him. "Your gifts, sir, have been wisely invested. As a result I am now a very rich man and am able to give out presents myself." He pointed to a Rolls Royce parked nearby and handed the keys to his astonished benefactor.

"Because of your generosity," he cried out, "I can now bid a farewell to alms!"

THE JAGGED JENNET

Convict DiHoti had been incarcerated in a Mexican panopticon for trafficking in "keys." Three hebdomads later his coadjutor, Pancho Sanza, dexterously engineered his clandestine nocturnal liberation from the Stygian calaboose.

Sanza had provided a robustious, animated Arab for DiHoti, while he himself was borne on a burro bearing the appellation Dribble. Shrouded in tenebrity, the duo commenced their noctivagation through an arboreous region.

At cockcrow they emerged onto a *camino* and perforce approached an opulent *hacienda*. Suddenly a detonation occurred within that sumptuous structure. The concussion caused vitreous particles from the casements to circumfuse the nefarious twosome. One fragment struck Sanza's jennet in the costal area and generated a jagged aperture in its epidermis. Dribble collapsed into a recumbent, moribund position.

DiHoti exhorted Sanza to absquatulate, but his cohort would not abandon his stricken mount. While they indulged acrimoniously in logomachy, the *policia* materialized and apprehended them both.

"Eheu!" exclaimed DiHoti. "What a horrendous section of an oriel in the burro!"

DONKEY BUSINESS

Con DiHoti had been imprisoned in a Mexican jail for buying and selling kilograms of marijuana and heroin. Three weeks later his assistant, Pancho Sanza, cleverly contrived his secret escape at night from the hellish and gloomy jail.

Sanza had supplied a sturdy, spirited horse of Arabian stock for DiHoti, while he himself rode an ass named Dribble. Shielded by darkness, the two began their nightly wandering through a heavily wooded forest.

At dawn they came out onto a road and, by necessity, passed a home owned by a rich farmer. Suddenly an explosion took place inside that splendid house. The shock caused pieces of window glass to pour all around the villainous pair. One piece hit Sanza's donkey in the ribs and produced a rough, sharp hole in the outer layer of its skin. Dribble lay down dying.

DiHoti urged Sanza to flee, but his partner in crime would not leave his wounded beast. While they argued bitterly, the police arrived and arrested them both.

"Alas!" cried DiHoti. "What an awful pane in the ass!"

A CAESAR'S SEIZURE

Extant once was a palatinate renowned for its vineyards. Whether the delectability of the singular spirits of Bacchus resided perdu in the vitaceous globules, in the *terra firma,* in the clime, or in the fermentative *modus operandi,* no one could fathom. The eventuation was, nonetheless, no cause for pilpul. The vinous products were so dulcified and so demulcent that they appeared celestial. The imbiber attained a euphoric condition akin to that of the Pantheon.

In a biennial jubilee, the aggregate of the dominion rendezvoused to solemnize erstwhile achievements and to importune the deities for their enduring munificence. The distinction of being the sommelier was universally coveted and on each occasion devolved upon a vintner designated by the assemblage. The observance was centuried and had remained inviolate through the regnancies of incalculable sovereigns. Till such time as King Stitt appeared, *id est.*

From the onset of his ascendancy Stitt manifested a supercilious and peremptory mien incongruous with this equanimous realm. As the day of the *fête champêtre* became proximate, the populace speculated as to whether Stitt would tyrannize over this proceeding too. As soon as the goblets were meted out and the carafes uncorked, Stitt asserted himself. He commandeered the primary decanter and, filling a propinquant chalice, promulgated: "Whenas Stitt predominates, Stitt decants!"

A KING'S TAKE-OVER

There once was a kingdom well known for its wine fields. Whether the delightful flavor of the special wines was concealed in the grapes, in the soil, in the climate, or in the wine-making process, no one knew. The result, however, was not disputed. The wines were so free from acidity and so soothing that they seemed not to be a product of this world. The drinker reached a state of happiness similar to that of all the gods.

In a feast held every two years, all in the kingdom met to celebrate past successes and to ask the gods for their continued kindnesses. The honor of being the wine steward was one everybody wanted and each time fell to a grower chosen by the group. The tradition had existed for centuries and had remained unchanged through the reigns of countless kings. Until Stitt, that is.

Since taking the throne, Stitt had shown an arrogant and domineering manner out of tune with this genial land. As the day of the celebration drew near, the people wondered if Stitt would use his power arbitrarily at this event too. As soon as the wineglasses were distributed and the bottles opened, Stitt advanced. He grabbed the first bottle and, filling a nearby goblet, announced: "When Stitt reigns, Stitt pours!"

NENDELIAN NONSENSE

One day while the renowned Spermatophyta taxonomist Gregor Hojann Nendel was on his tract crossbreeding his pinnate-leaved legumes, a page ingressed apace.

Anhelous, he exhorted, "Lord, excuse this obtrusion upon your indagations in the leguminous sphere, but I am an emissary from the urban thespians. One of our personnel is insalubrious and unable to execute his role this eventide. The coryphaeus of our histrions has propounded that you, liege, could serve as a surrogate."

"And wherefore me?" queried the dumbfounded Nendel, who subsisted as an anchorite in his bower.

"Because the function is that of a horticulturist. There is merely one sentence for you to articulate. You will be indefectible!"

With some disinclination Nendel acquiesced. He rehearsed his tableau with the troupe while Phoebus shone. It was not problematic; his desideratum was simply to eradicate extraneous vegetation from a plot of legumes on the proscenium. His single enunciation ensued the verbal stimulus, "Confound that caitiff!"

At gloaming the dramalogue transpired faultlessly until Nendel descried the orbs of those assembled fixed on him. He became immobilized. The tragedian delivered the verbal stimulus, "Confound that caitiff!" Nendel remained in a state of obmutescence. "Confound that caitiff!" his confrere iterated thunderously. Nendel was yet paralyzed.

The assemblage waxed restive and clamorous. Eventually an individual vociferated, "Nendel may be conversant with his pinnate-leaved legumes, but indeed he has not apprehended his verbal stimuli!"

THE WORDLESS WEEDER

One day while the famous botanist Gregor Hojann Nendel was in his garden doing his hybrid experiments with sweet peas, a servant came running toward him. Out of breath, he cried, "Sir, I am sorry to interrupt your pea experiments, but I am a messenger from the drama group in town. One of our members has fallen ill and cannot perform tonight. The director of our actors has suggested that you, sir, could act as a substitute."

"And why me?" asked the surprised Nendel, who lived a hermit's life in his rural cottage.

"Because the role is that of a gardener. There is only one line. You will be perfect!"

Reluctantly Nendel agreed. He practiced his scene with the group all afternoon. It was easy; all he had to do was weed a pea garden on the front part of the stage. His one line followed the cue, "Damn that coward!"

That evening the play went well until Nendel noticed the eyes of the audience upon him. He froze. The actor gave him the cue, "Damn that coward!" Nendel remained silent. "Damn that coward!" his fellow actor repeated loudly. Nendel still didn't move.

The audience became impatient and noisy. Finally someone yelled out, "Nendel may know his peas, but he certainly hasn't learned his cues!"

THE SAPIENT RHETORICIAN

In his postprandial ruminations, Dr. Schlepper (an estimable deipnosophist) descanted for our edification. Accumbent, he discoursed on a farrago of subjects, ranging from xyloglyphy and psychopharmacology to cynegetics and typhlology. Even misologists among us were impelled *nolens volens* to admire this savant's acroamatic disquisitions. His lore was pansophical!

However, one sciolist on the purlieu of the assemblage cachinnated deprecatingly during the sage's protracted exposition on the dissimilitudes between exegesis and isagogics. But that cynocephalus was relegated forthwith. Erubescent, we apologized to our mentor for our condisciple's contumelious irruption.

An onomasticon could be compiled from the appellations we heaped upon the scapegrace as he was summarily ejected from the premises. Acrimonious epithets such as "Charlatan," "Philistine" and "Yahoo" emanated from our rankling coterie.

But our pantologist displayed seraphic serenity and attempered our acerbity with a homily on the ecological causations for stultification, hebetude and mordacious deportment. Ah, such sophrosyne, commingled with atticisms, made us his sequacious adherents sempiternally.

Wellaway! This vignette has a lugubrious coda. On the morrow, *subito,* Dr. Schlepper became a valetudinarian. His helpmeet asseverated that he had been afflicted with logorrhea!

THE WISE AND ELOQUENT SPEAKER

In his meditations after dinner, Dr. Schlepper (a man highly esteemed for his skill in the art of table talk) made a great number of observations that increased our knowledge. Reclining, he spoke with regard to a mixture of topics, covering a wide area from artistic wood carving and the study of the effects of drugs on mental states to the art of hunting and the science dealing with blindness. Even those of us who reacted against new learning were forced willy-nilly to have great respect for this wise man's oral inquiries into various subjects. His store of knowledge could fill an encyclopedia.

However, one pretender to scholarship on the edge of the gathering laughed out loud in a belittling way during the wise man's lengthy explanation of the differences between critical interpretation of the Bible and the study of its literary history. But that baboon was banished immediately. Reddening, we begged our counselor to forgive our schoolfellow's insulting and humiliating intrusion.

A printed collection of nouns could be put together from the names we called the rascal as he was hastily and arbitrarily ousted from the room. Bitter names such as "pretender," "ignorant outsider" and "barbarian" sprang from our angry group.

But our man of all knowledge showed angelic calm and made us less harsh with a solemn talk on the environmental reasons for stupidity, dullness and sarcastic behavior. Ah, such self-control mixed with well turned expressions made us his slavish followers forever.

Alas, this little sketch has a sad ending. The next day, suddenly, Dr. Schlepper became an invalid. His wife stated that he had come down with a case of excessive talkativeness!

THE VOCAL VENDOR

One autumn the family breadwinner was on sabbatical leave and instructing at a Gallic *gymnasium*. So we tremulous and inquisitive offspring also took up residence in modern Gaul for a twelvemonth. Through those aureate spectacles of Mnemosyne, I recollect in particular the antemeridian excursions for comestibles, and I can still envision my kinfolk circumambulating an alfresco emporium in the harborage of Nantes.

Our quotidian routine was to peregrinate in this uncommon setting, beneficently allocating blandishments among the jovial laborers. All their displays of edibles intermixed as one pullulating organism of commerce: we gazed upon heifers' glossal processes recently transported out of an abattoir, tureens of animated elvers, and myriads of mangel-wurzels, rutabagas, worts, et cetera. On our circumforaneous route we became inured to occasional eruptions of billingsgate among the rival vendors. Their argot did not disturb our equanimity, but one eccentric entrepreneur addled us indeed.

"*Les jolis champignons, madame!*" this matron vociferated as we traversed the site. And so we halted to purchase some of her succulent mycological specimens. Not a single one on display! As inveterate mycophagists, we experienced a surge of vexation.

"*Quoi?* They're all vended!" *Maman* ejaculated. "But your announcement—can you explicate?"

"Oh, it's just an acquired mannerism," rejoined the *vendeuse*, "from incessantly marketing morels. I vocalize even if all are exhausted—but when in stock, they're *la crème de la crème!*"

We concurred, on quitting the scene, that *she* was indubitably the "belle of the yell!"

THE YELLING SELLER

One fall Dad took a leave from his college work and taught at a French high school. So we timid and curious kids also got to live in France for a year. Through those golden-tinted glasses of memory, I recollect especially the morning shopping trips for food, and I can still see my family walking around an open-air marketplace in the commercial seaport of Nantes.

Our daily practice was to wander in this new place, generously giving out kind works to the merry workers. All their food stands blended into one teeming body of trade: we saw cows' tongues newly shipped out of a slaughterhouse, large bowls of live young eels, and a great number of beets, turnips, herbs, etc. As we went from one booth to another we became used to the curses hurled at one another now and then by the people competing to have their wares bought. Their vulgar language didn't bother us, but one strange seller certainly confused us.

"Pretty mushrooms, my lady!" this elderly woman cried as we passed her. And so we stopped to buy some of her delicious varieties of mushrooms. Not a single one to be seen! As confirmed mushroom eaters, we were keenly annoyed.

"What? They're all sold!" Mother cried. "But your call—can you explain?"

"Oh, it's just a habit I got into," replied the tradeswoman, "from selling mushrooms all the time. I call even when they're sold out—but if I have some, they're the cream of the crop!

We agreed, as we left, that *she* was definitely the "scream" of the crop!

MY BEASTLY BENEFACTORS

W hen a neophytic scholar, I made the acquaintance of a singular professor. He was a polyglot as well as a bibliomaniac.

Confident that his passion for classics would fructify in me, he once tendered me on a temporary basis a scarce edition of *Aesop's Fables*. In truth, I was apathetic about the *oeuvre*. . . . On the eve of the day set for restoring it to its owner I discovered I had mislaid it! Reconnoitering to no avail, I finally passed into slumberland distraught.

In a somnolent vision I meandered over bouldered terrain questing for my neglected volume. The route bifurcated, and when I opted for one channel, it trifucated! My undertaking seemed obfuscated.

Subsequently a duad of creatures with shining orbs instantaneously materialized. One was a chanticleer and the other a taurine beast. "What direction should I pursue to locate my text?" I uttered optimistically.

"Why should we enlighten you?" they retorted *a due* with sardonic smirks. "You're no bibliophile!" But perceiving that I was mortified, they ultimately became ruthful. "The opus is behind your chiffonier— why not contemplate it now?"

I returned to reality and wrenched the bureau away from the partition. *Voila!* The vanished storybook! Needless to elucidate, I never related to my mentor this gallinaceous and bovine narrative!

WITH A LITTLE HELP FROM MY FRIENDS

W hen a college freshman, I knew a teacher who was unique. He was a master of many languages and a fanatic about collecting books.

Hoping his love of ancient literature would bear fruit in me, he once lent me a rare copy of *Aesop's Fables*. Frankly, I wasn't interested in the book. . . . The evening before I had promised to return it I realized I'd lost it! I looked all over for it but couldn't find the book, and finally fell asleep very upset.

In a dream I wandered aimlessly on rocky land in search of my lost book. The path split into two branches, and when I went one way, it split again—this time going in three directions! My job seemed increasingly difficult.

Then two animals with bright eyes suddenly appeared. One was a rooster and the other a male cow. "Which way might I find my book?" I said hopefully.

"Why should we tell you?" they answered together with scornful smiles. "You're no lover of books!" But seeing that my pride was severely wounded, at last they relented. "The book is behind your dresser —why not study it now?"

I awoke and pulled my dresser away from the wall. Hurrah! The lost text! Needless to say, I never told my professor this cock-and-bull story!

AN ALLY OF TRUE ALLOY

The industrious population of a Pennsylvania steel mill felt disgruntlement because their superiors continually negated petitions for grievance hearings on environmental factors. Unfortunately their regional union representatives lacked the intellectual wherewithal to initiate a *modus operandi*.

Hence an *ad hoc* committee sought the services of "Steel Eye" Sam. Presently emeritus, Sam had hitherto received réclame as a *par excellence* national unionizer. Moreover, he had participated in all the processes of production, from liquefying the crude ferrum to extracting the scoria and preparing the molten metal for molding. Sam was favorably disposed to their overture.

One day, in accordance with Sam's expedients for exigency, a wildcat strike affected the plant—precisely when the giant crucibles were replete with simmering iron. The oligarchy in charge was flabbergasted; if not cast, the steel would solidify—monolithic and immovable.

Posthaste the moilers apprised the overseers that if protestations could be audited, operations would resume *de novo*. Management capitulated; Sam's machination had been a masterstroke. And as they parted company, Sam lectured the union fuglemen, "Remember: oppose when the ore flows!"

THE WELL-TEMPERED FRIEND

The laborers in a Pennsylvania steel mill were unhappy because their bosses always refused to hear complaints about poor working conditions. Unfortunately their local union leaders didn't have enough intelligence to design a plan of action.

So a group of them formed for the purpose of calling on "Steel Eye" Sam. Now in retirement, Sam had once been famous as the best steel-union organizer in the country. And he'd worked at every step of steelmaking, from melting down the raw material to removing the impurities and getting the stuff ready for shaping. Sam accepted their offer.

One day, in keeping with Sam's strategy for urgent measures, all the workers left their posts without any notice—just as the large vats were full of burning ore. The bosses were taken by surprise; if not poured into molds, the metal would harden into huge blocks and be impossible to move.

Quickly the workers explained to the foremen that when the company was ready to hear complaints, work would begin again. The company gave in; Sam's plan had been simple and ingenious. And as he left, Sam said to the union leaders, "Remember: strike while the iron is hot!"

SIBLINGS AND SAPLINGS

A domicile was newly being established in the abandoned lakeside inn. In addition to refurbishment of the structure, the owners aspired toward the conservation and rejuvenation of their sylvan acreage. Consequently they besought an indigenous dendrologist to assist them.

Their two children gamboled in the vicinity as the adept counseled, "Fell those moribund robles in the paludal sector," and "Destroy the noisome, omnipresent squawbushes, thus ameliorating the opportunity for the loblollies to flourish." According to him, multiple elm saplings were incipient in the coppices. "A rarity in this terrain," the specialist commented. "Nurture those ulmaceous growths!"

In the nocturnal hours, while in a state of sopor, the two adults were startled into consciousness by an eldritch, tum-tumming charivari from the outdoors. "Incline your auricle," recommended the husband.

Timorously the pair progressed toward the exit. Reaching the deck, they espied their two moppets, the daughter cradling her decrepit humstrum. "What is transpiring?" their maternal progenitor queried.

"We're attempting to communicate with the elves!" they replied without guile. Chortling, their father interrogated them as to why they postulated the presence of fey creatures.

His diminutive scion responded, "That dendrologist informed us did he not?"

The couple both found the situation risible now. "*Elms*—flora, not fauna!" explained their mater.

LITTLE CHILDREN AND LITTLE TREES

A new family had just moved into the vacant inn near the lake. Aside from renovating the building, they wished to preserve and give new life to the trees in the forest on their acres. And so they asked a local expert to help them.

While their two kids played nearby, the pro advised, "Cut down those dying oaks in the marshy area," and "Get rid of that foul-smelling sumac everywhere so those pines can have a chance to grow better." He said they also had a lot of little elm trees starting to grow in the thickets. "That's unusual around here," he observed. "Treat all those little elms well!"

While asleep that night the couple were rudely awakened. "Listen!" said the husband. Coming from outside was a strange twanging mixture of sounds.

Full of fear, the couple moved to the door. They stepped onto the porch—and there they saw their two children, the girl holding her battered old guitar. "What is going on?" the mother asked.

"We're trying to meet the elves!" they answered innocently. The father laughed and asked them why they assumed elves lived nearby.

The little boy answered, "That man here today, who knew about the woods, he said so. . . . He said there were lots of little elves over in the woods—didn't he?"

Both adults laughed. *"Elms*—not elves!" the mother told them.

IN VINO, VERITAS

To conclude this chapter, here is a once-told tale. You are asked to select the proper words in the list below and fill in the blanks in the story. The answers appear on p. 436, in the Appendix.

Incidentally, you may wish to write the simplified story yourself and compare your version with the one on p. 436, in the Appendix.

My (1) _____ grandfather has reached his
(2) _____. Recently he related the story of how he had once decided to (3) _____ his estate in order to
(4) _____ himself from financial problems that were causing him to worry about eventually becoming (5) _____.

Grandpa had two friends who were (6) _____
and also (7) _____. So he asked them if they would allow him to be one of their tasters. He figured it would be the first step toward becoming a (8) _____.

Well, Grandpa's friends (9) _____, but the plan backfired. It seems that the wine was (10) _____! He kept dozing off on his regular job as a con man at carnivals. Worse yet, he discovered that whenever he became (11)_____ he would forget his (12) _____ for (13) _____ and would actually tell the truth!

mythomania	anecdotage	somnolent	indigent
somniferous	vintners	sommelier	aggrandize
acquiesced	extricate	paternal	propensity
oenologists			

CHAPTER 12

Some "Immortal" Mortals

Hundreds upon hundreds of nouns, verbs and adjectives in our dictionaries bear the names of actual people. Such words are called *eponyms,* which is an example of how elastic our language is. Originally an *eponym* applied only to a person, real or mythical, whose name was adopted by a family, tribe, race or other group. Thus Hellen was the *eponymous* founder of the Hellenic people, or Greeks, and Christ was the *eponymic* leader of the Christians. But when we started to designate objects, creations and activities according to the names of the people uniquely associated with them, we cast around for a suitable term and fell back on *eponym.* Hence John Hancock became an *eponym* for a signature and Casanova for a lover. Such extensions were altogether fitting and proper, because the original Greek source for *eponymous* meant "after the name."

How does a mortal become "immortalized" in our language? Well, it's helpful to be born into royalty or to be some kind of ruler. The chances for a Croesus, Prince Albert, Caesar or Napoleon to become perpetuated in an *eponym* are tremendous, whereas the average citizen is a million-to-one shot in this linguistic competition.

Statesmen, generals, inventors, botanists, physicists and writers come in second. Chefs, bartenders, actors, artists and physicians have an outside chance. But if you are none of the above, your best bet at getting your name into the dictionary is to do something crazy, cruel, nasty or treasonable.

Take, for instance, Steve Brodie, a newsboy who claimed he had survived a leap off the Brooklyn Bridge. A *brodie* is a suicidal dive; hence in slanguage it's a flop or a blunder.

Or consider Comte Donatien Alphonse Francoise de Sade and Tomás de Torquemada. The former, who was a French soldier and novelist, described sexual aberrations involving pleasure obtained from mistreating one's partner. He gave us a cluster of cruel words: *sadism, sadist, sadistic* and *sadomasochism.**

---

* *Sadomasochism* (or S-M) is unusual because it combines two eponyms. Masochism is named for Leopold von Sacher-Masoch, an Austrian author whose writings describe how some people get sexual pleasure from being abused or dominated by their partners.

Torquemada was a Dominican prior. Ferdinand and Isabella made him the first inquisitor general for Spain in 1483. He organized the Spanish Inquisition and became infamous for the severity of his punishments. Thousands of his victims suffered death. Today his name is a synonym for persecutor.

Incidentally, several decades ago a crossword puzzle constructor who wished to remain anonymous used *Torquemada* as a pseudonym. The name was well chosen because the puzzles were brain-breakers.

Another fellow who lives in infamy is Mr. Hooligan, of Southwark, London. He and his family are reputed to have caused many a ruckus around the turn of the century. Now *hooligan* and *hoodlum* are synonymous, and we have even formed a derivative, *hooliganism,* which means "disorderly conduct."

It's interesting to note that the verb *hoolihan* probably also stems from a person's name. Mr. Hoolihan apparently was a clever bulldogger. To *hoolihan* is to bring down a steer by leaping well forward on the animal's horns.

Two men whose descendants must be embarrassed are William Burke and Captain William Lynch. The former suffocated his victims, leaving their bodies unmarked and fit for dissection. After his execution in Edinburgh in 1829, anybody who had been murdered in the above way was said to have been *burked.*

As for the captain, he was a member of a vigilance committee of Pittsylvania, Virginia, in 1780. Some lexicographers say that his methods led to *lynch law* ("condemnation without due process"). Others say that the term and the verb *to lynch* are probably derived from Charles *Lynch,* an American planter who held the position of justice of the peace. Reputedly, he presided over an extralegal court that endeavored to suppress Tories during the Revolution. At any rate, it's fascinating that both *Lynches* were contemporaries and participated in similar activities.

While we're on this unpleasant tack we might as well include Dr. Joseph Ignace *Guillotin.* He proposed in 1789 that the privilege of decapitation should not be reserved only for the nobles of France. Furthermore, he suggested that some sort of machine should be constructed to perform the act quickly and humanely. His idea was accepted and a German mechanic named Schmidt put together a device that the officials adopted. But the French preferred not to say that the victims of the machine had been *schmidted*—no, it seemed more proper to use *guillotined.*

I am sure that members of the *Quisling* family are not happy about the fact that their name has become a common noun meaning "traitor." Vidkun *Quisling* was the head of the Norwegian puppet regime that cooperated with the Nazis in World War II. Like his counterpart, Pierre Laval of France, he was executed in October 1945. Strangely enough, the Laval family has escaped the ignominy of having their name eponymized.

––––––––––

But for better or for worse, to achieve linguistic immortality it certainly helps to be a ruler. Take Julius Caesar, for instance. He has become a synonym for autocrat. The *Caesar weed*, a tropical shrub, bears his name probably because its fiber is so strong. And the month of July was so called in his honor, just as August is a shortening of Augustus.

Physicians speak of a *Caesarean section*, a surgical operation performed by cutting through the abdominal wall to extract the fetus. The term possibly arose from the rumor that little Julius was born in that manner. More likely is the supposition that *caesus*, the past participle of the Latin verb *caedere* ("to cut"), gave rise to *Caesarean*.

The *Caesar salad*, by the way, is not directly related to the Roman dictator. It is reputed to be the recipe of Caesar Gardini, a Mexican restaurateur.

But *kaiser* is a Germanic borrowing from *Caesar*. Its extensions include *kaiserin* (wife of the ruler), *kaiserdom, kaiserism, kaisership* and even *kaiser brown* (the color ginger). Incidentally, czar, tsar, czarina and tsarina are also derivatives of *Caesar*.

Almost two hundred years before Caesar was born, King Pyrrhus of Epirus defeated the Romans in a bloody battle during which a large part of his army was destroyed. Afterward he exclaimed, "One more such victory over the Romans and we are utterly undone." And so a *Pyrrhic victory* is any triumph or success gained at tremendous cost.

Two other rulers got into our dictionaries as coins. The *bolivar* is the monetary unit of Venezuela, and a *louis d'or* is an old French coin named in honor of Louis XIII. His successor did even better; *Louisiana* bears his name. And the *Louis heel* on a shoe was probably thus called as a tribute to Louis XV.

King Croesus of Lydia (560–546 B.C.) was so opulent that today he figures as part of the simile *rich as Croesus*, and Nero was so depraved and despotic that he has become an adjective and a verb—*Neronian* and *Neronize*.

––––––––––

Cicero was only a senator, but his voluble discourses caused sightseers' guides to be named after him. Those *cicerones* are also talkative.

A more modern senator has also achieved unenviable immortality. *McCarthyism* is the use of indiscriminate, usually baseless accusations for the purpose of suppression.

President Theodore Roosevelt received kinder treatment. The *teddy bear* was named for him. But a Revolutionary patriot, Elbridge Gerry, got himself into hot water in 1812 as governor of Massachusetts when he pushed through what eventually became known as the

Gerrymander Bill; it limited the power of his Federalist rivals by redistricting the state so that their votes would be concentrated in only one district. On the map, one elongated district seemed to form the shape of a salamander, so Gerry's opponents wittily coined the verb *gerrymander*—which means "to divide election districts unnaturally and unfairly." But Governor Gerry was apparently unscathed by the nomenclature. He became Madison's vice-president shortly thereafter.

Two high-ranking Frenchmen, whose names rhyme, have been reduced to common nouns. They are Jean Martinet and Étienne de Silhouette.

In the era of Louis XIV, officer Martinet devised a new system of military drill which required rigid adherence to rules. Soon the courtiers in service complained so much that a *martinet* came to mean "a strict disciplinarian." Today we hear advocates of harsh methods in school systems proclaiming the need for more *martinets*.

Silhouette was a French minister of finance in the eighteenth century. Scholars do not agree as to why his name was attached to solid-color drawings showing only the outline. One theory is that his ephemeral career (hence, dark) is the cause. Another is that his parsimonious fiscal policies combined with his amateurish attempts at portraits caused his name to be attached to the art form.

A Prussian army officer named Karl von Clausewitz (1780–1831) obtained a reputation as a master of strategy, largely because of his writings. Thus a *Clausewitz* is an expert on military science.

Baron von Roorback never existed, but his name lives on in our lexicons. *Roorback* means "a scurrilous, false tale used for political advantage." Opponents of James Polk in the presidential election of 1844 announced that Roorback had written a book and actually pretended to quote passages that made charges against Polk. Their ruse failed; he was elected.

But Captain Charles C. Boycott (1832–97) was not a figment of anyone's imagination. That British army officer became an agent for the owner of a large estate in Ireland. When he refused to accept rents lower than those to which his employer was legally entitled, he was ostracized and vilified by the tenants. About six hundred soldiers had to be brought in to protect the owner's property during harvesting. Today *boycott* means "to join in refusing to deal with or patronize a seller, employer, other person or a group."

Another army officer who has enlarged our vocabulary is Henry Shrapnel (1761–1842). As a British general in the artillery he devised a projectile filled with small metal balls that would scatter in the air when exploded over the objective. In present usage, *shrapnel* refers to the fragments strewn by a shell that has burst. Many a soldier has been slain by such flying debris.

Nicholas Chauvin, a legendary French soldier whose devotion to Napoleon was loud and bellicose, would be amazed today if he could return to life. *Chauvinism* has not only been equated with excessive, blind patriotism but also has been extended to mean "undue attachment to one's own group."

The feminists have latched onto the word with fierce abhorrence. In their opinion, *male chauvinists* use and abuse women and either deliberately or inadvertently discriminate against them and keep them down.

> Poor Nicholas, how fickle is
> The world you loved a lot;
> Now you're condemned by angry femmes
> For all that you were not.
> But, sir, you rate some hoots of hate
> As superpatriot!

Nevertheless the feminists have a point. Men have been so dominant through the centuries that women have had few opportunities to achieve linguistic longevity. Only a handful have reached the eponymic pinnacles. Here are some examples:

victoria—a pleasure carriage named for the queen
Queen Anne's lace—wild carrot
curie—unit used in measuring radioactivity
bloomers—garb recommended by Mrs. Amelia Bloomer, an American pioneer in social reform
pompadour—hairdo named for the mistress of Louis XV
Mae West—inflated life jacket for aviators downed at sea
melba toast—named for Dame Nellie Melba, Australian soprano
jezebel—shameless woman, from Ahab's wicked wife in the Bible

Annie Oakley (1860–1926) and *Calamity Jane* (1852–1903) have also found their way into our dictionaries because of their marksmanship. The former lives as a free ticket or pass, because her targets were so small that they resembled punched tickets. Frontierswoman Martha Jane Burke has suffered a different fate. To a female pessimist or hypochondriac someone is apt to exclaim, "Don't be a Calamity Jane!"

Incidentally, how Ms. Burke acquired her nickname is a story in itself. She is alleged to have warned that any man who offended her would be courting calamity. Her last years were indeed calamitous; she died in poverty.

Martha Washington seems to have won the most eponymic honors for women. A chair, a table and a geranium bear her name.

It is interesting that horticulturists who raise different varieties of roses love to name their blossoms after famous people. The *Mister*

Lincoln and the *Herbert Hoover* are two of the many flowers in this category.

Quite a number of botanists have staked out their claims to etymological perpetuity. Among them are Alexander Garden of Scotland (*gardenia*), Mathias Lobel of Flanders (*lobelia*), Pierre Magnol of France (*magnolia*) and Johann Zinn of Germany (*zinnia*).

A French navigator named De Bougainville named the *bougainvillaea,* and a Jesuit missionary, G. J. Kamel, gave his name to the *camellia* when he discovered that evergreen in the Far East. The *sequoia* might well be called a *guess.* It was named for George Guess, a Cherokee scholar whose Indian appellation was Sequoya.

The grass called *timothy* bears the first name of one Mr. Hanson, who carried the seed from New York to the Carolinas around 1720.

A Canadian named John *McIntosh* was the first to cultivate a certain delectable red apple.

My personal favorite in this area is the *Jim Hill mustard* weed, which was so called because it flourished alongside the railroad lines promoted by Mr. Hill.

But one of the best approaches to getting your name into a dictionary is to become a physicist, especially in the field of electricity. Consider *Ampère, Gilbert, Henry, Maxwell, Ohm, Volta* and *Watt,* among others.

Messrs. *Fahrenheit* and *Celsius* got themselves associated with thermometers, and Wilhelm Konrad *Roentgen*'s name has proliferated into many words, all because he discovered X-rays. For example, there are *roentgenization, roentgenograph, roentgenologist, roentgenoscope, roentgenotherapy* and a score of others.

Devising a weapon is another method of achieving linguistic longevity. A *bowie* is a steel knife more than a foot long and usually carried in a sheath. Jim *Bowie,* the famous frontiersman, popularized the article. Either he or his brother Rezin created it.

Inventors of guns include Samuel *Colt* (revolver), John C. *Garand* (rifle) and Sir Hiram S. *Maxim* (machine gun). Somehow Henry *Deringer* had his name lengthened into *derringer* when he created a pocket pistol. The opposite happened to Richard J. *Gatling*. His name became associated with a *gat* (slang for pistol).

Coming up with a new mode of transportation is often an easy path to eponymic fame. Kinds of carriages are especially conducive to such repute. A Scottish jurist named Henry Peter *Brougham* devised one in the nineteenth century. Around the same time an English architect named Joseph Aloysius *Hansom* designed his popular cab. But whoever invented the *clarence* named his carriage for royalty instead. The honor went to the Duke of Clarence, later William IV.

George M. *Pullman,* an American, patented a comfortable railroad passenger car with facilities for sleeping overnight. And a German mechanical engineer named Rudolf *Diesel* invented a new type of engine. Another German, Count Ferdinand von *Zeppelin,* devised an airship circa 1900. Its cousin the *blimp* was not named for cartoonist David Low's famous colonel. Low gave the name to his character because the colonel's corpulent body resembled the airship.

Europeans appear to be good at this name game. A French painter named Louis J. M. *Daguerre* developed a photographic method (*daguerreotype*) that became very popular in the nineteenth century. Another Frenchman, Louis *Braille,* came up with a system for teaching his blind students. His raised dots have been adapted for writing various languages.

Adolphe *Sax,* a Belgian maker of musical instruments, gave us the cousin of the clarinet. And a German chemist, Robert W. *Bunsen,* invented a burner that can be found in any laboratory.

An American named W. L. *Murphy* got into the act with his folding bed. Subsequently P. N. *Nissen,* an engineer in the Canadian army, devised a prefabricated hut that was first used by the British in World War I. Its relative, the *Quonset hut,* was not named for a person but for a place called Quonset Point, in Rhode Island, where it was first manufactured.

Some creative people become verbs as well as nouns or adjectives. Our milk is *pasteurized* (for Pasteur) and our roads *macadamized* (for McAdam). An Austrian physician named F. A. Mesmer practiced a form of hypnosis so well that people became *mesmerized* (spellbound).

Then there was Luigi Galvani, an Italian physicist and physician. His discoveries in the field of electricity in the eighteenth century have caused his name to appear in a score of English words. Best of them all is *galvanize.* In a nontechnical sense it means "to electrify or startle into sudden activity."

Furniture designers and cabinetmakers, such as *Adam, Chippendale, Eames* and *Hepplewhite,* have added their names to our language. *Buhlwork,* a style of furniture decoration, was the creation of André C. *Boulle* (1642–1732).

It's especially fascinating to note that a famous English poet-artist-decorator-designer-manufacturer-printer and socialist leader devised a comfortable chair that has retained its popularity since it was produced in the nineteenth century. His name was William *Morris.*

Creators of clothes styles have done well in the eponymic field. In millinery, a Frenchman named *Gibus* invented the opera hat of that name and the John B. *Stetson* company produced the Texans' ten-gallon hat.

In 1780, Edward Stanley, twelfth Earl of *Derby,* founded a horse race at Epsom Downs. It was given his name, and subsequently other famous races, such as the Kentucky Derby, were so called. The round hat that was worn so often at such events then acquired the appellation too.

Another nobleman, James T. Brudenell, seventh Earl of *Cardigan* (who led the disastrous charge of the Light Brigade), popularized the sweater or jacket that bears his name. His superior officer in the Crimean War was Lord *Raglan.* He adopted a loose overcoat with sleeves that continue in one piece to the collar. The coat and the sleeve now bear his name.

Meanwhile *Prince Albert* Edward (later Edward VII) stimulated the fashion of wearing a long double-breasted frock coat. A slipper, a fir and a yew were also named for the prince.

Earls, however, seem to have been the chief style-setters. Another nineteenth-century nobleman, the nineteenth Earl of *Chesterfield,* took to wearing a beltless topcoat with a velvet collar, flap pockets and a fly front. Not only does the coat bear his name but so does a davenport, or sofa.

Arthur Wellesley, the first Duke of Wellington, wore high boots during his campaign against Napoleon.* Thus his name was applied to an article of footwear. There are also *half Wellingtons,* which look somewhat like a pair of galoshes and are worn under trousers. Finally, an admirer of the duke coined a synonym for the sequoia; he called it the *wellingtonia.* As I have stated before, it pays to be a nobleman if you wish to be an eponym.

As just another example, Sir Henry *Havelock,* an English general who quelled an Indian mutiny in 1887, wore a cloth cover with a flap hanging down from his military cap. That protection from the elements still bears his name.

> Dear Havelock, you have a lock
> On names for flaps for caps.

Another British officer, Sir Samuel James Browne, set the style for wearing a leather belt supported by a light strap passing over the right shoulder. Today it is called the *Sam Browne* belt.

In modern times two other leaders have achieved fleeting fame in the area of apparel. The distinctive jackets of *Eisenhower* and *Nehru* set fashions for a while.

Charles MacIntosh, a Scottish chemist and inventor, devised the *mackintosh,* a waterproof raincoat or the fabric of rubberized cotton used to produce the coat.

---

* Not to be outdone by his adversary, *Napoleon* has also had a boot named for him.

A predecessor of Étienne de Silhouette as the French minister of finance was Jean Baptiste Colbert (1619–83). *Colberteen,* a lace with a coarse network, is named for him.

Beau Brummell was not a Frenchman but an Englishman who lived early in the nineteenth century. Born George Bryan Brummell, he became famous for his stylish clothes and manners. Today his name is a synonym for a fop or dandy.

Pantaloons have an intriguing history. Their eventual source is Saint Pantaleone, the patron of Venice. The Italians made him into an old fool in comedies and dressed him in long, tight trousers. The character came to be called *Pantaloon,* and his distinctive garb was soon given the same name.

What's most interesting is that *pants* is a shortening of the word. Thus an Italian saint is inadvertently responsible for such terms as *panties, pantywaist* ("sissy, sissified") and *pantyhose.*

The Duchess de *La Vallière* was no saint, but she has made her own contribution to our language. As mistress of Louis XIV, she popularized the fashion for wearing a certain type of necklace consisting of a pendant ornament attached to a fine chain. The word can be spelled three ways: *lavaliere, lavalier* or *lavalliere.*

In contrast to the dainty duchess, a British pugilist named James *Belcher* has given us another form of neckwear. A *belcher* is a blue neckerchief with white spots or any multicolored neckerchief. Because its sound causes association with "one who belches," it is predictable that the name for the neckwear will become obsolete. In fact, most modern dictionaries have already dropped it.

The *dickey* has no such problem. It's an extension of *Dick* and was so named because originally it was a detachable shirtfront worn by men only. Today it is seen more often on women. Their *dickeys* are detachable collars or blouse fronts. A child's bib or apron is also called by the same name.

At least two manufacturers associated with clothing have added their names to our language. *Levis* are close-fitting trousers made of heavy denim; the trademark stems from the name of *Levi* Strauss, who first manufactured the garb in San Francisco. And *Sanford* L. Cluett (1874–1968) invented a preshrinking process. A fabric or garment so treated is said to be *Sanforized.*

In the area of hair styles *Marcel* Grateau has become immortal because that French beautician devised a method for creating a series of deep, soft waves by using a heated curling iron on the hair.

Ambrose Everett *Burnside,* a Union general, wore full side whiskers and a mustache but shaved his chin, giving a name to the style called *burnsides*. By back formation, the word *sideburns* was developed as a term for the hair in front of the ears on a man's face.

The Flemish painter Sir Anthony *Vandyke* (or *Van Dyck*) often drew portraits of men with trim, pointed beards or with wide collars. His name now lives in our language in association with both the beard and the collar. There are also two shades of color named for him—*Van Dyke brown* and *Van Dyke red*.

The Italian artist *Titian* is famous for the unique brownish orange color in his paintings. Today we often hear hair described as *titian*.

Turning from art to literature, let us begin with characters from the Bible. Here are just a few of the names that have taken on various connotations.

Adam's ale—water
Adam's apple—projection in the neck
Ananias—liar
Jehu—reckless driver
Jonah—jinx
Joseph's coat—many-colored plant
Joshua tree—yucca
Judas—betrayer
Methuselah—aged person; oversize wine bottle
Nimrod—tyrant or hunter
raise Cain—become angry, violent or boisterous
Solomon—wise man

In literary circles a common way to eponymize one's favorite author is to convert him into an adjective. Thus we have such words as *Aesopian, Chaucerian, Gilbertian, Rabelaisian, Shakespearean, Shavian* and scores of others. Probably the most interesting is *Machiavellian,* which has come to mean "crafty or deceitful" because of the unscrupulous principles and theories expounded in the Italian author's THE PRINCE.

Another eponymous ploy is to add *ese* to the writer's name in order to characterize his style. Examples are *Carlylese, Johnsonese* and *Ruskinese.*

Sometimes the author's name is transformed into a verb. If you write an account of someone else's life in the style of Samuel Johnson's biographer, you are *Boswellizing.* Incidentally, a hero-worshipper who hangs around the object of his admiration and is in constant attendance on him is said to be a *Boswell.*

The surnames of Thomas *Bowdler* and James *Granger* have evolved into pejorative verbs. The former edited an expurgated edition of Shakespeare for family use. It omitted whatever he considered off-color or indelicate. Hence to *bowdlerize* a work is to remove prudishly and arbitrarily anything objectionable—in other words, to emasculate it.

In his BIOGRAPHICAL HISTORY OF ENGLAND, *Granger* included blank pages for illustrations to be snipped from other books and pasted in. That practice is now called *grangerism.* Also, to *grangerize* is to mutilate a book.

Mr. *Bowdler* and Anthony *Comstock* were kindred spirits. As secretary for the Society for the Suppression of Vice, the American reformer's puritanical zeal led him to confuse real pornography with such works as Shaw's MRS. WARREN'S PROFESSION. Shaw then coined the term *comstockery,* and it has entered our lexicons as a synonym for overzealous moral censorship, or prudery.

In contrast, we have the word *Comtism,* which means "positivism." It is derived from the philosophical tenets of the French philosopher Auguste *Comte* (1798–1857).

Two literary derivatives that may be unfamiliar to most people are *ascham* and *brocard.*

Roger *Ascham,* an English scholar in the sixteenth century, wrote a treatise on archery. Consequently a tall, narrow locker for arrows is called an *ascham.*

In the eleventh century Bishop Burchardus *Burchard* of Germany compiled a book of ecclesiastical rules and laws. Folks in England altered his name to *brocard* and used it as a synonym for a maxim or short proverbial guide to conduct.

An altogether different sort of guidebook was published by John Mottley in 1739. The author admired a British comedian named *Joe Miller.* Hence he named his collection of jokes JOE MILLER'S JEST-BOOK. Other comics used the publication so much that the quips lost their appeal, and today a *Joe Miller* is a stale joke, or an oldie.

I am reminded of the story of the Englishman who was incarcerated in a U.S. prison. His fellow convicts had access to a single jokebook, which they passed from cell to cell all year. The jokes were numbered, and after a while the prisoners could simply call out a certain sure-fire number and be assured of getting guffaws from neighbors.

The Englishman decided to try it. Thumbing through the book, he picked out one that seemed especially funny. Then he called out, "Forty-four." The response was complete silence, punctuated by a few groans.

"Did I choose an inferior jest?" the Englishman asked his cell mate.

"Naw," came the reply. "It ain't the joke; it's the way you tell it!"

———

Another way to get your name into the dictionary is to concoct a drink. Bartenders *Tom Collins* and Henry Charles *Ramos* did just that. The *martini* had a different source; it's probably derived from the name of a liquor firm—*Martini* and Rossi.* The *Rob Roy,* a Scotch cocktail, presumably was so called in honor of the Scottish freebooter Robert Macgregor. His nickname was *Rob Roy.*

Negus is a drink I have never seen or tasted, but it's a crossword puzzle repeater. Made of wine, hot water, sugar, lemon juice and nutmeg, it was invented in the eighteenth century by a British colonel named Francis *Negus.*

Note again how the military men and nobles keep getting linguistic publicity. *Napoleon* had a rich pastry named for him, as well as a card game and a weeping willow. Another Frenchman, Vicomte Françoise René de *Chateaubriand,* lives as a thick steak—probably the bequest of his chef.

Culinary artists do have a knack for promoting their patrons. Take the case of Count Karl Robert *Nesselrode* (1780–1862), a Russian diplomat and statesman. His chef invented a mixture of nuts, preserved fruits and other ingredients; the concoction is used as a sauce for ice cream. Two popular offshoots are *Nesselrode pie* or *Nesselrode pudding.*

But John Montagu, fourth Earl of Sandwich (1718–92) used his own ingenuity rather than his chef's when he contributed a luncheon snack to us. The story goes that he ordered his servants to bring him pieces of bread with a filling, such as meat, so that he would not have to leave the gaming tables. Even more interesting is the fact that we have converted *sandwich* into a verb. When you are *sandwiched* between two other persons (as in rush hour) or between two things, the squeeze is on.

An adjectival derivative occurs in *sandwich man*—the fellow who parades on the streets between two signboards—one in front and another in back. Finally, it should be noted that Captain Cook originally named Hawaii the Sandwich Islands, not because of the food there but in honor of the earl.

Not to be forgotten is Louis de *Bechamel,* steward to Louis XIV. He created a white sauce made of cream, flour and other ingredients which is still a prime feature at French restaurants.

And then there is Sylvester *Graham* (1794–1851). That American dietary reformer donated a cracker made of ground whole wheat flour.

Last, in the alimentary area, let's consider *salmonella,* a type of food poisoning that has no relation to the parr, grilse, smolt, sockeye,

* John Doxat, an expert on cocktails, believes that the *martini* was invented for John D. Rockefeller by a bartender named Martini, at the Knickerbocker Hotel in New York, in 1910.

humpback or other fish. The word stems from the name of Daniel E. *Salmon,* an American veterinarian, who died in 1914.

In the field of the theater, the meaning of *Chaplinesque* should be obvious. But *guignol* and *talma* are not so obvious. The former is a hand puppet, probably named for a silkworker of Lyon who worked in a puppet theater and gave his own name to the character he manipulated. And François-Joseph *Talma,* a French actor in the nineteenth century, popularized a large cloak that bears his name.

Another French actor, *Cabotin,* was such a ham in the seventeenth century that his name has become a common noun. *Cabotinage* is a synonym for theatricality.

Beau Gregory may sound like an actor or a dude, but it's actually a fish caught off Florida and the West Indies. Some unknown person named *Gregory* is probably responsible for the name.

Guppy seems like a perfect name for the fish often seen in little tanks and aquaria. From its open-mouthed actions one would assume its name is a variation of "gulpy." Instead, it is so called because a man named R. J. Lechmere *Guppy* of Trinidad first presented specimens of the brilliant fish to the British Museum.

Another member of the animal kingdom is the *maverick*—an unbranded steer, especially a strayed calf. In the old days such an animal became the property of the first person who put his brand on it. The name dates back to Samuel *Maverick* (1803–70), a Texas rancher who refused to brand his cattle. That wanderer on the range has been personified. A *maverick* in a political party, or in any other group, is one who refuses to conform.

Bird lovers will be interested to hear that the small European swallow called the *martin* was named for Saint *Martin* of Tours. The birds' habit of migrating at Martinmas (Indian summer) gave rise to its appellation.

Another of the many saints that have been etymologically perpetuated is Peter. One of his contributions to English is *Peter's pence,* an annual donation to the Vatican made voluntarily by Roman Catholics.

To conclude this chapter, here is an eponymic quiz. The answers appear on p. 436, in the Appendix.

1. What British statesman is a traveling bag?
2. Name the Apache chief who has become a battle cry for paratroopers.
3. In the nineteenth century a jockey became famous for his come-from-behind victories. What is the phrase that carries his name?
4. What poisonous water-soluble alkaloid was introduced into France by the ambassador to Portugal Jean Nicot?

5. Who is the imaginary colonel whose name is used for a one-over-par golf score?

6. Charley Noble is a synonym for:
   a. stiffness in the leg
   b. French courtier
   c. smoke pipe for a ship's kitchen

7. A French chemist, Nicolas-Jacques Conté, invented:
   a. a crayon
   b. a type of narrative
   c. a variety of litmus paper

8. An English physician, who was also a colonel, is reputed to have devised the:
   a. iron lung
   b. condom
   c. radiometer

9. The liveryman who required every customer to choose the horse that stood nearest to the door was:
   a. Davy Jones
   b. Richard Roe
   c. Thomas Hobson

10. An early minstrel song with racial overtones was:
    a. "Jim Crow"
    b. "Mr. Bones"
    c. "John Henry"

This chapter, like many others, has only scratched the surface. Hundreds of other names lie hidden in our dictionaries. If you wish to add your name to that company, don't just sit there—do something!

CHAPTER 13

The Place Is Familiar

W ines, foods, fabrics, clothes, chinaware, pets, dances, weapons and vehicles have something in common: many of them were named for the places where they originated. It's amazing to discover how many hundreds of cities, towns, regions and other geographical areas have become common nouns in our dictionaries.

Let's begin with wines and liquors. *Champagne, Burgundy* and *Beaujolais* are all regions in France. *Bordeaux* is a seaport in the southwestern area of that country. Not only does a wine bear its name but also a red dye, a turpentine and a sauce called *bordelaise.**

Montilla is a pale dry sherry named for a town in Spain. Its more popular cousin is *amontillado*. The word *sherry* itself has an interesting history. It was once spelled *sherris* ("wine of Jerez"). That's the old name for Xeres, the Spanish town where the drink originated.

Chianti is a mountainous region in Italy famous for its red table wine. Another Italian area noted for its vineyards is *Asti*. If you have listened to TV commercials lately, you know about the bubbly beverage that comes from there.

Carlowitz is a strong, sweet, red wine produced in a Yugoslavian town of that name.

Brandy drinkers probably know that *cognac* is named for a commune in western France and that *calvados* is called after a department in the Normandy area. *Bourbon,* of course, is not a French whiskey; it was named for the county in Kentucky in which it was first distilled.

Even some cocktails fall into this category. The origin of the name for the *Manhattan* is easy to discern, but *daiquiri* is not so familiar. This rum drink takes its name from a district in Cuba.

Bock beer was first produced in *Einbeck,* Germany. Its shortened form and the alteration of *beck* to *bock* are largely due to the vagaries of the Bavarian dialect.

---

* A medium-dry white wine from Montefiascone, Italy, does not bear the name of that town but deserves mention anyway because of its unusual name. The monks who created the wine dubbed it *Est, Est, Est*—literally, "It is! It is! It is!"

In the district of *Tequila* the Mexicans distilled a form of mescal that has given many a U.S. tourist a fierce hangover.

Far less potent are two other beverages, *darjeeling* and *sunglo*. Both are teas. The former was named for a district in West Bengal and the latter for a mountain in China. I must confess that when I first saw the word *sunglo* I assumed that the tea had been named by a clever adman.

The above is only a smattering of the beverages named for places. Let's go to some foods. Cheeses are often likely to be named according to their geographic origins. *Camembert* is a village in Normandy; *Cheddar* is an English village in Somersetshire; and *Edam* is a Dutch town. *Parmesan* cheese is named for an Italian commune called *Parma*.

Your local deli features place-names too. Among them are *Bologna,* in Italy, and two German cities, *Frankfurt* and *Hamburg.* As I mentioned in a previous chapter, the German appellation for Vienna is *Wien,* whence we get *wiener, wienerwurst* and *wiener* schnitzel.

Obviously *Brussels sprouts* were named for the capital of Belgium. But the origin of the *casaba* will probably give most people pause. It was introduced in *Kasaba,* a Turkish city that has since been renamed Turgutlu.

At a former papal villa, *Cantalupo,* a new form of muskmelon was developed. Today it is called a *cantaloupe.*

Currants have quite a fascinating etymological history. Briefly, they were called *raysons of Coraunte* ("raisins of Corinth")* in Medieval English.

In the above case the influence of the French is apparent. It is also seen in *mayonnaise.* The word can be traced back to *Mahon,* a seaport of Minorca. Lexicographers aren't sure why. Some guess that the name arose in commemoration of the capture of the port in 1756 by the Duke of Richelieu.

Finally, let's consider *finnan haddie,* a Scottish dish of smoked fish. The name is an alteration of *Findon haddock,* which in turn was once called *Findhorn haddock,* after a fishing port in Scotland.

As we move over to the areas of fabrics and clothes we are surprised to discover that so many laces bear the names of the towns that created them. Consider *Alençon, Chantilly* and *Cluny,* in France—also the city of *Valenciennes. Nottingham,* in England, is another example.

The fine linen or cotton fabric called *cambric* is an alteration of

----

* Corinth has also provided us with *Corinthian*—a lover of luxury or a wealthy *bon vivant.* As an adjective, *Corinthian* is a synonym for dissolute. Obviously the inhabitants of that ancient Greek city were rich and profligate.

Cambrai, a town in northern France. The change in spelling came about through Flemish dialect. By the way, a mixture of weak tea with milk, sugar and water is called *cambric tea.*

The French also gave us the tapestry *arras* and the fabric *cretonne.* The wall hanging was named for the city of its origin, and the cloth was first made in *Creton,* another creative village, in Normandy.

Denim was originally called *serge de Nîmes.* The cousins of denims are *jeans,* fashionable among people of all walks of life. They were not named for a girl but for *Genoa.* In the Middle Ages orthographic changes affected the initial letter.

Scotland is the home of several patterned fabrics, mainly because the clans developed distinctive designs. *Argyle* is one of the patterns; it originated in a former county called *Argyll.* Another is *glen plaid,* a creation of a clan in *Glen Urquhart,* a valley in the northwestern part of the country. *Paisley* is a city in Scotland. Its woolen shawls with colorful, complex patterns became very popular. Soon the term *paisley print* was coined for this type of design, which often appears on scarfs and neckties.

Areas now in the U.S.S.R. have contributed too. The coarse cloth called *buckram* was named for the city of *Bukhara.* The weasel *kolinsky* and the fur it yields can be traced back to *Kola,* a district in northern Russia. Similarly, the sheep *karakul* is a denizen of Russia. Its name stems from *Kara Kul* (literally, "black lake") a body of water in the U.S.S.R. Another spelling of the animal and its fur is *caracul.*

Also from Asia is *cashmere,* which has several meanings:

1. a soft wool obtained from a Himalayan goat
2. fine woolen yarn used for sweaters, coats, shawls and other knitted objects
3. a sweater, coat or shawl made of the wool

The goat and its wool are named for *Kashmir,* a region in Asia between Tibet and Afghanistan.

From India we have obtained such fabrics as *calico* (after the city of *Calicut*) and *madras* (after the city of the same name). Those pants called *jodhpurs* that equestrians wear are also named for a city in India. Interestingly enough, there has also emerged the ankle-high, buckled *jodhpur boot* or *jodhpur shoe.*

Like the above, the article of clothing called the *jersey* has the exact spelling of the island that it is named for. So has the leather called *morocco.* Another leather, *cordovan,* has undergone a slight change. It was first manufactured at *Córdoba,* a city in Spain. The English changed the *b* to a *v* and dropped the accent.

Several styles of men's headgear are derived from place-names. The *Panama hat* is an example. *Homburg* is a town in Germany that first produced the diplomats' toppers. And the *Glengarry* is a cap or bonnet that originated in a valley of Inverness-shire in Scotland.

Proceeding from the head down to the toes, we find the *oxford shoe* from England and the *crakow* from Poland. The latter had a long, pointed toe and was quite stylish in Europe between 1300 and 1600 A.D. Shakespeare probably got quite a kick out of it.

The United States is a relatively young country. Hence our cities, towns and regions have not become part of our language as often as those in other parts of the world. *Buncombe County* in North Carolina has been discussed in a previous chapter. Two groups of itinerant agricultural workers during the Depression—the *Okies* and the *Arkies* —have not helped the reputations of their respective states. *Boston* and *Michigan* have become card games, and *Chicago,* a poolroom game. And of course there are *New York steaks, New York cuts* and even *New York weasels* (not city slickers!). Some writers have tried to coin *New-Yorky* as a synonym for sophisticated, but the public hasn't bought it in the same way that our dancing grandmas adopted the *Charleston* in the roaring twenties.

But to get back to our discussion of clothes, the prize in the United States must go to either *Mackinac,* an island in Michigan, or *Mackinaw City,* a resort in that area: philologers disagree as to the credit lines. In any case, take a look at the wealth from that linguistic mine.

> *mackinaw*—short double-breasted heavy coat or jacket
> *mackinaw blanket*—covering once used by Indians, traders and trappers
> *mackinaw boat*—former Great Lakes craft
> *mackinaw cloth*—heavily napped felted material
> *mackinaw trout*—food fish; namaycush

Finally, let us not forget *tuxedo*. This semiformal attire was the creation of one of the rich men who attended formal parties at a country club in *Tuxedo Park,* New York, during the Gay Nineties. The fellow apparently rebelled against the formal "soup and fish."

It's interesting to note that a *tuxedo sofa* has also emerged.

Now let's turn our attention to the animal kingdom. Dogs and horses seem to have the edge in this place-name category. It's probably no news to canine lovers that the *Airedale* comes from a valley of the *Aire* River bearing the same name. The stream is in *Yorkshire,* and, sure enough, another breed of terrier is so called. Incidentally, these Yorkshiremen are obviously a creative group with good press agents. They have donated to our language a breed of swine, a canary, a chair, a coach horse, a velvet grass (*Yorkshire fog*), a type of grease, a window (*Yorkshire light*) and a famous pudding.

> I've never sailed along the Aire,
> But people there are really rare—
> Linguistically they've done their share
> Like no one else from anywhere.

But let's go to the dogs again. Along with the *Scottish terrier* we have the *Clydesdale terrier.* And the valley of the Clyde River also developed a heavy draft horse, the *Clydesdale,* capable of pulling wagons loaded with barrels of beer or other weighty goods.

From Mexico comes the tiny *Chihuahua,* which takes the name of a city or state in that country. In contrast is the tall, swift, keen-eyed *Saluki,* a hunting dog named for the ancient city of *Salug,* in southern Arabia.

The *Lhasa Apso* has achieved great popularity in recent decades. This little terrier with a leonine appearance gets its first name from the capital of Tibet. *Apso* means "sentinel."

Among the equines the award for place-names must go to the British. Aside from the aforementioned *Clydesdale,* there is the *Suffolk*— another draft horse. Also, a breed of sheep carries the name of that county. A third group of English draft horses are the *Shires,* which originated in the Midland region.

Hanoverians were bred by crossing German horses with a swift English type called Thoroughbreds. Their designation stems from *Hanover,* a city in Germany that is also famous for another reason: it gave its name to a royal family, including Queen Victoria.

Most interesting among the British breeds is the *Hackney.* Named for a former town that has since become a borough of London, the horse has taken on other connotations by metonymy. The carriage behind it now bears the same appellation. When we call a taxicab a *hack* we are using a shortened form of the name.

In earlier days these horses were employed so often for ordinary riding that they apparently became worn out. Consequently a *hackney* became a synonym for a nag. Other extensions, which are now obsolete, emerged: drudge, slave, and even prostitute. But the adjective that evolved is still in general usage. *Hackneyed* means "made trite, vulgar or commonplace from overuse."

A rugged Gallic equine entry is the *Percheron.* This draft horse originated in the *Perche* region of France but is now used in many other parts of the world.

Names of British places have been lexicalized on the ovine front too. The *Cheviot* Hills, in England and Scotland, are the original home of a breed of hardy, hornless sheep. *Romney Marsh,* in southwestern England, developed a long-wooled type that provides the Londoners with mutton.

In the piscine area the English are famous for their *Dover sole,* and among the felines the tailless *Manx* cat was first bred on the *Isle of Man.*

Two counties, *Kilkenny,* in southeast Ireland, and *Cheshire,* in northwest England, are also famous for cats—but not because their citizens have developed special breeds of the pets.

"To fight like *Kilkenny cats*" is an expression carrying the idea of battling it out until both sides are bloody and bowed. Irish legend has it that during the rebellion of 1798, Hessian soldiers garrisoned at *Kilkenny* amused themselves by tying the tails of two cats together and tossing the poor animals over a clothesline, where they fought to get free.

Lewis Carroll made the *Cheshire cat* famous in ALICE IN WONDER-LAND, but it is said that he got the idea from an old tale about cheese once sold in that county. The cheese was apparently shaped in the form of a cat that seemed to be grinning. *Cheshire* has also earned its way into the dictionaries via its present-day cheese and its unique breed of white swine.

Finally, the coop group has attained its share of place-name fame. The *Rhode Island Red* is not a communist but a breed of chickens. There is also a *Rhode Island White. Dominique,* named for the island of *Dominica* in the West Indies, is another domestic fowl.

The *Bantam* is a very small hen or rooster. The name stems from a town in Java where the Dutch first settled. It is believed that the fowl was native to *Bantam.* Because of the breed's dwarfish size and aggressive ways, its name became associated with small, combative people. A further extension is *bantamweight,* a boxer who weighs between 113 and 118 pounds.

As an adjective, *bantam* can have several meanings:

1. diminutive; miniature
2. small and aggressive
3. pert; saucy
4. of the junior-age group in baseball

Java, by the way, seems to have won the lexicographic prize. Its name has been applied to an almond, a bean, a citronella oil, a cotton, a type of grass or jute, a pepper, a plum, a sparrow and a type of tea— among other things. And of course the name is a slangy word for coffee.

Leghorn is a Mediterranean fowl noted for laying eggs in abundance. Its title is actually the English name for *Livorno,* an Italian seaport. The lexicographers inform us that the alteration is the result of "folk etymology." I wish that one of them could tell me by what steps such a vast change occurred!

At any rate, that city also deserves some kind of award for a perfect parlay. *Leghorn* is not only a biddy but also a type of straw made from Italian wheat, a fabric produced from that straw, a hat made from the fabric, and ultimately, a pale-yellow color resembling straw. Now, there's a marvelous example of how we build one layer of meaning atop another. Yes, the pun was intended, and it probably laid an egg!

On the subject of colors, we note that another Italian city has given us *Siena,* a synonym for *Venetian red.* Somewhere along the line the second consonant was doubled, probably by a poor speller. Thus *sienna, burnt sienna, sienna brown* and *sienna drab* came forth.

Since the Italians are noted for their skill in art, it's only natural that their cities should be so "colorful." *Magenta* in northern Italy is still another example. Its namesake is defined as "a deep purplish red."

Among the colors donated to our language by the French is *chartreuse.* Actually, this word should have been cited earlier in this chapter during the discussion of beverages, because the name was originally given to a greenish-yellow liqueur made by the Carthusian monks at La Grande *Chartreuse,* a monastery near Grenoble.*

Charterhouse is a close relative of the liqueur and the color. Originally a Carthusian monastery, it later became the name for a charitable hospital and institution founded in London in 1611. Later the hospital was converted into a school but retained the same name. The eventual ancestor of all the above is *Chartrousse,* a village in Dauphine near which the monastic order was founded.

Isn't it fascinating to think that some sophisticated interior decorator or couturier who leans toward *chartreuse* is harking back to a tiny spot in a former province of southwestern France? Antique collectors will know what I mean.

Killarney is another yellow-green color with Irish overtones. It is closely related to *Gretna green,* a bit paler in hue. Of course it should be noted that *Gretna Green*—a Scottish village on the English border —is widely known as the place where British elopers were quickly united in matrimony. In Maryland, the town of Elkton once followed the same no-questions-asked procedure, but the chamber of commerce missed out on a good publicity gimmick. *Elktonize* might have meant "to perform a marriage ceremony in haste."

As I have pointed out before, chinaware and related products also represent place-names. *China* itself was named for the country.

The decorated porcelain called *Dresden china* was named for the East German city where it originated. *Limoges* is another superior

---

* This is just one of the many liqueurs created by monks. *Benedictine* is another. And at the Basilica of St. Paul's in Rome, that same order has concocted *abbazia.* Legend has it that if a person imbibes too much of this spiritous drink he will "die and go to Heaven."

variety of porcelain; it takes the name of a city in France. Both of the preceding are familiar to most people, but I wonder how many know about *Buen Retiro* (literally, "good retreat"). This place, located near Madrid, once produced a soft-paste porcelain under the aegis of the Spanish king.

Kaolin merits mention in this area. It's a fine white clay used in making porcelain. The place in China where it was found is called *Kao-ling* ("high hill").

———

Now let's consider just a few vehicles whose names have sprung from their places of origin. American pioneers on the Santa Fe and Oregon trails often made use of the *Conestoga wagon,* which was larger than the prairie schooner. It was so named because it was manufactured in *Conestoga Valley,* a part of Lancaster County in Pennsylvania.

In a town in southwestern Germany a manufacturer produced the *landau,* a four-wheeled covered carriage.

The *limousine* deserves special attention. The vehicle comes to us via a region called *Limousin* in west-central France. The distinctive cloaks or hoods worn by the natives of that area gave rise to *limousin,* a synonym for such a garment. When the car was manufactured, it featured a closed compartment that separated the passenger from the driver. It is probable that this "cloak" of privacy generated the name *limousine,* although some experts believe that the costumes of the chauffeurs were the cause.

———

Weapons are sometimes named for the cities where they were first made. The *bayonet,* for instance, was produced in *Bayonne,* France. And a *Toledo* is a finely tempered sword named for a well-known city in Spain.

Shillelaghs are clubs or cudgels. Their name stems from a village in County Wicklow, Ireland, famous for its oaks and other hardwoods.

Bilbo was once a type of sword or rapier. Today it's a long iron bar with sliding shackles and is used to fetter a prisoner's feet. The name is an alteration of *Bilbao,* a Spanish seaport formerly famous for its ironworks.

———

As in the case of the *Toledo,* it often happens that no changes in the spelling of the place-name occur, except that the initial letter may no longer be capitalized. Here are some examples:

> *Axminster*—type of carpet—town in southwestern England
> *Calcutta*—fishing rod or form of auction pool—seaport in India
> *Calvary*—anguishing experience—crucifixion site near Jerusalem
> *Castile*—type of soap—region in Spain

Christiania—skiing turn—city in Norway (now Oslo)
cologne—toilet water—city on the Rhine
Cremona—fine violin—commune on the Po
El Dorado—any reputedly rich place—legendary South American
    country
etna—heating device—volcano in Sicily
guinea—former English coin—coastal region of western Africa
Havana—Cuban cigar—capital of Cuba
Malacca—cane; walking stick—state of western Malaya
Mecca—center of activity; goal—city in Saudi Arabia
Santa Ana—strong hot, dry wind in California—range in California
Wilton—type of carpet—city in southern England

Blarney and *limerick* also fit into the above list but merit elaboration. The former is derived from *Blarney Castle* in County Cork. A legend arose in Ireland about a certain stone on the wall of the castle. Located about twenty feet from the top, this *Blarney Stone* is difficult to reach. An inscription on the stone indicates that anyone brave enough to obtain access to it and to kiss it will be rewarded with the power to influence people by cajolery. Thus when a fellow is facile in speech and very persuasive, the Irish say, "He kissed the *Blarney Stone.*" Eventually *blarney* became a synonym for smooth talk, cajolement or flattery.

A *limerick* is a humorous poem containing five lines in anapestic-iambic meter and using *aa bb a* as a rhyme scheme. It is named for a county in Ireland, but it probably wasn't created there. An English writer, Edward Lear (1812–88), popularized the verse form in THE BOOK OF NONSENSE, but no one knows exactly where and by whom it was first devised.

Philologers take an educated guess that the *limerick* was given the name of the Irish county about ten years after Lear's death. At that time, in the pubs and at parties, it became the custom for people to sing in chorus, "Will you come up to Limerick?" while individuals were reciting or extemporizing the verses.

Lear's nonsensical lines were not the bawdy type that we now hear. Below is one of his typical creations. Note how he repeats the last word of the first line when he ends the verse. That's not considered good form today.

> "There was an Old Man with a beard,
> Who said: 'It is just as I feared!
>   Two owls and a hen,
>   Four larks and a wren
> Have all built their nests in my beard.' "

But if *Limerick* is not the original home of such doggerel, it has earned its way into our lexicons via its lace. Moreover, a type of fish-hook that was first made in Ireland bears the name of the county.

––––––––

Two other place-names that became common nouns with no change in spelling are *agapemone* and *billingsgate*.

Agapemone literally means "stopping place for love," and that's exactly what it was at a communistic establishment founded around 1850 at Spaxton, England. The *Agapemone* group had unconventional ways that shocked the staid Victorians. Hence the name they chose has come to mean "an institution for free love."

Billingsgate is an old gate and market in London. Fishmongers and others who gathered there were notorious for using certain four-letter words and shouting curses at each other. By metonymy the name of the place became associated with vulgar and abusive language. Therefore, if a person indulges in *billingsgate,* he is guilty of foul-mouthed vituperation or scurrilous name-calling.

Finally, let's consider *Aceldama*. In the Bible it is designated as the field that was bought with the money Judas was given when he betrayed Christ. Hence an *aceldama* is a field of bloodshed or place with ugly associations.

Unlike the above, *Armageddon* has incurred a slight orthographic change. In Low Latin it was spelled *Armagedon*. It is assumed that the word can eventually be traced to the plain of *Megiddo,* a legendary scene of decisive, bloody battles. At any rate, *Armageddon* is mentioned in the Bible as the scene of the last conflict between the forces of good and evil just before the Day of Judgment. In modern usage the word has come to be associated with a war that will put the quietus on mankind.

Two other Biblically derived words that have vastly different connotations are *Samaritan* and *sodomy*. In common usage a *good Samaritan* is a person who unselfishly helps another human being in distress. The expression comes from a New Testament parable in which a native of *Samaria* was the only passerby to give aid to a man who had been beaten and robbed (Luke 10:30–37).

Sodom, along with its neighbor Gomorrah, was destroyed by fire because of the homosexual practices of its male denizens (Gen. 19:1–11). *Sodomy* now relates to various forms of "unnatural" copulation. It should not be confused with *simony*—the buying or selling of church offices, ecclesiastical pardons and sacred benefices or things. That word was given to us by *Simon* Magus, a Samaritan who apparently wasn't so good. He offered money to two Apostles for the power of conferring the Holy Ghost on other people (Acts 8:18–19).

Another pair of ancient cities that have entered our dictionaries are *Abdera* and *Sybaris*. The Thracian inhabitants of the former place were reputed to be stupid yokels who contented themselves with irrational derision of others. As a result, *Abderian laughter* has come to be associated with foolish chuckling about something that is over one's head. An *Abderite* is a simpleton or a scoffer.

The Sybarites were noted for their love of pleasure and luxury. Living in the lushness of southern Italy, those Greeks became hedonistic.* Their life-style has given us *sybarite* ("voluptuary"), *sybaritic, sybaritical, sybaritically, sybaritish* and *sybaritism*.

Also of ancient origin is the adjective *avernal,* which means "infernal or hellish." The word is derived from *Avernus,* a small lake located on the site of an extinct volcano near Naples. It was reputed to be so deep and so malodorous that the ancients decided it must be the entrance to the underworld. And so, in Roman mythology, *Avernus* became a synonym for Hades.

Another geographic sight, the *Geysir* (a hot spring in Iceland) is the source of our *geyser*. That alteration in spelling is slight compared with the change of the name of *Birmingham,* England, to *brummagem* —a word stemming from a vulgar pronunciation of the city by some of its natives. *Brummagem* means "cheap; showy, gaudy but inferior." The reason is twofold: in the seventeenth century, counterfeit silver coins (called groats) were traced to *Birmingham;* later, in the nineteenth century, the city became notorious for manufacturing cheap jewelry and tawdry toys.

That word *tawdry* has its own interesting background. But for the foibles of folk etymology, it might have become *norwichian*. It seems that in Norwich, England (at *St. Audrey's* fair), cheap, gaudy women's lacy necklets were sold. Instead of the city, poor *St. Audrey* was given the blame linguistically. The adjective is an elision of her name.

In contrast with fortunate Norwich, the town of *Donnybrook,* near Dublin, has not enjoyed "the luck of the Irish." Its annual fair became notorious for fist fights and rowdyish behavior. Since there was apparently no saint involved, the town itself had to take the rap. Hence a *donnybrook* is a free-for-all or noisy, disorderly brawl.

Nor has the town of Coventry in England been as lucky as Norwich. To be *sent to Coventry* is to be ostracized. Lexicographers have different theories as to the origin of the phrase. Some say that it arose among the Cavaliers in the seventeenth century because *Coventry* was a stronghold of their opponents, the Roundheads. Others guess that the phrase came into use because of the practice of sending Royalist prisoners to *Coventry* during the English Civil War.

---

* *Hedonistic* means "devoted to pleasure." The Greek root is *hedone* ("pleasure").

While I was a young teacher in New York City I used the phrase as a jocose sort of threat. When one of my teenage boys started to cause a disturbance I sometimes would say, "Behave yourself or I'll *send you to Coventry!*" To the recalcitrant student, *Coventry* sounded like the name of a reform school. The ruse usually worked.

At other times I would waggle a finger ominously and warn, "If you don't quiet down, I'll ostracize you!" That verb apparently carried overtones of dismemberment. So did *coventrize*—a verb I coined. In any case, either verb did the trick.

But *Coventry* does receive a few complimentary entries in the dictionary. The *Coventry bell* (sometimes called *Canterbury bell*) is a type of pasqueflower. And *Coventry blue* is a blue embroidery thread that was first made in that town.

Another place that has taken on a pejorative connotation is *Gascony,* a region in southwestern France. Whether deservedly or not, its natives gained a reputation for being garrulous braggarts. Hence dictionaries define *gascon* as "a braggart or swaggerer." As an adjective the word means "boastful." And the verb *gasconade* means "to boast." Sometimes it is also used as a noun.

The citizens of *Coxsackie,* a town on the Hudson, probably aren't happy about their single addition to our vocabulary—*Coxsackie virus.* The phrase arose because a patient in that town was the first discovered to be carrying the virus. And I wonder if the Belgians who live in *Waterloo* resent the fact that their city has become a common noun meaning "decisive defeat."

Similarly, folks in *Taranto* must feel disgruntled because their seaport has given its name to *tarantism,* a nervous disease characterized by hysteria.* The Italians had divided opinions on the association of dancing with the ailment. Some believed that it could be cured by terpsichorean exercise; others declared that a mania for tripping the light fantastic was a symptom of the disease. At any rate, it's interesting to note that the most popular Italian dance—the *tarantella*—is a diminutive form of *Taranto.*

The reader may wonder how certain places themselves got their names. One obvious source is the choice made by a discoverer. For example, Columbus named San Salvador—the spot in the Bahamas where he first landed in 1492. And John Cabot, an Italian explorer in the employ of Spain, entitled Cape Bona Vista ("good view") in Newfoundland (new-found-land).

But sometimes the original explorers got thwarted. Balboa named

---

* *Tarantism* has been erroneously associated with the *tarantula.* It was formerly believed that the disease resulted from the bite of the hairy spider.

his discovery the South Sea. Magellan renamed it the Pacific, and his designation took hold. As I noted in the previous chapter, Captain Cook decided to honor a nobleman by calling Hawaii the Sandwich Islands. The natives negated his choice.

Changes in place-names occur often. Here's a quiz on that subject. Can you match the items in the two columns? The answers appear on p. 436, in the Appendix.

PRESENT NAME	FORMER NAME
1. Bahamas	a. Christiania
2. Helena, Mont.	b. Persia
3. Oslo	c. Lutetia
4. Leningrad	d. Last Chance
5. Iran	e. Stalingrad
6. Tokyo	f. Hierosolyma
7. Paris	g. Lucayos
8. Jerusalem	h. New Helvetia
9. Volgograd	i. Edo
10. Sacramento, Calif.	j. St. Petersburg

In several instances places are named for the explorers themselves. Hudson Bay, the Hudson River and the Straits of Magellan are a few examples.

In this connection we cannot omit Amerigo Vespucci (in Latin, Americus Vespucius). If his alleged account of a voyage in 1497 is authentic, he reached the mainland of the American continent about a week or two before the Cabots and more than a year before Columbus. A German geographer, Martin Waldseemüller, was the first to suggest that the new continent be named for Vespucci.

What is really strange is that the surname was not chosen. Otherwise our land would be Vespucius and we would be called Vespucians—which sounds almost like people from outer space!

Most often, place-names are chosen in honor of a ruler or nobleman, a saint or a famous leader. Consider such cities as Jamestown, Baltimore, San Francisco, Houston and Dallas. In case that last one puzzles you, George M. Dallas was vice-president under Polk.

Dallas, by the way, was not a Texan. He was born in Philadelphia —a city named by the Quakers. Literally, in Greek, Philadelphia means "brotherly love."

Cities get named in a variety of interesting ways. Here are the origins of a selection of others in the United States.

CITY	ORIGIN OF THE NAME
Atlanta, Ga.	Western & Atlantic Railroad
Boise, Idaho	*Boisé* (French—"wooded")
Buffalo, N.Y.	Alteration of the name of a Seneca Indian who lived there

Butte, Mont.	*Butte* (French—"mound, hillock")
Chicago, Ill.	Algonquin—"place of the wild onion"
Cincinnati, Ohio	Society of the Cincinnati, formed (1783) by ex-Revolutionary officers, after Cincinnatus, Roman statesman
Cleveland, Ohio	Moses Cleaveland (1764–1806), surveyor from Connecticut
Corpus Christi, Tex.	Latin—"body of Christ." The city was first called Kinney's Trading Post.
Denver, Col.	James W. Denver (1817–92), governor of Kansas Territory
Des Moines, Iowa	French—"of the monks"
Detroit, Mich.	Détroit (French—"strait"); first applied to the Detroit River
El Paso, Tex.	Spanish—"the ford" (shortening of El Paso del Norte, referring to the passage of the Rio Grande). The city was once called Franklin.
Evansville, Ill.	General R. M. Evans, War of 1812
Fresno, Cal.	Spanish—"ash tree"
Honolulu, Haw.	Hawaiian—"sheltered bay"
Las Vegas, Nev.	Spanish—"the plains"
Little Rock, Ark.	Rocky promontory in Arkansas River
Los Angeles, Cal.	Spanish—"the angels." (The original name was El Pueblo de Nuestra Señora la Reina de Los Angeles de Porciuncula.)
Memphis, Tenn.	After capital of ancient Egypt
Milwaukee, Wis.	Algonquian—"good land; council place"
Minneapolis, Minn.	After nearby Minnehaha Falls: Sioux—"water fall"; Greek—*polis* ("city")
Orlando, Fla.	Orlando Reeves, an Indian runner
Pensacola, Fla.	Choctaw—"hair people"
Phoenix, Ariz.	After the mythical desert bird
Pittsfield, Mass.	William Pitt (1708–78), English statesman
Pittsburgh, Pa.	Same as preceding
Plymouth, Mass.	After Plymouth, Eng. (named for junction of Plym and Tamar rivers)
Reno, Nev.	General J. L. Reno, Civil War hero
Rochester, N.Y.	Nathaniel Rochester, pioneer and Revolutionary officer
Seattle, Wash.	Seathl, an Indian chief

Now let's consider the origins of the names of the fifty states. Approximately half of them are derived from American Indian dialects, sometimes altered by the French or Spanish. Interestingly enough, references to water figure prominently in the names of many such states:

Arizona	"little springs"
Arkansas	"downstream people" (possibly a Siouan tribal name via French)
Connecticut	"place of the long river"
Kansas	See Arkansas.
Michigan	"great water"
Minnesota	"milky blue water"
Mississippi	"big river"
Missouri	"people of the big canoes"
Nebraska	"flat water" (Siouan name for the Platte River)
Ohio	"fine or large river"
Oregon	"birch-bark dish" (in reference to the Columbia River)
Wisconsin	"gathering of the waters" (via French— *Ouisconson*)

Idaho probably has the most poetic appellative origin—the Shoshoneans' *E-da-how*—"Behold the sun coming down the mountains."

Etymologists guess that Alabama means "thicket clearers" and that Massachusetts comes from the Algonquian expression *Massa-adchu-es-et* ("at the big hill"), with reference to the Blue Hills, near Boston.

Iowa is named for an Indian tribe that was scornfully called by others "the sleepy ones."

Through the French, the Indian word *ileniwe* ("man") became Illinois, and Indiana is a Modern Latin word meaning "land of the Indians." Why one state was singled out for that distinction puzzles me. After all, the Indians were spread out through the entire mainland.

North and South Dakota are so called because the Dakota tribes lived in the region. Their names can be construed to mean "allies": *da* ("to think of as"), *koda* ("friend").

The Caddoan people helped the Spaniards fight the Apaches. Hence a Caddoan-Spanish word evolved—*techas* ("allies"). As a proper noun the word became the name of the state of Texas.

The Spanish also played a part in the naming of Utah. They developed the word *Yutas* for the Shoshonean group that we call the Utes. Lexicographers guess that the original tribal word meant "hill dwellers."

There is also some question about the source of the name Tennessee. Possibly it stems from *Tanasi,* a Cherokee village.

Kentucky's name comes from an Iroquoian designation meaning "level land." Wyoming means "large plains," probably in reference to Wyoming Valley. Considering the topography of the state, one would think that the Indians should have been more impressed by the mountainous terrain than by the level land.

The name Oklahoma comes from a Choctaw expression—*okla* ("people"), *homma* ("red").

Alaska is *Alakshak* to the Eskimos. It's their name for the mainland portion of northwestern North America. *Hawaii* is probably a native name. The meaning is unclear.

Several names of states come directly from Spanish, with no etymological influence by the Indians. Colorado (in reference to the river) means "red, ruddy or colored." Florida, which was named by Ponce de Leon, means "abounding in flowers"—certainly appropriate!

Montana is the feminine form of *montano,* a Spanish adjective meaning "mountainous." Nevada is a shortened form of *Sierra Nevada* ("snowy range").

New Mexico's nomenclature is eventually derived from the Aztec war god *Mexìtili,* changed by the Spanish into *Méjico.*

The origin of the name California is in doubt, but many historians claim that the source is an old Spanish romance in which a woman named *Calafia* ruled over an island bearing the name that was given to the state.

Surprisingly, the names of only a few states come directly from the French colonists, with no Indian influence whatsoever. Vermont is a shortened form of *Verd Mont,* which literally and aptly means "green mountain."

Maine's name may have a Gallic appearance because of the extra vowel at the end, but that extension is probably the embellishment of colonists. In the great charter of 1606, given to the Plymouth Company, the region was called "Province of Main"—possibly to distinguish it from the islands or perhaps to indicate that it was the principal area of the Northeast.

Louisiana, a name associated with the earlier Louisiana Purchase, definitely has a French background. The Mississippi Valley was called *La Louisianne* after King Louis XIV.

The British penchant for naming places in honor of royalty or other noble personages is revealed in the names of many eastern states. Virginia and West Virginia were so dubbed in honor of Elizabeth I—the *virgin* queen. Delaware was named for Baron *De La Warr,* the title of Thomas West, first governor of the colony of Virginia. A river, a bay and a water gap in the area of the state also were given his title. And the Lenape tribe in the region were called the Delawares.

It would be interesting to learn how, when and why *Warr* became *ware.* I imagine that modern Delawareans are happy about the change. The original last syllable sounds so belligerent, especially when we note that the rich du Ponts of Delaware got their start through the manufacture of gunpowder.

A neighboring state, Maryland, was named for Queen Henrietta *Maria,* wife of Charles I. And Georgia, of course, is a tribute to an English king—in this case George II. New York must settle for a nobleman of slightly lesser rank—the Duke of *York* and Albany. However, Gothamites and upstaters can take consolation in the fact that the duke later became James II.

In the case of New York, a fascinating phenomenon occurred. The state was named for the city, which was originally settled by the Dutch and called New Amsterdam. The British captured the city in 1664 and renamed it New York. What a difference a few decades can make! Twenty-one years later the Duke of York was crowned. Obviously New York City would have then been called Jamesburg or James City.* Can you picture Harold Ross as the editor of a sophisticated magazine called THE JAMESBURGER?

As an aside, residents of the great metropolis may be interested to learn why their city has been nicknamed Gotham. It seems that a village in Nottinghamshire, England, bore that name, and the inhabitants deliberately developed a reputation for acting like fools back in the thirteenth century. At that time King John wanted to convert some of their acres into public roads. When they refused, he sent his men into the village to punish them. But they averted his wrath by acting like escapees from the cuckoo's nest. Thereafter Gotham traditionally became equated with "home of the fools."

Five centuries later a nursery rhyme subtly ribbed the Gothamites for their stupidity:

> "Three wise men of Gotham
> Went to sea in a bowl:
> And if the bowl had been stronger
> My song would have been longer."

But it was a native New Yorker who pinned the name Gotham on the scene of his entrance into this world. Washington Irving left the city and moved to Tarrytown, a residential village about twenty-four miles north of his birthplace. With two colleagues he wrote SALMAGUNDI, and in that humorous work New York City was called Gotham because of the wiseacres there.

Times do not change! Any student of social science or politics can attest to the fact that most upstaters in Albany, Syracuse, Utica and

---

* There actually is a Jamesburg, in New Jersey, and a county called James City, in Virginia. Incidentally, the Dutch recaptured New York City in 1673 and gave it a third name, New Orange (after the Prince of Orange), but it was ceded to the British a year later as part of the New Netherland deal and once again became New York.

other cities in northern New York State still regard Gothamites as "a bunch of wise guys."

Getting back to our states, we find two more that were named after a king. The original colony of Carolina is a feminine adjectival form of Carolus, a Latinized name for King Charles I, a Scotsman who ruled England from 1625 to 1649. The original colony included parts of Florida and Georgia, but only North Carolina and South Carolina carry the monarch's name today.

Some states take their names from places in Europe. Just as there is the county of York in England (also named for the duke), it's no secret that New Jersey is a throwback to the island of Jersey in the English Channel. "Why Jersey?" I inquired because it's my home state. The reason is interesting. Our friend the Duke of York originally was given the tract by his brother, Charles II. In turn the duke ceded the territory to two court favorites, Lord Berkeley and Sir George Carteret. It so happened that Carteret had successfully defended the island of Jersey during England's Parliamentary wars. Berkeley took a back seat. He let the area be called New Jersey in honor of his partner's feat. In today's world, when acronyms and combinations of names are so prevalent, the state would probably be called Berkarteret.

New Hampshire is so called in tribute to a former county on the southern coast of England. Captain John Mason, a British subject who had received a grant for the territory, chose the name for reasons I have not yet discovered. Natives of the Granite State may be interested to hear that he sold his rights to New Hampshire to Governor Samuel Allen in 1691.

Rhode Island's etymological birth is in dispute. Some scholars guess that the name was derived from the Dutch term *Roodt Eylandt* ("red island"). Others assert that the island of Rhodes is the source. According to their story, the Italian navigator Giovanni da Verrazano visited Narragansett Bay in 1524 and observed that a certain island (Aquidneck) reminded him of the Mediterranean. If this assumption is true, it's another instance of the entire state being named for one of its areas.

The origin of Pennsylvania is easy to ascertain. The Penn family and their Society of Friends obtained title to the lands from the ubiquitous Duke of York in 1682. Latin students will recognize *sylvania* as an extension of *sylva* or *silva* ("forest").

Last, but really first, is Washington—the only state named for a white man born in the Western Hemisphere. "First in war, first in peace, and first in the hearts of his countrymen."* our first President

---

* The quotation comes from "Lighthorse Harry" Lee (1756–1818) in Resolutions presented to the House of Representatives on the death of Washington (Dec. 1799).

certainly deserved the honor—and it's also fitting that our national capital bears his name.

So much for the states. Except for the names derived from Indian speech, few of them display much imagination. But the Americans who followed the original settlers more than made up for that lack. Pathos, bathos, humor, respect for the past, interest in literature and many other qualities are revealed in the titles they chose for thousands of places in the United States.

Typical of the American spirit is the city of Hope (Ark.). Other felicitous designations are Joy (Tex.) and Happy (Ky.). The ideal is reached in Eden (Ariz.), Promised Land (Ark.), Paradise (Tex.) and Utopia (Tex.). Two other towns in our second-largest state are called Blessing and Comfort.

Other upbeat names are Sunnyside (Wash.), Delightful (Ohio), Point Pleasant (N.J.), Welcome (N.C.), Prosperity (S.C.) and Yum Yum (Tenn.). Seat Pleasant (Md.) and Social Circle (Ga.) also fit into this gladsome category. Even Newfoundland joins the jubilant crowd with Heart's Content. Nor should Bountiful (Utah) be omitted.

The spirit of comradeship is exhibited in Concord—the name of three different cities. The most famous one of course is in Massachusetts. The others are in New Hampshire and North Carolina. In the same vein we have Harmony (Pa.) and New Harmony (Ind.). Friendly (W.Va.) seems like a nice place to live, and a recent novel has publicized Amityville (N.Y.).

The quest for the best has inspired the naming of Truth (N.C.) and Truth or Consequences (N.M.). Similarly, we are blessed with Freedom (Pa.), Liberty (in at least seven states), Equality (Ala. and Ky.) and Union (N.J.).

Our pioneers' indomitable spirit is evident in such names as Pluck (Tex.), Persist (Ore.) and Rough and Ready (Cal.).

On the other hand, just to show that Americans are not confirmed optimists, consider Worry (N.C.) and Anxiety Point (Ark.). Hostility Branch (Tenn.) doesn't sound like a place that would put out the red carpet for visitors. Residents there might be better off in Worse (Ga.). The ultimate is reached in Total Wreck (Ariz.)!

On the same note, Cape Fear (N.C.) sounds ominous. Nor would I relish climbing Purgatory Peak (Col.), visiting Chagrin Falls (Ohio) or spending my days of retirement in Tombstone (Ariz.). Even more hair-raising are Cannibal Plateau (Col.) and Maneater Canyon (Wyo.).

I would rather take a trip to such romantic spots as Kissimee (Fla.) or Swainsboro (Ga.). And what place seems more inviting for a honeymoon than Bridalveil, a waterfall in Yosemite National Park (Cal.)!

If ancient cities excite you but you want to remain in the good old U.S.A., visit New York State. There you will find Athens, Carthage, Ithaca, Nineveh, Rome, Sparta, Syracuse and Troy! Incidentally, some of those places are also the names of cities or towns in other states. For example, Athens and Rome can also be found in Georgia.

Speaking of the ancients, Cicero lives in Illinois and Hannibal in Missouri. Ovid found a spot in a New York village, as did Homer and Manlius. And Ulysses was rejuvenated in a city in Kansas.

If you desire a literary itinerary, you might start with Byron, Dryden and Milton (N.Y.), and follow up with Emerson (N.J.). Traveling to the Midwest, you'll find Kipling (Ohio), Bryant (Iowa), Keats and Hiawatha (Kan.). Moving northward, be sure to visit Ivanhoe (Minn.). In the West you must take in Twain-Harte and Whittier (Cal.). On your return, via the Southwest, stop off at Ben Hur and Tennyson (Tex.), as well as Thoreau (N.M.). And before heading home, don't miss Pippa Passes (Ky.)!

As I have noted earlier, many of our place-names exhibit a sense of humor that is typically American. Nowhere else in the world can we find such outrageously funny names as Ticklenaked Pond (Vt.), Killpecker Creek (Wyo.), Pizzlewig Creek (Cal.), Suckabone (N.Y.), Washes Bottom (Ky.), Rabbit Ears Pass (Col.) and Jackass Flat (Cal.). Nor should we neglect to mention Yellville (Ark.), Sleepy Eye (Minn.), Cheesequake (N.J.), Shickshinny (Pa.), Pinch-Em Tight Ridge (Ky.), Pass Christian (Miss.) and Peekamoose Mountain (N.Y.).

Inadvertently the Indians have given us some place-names that can cause a few chuckles. Punxsutawney (Pa.) and Lake Winnipesaukee (N.H.) are examples. The Okefenokee Swamp (Fla.–Ga.) has a risible ring to it, as does Pongokwayhaymock Lake (Me.). The Chickahominy River (Va.) sounds as if it runs through a coop. And in Oklahoma there once was Chickiechockie, a name that the natives cut in half in 1964. My own favorite is the Itchepuckesassa River (Fla.); it makes me think of a rough hockey game.

Some names seem to go together hand in glove. The natives of the city called Thief River Falls (Minn.) ought to make friends with the residents of Shooters' Island (N.Y.). Also consider the following mountains: Black Brothers (N.C.), Three Brothers (Wash.) and Three Sisters (Ore.).

Of course we name places for almost every one of our Presidents, but other famous people also receive such honors. Two movie cowboys are celebrated in Tom Mix (Wash.) and Gene Autry (Okla.). Other examples are Kit Carson (Cal.), Lilypons (Md.), Jenny Lind (Ariz.) and Clemenceau (Ariz.).

Mt. Crosby (Wyo.) was probably not named for Bing, nor was Great Crosby—a borough in England—but Edith Cavell Mount, in Canada, is definitely a tribute to the great English nurse. And you can be sure that General Motors had nothing to do with the naming of the Edsel Ford Range, in Antarctica.

While we're on the subject of places in foreign lands, here are just a few that may tickle your fancy:

> Hecla and Griper—bay in Canada
> Medicine Hat—city in Alberta, Canada
> Post Office—bay in Galápagos
> Barking Town—suburb of London
> Rotten Row—fashionable thoroughfare in Hyde Park, London
> Popocatépetl—volcano in Mexico
> Poopó—lake in Bolivia
> Titicaca—lake on border of Peru and Bolivia

And here are three beauties from Scotland:

> Sound of Sleat—body of water off west coast
> Arthur's Seat—hill in Edinburgh
> Rattray Head—cape on northeast central coast

A retired sea captain with whom I correspond swears that Nome, Alaska, was so called because a cartographer scribbled *"Name?"* in that spot on the map and someone else misread his writing. The ex-skipper also tells me that when Magellan's ship anchored in the Philippines, a sailor hailed a fisherman.

"What's the name of this place?" he asked.

The fisherman yelled back in Tagalog, "Luzon?" ("What did you say?")

That reminds me of a funny story about a street in the East Bronx. The people who live there call it Fitelli Street. I assumed it had been named for a prominent Italian American. Finally I visited the area, and you can imagine my surprise when I gazed up at the stanchion on the corner. There, in bold letters, the sign announced: "Ft. Ely St."

CHAPTER 14

Literary Largess

J ust as myths and legends have contributed to our language, so have the great writers—and some who are not so great. Most of them have been novelists and playwrights; strangely enough, the pickings from poetry are comparatively meager. One of the reasons for this phenomenon is that the poets often write about such mythological and legendary personages as Hyperion, Prometheus, Merlin and Tristram. When they do invent a character, he or she is subtly or romantically depicted rather than broadly portrayed. For example, think of Eliot's J. Alfred Prufrock, Byron's Childe Harold and Browning's Pippa. We get different feelings about each of those characters, but they are not the kind that tempt us to equate the individual with a certain idiosyncrasy. In essence, none of them is a caricature.

E. A. Robinson's Miniver Cheevy comes close to becoming lexiconized. In a recent conversation one of my friends expressed a longing for the good old days, and my wife said to him, "You're beginning to sound like a Miniver Cheevy."

On the other hand, novelists and playwrights often emphasize and exaggerate a single trait or feature of a character, thus inadvertently paving the way for that individual's entry into our dictionaries. Take *pollyanna,* for instance. In 1913 Eleanor Porter published a book with that title. The heroine is a confirmed optimist who finds good in everything. Hence we now refer to any irritatingly cheerful person as a *pollyanna.*

Most of the time the characters retain their initial capitals when they become part of our vocabulary. In this connection let's look at some of Charles Dickens' creations.

Even though old Ebenezer reformed at the end of A CHRISTMAS CAROL, a mean and miserly person is a *Scrooge.*

A *Micawber* is a thriftless person who constantly looks forward to an improvement in his fortunes, just like the lovable character in DAVID COPPERFIELD. *Micawberish* means "habitually hopeful," and *Micawberism* is optimism accompanied by a lack of frugality or foresight.

In MARTIN CHUZZLEWIT, Seth *Pecksniff* is a hypocrite who talks in pious terms and simultaneously employs every means to enrich himself. *Pecksniffery* therefore is religious hypocrisy, and *Pecksniffian* means "sanctimonious."

From the same novel the British have obtained a lowercase noun. Sarah *Gamp* was a nurse who carried a big cotton umbrella. Hence to a Londoner a *gamp* is a large umbrella.

The hero of THE PICKWICK PAPERS is a generous fool. Hence *Pickwickian* people are benevolent simpletons. The adjective also applies to expressions that a speaker or writer uses in a special or recondite sense; the reason is that members of the Pickwick Club often employed words and phrases in a nonliteral way.

Satirists have also placed their stamp on our language. Jonathan Swift in GULLIVER'S TRAVELS conceived the land of Lilliput, where the inhabitants were only six inches tall. Consequently *Lilliputian* means "very small" and has been extended to mean "narrow-minded." It can also be used as a noun: *Lilliputians* are tiny people or petty, provincial persons.

Gulliver also visited Brobdingnag, a land in which the giants were sixty feet tall! Thus *Brobdingnagian* has become a synonym for colossal or huge.

In the same book the *Yahoos* are described as beastly creatures. Today a *Yahoo* is an uncouth person, and *Yahooism* is rowdyism.

Finally, Swift invented the flying island of Laputa, inhabited by philosophers. We have gained *Laputan*, both adjective and noun, from his creation. The adjective means "fanciful; preposterous; absurd"; and the noun means "a visionary."

Another satirist, François Rabelais, has contributed a different synonym for huge. In GARGANTUA AND PANTAGRUEL his hero is a gigantic king. From that source our adjective *gargantuan* was coined. By the way, Rabelais didn't really invent the word "Gargantua"—in medieval folk literature the character was a mammoth hero—but it must be admitted that the French writer was the chief catalyst for the giant's entrance into our language as an adjective.

Pantagruel, which literally means "all-thirsty," was the equally colossal son of Gargantua. Because of the prince's penchant for coarse wit with derisive undertones, we have been given *Pantagruelism*—a synonym for cynical humor. The adjectives *Pantagruelic* and *Pantagruelian* mean "having crude humor with a serious intent."

In the same work, Panurge is a friend of Pantagruel. This high-spirited rascal is ready to do anything. Rabelais borrowed the name from the Greek *pan* ("all") *ergon* ("work"). In English *panurgic* means "prepared for all kinds of work." A jack-of-all-trades is truly *panurgic*.

Those three first letters, *p-a-n,* have been especially prolific in the production of literary words in our language. *Pantaloons* has already been discussed in Chapter 12.

Panjandrum now signifies a pretentious official or pompous personage. In some nonsense lines the playwright-actor Samuel Foote coined the word back in the eighteenth century.

Pangloss is an optimistic tutor in Voltaire's CANDIDE. Somewhat like *pollyannaish,* the adjective *Panglossian* now means "all is for the best in this best of all possible worlds."

By the way, CANDIDE is not the mother of *candid.* Quite the opposite is true. Both have their origins in the Latin adjective *candidus* ("white, bright").

Finally, let's consider *Pandemonium,* a word that John Milton created in PARADISE LOST as a synonym for Hell. Literally, it means "all demons." The evolution of various senses of the noun is fascinating. From the infernal regions ruled by Satan, it developed into any center of evil; then it became a wild, disorderly place, and that idea led to our present connotation: an uproarious condition or a state in which noise and tumult prevail.

Milton proved that at least one poet could conjure up a new word. So did Edmund Spenser when he created *Braggadocio,* the personification of boasting, in THE FAERIE QUEENE (see Chapter 7).

Shakespeare, who can certainly be classified as a poet, has popularized *Shylock* as a relentless creditor and *Romeo* as a lover. Interestingly enough, a *romeo* is also a man's slipper, and a *juliet* is a woman's slipper.

Robert Burns and W. S. Gilbert have also contributed. The Scottish cap called a *tam* is named for Tam o'Shanter, a hero of a Burns poem. And in THE MIKADO, Gilbert created a character called *Pooh-Bah* whose title was Lord-High-Everything-Else. Hence the name is applied to any official who holds a variety of public and private positions. It also designates a person who gives the impression of being a V.I.P.

An Italian physician, astronomer and poet named Girolamo Fracastoro has, I regret to report, given us *syphilis.* In his poem "Syphilis sive Morbus Gallicus" the hero suffers from venereal disease.

But probably the most amazing endowment from poetry is our word *pamphlet.* In the twelfth century a Latin poem called "Pamphilus, seu de Amore" became very popular. This small, thin book served to create a new word in our vocabulary.* *Pamphleteer* is a derivative.

But the writers of prose dominate in this area, largely for reasons previously mentioned. For example, Harriet Beecher Stowe created *Uncle Tom* and *Simon Legree.* Today the former is a term of contempt,

* *Pamphilus* was originally a disciple of Plato's.

signifying a black person who toadies to whites. A *Simon Legree* is a cruel taskmaster.

In ROBINSON CRUSOE, by Daniel Defoe, the devoted servant of the hero is named Friday. In modern usage a *girl Friday* or *man Friday* is a faithful and efficient aide.

Robert Louis Stevenson created Doctor Jekyll, a virtuous physician who drinks a potion by which he transforms himself into a vicious brute. Calling himself Mr. Hyde, he commits various crimes. Thus a *Jekyll-Hyde* personality in our modern vocabulary is similar to one suffering from schizophrenia.

In connection with crime, British author A. Conan Doyle has given us a master of deduction who constantly humiliates Scotland Yard. *Sherlock Holmes,* or simply *Sherlock,* is a synonym for detective. To *sherlock* is to ferret out the answers to a crime via analytical inferences, or to do a good job as a detective. *Sherlockian* is an adjectival outgrowth. The word is used in sentences such as the following: "The police will need *sherlockian* skill to uncover the madman who has terrorized the city."

Anyone who has seen the great musical called THE MAN OF LA MANCHA will remember Miguel de Cervantes Saavedra's chivalrous hero, Don Quixote. He had a romantic imagination and even tilted at windmills. Today a *Quixote* is a rash, idealistic person, and *quixotic* means "visionary, imaginary or impractical."

Mary Shelley, second wife of the great poet, wrote a Gothic romance called FRANKENSTEIN OR THE MODERN PROMETHEUS. In the book a young scientist named Baron Frankenstein brings to life a monster out of soulless corpses and is ruined by his own creation. For some reason folks have confused the inventor and the invention. Today a *Frankenstein* is a man-made monster with a human shape. It can also be construed as any agency that troubles or destroys its creator. For example, the H-bomb may be the *Frankenstein* that puts an end to us earthlings.

John Lyly, an English author of the sixteenth century, wrote two prose romances in which the chief character was Euphues. The author's artificial, affected style gave rise to *euphuism*—a synonym for high-flown diction.

Incidentally, the above should not be confused with *euphemism,* which is the substitution of an inoffensive word for an objectionable one. The Greek ancestry for that noun can be loosely translated into "good speech."

It's interesting to see how *John Bull* emerged as a synonym for the English nation or for the average Englishman. Early in the eighteenth century a writer named John Arbuthnot dreamed up the nickname. This Scottish-born author depicted his British kin as affable people who could also be crusty; Arbuthnot's personification of England was a bull-headed farmer. The French were represented by Lewis Baboon and the Dutch by Nicholas Frog.

Fairy tales and similar stories have also provided us with characters whose names are part of our vocabulary. In 1697 a Frenchman named Charles Perrault was the first to put down on paper an old folktale about a man named Bluebeard who has murdered six wives and hidden them away in his castle. His seventh wife, Fatima, discovers his crime and he tries to kill her too. But in the nick of time her brothers rush in and slay the villain.

A *bluebeard* is now a man who slays a succession of women, whether they are his wives or not. Because Fatima was told not to enter the chamber of horrors, the adjective *bluebeard* means "forbidden."

Hans Christian Andersen published THE UGLY DUCKLING around 1835. It concerned a swan that had been hatched by a duck and was despised by the other ducks for its ugliness; later it matured into beauty. Today an *ugly duckling* is any person or thing that looks unpromising but develops marvelously and gains admiration and respect.

In an early beast epic, REYNARD THE FOX, *Bruin* was the name of a bear. That epithet for the animal exists in our language. Also, a fox is called a *reynard*.

In THE ARABIAN NIGHTS, a prince named Barmecide invited a beggar to dine with him. Then he pretended to serve a variety of viands, but the plates were empty. When the beggar good-naturedly went along with the joke, Barmecide relented and gave him a hearty meal.

Despite the happy ending, a *Barmecide feast* now retains the idea of fakery. Here are some definitions for the phrase:

1. illusion of plenty
2. make-believe feast
3. pretended hospitality or generosity

Barmecidal is an adjective that is less murderous than it sounds. It means "seemingly but not actually abundant; illusory; deceptive; unreal."

THE THREE PRINCES OF SERENDIP is a Persian fairy tale in which the itinerant heroes constantly discover valuable or pleasant things that they are not seeking. Around 1754, Horace Walpole coined the word *serendipity* in allusion to the Persian story. It carries the idea of having an aptitude for making fortunate discoveries.

Serendipitous is the adjectival derivative. When Sir Alexander Fleming and his colleagues accidentally left some culture plates exposed, a mold developed and prevented the spread of bacteria on the specimens. Fleming was about to throw the plates away when he suddenly realized that some unknown substance on the mold had the power to kill bacteria. That was indeed a *serendipitous* series of events. Incidentally, he called the substance Penicillium, which is the genus name of the mold. The antibiotic compound from it is penicillin.

In THROUGH THE LOOKING GLASS, Lewis Carroll coined the word *chortle*—probably as a combination of "chuckle" and "snort." To *chortle* is to sing or chant gleefully or to chuckle laughingly. Recently the verb has taken on additional senses:

1. to progress noisily
2. to express amused contempt
3. to speak exuberantly or with bubbling excitement

Chortle is a portmanteau* word—that is, an arbitrary combination of two words. *Smog* is a good example, combining "smoke" with "fog." Lewis Carroll loved such words. Take, for instance, " 'Twas brillig, and the slithy toves . . ." My guesses as to the combinations are as follows:

brillig	=	brilliant	+	lighted
slithy	=	slimy	+	lithe
toves	=	turtle	+	doves

Carroll is also responsible for *jabberwocky* or *jabberwock,* which is gibberish or meaningless speech. Here is a famous stanza from THROUGH THE LOOKING GLASS:

> " 'Beware the Jabberwock, my son!
> The jaws that bite, the claws that catch!
> Beware the Jubjub bird and shun
> The frumious Bandersnatch!' "

The gift of playwrights to our vocabulary are numerous and interesting. What follows is a sampling.

A *lothario* is a gay blade who seduces women. The noun comes from the name of a young rake in THE FAIR PENITENT (1703), a play by Nicholas Rowe.

If you have ever wondered why we use *simon-pure* as a synonym for genuine or authentic, rather than peter-pure or paul-pure or tom-dick-and-harry pure, the answer is that Simon Pure is a Quaker in A BOLD STROKE FOR A WIFE (1718), a play by Susanna Centlivre. An impostor claims that he, and not Simon, is Pure, but in the end our hero proves that he's the real McCoy—I mean the authentic Pure.

Not so pure as Pure is Tartufe, in a Molière play (1664) of the same

---

* *Portmanteau* is a French-English word for a type of traveling bag. Literally, it means "carry a cloak." *Portmanteau* words carry a double load.

name. This imposter dupes his host into giving him title to all the property owned by his victim. Meanwhile, like Dickens' Mr. Pecksniff, he pretends to be a very pious man. Luckily he is finally undone by a ruse and is hauled off to jail. Today a *tartufe* (or *tartuffe*) is a religious hypocrite.

Mrs. Grundy is religious, but she's no hypocrite. In Tom Morton's play SPEED THE PLOUGH (1798) she is a prudish neighbor of the main characters. Although she never appears onstage, her role is important, because the characters keep asking one another, "What will Mrs. Grundy say?" Hence any person with a narrowly conventional or intolerant attitude is a *Mrs. Grundy* or simply a *Grundy*. An offshoot is *Grundyism*.

Another married woman who has made quite a name for herself in our language is Mrs. Malaprop, a character in Richard Sheridan's THE RIVALS (1775). Words are her chief problem; she mixes them up. For instance, she talks about being "as headstrong as an *allegory* on the banks of the Nile." She *reprehends* when she should be apprehending, and so on, and so on.

Malapropism,* therefore, is gross or ludicrous misuse of words, especially through confusion of those that sound alike. Some of my favorites are:

> "That young violinist is certainly a child *progeny!*"
>
> "If you lead the way, I'll *precede*."
>
> "When we visited Athens, we saw the *Apocalypse*."
>
> "You're in for a *shrewd* awakening."
>
> "Beware of sexy women like those *lymphomaniacs*."
>
> "Send the package by *partial* post."

Then there is the little Catholic girl in New York City who said she was taught *cataclysm* in school. She may be the same one who, when saying her prayers at bedtime, recited, "Lead us not into Penn Station."

It should be noted that Sheridan took the name for his blundering character from *malapropos,* which means "inappropriate." His choice was truly apropos!

To that little moppet, Penn Station could certainly be converted from a terminal into a *termagant* if she happened to have come across that synonym for a shrew. I distinctly recall the first time I ran into the word. As a boy, I was reading Washington Irving's story about Rip

---

* *Malapropism* has a brand-new synonym: *Archie Bunkerism,* or just plain *Bunkerism,* from the TV character so well played by Carroll O'Connor. Archie's verbal blunders are part of the fun of the program.

Van Winkle. The author referred to Rip's wife as a *termagant,* and the context must have helped me, because I immediately knew that the word meant "a quarrelsome woman." I wonder how many readers have had the same experience; it's probably not unique to remember the exact place where you discovered a new word and subconsciously or consciously added it to your vocabulary.

But many years elapsed before I discovered the original source of the shrew. Originally she was an imaginary Moslem male deity, probably invented by the Crusaders. In medieval plays Termagant was depicted as a boisterous, overbearing character. He caused lots of tumult onstage. Note how his sex changed when he entered our dictionaries. This looks like grist for the feminists' mill.

Termagant as an adjective means "turbulent." *Termagantish* means "shrewish," and *termagancy* means "habitual bad temper." Some teachers seem to develop that disposition around midterm. I am reminded of an old Joe Miller joke:

Q. Why is a teacher like a Model-T?

A. Because she's a crank in front of a bunch of nuts!

Such devilish statements provide me with a nice transition to *Mephistophelian* or *Mephistophelean,* which means "fiendish, surly, sardonic, crafty or malevolent."

Mephistopheles, a devil in medieval legends, was made into a real character by Goethe when he wrote Faust (1808). In that play the fiend becomes an urbane cynic—"the spirit who always negates"—and an agent of complete destruction. He tempts the old scholar into a pact by which Faust will sell his soul in return for comprehending all experience.

Variations of the Faust legend appear in Christopher Marlowe's Dr. Faustus and Thomas Mann's Doktor Faustus. Several operatic composers have been intrigued by the story. Gounod's Faust is probably the most famous musical offshoot.

Works of literature, good and bad, have also added to our stock of words in the area of clothing. Let us start with the play Trilby (1894), which was based on George du Maurier's novel with the same name. A soft felt hat with an indented crown was worn by one of the characters in the drama. The British milliners seized on the popularity of the play and produced a hat called a *trilby.* I am told that some Londoners still prefer it.

But *trilbies* are also feet! The reason for the confusion is that Trilby, an artist's model, had feet that evoked wonder and delight. If I may coin a word, her admirers were *pedolaters,* who placed her on a pedestal because of her pedal pulchritude.

Du Maurier's novel also expanded our vocabulary in another direction. Svengali was a Hungarian musician with hypnotic power who could control Trilby's singing on the stage. Today a *Svengali* is a person who can mesmerize others in a sinister way and force them to do his bidding.

The *trilby* is a relative of the *fedora*. Whence comes that hat? Well, in 1882 (thirteen years before the du Maurier novel became a play) a Frenchman, Victorien Sardou, wrote a drama called *Fédora,* which starred Sarah Bernhardt. The hat she wore created a sensation, and the milliners again responded to opportunity's knock.

Dropping down from the top of the head to the neck, we find the *Peter Pan collar,* named for the traditional close-fitting article worn by J. M. Barrie's little boy who ran away to Neverland to escape growing up. Incidentally, a *Peter Pan* in today's lingo is a person who is young in heart and spirit though old in years. The expression may be used with affection or contempt, depending on one's point of view.

> Let's give the hook to Peter Pan!
> He never got to be a man;
> Yet maybe Peter had the key
> That didn't come to you or me:
> He never got the can or axe
> And never paid an income tax!
> He took life easy, on the wing,
> And all he did was prance and sing—
> He zipped around without a care;
> Well, maybe he had something there!

That little boy reminds me of Frances Hodgson Burnett's hero in the novel LITTLE LORD FAUNTLEROY (1886). A *fauntleroy* outfit is one that features a short jacket, trousers reaching to the knees, a wide collar on a frilly shirt—just like the garb of the boy in the book.

In slanguage a *Fauntleroy* is an effeminate man or sissy. A derivative is *Flauntleroy,* designating a white-collar worker.

Finally, on the subject of clothes made notable by literature of all sorts, we come upon a *Mother Hubbard.* It's a full, loose gown worn by women. Why? Well, artists who depicted the woman in futile search of a bone for her hungry canine always showed her in that kind of garb.

———

Now let's look at a few additions to the English language from the literature of our own century. *Babbitt* is the prime example, stemming from the novel of that name published by Sinclair Lewis in 1922. George Babbitt is portrayed as a smug businessman, living a conventional and comfortable life and having no cultural values whatsoever.

Hence a *Babbitt* has become a synonym for a self-satisfied, unthinking, middle-class conformist striving for material success and little else.

Some derivatives are *Babbittical, Babbitty, Babbittry* and *Babbittism.* Can you imagine what Mrs. Malaprop would do with that last word?

Edgar Rice Burroughs created Tarzan when I was a boy. Naturally, I devoured all the Tarzan books, just as I had consumed such juvenile fodder as stories about the Merriwells, Rover Boys and Tom Swift. Today a *Tarzan* is a virile, agile, heroic man.

Incidentally, do you know about *Tom Swifties?* Because of the stilted use of adverbs in Edward Stratemeyer's series, a satiric word game has arisen. A few decades ago Father Edward O'Brien transferred the idea to Sunday TIMES crossword puzzles. Here are a few examples of this form of satire:

"Who cares about the grapes?" said Tom *sourly.*

"I feel glassy-eyed," said Tom *transparently.*

"You Jezebel! Don't caress me like that!" said Tom *touchily.*

Sportswriters have given us some new words too. One example is *Tom and Jerry,* which is not so modern. In 1821, Pierce Egan—an English expert on outdoor games—wrote LIFE IN LONDON. In that book he described Tom and Jerry Hawthorne, who liked *la dolce vita.* Today their first names are a hot, eggy, spicy but sweet rum drink.

An up-to-date contribution is from Jack Conway, a baseball player and sportswriter who is reputed to have coined the word *palooka,* which now hovers between acceptance and rejection by lexicographers. The word originally referred to an inept boxer or other athlete. More recently it has evolved into a synonym for any clumsy person or oaf. Cartoonist Ham Fisher gave the noun lots of publicity when he created a boxer named *Joe Palooka.*

Cartoons and comic strips are not exactly literature, but those media have also been adding words to our language—from David Low's Colonel Blimp to H. T. Webster's Caspar Milquetoast.

Thomas Nast invented the Democratic donkey, the Republican elephant and the Tammany tiger. Moreover, T. A. Dorgan ("Tad") originated such slang expressions as "Twenty-three skiddoo" and "Yes, we have no bananas."

You won't find Bud Fisher's Mutt and Jeff in your dictionary, but I've heard their names all my life. Because I'm six feet five, whenever I stand next to a very small person someone is sure to remark, "Mutt and Jeff!"

Superman is one of our words, but not because of the comic strip.

He's a superior human being considered by philosopher Friedrich Nietzsche as the idealized goal of our evolutionary struggle for survival.

Earlier in this century an artist named Richard F. Outcault created a lad named Buster Brown. His pageboy haircut and his distinctive suit and collar became very popular. In my family's album a picture of me as a five-year-old is in the *Buster Brown* mode from head to toe. Immodestly, I must admit I look cute.

Walt Disney's Mickey Mouse has become a slangy adjective with several meanings:

1. corny, as dance bands or music
2. childish; unrelated to reality
3. commercially slick

In some areas of the country a *Mickey Mouse* is a police car. I have no idea why. Incidentally, my favorite definition for Disney is: "He gave the world a Mickey."

Cartoonist George Baker took his character *Sad Sack* from an old U.S. Army term for a bottom-of-the-barrel private who is "a *sad sack* of s—t." But Baker's comic-strip certainly gave the soldier a place in our language. *Sad sack* is still listed as a slang expression in most dictionaries, but it may someday become legitimized as a synonym for a ludicrous, inept misfit, whether in the service or not. Usage dictates that our lexicographers sanction the term.

Finally, *Rube Goldberg* should not be left out, though I will admit that his name rightly belongs in the chapter "Some 'Immortal' Mortals." In any event, the ingenious creations of that cartoonist-sculptor have become famous. Any complicated diagram or contraption designed to achieve a simple result is now called a *Rube Goldberg*.

I must point out that this chapter, like so many others in the book, is not meant to be comprehensive or encyclopedic. Various readers may be disappointed to see that their own favorites from literature have been omitted. All I can say is that I have tried to offer a representative sampling of our literary largess.

CHAPTER 15

Eyebrow Raisers

If you're squeamish about sex you may wish to skip this chapter. The reason for its inclusion is certainly not to shock prudish people or, on the other hand, to pander to prurient tastes. The fact is that our dictionaries are filled with terms pertaining to biology, physiology, scatology, lovemaking and the sexual drive. Only a comstocker would decide to omit any reference to them in a book on vocabulary.

It is also true that many words appear on the surface to have no relation to any of these areas, but actually do, either through usage or their etymological background. It seems proper to bring some of them into focus.

For example, *meretricious* looks innocent enough. Most people think of it as a synonym for tawdry, showy, gaudy, specious or deceitful. All those connotations are correct, but the first meaning of the word is "pertaining to a prostitute." Since women of the earliest profession often bedeck themselves with cheap ornaments and are not known for straightforwardness or honesty, it's easy to see how *meretricious* became synonymous with cheap ostentation and deception.

The Latin root is *meretrix,* a word we have borrowed without alteration. Its meaning is "whore." The last syllable of the word has led to some obvious puns.

Most fascinating is the ultimate root—*merere* (or *mereri*), *meritus.* The verb means "to earn." And so it's ironic that *merit, meritorious, emeritus* and other such derivations are all linguistic kin of prostitutes.

Lupanarian is another fooler. *Lupa* means "female wolf" in Latin. Probably by association, in our language *lupanarian* means "pertaining to brothels."

A *pom-pom* is a large automatic gun. Interestingly enough, it's also called a *Chicago piano,* probably with reference to the use of such guns by the Al Capone gang in the Windy City. For some reason the term *pom-pom girl* evolved as a synonym for a prostitute or girl who can easily be picked up.

There are also *pompon girls,* or cheerleaders who wave chrysanthemums. The *pompon* is a variety of the fall flower. But erroneous usage has been changing those cheerleaders into *pom-pom* girls—thus prostituting them. Do they merit the alteration? I leave the answer to the reader's personal opinion.

Roger is a word we all know. A pirate's flag is called a *Jolly Roger.* And in recent usage *roger* has become a code word for the letter *r* and stands for "received." When a radio operator says "*Roger!*" he is telling his communicator that he's got the message.

But *roger* is also a vulgarish verb meaning "to copulate with or have sexual intercourse." No less a poet than Ezra Pound wrote ". . . occasionally *rogered* the lady." The word is believed to have arisen because of the use of *roger* as a name for the penis. Peter and Dick also fall into the same category, whereas John has taken a different course. He's either a lavatory or a prostitute's client.

Rut is another word with more than one meaning. Actually, there are two basic ancestors of *rut,* both from Old French: *rote* or *route* ("way") and *rut* or *ruit* ("to roar"). As an English noun it means a male deer's annual state of sexual excitement. When a stag is *in a rut* he bellows.

The word has been broadened to mean sexual excitement in any mammal. A related word is *estrus* (from Latin *oestrus,* "gadfly or frenzy"). When a bitch is in heat, it is said to be *estrous* or *estruating.* Some lexicographers say that *estrus* and *ire* are etymologically related.

Incidentally, the period of sexual quiescence after the cycle is over is called *anestrus.* And it should be noted that *estrogen,* from the same frenzied root, is a female hormone.

Vanilla beans are podlike capsules of a tropical plant that yields a delicious flavoring extract used in confectionery, cooking and perfumery. *Vanilla* comes to us via the Spanish word *vainilla* ("small pod or husk"). The ultimate source is *vagina,* a Latin word meaning "sheath or scabbard."* Botanists call the ensheathing part of the base of a leaf a *vagina.* And, of course, it is a canal between the uterus and vulva.

Salep, which is familiar to addicts of the black and white squares, is another innocent-looking word with a raunchy background. It means "dried tubers of orchids." But its Arabic ancestor, *sahlab,* refers to a fox's testicles.

---

* When Caesar put his *gladius* into the *vagina,* he was inserting his sword into his scabbard.

Pumpernickel is such a tasty bread that I hesitated to reveal its scatological source. In an early form of German, *pumpern* meant "to break wind." *Nickel* meant a "goblin or demon," specifically the Devil. Since the sourdough bread caused gas and was as hard as the devil to digest, its high-sounding (or low-sounding) name evolved.

Shyster has caused a rift among the experts. They have different opinions as to the origin of this term for an unscrupulous lawyer. Take your pick:

1. probably after Mr. Scheuster, a nineteenth-century attorney frequently chided in New York courts for his quibbling tactics
2. possibly from *shy,* a slangy synonym for disreputable, plus *ster* ("one who is")
3. possibly from *shuyster,* alteration of the German word *Scheisser* ("defecator")

My first contact with *defecate* came when I was a nine-year-old boy who owned a dog named Prince. Unfortunately the mongrel was too clever for me. He found several ways to get out of the house clandestinely. An angry neighbor screamed at me, "Stop your dog from *defecating* on my lawn!"

Now you can imagine my bewilderment! What had Prince done? I knew he was a Casanova whenever a female dog wandered into the area. So that's what the rascal was doing! Finally I looked the word up, and it wasn't easy. At that age my knowledge of orthography was shaky. Then I discovered the definition—or I should say definitions. Number Two seemed to be the most applicable.

1. to clear from impurities; to clarify; purify or refine. (Certainly Prince wasn't refined!)
2. to void excrement. (What the heck was excrement?)
3. in sugar manufacturing, to clarify juice

I zeroed in on "excrement" and discovered it was "fecal matter." Fecal? The dictionary referred me to "feces." There I learned that feces meant "ordure." Okay, what's ordure? The answer was dung. Now I was getting close. Dung, the dictionary said, was manure. For some reason I knew the meaning of that word. In those days horses outnumbered automobiles and often spoiled our games of Skelly and hopscotch in the middle of a street.

I looked up from the dictionary and exclaimed, "So that's what Prince did! Oh, s—t!"

Those other definitions of *defecate* remind me of crossword puzzle fans who **leap** before they look. One woman wrote to me that *fearful* meant "afraid," **not** "dire." She had failed to check any good dictionary.

A man in New Jersey couldn't understand how *arise* was defined as "rebel." To him it meant "go up" and nothing else. We do get stuck with our first impressions, and some of us don't budge beyond our earliest notions.

My personal example is *petard.* Sometime in my salad days I learned the expression *hoist with one's own petard,* meaning "hurt by one's own schemes." I always assumed that a *petard* was some kind of shaft. If someone had told me it was a firecracker, I might have demurred. But that's exactly what a *petard* is. Originally the word referred to a case containing an explosive for breaking down bridges, barricades and gates.

Like that of *pumpernickel,* the derivation is a bit offensive. The word comes from the French verb *péter* ("to break wind") and ultimately from the Latin infinitive *pedere* (which has the same meaning). Hence a *petard* is a sort of human bomb. If a gassy chap is thrown out of a restaurant because of malodorous emanations, he has been literally *hoisted on his own petard.**

In the same category as the above we must include *fizzle.* Today if your attempts *fizzle out,* they fail or end feebly. That last adverb is a vestige from the obsolete meaning of the word—"to break wind quietly." Appropriately, another modern definition for *fizzle* is "to make a hissing or sputtering sound."

Also, the colloquial adjective *feisty,* meaning "lively or quarrelsome," comes from the adjective *feist,* a relative of *fizzle.* It originally meant "breaking wind."

Of course our most common word for the emission of gas from the intestines is *fart.* The word has a long history, dating back to the original Indo-European great-great-grandparent. In Middle English the verb was *ferten* or *farten.* Obviously, gastric problems have afflicted mankind for ages and ages.

———

Can you imagine the howl that would arise from addicts of black-and-white squares if a crossword puzzle editor ever defined *avocado* as "fruit from the testicle tree"? The word can be traced to a Spanish alteration of a Nahuatl term. That ancient Mexican tribe believed that the fruit had power as an aphrodisiac.

Aphrodisiacs, by the way, have been overrated. Sex-oriented men have been in search of such stimulants since (and maybe before) the days of Aphrodite, for whom they were named. Oysters, certain wines, perfumes, chemicals, drugs and other substances are said to stimulate

———

* The first syllable of *petcock* ("small faucet or valve") has the same Gallic root as *petard.*

sexual desires, but there is really no proof that any of them are universally potent. The human psyche is the variant that must be considered. Just think of what would happen if a scientist invented an *aphrodisiac* that never failed. Our wives and daughters would have to wear those old chastity belts forced upon women by the Crusaders.

Testicles presents a different linguistic problem. Would you believe that they are related to such words as *testament, testify* and *attest?* The Latin root is *testis* ("witness"). *Testicle* is a diminutive derivation. The experts guess at the connection: those male sex glands, they say, might be "witnesses to virility." I leave it to the reader's imagination to figure that one out.

When I taught in Harlem the boys had trouble pronouncing plurals of words ending in *est*. Thus *nests* became *nestés* and *chests* came out as *chestés*. I'll never forget the day when a student asked, "Mr. Maleska, when will you give us our final testés?"

An obsolescent Spanish word for *testicle* has found a spot in vulgar English. Recently my partner and I were losing a bridge game. He exclaimed, "I guess they've got us by the cojones [co-hó-naze]!"

In that connection, *anorchous* is a high-sounding word that means "having no testes." Some equestrian owners castrate certain male horses, which then become *anorchous* and are called geldings. Castration is the removal of testes or ovaries. When applied to females it is called spaying. Both words have a Latin background: castrate literally means "to prune with a knife"; the Romans inherited the word from Sanskrit. Spay comes from *spatha* ("broadsword").

Eunuchs are castrated men who protect a sultan's harem. Their name has a Greco-Roman ancestry and literally means "guardian of the bed."

In contrast to pumpernickel, petard and other innocent-looking words that have ribald histories, there are many that sound lewd or vulgar but are really as pure as the driven snow. Here are just a few examples:

> *coal tit*—small black-capped European bird
> *cockup*—hat or cap turned up in front
> *crapulence*—gross intemperance in drinking beverages
> *cunner*—small blue fish
> *shittim*—the wood of the shittah, a tree mentioned in the Bible; small U.S. shrub or tree
> *stinkhorn*—type of fungus

Some words have two meanings, one of which is vulgar or suggestive. Again a few examples will suffice:

ass—beast of burden; also buttocks

bastard—illegitimate child; also obnoxious person

bum—loafer; hobo; vagrant; also buttocks

(The use of the word to refer to the posterior is chiefly British. In Londonese, *bum*—short for *bum fodder*—is toilet paper; hence, official documents. Most interesting is *bumfreezer,* the British synonym for the Eton jacket; it comes down to a bit below the waistline.)

bung—stopper in a cask; also anus

butt—rifle end; laughingstock, victim, mark, etc.; also buttocks

diddle—waste time; dawdle; also copulate

dingus—thingumbob

faggot—bundle of sticks; also male homosexual

goosey or *goosy*—foolish; also ticklish when touched between the buttocks

horny—having antlers; hard, callous, etc.; also lascivious

hung—suspended; also having a large penis

lust—vigor; also lechery

moon—earth's satellite, etc.; also buttocks

(*Mooning* is the practice of exposing one's buttocks, as through the open window of a car or bus.)

Admittedly, some of the second definitions in the above list are slangy, but it cannot be denied that they are in common usage. TV comedians make sly jokes about them, writers bandy the words about, and people in every class of society either utter or hear such terms almost daily. My list could be extended to such words as *pecker, prick, pussy, snatch, whang* and other double entendres, but why belabor the point?

Mankind's almost obsessive interest in sex is remarkably revealed in synonyms for *prostitute* (from *prostituere*—a Latin verb meaning "to expose in public"). Aside from *meretrix,* we have the following samples: *harridan, strumpet, drab, harlot, trull, doxy, chippy, whore,* trollop, hooker, floozy, slut* and *hustler.* The Parisian version, *cocotte,* has also been added to our dictionaries; literally, it means "hen." A related noun is *cocodette*—a French call girl. Another import from France is *fille de joie* ("young woman of pleasure"). And the Italians have donated *bona roba* ("good material").

Recently I read an article in *The New York Times* about a West German peddler of sex. His term for the women that he employed was *erohostesses* (from Eros, god of love)!

---

* *Whore* has an interesting history. It can be traced to Old High German (*huara*), Old Norse (*hōra*), Gothic (*hors*). But lexicographers say that it is also related to the Latin adjective *carus* ("dear") via *kāma,* the Sanskrit word for "love or desire."

Caress and *cherish* are members of the family. So is *charity*—and that's a laugh!

Additionally, one of my dictionaries of slang lists more than a hundred synonyms for these so-called loose women. They have obviously attracted the attention of neologers.

Houses of ill repute have also intrigued the slangsters. There are at least fifty vulgar words or phrases for such places, including *cathouse, notcherie, service station* and *shooting gallery*.

Brothel is the "refined" term for the above. It comes from a Middle English verb meaning "to waste away." The word was originally applied to lewd men or women; then it became associated with the scene of their activities.

The Italian synonym, which we sometimes employ, is *bordello*. The Spanish call it a *casa de trato* ("house of treatment or deal") and *casa de putas* ("house of whores").

———

Putage is fornication by women, and *putanism* is habitual prostitution. *Pornocracy* is government by harlots. Someone has said that such an administration wouldn't make much difference, because most of our present politicians are already lying down on the job. But who would vote for such *pornerastic* women? *Philopornists* of course!

Courtesans are high-class harlots. Usually the mistresses of noblemen are given that euphemistic name. *Concubine* can also be defined as "mistress." But in more common usage such a woman is one who cohabits with a man although not married to him. The name is derived from *concubare*, "to go to bed together." The sleeping compartment called a *cubicle* has the same ancestry.

Speaking of "shacking up," the Australians have created *combo* as a term for a white man living with a female aborigine. One would expect them to make beautiful music together.

The above remark is said only tongue-in-cheek—which reminds me that a *soul kiss* does not seem to have any relationship to *soul music, soul food* or *soul brother*. But because the kiss is deep, it is probably akin to *soul mates*—men and women who have intimate personal relationships, often illicitly.

But *soul mates* can also be described as two people who merely have an affinity for each other. They could possibly be *Platonic lovers,* a phrase that really belongs in the chapter on eponyms. Plato's concept of love was an urge to unite with the beautiful in a way that transcended animal passion and reached for the ideal. Hence lovers who follow this philosophy sublimate or suppress their libidos.

Libido has been popularized by the psychoanalysts of the Freudian school. In recent decades it has been equated with desire for sex. The ultimate Latin ancestor is *libere* ("to please or gratify"). *Love* has come to us via the same root or route.

Speaking of routes, we note that the *libido* can take many different courses. Most humans are *heterosexual:* the object of their desire is a person of the *other* sex. But some are *homosexual:* the Greek root *homo* * means "same."

Here again our polite language seems to concentrate on the women more than the men, although the opposite is true of slang expressions. In any case, the most common designation for a female who prefers sex with others of her own gender is *lesbian*. The source for the word is the island of Lesbos, in the Aegean. There the poet Sappho and her feminine followers were reputed to have had sexual relations with one another.

Sapphist therefore is a synonym for *lesbian,* and *sapphism* is erotic desire of one female for another.

Furthermore, a *tribade* is a woman who attempts to simulate heterosexual practices with another woman. Their activities are called *tribadism* or *tribady*. The source is the Greek verb *tribein* ("to rub").

Such females may use a *dildo,* which is an object shaped like an erect penis. The origin is uncertain, but it is possible that the word may be a corruption of *dill,* the pickle. Some experts guess that *diletto* is the source. In Italian that word means "delight."

Dyke or *dike* is a term for a mannish female homosexual. The original expression was *bulldyke* or *bulldike*. One can readily understand the use of *bull,* but the second syllable is an etymological puzzler. Perhaps it is related to the Lithuanian *diegti* ("to prick"). Also, in British dialect a *dike* is a ditch or watercourse—but I cannot see the connection. Nor do I find any link with the kind of dam that prevents flooding.

In slanguage, male homosexuals have been given such derogatory names as *queers, fairies, pansies, fruits, fags* and *queens.* The last of that list often appear in *drag,* meaning that they dress up in women's clothes. Nobody seems to be sure how *drag* acquired that connotation. My own theory is that it is derived from the fact that *drag* is a slang word for a girl that a man is escorting (or pulling along with him). Since *drags* wear dresses, metonomy takes over.

Incidentally, *drag* has also taken on another sense; it can be a homosexual party. Is your bag chewing the rag or doing the shag with a fag at a *drag*—or do you prefer a stag where nary a hag or a nag will make you sag and gag?

All of the above people are *paraphiliacs;* like sadists and masochists (see Chapter 12), they go in for sexual practices that the majority of people consider abnormal. Such deviations are called *perversions* (from a Latin verb meaning "to turn the wrong way"), and a *pervert* is

---

* *Homo* is also a Latin noun meaning "man." Its most familiar use is the phrase *Homo sapiens* (literally, "wise man"), referring to mankind as a distinctive organic species.

construed to be anyone from a misdirected person to a morally corrupt individual.

A euphemistic term that has gained popularity in recent years is *gay.* That word stems from Old High German *gāhi* ("hasty or rash"). Its first meaning today is "excited and merry." Because orgies are often arousing and mirthful, *gay* also came to mean "loose, dissipated, unchaste." Thus it's easy to see how homosexuals became *gays* in the eyes of the "straights."

As I've said before, our language keeps building one word upon another. *Gayola* is a magnificent example. As an alteration of *payola,* it is a term for payment made to police or criminal syndicates by establishments catering to homosexuals.

The general term for the practices of homosexuals is *sodomy,* which has already been discussed in Chapter 13. A synonym is *buggery,* which has an ecclesiastical background. The word can be traced to a Middle English corruption of Bulgarian. It seems that Bulgarians preferred the Eastern Church, which the majority of religious Europeans regarded as heretical. Hence *bugger* arose as a term for a worthless fellow and then was extended to signify a *sodomite.*

Some homosexuals are *pedophiliacs:* their sexual desires are directed toward children. A *pederast* is a lover of boys, and *pederasty* is anal intercourse with a boy. In this case the boy is called a *catamite*— from an old Etruscan alteration of Ganymede, the cupbearer of the gods.

But in one sense *sodomy* is not restricted to homosexuals. The word is often used as a synonym for *fellatio,* a practice involving oral stimulation of the male organ, whether by another male or by a female. *Fellatio* comes from *fellatus,* the past participle of a Latin verb meaning "to suck." Other spellings for the word are *fellation* and *fellata.*

Oral stimulation of the female organ is called *cunnilingus,* a word that comes straight to us from Latin; it means "one who licks the vulva."

Vulva is also from Latin. In that language it means "integument, wrapper, covering or womb"; the parent verb is *volvere* ("to roll or turn"). In English *vulva* has come to mean "the external female genital organs."

The Romans' noun for those genitalia was *cunnus.* It's interesting to note that the word *kunte* sprang up in Middle Low German, and later, in Middle English, the spelling was *cunte.* Both nouns, as well as our own shortened form, designate the female pudendum.

An obsolete word, *cunny,* meant "woman or rabbit" and was probably an alteration of *coney* or *cony.* It has endowed us with *cunnythumb,* which means "with thumb bent inward behind the second finger of the closed hand." Because of the awkwardness of that placement of the fingers, *cunnythumb* has evolved into a synonym for inexpertly. And as a verb it means "to shoot marbles ineptly."

Pudendum has an intriguing etymology. This synonym for the *vulva* is the gerundive of *pudēre*, "to be ashamed." Related words are *pudency* ("modesty, prudishness") and *pudibund* ("prudish").

The most sensitive part of the *pudendum* is the *clitoris* (pronounced with the accent on the first syllable). It's an erectile organ that corresponds to the male's penis.* The source is *kleitoris*, a Greek word meaning "small hill." An interesting relative is *matroclinous*— "having predominantly maternal hereditary traits."

Because female genitals are sometimes thought to resemble *figs,* a derisive gesture in which the thumb is placed between two fingers is called a *fig*. Similarly, the gesture in which the third digit is angrily thrust upward into the air is called *the finger*. In this case the connotation is anal. *Giving the finger* and *getting the shaft* are related expressions.

You may be surprised to learn that *penis* is a Latin word for tail. The Romans called it *membrum virile* ("male limb"). *Membrum* comes from a Sanskrit word meaning "a decaying thing" or "a thing grinding in the socket."

Penis envy is a phrase that psychiatrists like to bandy about. It refers to the presumed subconscious desire of a female to be a male. I am reminded that a tomboy is often called a *hoyden*. That word earlier meant "rude fellow" and possibly can be traced to a Dutch term for *heathen*. Linguistically, therefore, a girl who wants to play football may be a pagan.

The Romans are also responsible for our word *pubes*—the hair appearing on the lower abdomen during adolescence. The eventual root of those hairs is *puer* ("boy"). Some related words are:

> *puberty*—stage of life at which the individual becomes capable of reproduction; hence, youth
> *puberulent* ⎫ minutely downy
> *puberulous* ⎭
> *pubescent*—adolescent; having a fuzzy surface; downy

In this category we find *merkin,* which lives, along with *muff* and *beaver,* as a slang word for the hair covering the female genitals. In nonslang it is false hair for the same area—a kind of nether wig, if you will.

---

* *Clitoridectomy* is female circumcision.

Phallus is a word that the Romans borrowed from the Greek *phallos* ("penis"). The Indo-European source is said to be *bhel* ("to swell"). In modern English the noun refers to the penis or clitoris, but the latter word gets short shrift in actual usage. This is probably because an image of the penis as the organ of reproduction was worshipped in Grecian festivals honoring Dionysus. This practice is now called *phallicism*.

One of the ancestors of *phallus* is the Latin verb *flare* ("to blow"). I have no evidence to support the notion that there is a connection with *fellative* (my coined word) practices.

Incidentally, the previously mentioned *stinkhorn* is a member of the *Phallus* genus because of the shape of that fungus.

But the most startling member (no pun intended) of the family is *ithyphallic*. It means "having an erect penis." Consequently other definitions have evolved—"obscene" and "lustful," for example.

As is often the case in other areas of our language, our more refined vocabulary has a Greco-Roman background, while our vulgar "four-letter words" usually have a lusty Anglo-Saxon or Teutonic heritage. For instance, sometime between the twelfth and fifteenth centuries our ancestors developed the word *fucken* from a Germanic word meaning "to strike or penetrate." In the same period the Dutch came up with *fokken* ("to strike or copulate with"). The lower classes held onto such words through the centuries, while the literati preferred classical terms.

Copulate is a good example. It doesn't carry with it any tinge or nuance of vulgarity. Its source is *copulare* ("to unite or couple"). We have also perpetuated *copula,* the Romans' term for a bond or link. It has different significance to grammarians and logicians, which the reader may wish to pursue, but it also can mean "sexual union" today.

Another polite substitution for our four-letter shocker is *coitus,* which literally means "meeting" in Latin. When the male withdraws purposely prior to his orgasm,* the procedure is called *coitus interruptus*.

Somewhat less refined is *fornication,* because the copulatory activity is not sanctioned by matrimony. When one or both of the partners is unmarried, they *fornicate*. The derivation is fascinating. In ancient Rome a *fornix* was an arch, and in the late republican period a vaulted underground dwelling with that name was frequented by prostitutes. Hence a *fornix* became a synonym for a brothel, and the other derivatives emerged.

---

* *Orgasm* can be traced to *orgasmos,* a Greek noun derived from the verb *organ* ("to grow ripe, to swell with moisture or lust"). *Orgy* is not a relative. Its Greek root is akin to *ergon* ("work")!

An obsolescent synonym is *scortation* (from *scortari*—"to associate with harlots"). It has no relation to the slang verb *score,* which is a logical extension of *get to first base.* Incidentally, a cartoon in PLAYBOY recently showed some tourists at the Lincoln Memorial. One of them is saying, "If Abe Lincoln made only four scores in seven years, he wasn't much of a ladies' man."

By the way, it's important not to mix up *fornication* with *formication.* In a way the latter might be taken to mean "ants in the pants," but its proper definition is "an abnormal feeling that ants are crawling over one's skin." To *formicate* is to creep or crawl like ants or to teem with ants.

Young men who fornicate may be afflicted with *colt's tooth,* or concupiscent desire. *Concupiscence* is lust. And when a wife fornicates, her husband becomes a *cuckold.* Lexicographers guess that *cuckold* is related to an Old French word *cucu* ("cuckoo"). That bird is notorious for leaving its eggs in other birds' nests, and the female habitually changes mates.

A *cucking stool* is a chair to which such persons as shrews, prostitutes and cheats were fastened and exposed to public mockery. Its Middle English ancestor, *coking-stole* or *cucking stol,* was literally a toilet seat.

Among the women who are not necessarily fornicators we must consider *flirts* and *hussies.* The ancestor of the former is an Old French verb, *fleurter* ("to touch lightly; to move from flower to flower").

Hussy comes from a Middle English word for housewife. Today it has acquired other meanings:

1. pert, impudent girl; minx
2. lewd or brazen woman; strumpet

When I was a college freshman I learned a new expression for a hussy of sorts. My roommate, a rough-and-tumble fellow who had received an athletic scholarship, had only two interests in life—sports and scoring. After one of his many dates with a coed he ranted: "A lousy C.T., that's what she was! That bimbo let me get to third base and then threw me out. How I hate those teasers."

If my roommate had studied French and had been more refined, he might have called the hussy a *demivierge.* To a Parisian that's a half virgin. One of my dictionaries defines the word as "a girl or woman who engages in lewd or suggestive speech and usually promiscuous petting but retains her virginity."

In Italian *bimbo* and *bambino* are synonymous: both mean "baby." We have retained the meaning for *bambino,* especially in representations of the infant Christ. But *bimbo* has undergone many a change in our slanguage. It was first used disparagingly to refer to a lazy lout or unlikable fellow. Though it still retains that sense, it is now also employed as a synonym for a promiscuous* woman. Purists would say that the proper form should be *bimba*.

Broad is another slang word for a woman, especially one with loose morals. Some philologers claim that the word is an alteration of *bawd* ("a woman who keeps a brothel"), but others state that it is a shortening of *broad-minded*.

In a punny sense, *lechers* are broad-minded. Such lewd men owe their name to an Old French verb that literally means "to lick." They lead a life of *debauchery*—and there's another word from Old French. Its ancestor meant "to separate branches from the trunk." This connotation caused the definition of the verb *debauch* to evolve into "to lead astray"—hence, "to seduce."

Two other men of the lecherous ilk are *reprobates* and *profligates*. Both have Latin roots. The former comes from *reprobare* ("to disapprove of or condemn"); the ancestor of the latter is *profligare* ("to strike down to the ground; to ruin"). *Rakehells, rakes* and *roués,* by the way, are kin to the above lechers.

All the foregoing men can be described as lustful and lascivious. They are also *salacious*—a word that can be traced to the Latin verb *salire* ("to leap, or cover sexually").

Salacious does double duty. It's not only a synonym for lecherous but also for pornographic. Incidentally, *coprology* is a synonym for pornography, and *coprophilous* people are fond of writings or pictures calculated to arouse sexual desires.

In its literal sense, from its Greek root, *pornography* means "writing of harlots." In one modern usage it still is a description of prostitutes. But chiefly it's a synonym for *curiosa* or *erotica*.

Eros has provided us with another word, coined by Havelock Ellis —*autoerotism,* which means "sexual arousal or satisfaction obtained without a partner." It can be contrasted with *alloerotism* ("sexual feeling or activity finding its object in another person").

A common *autoerotic* practice is *masturbation*. Lexicographers assume that the word eventually comes from the Latin *manus* ("hand") and *stuprare* ("to defile").

In Genesis 38:9, Onan is described as practicing *coitus interruptus*. Such withdrawal before ejaculation is now called *onanism,* but Judah's son's act has also come to be equated with masturbation. In old wives' tales, addiction to *autoerotism* is supposed to cause *cecity* ("blindness") but it's more likely to lead to *oligospermia* ("scantiness of semen").

---

* *Promiscuous* comes from a Latin word that literally means "mixing forth or forward."

Autocopulation has nothing to do with back seats. It's defined as "self-copulation that infrequently occurs in some hermaphroditic worms." That's carrying *autoerotism* to an extreme! Those worms are certainly *ambisextrous*. They are also *androgynous* (simultaneously male and female).

In connection with the lower animals, here are four other eyebrow raisers:

> *amplexus*—the mating embrace of a frog or toad
> *clicket*—to be in heat or copulate, as foxes and hares
> *go to buck*—copulate, as female hares with male hares
> *pizzle*—the penis of a bull

As you will remember, Zeus came down as a bull and copulated with Europa. He also used other disguises. For example, as a swan, he fornicated with poor Leda. Such myths may or may not have given rise to the medieval *incubus-succubus* complex.

The *incubus* was a demon believed to lie upon sleeping women for the purpose of sexual intercourse. His female counterpart was the *succubus,* who somehow found a way to lie beneath soporose men in order to engage in coitus. Their names were well chosen: in Latin *incubare* means "to lie upon" and *succubare* means "to lie under."

Both words live in modern English in different ways. An *incubus* is a nightmare, literally or figuratively. A *succubus* is a fiend or another of the many synonyms for prostitute.

The male equivalent of a prostitute is often called a *gigolo*. This fellow escorts, dances with and/or makes love to a woman who pays him or supports him.

The word has a fascinating background, via the French. Let's trace its history. First there was *gigue* ("a leg or fiddle"). That word has entered our language as a medieval viol and a lively dance movement. It has also been altered into *jig*.

The next step is *giguer* ("to dance"). Subsequently, any girl who frequented dance halls in Paris and was an easy pickup acquired the name *gigolette*. By back-formation her male counterpart became a *gigolo*.

Also of interest is the fact that *gigolo* is related to *gigot*—a leg of lamb or mutton or a type of sleeve shaped like the cut of meat.

Gigolos are usually younger men, and their supporters are often buxom women who have passed their prime. I am reminded of my first introduction to spoonerisms. When I was seventeen an older man named Eddie asked me, in front of some young ladies, if I had ever heard of Professor Spooner of Oxford. When I shook my head, he explained that the eminent instructor was famous for reversing initial sounds. He gave me two examples: "It's kisstomary to cuss the bride" and "a well-boiled icicle." Then he suggested I spoonerize "Gloria is fair and buxom." I blurted out the answer and inadvertently shocked everybody except Eddie.

Buxom is another word with an incredible history. In Middle English it meant "humble, obedient." Then it evolved into "physically flexible, pliant" and "blithe or lively." But today it carries only two chief senses: "vigorously plump" and "having a full bosom." What a far cry from its humble beginnings!

In line with the above, it grieves me to report that *callicolpia* has become obsolete. It means "the state of having a fine bosom." Its next of kin is *callipygian* (described in Chapter 1), which has managed to survive. Does it mean that we are more interested in posteriors and derrières than in mammary glands? I doubt it.

At any rate, the Greeks' *pygos* ("buttocks") has endowed us with several other interesting descendants. Two of them are *macropygia* and *steatopygia*. The former is a genus of long-tailed pigeons. Literally, they have large rumps.

Steatopygous people have too much fat on their buttocks. The condition is especially notable among female Hottentots.

The Romans, via the Athenians, have also contributed to our rear views. *Gluteus maximus* and *gluteus medius* and *gluteus minimus* are all muscles in the buttocks. *Gluteal* means "pertaining to the buttocks."

To a Scotchman the same area is the *curpin*. As an aside, the Scots have also come up with a word for the familiar rumbling in our stomachs. Their word for that flatulent* state is *curmurring*.

We have a plethora of synonyms for our posteriors. Among them are *fundament, haunches, stern, dorsal region, lumbar region, hindquarters, bottom* and *rump*. Slangsters have come up with *fanny* (in honor of some anonymous female of that name), *arse, backside, can, prat, keister* and many other words.

By metonymy *can* has also become a toilet. *Prat* has led to *pratfall,* a favorite laugh-getter of low comics who tumble backward. In recent years that refugee from burlesque has developed into a synonym for any humiliating mishap or blunder. *Keister* has probably come into our language via Yiddish. Aside from being a slangy synonym for the buttocks, it is also a suitcase or satchel, especially one carried by an itinerant peddler. I wonder about the connection.

---

* *Flatulent* means "full of air or other gas, especially in the intestines or stomach." The Latin ancestor *flatus* means "act of blowing or breaking wind." Some synonyms for *flatulent* are: turgid, inflated, pompous, pretentious and bombastic. The adjective can appropriately apply to orators who are "full of hot air."

Speaking of nonconnections, here is a disjointed list of other words relevant to this chapter:

> *coprolalia*—obsessive use of obscene, scatological language, often for sexual gratification
> *aischrolatreia*—worship of filth; cult of the obscene
> *parthenic*—relating to virginity
> *colposcopy*—visual inspection of the vagina
> *anaphrodisiac*—absence or impairment of sexual desire
> *aproctous*—having no anal orifice
> *anacreontic*—amatory
> *atocia*—female sterility
> *algolagnia*—sexual pleasure derived from inflicting or suffering pain
> *schmuck*—jerk; clumsy, stupid person (slang—from Yiddish word for penis)
> *cyesis*—pregnancy

Let me conclude with a funny story about *cyesis*. When I was a junior high school principal in a New York inner-city school, occasionally one of the female students would have a baby out of wedlock. In such cases, when the girl was ready to return, the district office would transfer her to another school to avoid either discomfiture or adulation for her. On her record card *cyesis* was indicated as the reason for the transfer.

One day a new principal of a school near mine gazed at the record card of my latest transferee and reacted with shock. Using his scanty knowledge of Greek, he assumed that *cy* meant "cells" and *esis* meant "disease of." Immediately he phoned me.

"Do you realize that Luella Jones has *cyesis?*" he asked.

"Sure," I replied, "but she's over it."

"Over it? How can anybody whose cells have broken down get over it?"

Well, you can imagine his embarrassment when I informed him what the word really meant!

CHAPTER 16

How to Construct Crossword Puzzles

Why should a chapter with the above title appear in this book? Well, hear me out. First of all, it's debatable whether *solving* crossword puzzles will build your vocabulary. Critics sneer at "crosswordese," and they have a good point. However, I believe that among the useless words, the solvers often make interesting discoveries. For example, I remember the first time I came across *zenana* as a definition for harem. I also recall learning that *seraglio* is another synonym. I don't ever expect to see a *zenana* or a *seraglio,* or even to talk about such establishments, but it's nice to have these alternatives for harem tucked away in my mind.

When we were guests on a TV program in Chicago, Carol Channing told me that a French friend of hers was improving her English vocabulary while having fun with THE NEW YORK TIMES puzzles. There are certainly better ways to build one's command of English, but her friend had a pretty good idea. At any rate, I do know one thing from personal experience: *constructing* crossword puzzles definitely increases the scope of your knowledge of words. In fact, if you take the hobby seriously over a long period of time, you become a human encyclopedia in such fields as history, geography, the arts, zoology, botany, sports, television and comics. You even gain a foothold in many foreign languages.

So take my word for it. If you want to develop a greater command of your mother tongue, as well as other tongues, try to make up crossword puzzles.

But it's not easy!

Out of the millions of people in the United States, I would guess that there are only about five hundred who are able to put together an American-style puzzle that meets all the criteria. Maybe one of the reasons is that nobody with an extensive background in the field has ever given the public a thorough look at the do's and don'ts.

I hope this chapter will correct that grave omission.

Let me tell you how I started four decades ago. To begin with, I became a crossword addict. I tackled every puzzle I could get hold of, whether easy or hard. When I couldn't finish one, I would religiously consult the answers. Aha! A compendium is a PANDECT! I'll remember that beauty next time it comes around. And a LAET is a Kentish freedman. Who cares? But I'll keep that stupid word in mind.

The romantic story of my first amateurish puzzle creation is related in the introduction to this book. The coed for whom it was made encouraged me to reach for the stars.

And so I set about getting myself published. First I bought the newspaper every day and studied the style of the puzzle very carefully. Months later I submitted my first professional effort—and held my breath. Incidentally, I enclosed an S.A.S.E. (self-addressed stamped envelope) but did not bother to write an accompanying letter. I had too much *amour propre* to plead.

My bubble of self-esteem burst abruptly. Not even a formal rejection slip! I was tempted to give up right then and there. But persistence emerged to take the place of pride. To make a long story short, I set some sort of record for initial failure—over forty rejections from a silent editor in a two-year period!

By that time I had married the beautiful girl whom I had wooed in college. We were driving along a street near our home in New Jersey and she was glancing through the TRIB. Suddenly she yelled, "Your puzzle. It's in the paper!"

I was so nervous and excited that I had to pull over to the curb and stop the car. A winner at last!

After that the acceptances outnumbered the rejections by a wide margin. In fact, I sold most of the puzzles that had been turned down. Later I heard from the new puzzle editor at the HERALD TRIBUNE that her predecessor had suspected me of plagiarism. Newcomers usually make a lot of errors. They sometimes resort to a plethora of black squares; their puzzles have "unkeyed" letters; their definitions are often inaccurate or uninteresting; finally, in some cases, they fail to design an open pattern.

Here's an example.

Actually, the diagram at the right is not just one puzzle; it is three small puzzles.

At any rate, it's ironic to think that my careful research before contributing a puzzle probably caused all those rejections!

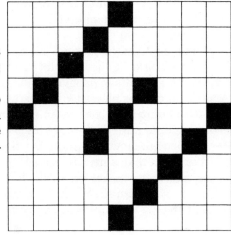

———

One of the features of published puzzles that captured my attention in those days was the frequent use of words that alternate consonants and vowels. Studiously, I compiled a list of such words as RECITAL, EMULATE, SARACEN, OPALINE and various others. I grouped them according to the number of letters in each word. The above were my "sevens." Longer words of this ilk were hard to find, but it was a thrill to dredge up such "tens" as DECELERATE, ECUMENICAL, ANEMOMETER and PALATINATE.

To show you what I mean about the value of such words to a budding constructor, here's an example of how it works.

```
P  A  R  A  P  E  T
A  L  A  B  A  M  A
T  E  T  A  N  U  S
```

Note how the vertical words fall into place. TAS is a French word meaning "heap" or "pile," but if I were constructing the puzzle I would probably expand that word to TASTE or TASSEL or even TASMANIA. Incidentally, as you examine the above, you will find ABA ("Arab robe") and EMU ("Australian bird"). Now you can see why such words are so popular with puzzle-makers.

The "alternating" technique can be overdone. An experienced pro seldom resorts to it. But it does give confidence to a beginner.

———

Another problem that I ran into early in my career was the handling of the ends of words. My diagram would call for a seven-letter word ending in RO. Of course the dictionary was no help. I had to rack my brain for a word that would fit. SOMBRERO? No, too long. BOLERO? Too short. ALLEGRO? Yes!

But there I was, stuck with only one word that would suit my Procrustean bed. There had to be a better way!

Well, I hit upon an idea that would not only solve my problem but possibly interest some publisher. I would prepare "Maleska's Reverse Dictionary." It would start with all the words ending in AA, then BA, CA and so on. The last page, of course, would include such words as BUZZ and FUZZ.

Armed with lots of paper and sharpened pencils, I visited the local library, which was blessed with three unabridged dictionaries. After I had spent four nights lucubrating, the librarian became curious about the strange young fellow with all those lexicons arrayed in front of him. She began a conversation. With a certain amount of pride in my creativity, I revealed my project.

I still remember her laughter. It was not derisive. It was kind of a sad laugh. Anyway, she walked about five yards to a shelf on my right and extracted a medium-size black book.

"I'm sorry for you," she said and handed me WALKER'S RHYMING DICTIONARY. It had first been published by an English schoolmaster in 1775 under the title THE CRITICAL PRONOUNCING DICTIONARY. The preface informed me that even Byron had found it useful.

My initial reaction was a feeling of chagrin. However, I couldn't help but be grateful, not only to the librarian but also to Mr. Walker. A few days later I bought his book. I still find it useful in a pinch.

Incidentally, here are the seven-letter words ending in RO that he lists. What a fascinating group of choices for a puzzle constructor!

ZINGARO—Gypsy
PIFFERO—Pipe; bagpipe
PRIMERO—Obsolete card game
LLANERO—Dweller on a llano
MONTERO—Spanish huntsman's cap
PAMPERO—Cold southwest wind of South America
VAQUERO—Mexican herdsman
ALLEGRO—Briskly (*mus.*)
ELECTRO—Electroplate; an electrotype

There are many other rhyming dictionaries, but they are designed only for poets. For example, BESTOW is found in the same category as HELLO.

While on the subject of lexicons, let me say that it is imperative for a puzzle-maker to arm himself with at least one reputable unabridged dictionary. Over the years I have acquired five such tomes.

WEBSTER'S NEW INTERNATIONAL DICTIONARY: SECOND EDITION (W-2)

This is known as the "constructors' Bible." It's a scholarly, no-nonsense book with thousands of entries and with definitions that are clear and accurate. The "Abbreviations" section is often helpful; the "Gazeteer" and the "Biography" are excellent.

W-2, as we call it, presents only a few problems. First of all, it is out of print. But trips to secondhand bookstores may reward the constructor or solver in search of this treasure. Also, it does not include words that have cropped up in our language during recent decades. You won't find *dognapping, kibbutz, megacycle, videotape* or such slang entries as *snow job* and *vigorish.* You'll have to consult W-3 for modernisms.

By the way, although W-2 does not list *vigorish,* it does give us *vigorist* as "an energetic or effective agent." The word cannot be found in W-3 or in any other of my unabridged dictionaries. This indicates another area of concern: some of the words in W-2 have apparently become obsolete. I feel sorry about *vigorist.* It says a great deal and has a nice ring to it.

One more point about W-2. Let's say you believe that George Eliot wrote ROMOLA but you're not sure. If you look this up in W-2, you will find not only the title and author but also a brief summary of the plot and mention of some of the characters. In other words, most of the works of past literature that are considered worthwhile are listed in the text. The same applies to literary characters. If you are uncertain as to what role Orsino played in what Shakespearean play, you can find out in W-2. Finally, it rivals Bullfinch in covering mythology.

WEBSTER'S THIRD NEW INTERNATIONAL DICTIONARY (W-3)

This calepin* has been roasted by most of the critics. They feel it is too wild and far-out. They complain about the format, the sins of omission and commission, the acceptance of ephemeral neologisms and slanguage, et cetera, et cetera.

Although many of the complaints are justified, W-3 is a valuable supplement to its predecessor. It is almost up-to-date (no dictionary can ever be perfect on this score), and it does recognize that usage by educated people alters the meanings, spellings and pronunciations of words. We conservatives may wince as the old order changeth, but it is futile for us to try to hold back the tide. I have been in the presence of Ph.D.s who say they are "enthused" and have heard others babble that certain unpleasant conditions make them feel "aggravated."

In consulting W-3 a puzzle constructor must be wary for two other reasons. Obsolete definitions are labeled as such, but they are mixed in with current ones. More important, if some obscure writer has stretched the meaning of a word, his concocted usage is duly recorded as a definition.

THE RANDOM HOUSE DICTIONARY OF THE ENGLISH LANGUAGE, unabridged edition (R.H.)

Here is the poor man's bonanza—a bargain for any puzzle-maker or -solver. It is not so new-fangled as W-3 and is more abreast of our times than W-2. Synonyms and antonyms are often appended to a series of definitions. Colloquial phrases are included in profusion.

One great advantage of this lexicon is the alphabetical placement of abbreviations and proper names (from Aachen and Aalto to Zworykin and Zyrian) in the text itself.

Other remarkable features are supplements. These include a list of colleges and universities, an extensive array of foreign words (French, Spanish, Italian and German), an atlas in full color and a rather thorough gazeteer.

---

* *Calepin* is another interesting word from W-2, but it is not listed in W-3. Here is the definition: "a dictionary; sometimes a polyglot lexicon; so called from Ambrogio Calepino, author of a widely used dictionary of Latin (1502); hence, one's customary chief book of reference."

On the negative side, it is apparent that R.H. editors solved their space problem by lumping together the definitions for various parts of speech. If one is accustomed to the neat separations of W-2, he sometimes gets confused when referring to R.H.

Naturally, too, a book with 1664 pages in the text proper must omit words that are included in W-3 (2662 pages) or W-2 (2987 pages).

Finally, puzzle-makers must double-check the spelling of proper names. Slips occur now and then in R.H. To give one example among many, I once published an acrostic by Thomas Middleton that included the name O'Kelley. That former president of Ireland spells his name O'Kelly—but Mr. Middleton and I trusted the spelling in R.H. Alert fans wrote in to ask humorously if we had made the error because we needed an extra E!

The American Heritage Dictionary of the English Language (A.H.)

This is another bargain. It is up-to-date, scholarly and well organized. The order in which the definitions are placed is excellent. But with only 1491 pages, it is necessarily less nearly complete than R.H., and it doesn't contain the latter's supplementary features. However, the section on derivations of English words is invaluable.

The Oxford English Dictionary (O.E.D.)

O.E.D. has rightly achieved fame as an extensive and accurate compilation of words and definitions. However, the American who uses it must beware of Britishisms. As H. L. Mencken once pointed out, there is an English language and there is an American language. They are often quite different.

I once owned a Funk and Wagnalls Dictionary, but I gave it away. For ordinary use it is fine. But it contains a host of abstruse entries that appear nowhere else. The constructor who consults it is tempted to use such words. It would be better for him if he had never come across them. Solvers confronted with esoterica can't be blamed if they become enraged.

Webster's New World Dictionary, second college edition (N.W.D.)

This is the lexicon that amazes me most. My edition was copyrighted in 1976, whereas W-3 came out in 1961. In those fifteen years a lot of new words were added to our language. As an aside, it should be noted that in 1976 W-3 issued a supplement called *6,000 Words*. I invested eight dollars and fifty cents and found it helpful.

But my N.W.D. has recently become a sort of linguistic Bible. Its 1692 small pages are packed with most of the information I need. The definitions are concise and accurate, and the format is splendid. Best of all, it contains a wealth of information on derivations of lowercase words and even proper nouns. It was in N.W.D. that I discovered the sources for such names as Chicago, Idaho and other place-names.

You won't find an atlas in N.W.D. or a dictionary of foreign words. In those respects R.H. is better. Nor will you find the marvelous section on Indo-European roots or the wealth of delightful illustrations offered by A.H.—but no single dictionary can be all things to all people. My feeling is that they all have their special fortes, and I am glad I invested in each of them. Maybe I'll buy a new copy of F. & W.

Some constructors use one or more of the umpteen crossword puzzle dictionaries that flood the market. These carefully written books are intended for solvers who are sometimes afflicted by inferior puzzles. They feature words such as IHI, AKU, ACARA, MEASE, PICI, HEER, PUNA, VETA, ASSI, HIR, POOAH. A good constructor avoids that sort of "crosswordese" like the plague.

New constructors often ask me what other books besides dictionaries would be useful to them. In a way it's a silly question, because any pro knows that reference books of all kinds are grist for his mill. Back in the forties, when I was a neophyte at the game, I set aside my puzzle checks to augment my library. Here are some of the reference books I have collected:

Several encyclopedias
Seven collections of quotations*
A few atlases
Some history books
VARIETY MUSIC CAVALCADE
THE AMERICAN THESAURUS OF SLANG
DICTIONARY OF PHRASE AND FABLE
Three books on classical music and art
Many paperback dictionaries of various foreign languages
Current and past almanacs
The READER'S ENCYCLOPEDIA and other books relating to literature
ENCYCLOPEDIA OF SPORTS
BOOKS IN PRINT
THE INTERNATIONAL ENCYCLOPEDIA OF FILM
Several Bibles
A concordance to the Bible
THE NEW YORK TIMES DIRECTORY OF THE THEATER
Several anthologies of poetry
ROGET'S INTERNATIONAL THESAURUS
Books on flora and fauna

---

* The chief reason for collecting such a large number of books of quotations is that I have been editor, since 1966, of Simon & Schuster's CROSSWORD BOOK OF QUOTATIONS series.

I should point out that the average constructor probably doesn't need half these books. But an editor of crossword puzzles requires all of them—and more!

Now, let's say that you have acquired a few unabridged dictionaries and several additional reference books. Let's assume, too, that for years you have solved enough puzzles (possibly in ink!) to consider yourself ready for your debut on the other side of the fence. What is your next step?

It may seem ridiculous to mention, but a typewriter is a necessity. Even when definitions are carefully lettered they are not acceptable. If, like me, you are a terrible typist—and your relatives are either unwilling or unable to help—then I suggest that you hire someone. For years I have employed top students taking commercial courses in local high schools. Their rates are reasonable and their work is usually good. Principals are happy to recommend young people who need the experience and the extra money.

Next, you need the proper grids for the diagrams. The squares in ordinary sheets of graph paper are too small. Drawing the lines yourself is too laborious and results in an amateurish appearance. Hence you should give a neighborhood printer some welcome business or employ the services of high school youngsters in the print shop. Specify that the sheets should be typewriter-size and the squares should measure a bit over one-quarter of an inch.

Once you have acquired the necessary materials and services you are presumably ready to apply your newly sharpened pencil to paper. At this point I cannot emphasize enough the importance of not biting off more than you can chew. In short, start with a puzzle that is no larger than 15 x 15 squares. Ninety percent of the tyros who attempt 21 x 21 and 23 x 23 puzzles fall flat on their faces. But those who practice on the smaller puzzles for a year or two find only a modicum of difficulty when they graduate to the Sunday toughies.

At this point you should already have familiarized yourself with the regulations stipulated by the editor to whom you wish to sell your puzzle. Assuming that you are aiming at the top—THE NEW YORK TIMES—here are the rules for a daily puzzle:

1. The pattern should be diagonally symmetrical. In other words, if you place a black square in the top-left corner, you must place another in the bottom-right corner.

2. The number of black squares should be kept to a minimum. In the old days the criterion was that the number should not exceed one-sixth of the total in the grid. A 15 x 15 puzzle has 225 squares. Thus 37–38 black squares were once considered to be the maximum. This

benchmark is constantly overlooked today, but any constructor who blacks in as many as 44 squares is skating on thin ice.

3. The maximum number of entries should be 76 unless the puzzle features a theme. In that case, 78 entries are permissible. A puzzle with 80 or more entries meets with automatic rejection.

4. Your pattern must be "open" (no corners closed off by black squares), and all your letters must be keyed. This means that every letter must fit into a word that goes across and simultaneously into another word that goes down. (British-type puzzles do not follow this rule.)

5. The minimum length of words is three letters.

6. Do not use colloquial phrases that are not found in any lexicon or book of quotations or as a title of a book, song, etc. Phrases such as SMELL A RAT or OVER A BARREL are acceptable, in whole or in part, because they are in the dictionary. An entry such as NO TIME is good if defined as "—— for Comedy," and A PLUM is fine if the clue is "He pulled out ——."

This is one of the areas where most new constructors invite rejections. For some reason many fail to see the difference between a made-up expression and one that can be defended via a reference book. Also, many fall by the wayside because of overdependence on strange, meaningless quotations.

7. Avoid obscure abbreviations even when you find them in the dictionary. Common abbreviations, such as C.I.A.. A.F.L., ETC., GOV., are all right, but it is best not to overload the puzzle with them.

8. Make every effort to keep "crosswordese" down to a minimum. Such words as ANOA, ASSE, IPIL, GHER, TOLA and other oddities appear in puzzles only because the constructor and the editor found it impossible to eliminate them. But the use of four or five words of that type in a 15 x 15 puzzle can only lead to a rejection.

9. The same applies to strange geographical places and to proper names. With regard to the latter, avoid entries that can be defined only as "Boy's name" or "Girl's name." Also shun the use of obscure surnames culled from encyclopedias.

10. Overuse of foreign words is another no-no.

11. Obsolete words are taboo, and so are most trade names. Avoid variants too.

12. Many puzzles are turned down because of a plethora of plurals. It's easy to load the diagram with words ending in S, but it will not impress the editor or the solver.

13. Words beginning with RE (such as *rehesitate* or *respark*) should be avoided or kept to an absolute minimum. Do not concoct a word beginning with RE (example: *redrown*).

14. If you do use an abstruse word, be sure that it crosses with easy words. Nothing can enrage a solver more than a "blind crossing."

15. Strive for interesting words, especially in the longer entries. Choice of consonants is important. A parade of R's, T's, D's, L's, N's and S's does not usually add up to an exciting time for the solver. Such letters as B, F, J, K, Q, W and X are too often neglected by mediocre constructors.

16. Most solvers do puzzles not only to sharpen their wits but also to get away for a while from the travails of life. Crosswords are definitely a form of escapism. Therefore it behooves the constructor to steer clear of diseases, bodily functions and innards, drunkenness, drug addiction, violence and vulgarity.

It is interesting to note that TIT is acceptable if defined as a "small bird," but TEAT is verboten. (Editors get letters from those little old ladies in tennis shoes.) ASS appears in many puzzles and is defined as "dunce" or "donkey." RAPE is a herb, but even if that clue is used, the editor will hesitate to publish the puzzle because of the painful associations of the more common meaning of the word. In short, a constructor must exercise good judgment when a questionable entry occurs to him. The general rule is When in doubt, leave it out.

But adherence to the rules is only one part of the game. The aspiring puzzle-maker has a blank 15 x 15 grid in front of him and he wonders how to get started. Should he draw up a diagram first or should he let it evolve?

Here is one way employed by many pros. They first gather together a list of long words, usually having a common theme, and they place these words in columns according to the number of letters in each word.

Let me give an example. Recently I decided to make up a 15 x 15 puzzle that would feature rhyming words ending in ADE. Consulting my WALKER'S RHYMING DICTIONARY, I found:

9 LETTERS

BARRICADE	COLONNADE
CAVALCADE	GASCONADE
AMBUSCADE	GABIONADE
MARMALADE	CANNONADE
DRAGONADE	CARRONADE
TWAYBLADE	GALLOPADE
EVERGLADE	CASSONADE
ESPLANADE	GINGERADE

10 Letters	11 Letters	12 Letters
NIGHTSHADE	FLANCONNADE	HARLEQUINADE
PASQUINADE	FANFARONADE	
TARDIGRADE	DIGITIGRADE	
MASQUERADE	RODOMONTADE	
VERMIGRADE	BALUSTRADE	
PINNIGRADE		
SALTIGRADE		
CENTIGRADE		
PRONOGRADE		
RETROGRADE		

Ordinarily my next step would have been to plot a diagram that contained at least four 9-letter words, because that list was the largest. It afforded sixteen choices, as opposed to only ten for the 10-letter words.

But then I noticed something. Seven of the 10-letter words ended in GRADE. That would certainly make the puzzle even more interesting! I checked W-2 and W-3 to make sure the *grade* words were all legitimate. (WALKER's sometimes includes obsolete words without labeling them as such.)

> TARDIGRADE—Slow-paced; sluggish (W-2 and W-3)
>
> VERMIGRADE—Creeping like a worm (W-2 only)
>
> PINNIGRADE—Walking by means of fins or flippers (W-3, defined; listed in W-2 but not defined)
>
> SALTIGRADE—Heavy feet or legs (W-2 and W-3)
>
> CENTIGRADE—A type of thermometer; consisting of a hundred degrees (W-2 and W-3)
>
> PRONOGRADE—Walking with the body approximately horizontal (W-2 and W-3)
>
> RETROGRADE—Moving or going backward; retreating (W-2 and W-3)

No obsoletes! Good, but I would place VERMIGRADE at the bottom of the list because of its omission from W-3. RETROGRADE or CENTIGRADE would be placed in the top-left section of the puzzle because those two are the most familiar. (It's a good idea to try to make the initial corner as easy as possible in order to get solvers off to a successful start.)

TARDIGRADE was my third choice. Even if a solver never had heard of the word, he would associate TARDI with TARDY. I hoped one of the other words would fit into the bottom-right corner. Any alert solver would by that time guess that the last five letters had to be GRADE. My job was to make sure that the crossings for PINNI, SALTI, PRONO or VERMI would be fair.

And so I drew up a diagram that looked like this:

1	2	3	4	█	5	6	7	8	9	█	10	11 R	12	13
14				█	15					█	16 E			
17 C	E	N	T	18 I	G	R	A	D	E	█	19 T			
20							█	21	22 R					
█	█	23				█	24			O			█	█
25	26	27 T			█	28				G	29	30		
31 A			█	32				█	33 R					
34 R		█	35				█	36 A						
37 D		█	38				█	39 D						
40 I	41				█	42		E						
█	43 G				█	44				█	█			
45 R	46			█	47				48	49	50			
51 A		█	52	53				G	R	A	D	E		
54 D		█	55				56							
57 E		█	58				59							

Note that the above diagram will contain only 74 entries. When I was a novice I probably would have been forced to add two or four more black squares to increase the word count to 76 or 78.

Notice also that the total number of black squares is only 34. Adding four more would not exceed the old one-sixth rule.

Originally I had placed CENTIGRADE in the top-right corner, but I switched to RETROGRADE because it is better to have 24-Across end in O rather than I.

Now the question will be asked, "Where did you go from there?" The answer is important. You don't plunge right in at 1-Across. Instead you examine the situation and try to determine where you will encounter the most trouble.

My decision was to work on 24-Across. A good choice seemed to be SEE TO (meaning "take care of"). If that didn't work out, I could try CARGO, CAIRO, ODE TO, CAN DO (motto of the Seabees), SEATO, HELLO or dozens of others. If nothing worked, I could move the two black squares down one notch. In that case, of course, I would have to remember to move up the two corresponding ones in front of 43-Across.

The second word that I tackled was 39-Down, because of that G at the end. Naturally I chose an NG ending. Placing a vowel before the G would vastly decrease my choices.

How did it all come out? Well, here is the completed puzzle.

P	A	P	A		A	L	L	O	T		E	R	A	S
I	V	E	S		G	U	I	L	E		C	E	L	L
C	E	N	T	I	G	R	A	D	E		A	T	T	U
A	R	T	E	R	!	E	S		T	E	R	R	O	R
		R	E	E	D		S	E	A	T	O			
L	A	T	I	N	S		C	O	R	T	E	G	E	S
E	R	A	S	E		A	R	L	E	S		R	A	M
P	E	R	K		P	R	I	E	D		C	A	S	E
E	N	D		G	R	E	E	R		Y	O	D	E	L
R	A	I	L	R	O	A	D		S	O	R	E	S	T
		G	A	I	T	S		S	T	U	N			
M	A	R	I	N	E		G	A	R	N	E	R	E	D
A	L	A	D		S	A	L	T	I	G	R	A	D	E
R	E	D	O		T	R	E	A	D		E	N	N	A
K	E	E	N		S	C	E	N	E		D	I	A	L

Attention should be paid to the two "ladders" of black squares in the middle of the puzzle. This is a favorite device of constructors. It helps to divide the puzzle into sections that can be handled almost separately. But as a pro I am not proud of the diagram. If I were less lazy I would reverse two black squares in each of the "ladders," thus creating a more open pattern. Then the diagram, in part, would probably look like this:

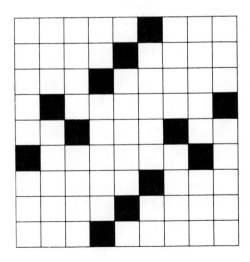

The use of themes has become very popular during the last two decades. Originally this idea featured groups of words on a given topic —for example: The Nine Muses, American Indians, Lakes Around the World, Members of the Hall of Fame. Sometimes a single word, such as TIME, would be repeated throughout the puzzle in phrases: "The Time of Your Life," "Make time," "Time and tide," "Sleepy Time Gal" and "Take time by the forelock."

But the type of theme that caught the fancy of most constructors and solvers was the "inner clue," usually accompanied by a catchy title. For example, a constructor would decide to make a puzzle called "Baker's Dozen." He would then search his mind and his reference books for words that fitted the title obliquely. His collection might include DRUM ROLL, NAPOLEON (defined as French emperor), MAKE DOUGH, DOUGHBOYS, BREADWINNER, CAKEWALK and scores of others.

But constructors and solvers are always looking for new and original ideas. Rebus letters got into the act. An Easter puzzle in THE NEW YORK TIMES required the solver to draw an egg whenever the letters E G G appeared in this combination. Thus PEGGY was shortened to P   Y and BEGGARS became B   ARS.

Puns proved to be a new attraction, especially when centered around a theme. Composers of music, for instance, have been mauled and mutilated as follows: PAT ON THE BACH, HAYDN GO SEEK and HANDEL WITH CARE. The above are delightful puns, but the problem that most constructors run into is the inability to maintain that same standard of excellence throughout the puzzle. Such inferior puns as WATCH THE VERDI or TAKE ME IN YOUR BRAHMS or MISS DEBUSSY rear their ugly heads. That is why so many efforts in paronomasia* are returned to the contributors.

The embodiment of a quotation or original verse in a puzzle is a bonus that pleases many solvers. Professional constructors usually include not only the author of the quotation but also the title, in whole or in part. In any case, it is not good form to split up a word in the verse. The following is an example of good work. After careful research the puzzler has chosen a quotation from an Emily Dickinson poem. He builds it into a 21 x 21 puzzle.

"THERE IS NO FRIGATE LIKE A (21 letters)
BOOK TO TAKE US LANDS AWAY" (21 letters)

People wonder where the constructors get so many new ideas. The answer is that it often takes hours of cogitation and research before

* *Paronomasia*—a play upon words; pun

the lightning strikes. And sometimes it happens that two people will simultaneously think of the same new gimmick. I once devised a theme in which symbols would be used as clues. Some examples:

DEFINITION		SOLUTION
$\dfrac{0}{10}$		TEN BELOW ZERO
2ND	2ND	SPLIT SECONDS

I sent it to DELL CROSSWORDS on the day that I became puzzle editor of THE NEW YORK TIMES. Lo and behold, my first batch of mail contained a puzzle called "Not So Symbol as π." It featured the same device! Of course I published it and was happy to receive a flood of fan mail.

But some themes can be dangerous. A point that all new constructors must keep in mind is the avoidance of what solvers call "write-ins" or "fill-ins." Too many contributors of 15 x 15 puzzles are intrigued by the "challenge" of stringing out three 15-letter words horizontally or vertically in the diagrams. I have published such puzzles for want of something better, but I am not happy about them.

Here is a favorite of many who think they have struck pay dirt but have only mined fool's gold:

ERNEST HEMINGWAY
A FAREWELL TO ARMS
THE SUN ALSO RISES

All the above add up to fifteen letters each, but they really don't present any challenge to most solvers. In fact, the average fan gets bored as he writes in the letters without any cerebration whatever.

On the other hand, a solver might be delighted with a puzzle that contained new words to add to his vocabulary, provided all the crossings were fairly easy. Take the field of magic, for instance:

ESCAMOTAGE—juggling; sleight of hand
THAUMATURGY—magic
PRESTIDIGITATOR—a performer of sleight of hand
LEGERDEMAIN—sleight of hand

Even if a solver already knows those four words—and I doubt that ESCAMOTAGE is familiar to most—he will be delighted to see them again, and he may hesitate about the spelling.

In that connection, the so-called "spelling demons" are excellent candidates for puzzles. Off the top of my head, here is a list of just a few:

SEPARATE	ACCOMMODATE	TITILLATE	TATTOO
SEIZE	CONNOISSEUR	BOURGEOISIE	SUBTLETY
SUPERSEDE	TINTINNABULATION	DIPHTHONG	PERSEVERANCE
PHARAOH	WEIRD	EXHILARATE	CANDELABRUM
VACILLATE	EXISTENCE	ONOMATOPOEIA	IRIDESCENT
PERSONNEL	FAHRENHEIT	MASOCHIST	SIEVE
BOOKKEEPER	KNICKKNACK	RECONNAISSANCE	WITHHOLD
VERMILION	EMBARRASS	INDEFATIGABLE	OCTAGON
OCCURRENCE	DISSIPATE	INDISPENSABLE	GAUGE
SILHOUETTE	INNOCUOUS	DAGUERREOTYPE	SATELLITE
RECONNOITER	INOCULATE		

Any good reference book on orthography will list hundreds more. I may be wrong, but I feel that improvement in spelling is one of the enlightening by-products of crossword puzzles. Incidentally, if you are a poor speller, my advice is to forget about becoming a constructor. Along with a good vocabulary and lots of patience and persistence, ability to spell is the keystone of good puzzle-making.

———

And now let us assume that you have successfully completed your first attempt at creating a puzzle. The long words in the diagram are interesting; you have reduced the use of foreign words, abstrusities and plurals to a minimum; the crossings are fair; and you have kept the word count low as well as the number of black squares.

Your task is only half completed!

First, you must inspect your puzzle carefully, just as a poet looks over his verses, and you must polish. How many hundreds of times have I found better words and fairer crossings after finishing a puzzle! Sometimes it is advisable to put away your endeavor for a few days and come back to it with a fresh viewpoint. You will often be amazed at the inadequacies that you had not noticed in the first flush of creation.

All right. You have taken a second look and even a third look. Your critical eye is satisfied. You have given birth to a beauty. But now comes the real test of your skill, creativity and ingenuity—the definitions.

Some constructors have confessed to me that once they finish putting the words into the diagram they find they lose interest. Defining becomes a chore. To them my reply is: Change your attitude or quit. The clues are the be-all, if not the end-all, of crossword puzzles. They are the final test of excellence.

Allow me to backtrack for a moment to give you more perspective. In the beginning, when constructors and solvers were new at the game, definitions were taken right out of the dictionary. A TREE was always a "woody plant" and a NEST was a "bird's home." Solvers were treated like Pavlov's dogs. Bells rang in their heads when they were given certain clues, and they automatically wrote in the answers. The whole experience became an exercise in lettering, whether in pencil or in ink. It was also a test of memory. ERA was EPOCH, and vice versa. You felt comfortable at first with that kind of spontaneous reaction, but after a while intelligent minds wondered: "Is that all there is?"

At that point I had become a regular contributor to the daily HER-ALD TRIBUNE. I asked the new editor if she would permit me, as an experiment, to try some jazzy definitions on a limited scale. She acquiesced with some trepidation.

I remember the first puzzle in which I broke the log jam. NEST was defined as "Nutcracker's suite" and the clue for NOON was "When both hands are up." For IRONER the solvers were confronted with "He has pressing problems."

Well, the fan mail was wonderful! Out of the woods came scores of people who cried for more. Constructors were encouraged to use other original clues in various places throughout their puzzles.

Today there are still some solvers who think we have gone too far. They are the conservatives who like to see EAR defined as "Organ of hearing." To them HIE is always "Hurry" or "Hasten." If you use "Shake a leg" or "Waste no time" or "Step on it," they feel discombobulated. But letters from solvers reveal that the diehards are in the minority. Most of the fans take pleasure in new clues as long as the practice is not overdone. Hence a good constructor and/or editor will sprinkle these offbeat definitions throughout the puzzle, like a pinch of salt and pepper, but will not smother his concoction in seasoning.

Let's try some examples. Suppose you have entered the word SIREN into the puzzle. You may have a choice of the following definitions:

1. Singer at sea
2. Alluring woman
3. Chased woman
4. Dangerous damsel
5. Femme fatale
6. "Debutantalizer"
7. "Irresistibelle"
8. C.D.A. apparatus
9. Police-car item
10. One of Odysseus' temptresses
11. Vamp
12. Klaxon
13. Lorelei
14. Circe

If most of your other definitions have been staid and sober, you might elect No. 3, 6 or 7. On the other hand, if you have already included several unconventional clues, No. 2, 4, 8, 9, 11 or even 12 would be suitable. If you have used French terms in the puzzle, shun No. 5. And if other mythological references have been made, avoid Nos. 1, 10, 13 and 14.

Here is another example of the vast selection of definitions available to a constructor who does his homework. In the 1930s an EEL was always an "elongate fish." Old Pavlov was in his glory. Now look at the variety of clues employed today—an array that I have recently collated from an inspection of a number of published puzzles.

Anguilla	Teleost fish	Use a pilger
Spitchcock	Elusive one	Silver —
Fish to be spitchcocked	Smorgasbord item	Slippery customer
Relative of a hagfish	Relative of a sand	Lamprey's next of kin
Congo or conger	launce	Voracious fish
Squirmer	South Sea tuna	Cusk —
Nine-eyes' cousin	Grown-up grig	Relative of an ophidid
Moray	Electric —	Aquarium sight
Herring's relative	Wriggly swimmer	Snipefish
Sniggle	Slithery thing	

Goodbye, Pavlov!

Some of the above definitions undoubtedly were spotted by the constructors in unabridged dictionaries; others probably came from careful research in encyclopedias and assorted reference books. At any rate, the pros are always on the lookout for new clues. Moreover, they vigilantly scan newspapers and magazines for new words. Some of them keep notebooks or file cards for recording words and definitions. The alphabetical entries are arranged according to the size of the words.

Rising celebrities always attract the attention of constructors. Because many words in a puzzle necessarily begin with a vowel, famous people whose names fall into that category get the lion's share (no pun intended) of publicity among the black and white squares. Fitzgerald and Raines had a new rival when Ella Grasso became governor of Connecticut. Kazan gave Charles Lamb a run for his money, just as Wallach had done to Whitney. When Erma Bombeck wrote a best seller, constructors jumped on her bandwagon. And of course people like Idi Amin and Evel Knievel get more attention than they deserve. Nor should I neglect to mention Edie Adams, whose first name has appeared in thousands of puzzles.

Here is a partial list of other luminaries whose lights are rekindled constantly by the puzzle-makers.

Aldo Ray
Alan Alda
Alec Guinness or *Alec* Templeton
Kingsley *Amis*
Aram Khachaturian
Arlo Guthrie
Peter *Arno*
Barbara *Eden*

Jack *Elam*
Elke Sommer
Elmo Roper
Emil Ludwig or *Emil* Jannings
Enid Bagnold
Erle Stanley Gardner
Evan Hunter
Igor Stravinsky
Ilka Chase
Oleg Cassini
King *Olaf* or *Olav*
Omar Sharif or *Omar* Bradley
Otto Preminger
Leon *Uris*

The above are only some four-letter names. Think of all the puzzles in which *Ava* Gardner and *Ida* Lupino have been publicized, not to mention such lesser stars as *Ina* Claire and *Una* Merkel.

Actress Claire, by the way, must have rued the day when entries of two or more words were permitted to constructors by the queen of puzzledom, Margaret Farrar. Before that Ms. Claire's only real competitor was "feminine suffix." Today a host of phrases have taken her place: "IN A rut," "IN A jiffy," "Tempest IN A teapot," "Pig IN A poke" and even Manet's "IN A Boat."

But let's get back to the fine art of defining. A constructor must have a thorough knowledge of grammar, diction and especially the parts of speech. Here are some recent errors that have crossed my desk:

WORD	CONSTRUCTOR'S CLUE	CORRECTION
COZY	Be comfortable	Comfortable
RISEN	Went up	Gone up
PALOS	From whence Columbus sailed	Whence Columbus sailed
APART	What lovers hate to be	Estranged
EARNS	Makes his salt	Makes one's salt
ENTHUSED	Excited	Excited: Colloq.

One acceptable device is to define an abbreviation with another abbreviation or slang with slang. Sometimes a prefix or a familiar foreign word will lend itself to the same kind of treatment. Examples:

WORD	DEFINITION		
P.T.A.	Schl. affiliate	TRI	Between bi and quadri
MINN.	Neighbor of N. Dak.	PRE	Opposite of post
C.I.O.	A.F.L. partner	SETTE	Due plus cinque
SAWBUCK	Two fins	TRE	Three, to Tonio
TWERP	Relative of a droop		

A type of clue that has recently come into vogue is the following:

WORD	DEFINITION
SALT	Kind of shaker or cellar
FRUIT	Word with cup or cake
WAVE	Follower of brain or heat

Sometimes the use of "Kind of" or "Word with" is omitted—although I'm not sure that this ellipsis is fair to the solver. Certainly it seems to be dirty pool to define SWEET as "Bitter or potato." It comes after *bitter* and before *potato.* Better to change *bitter* to *butter!*

One type of definition that fans abhor is "Word with up or down" or "Word with in or out." It is vague and meaningless. Also, since a multiplicity of words might fit, it is unfair.

An occasional clue that contains a pun or witticism is appreciated by most solvers if the crossings are simple enough. For instance, FOP can be defined as "Man after a fashion" or RAM as "He's never out of butts." In a puzzle recently published the clue for RUBAIYAT was "Poem that sounds like a red boat."

But the cornerstones of good defining are accuracy, clarity and economy of expression. These are the bywords of all lexicographers and all professional constructors and editors.

Speaking of editors, I should mention that they often change definitions. Constructors who have worked hard on clues sometimes wonder if the reasons for the alterations are capricious. Usually they are not. Here are only a few of the whys and wherefores:

The definition was used in another puzzle to be published at or about the same period.

The editor could not find the definition, because the constructor had not indicated his source.

The crossing seemed difficult; hence the editor chose an easier clue for the word.

The editor thought of a more specific clue. For instance, if THESE had been defined as "Pronoun," he changed the clue to "— Foolish Things."

Space problems dictated the abridgment of the definition.

———

Now comes the final step—preparing the puzzle for submission to a newspaper or magazine. Editors have different preferences and regulations, and therefore the new constructor should request a style sheet. In fact, it's a good idea to send for one long before tackling the diagram.

What follows is a description of THE NEW YORK TIMES rules.

Submit two diagrams on separate typewriter-size sheets, with squares measuring a bit over one-quarter inch. One pattern should contain numbers only. It will be used for test solving. The other should contain numbers and words. The words should be lettered in pencil to facilitate editorial changes. The black squares in both diagrams should be filled in *thoroughly* and *neatly*. They should be plainly visible.

The constructor's name and address (with zip code) and Social Security number should appear above both diagrams and at the top of the first page of definitions.

Definitions should be typed at the left side of the page and answers at the far right. Periods should not be used after either numbers or definitions. The following is a sample of the format.

ACROSS
1	Dashing young man	BLADE
6	Lion's ——	SHARE
11	Largest lake in Europe	LADOGA (Lipp. Gaz.)
24	Parcel: Abbr.	PKG. (W-3)

Definitions must be typed on typewriter-size paper. Erasable paper is forbidden, because it smears.

As indicated above, when using a blank in the definitions, type three hyphens. Also, when a word or clue is unusual, supply the source at the right of the word list.

Enclose a stamped, self-addressed return envelope with every puzzle. Puzzles may be folded for mailing.

Use paper clips. Do not use staples.

Submit only one puzzle at a time. Wait for a response before submitting another.

Finally, if you feel it is necessary to enclose a letter to the editor, make it brief and to the point.

———

You probably wonder how much you will be paid if you succeed in having a puzzle published. Well, it is practically impossible to make a living as a constructor. The competition is fierce, the markets are few, and the rates are low when compared with the time and effort expended. A 15 x 15 puzzle pays anywhere from $5.00 to $25.00. For a large Sunday-type puzzle you may receive as little as $35.00 and as much as $100.00. Of course, if you can sell your puzzle to a commercial firm, you will probably be paid a good deal more.

Who are your competitors? They come from all walks of life. One owns a construction company; at least two are engineers; some are teachers or professors; one is a network executive. There's a Texas millionaire, who has a secretary just for crossword puzzles! One man sells typewriters; another helps to produce movies. A convict has recently joined the ranks. Three or four are published authors, and two are rather well known actors. Another pair are eminent in the field of classical music, one as a conductor and the other as a recently retired first violinist for a philharmonic orchestra. A Washington bureaucrat is a regular contributor and so are a former cartoonist and a vice-president of a silver company. Nor must I forget a judge in the Midwest, a psychologist in the South, a lawyer in New England, and an accountant in New York City. But the majority, as you might expect, are housewives and retirees.

May your house be safe from rejections!

CHAPTER 17

Crosswords That Build Vocabulary

For me this is the most exciting and rewarding part of the entire book. Since the Thirties I have been deeply involved in crossword puzzles, and I have always said that they are not only a verbal barrel of fun but also educational. On behalf of DELL CROSSWORD magazines, in the 1950s, I once appeared before a congressional committee to testify that such puzzles are instructive and really do enhance an individual's vocabulary.

But the trouble has always been that a great number of those words are of little use. Who cares that an *anoa* is a Celebes ox, a *moa* is an extinct bird or an *Abo* is a member of an Australian tribe?

For some time it has been my ambition to present crossword puzzles that completely eschew esoteric words in the smaller entries but are simultaneously designed to enlarge the solver's vocabulary via the longer words. I believe I have achieved that goal in the puzzles that follow. Each crossword is deliberately constructed around two or more unfamiliar words of at least seven letters. The crossings have been purposely made easy in order to give the solver a chance to learn the meanings and spellings of the "vocabulary" words. In essence, this is the acme of the puzzle-maker's art, and I am pleased to offer these creations as a kind of culmination of my own devotion to the craft.

Finally, let me say that even if you have never tried to do a crossword puzzle before, you should have no trouble solving these. You will find the solutions on pp. 436 and 437, in the Appendix.

ACROSS
1 Meat from swine
4 Knock lightly
7 Pie ___ mode: 2 wds.
8 Hurry
9 Tear apart
11 Crow's call
12 Glassy; amorphous
16 Organ of hearing
17 Statute
18 Health resort
19 Henna is one

DOWN
1 Owned
2 Former heavyweight champ
3 Coloring for eyelashes or eyebrows
4 Jack London's "The Call of ___": 2 wds.
5 What we breathe
6 Vigor
10 Coolidge's nickname
12 "For ___ a jolly good fellow"
13 Sharp, shrill bark
14 Senator's "No!"
15 Female sheep

ACROSS
1 River obstruction
4 Mel Torme, "The Velvet ___"
7 Gold: Sp.
8 ___ Parseghian, former Notre Dame coach
9 Part of "C.I.A."
11 Road surfacing
12 Refined
16 ___ annum (yearly)
17 Stickum
18 Words at a wedding
19 Horatian creation

DOWN
1 One of the Seven Dwarfs
2 "Men ___ April when they woo": Shak.
3 Hunter's cap
4 Mixture or medley
5 "A feast ___ famine"
6 "My ___ Sal"
10 Playground game
12 Prefix with gram or graph
13 Conducted
14 Sign of approval
15 Part of a sock

ACROSS
1 Taxis
5 Letter before tee
8 Surmounting
9 Applaud
10 The sport of archery
12 Teachers' group: Abbr.
13 Bald-headed man
19 Fit to ____: 2 wds.
20 Fuss; commotion
21 Playground game
22 Bridge

DOWN
1 Jaguar
2 From ____ Z: 2 wds.
3 Carton
4 Kind of cake or bath
5 Inventor Whitney
6 ____ Mineo, memorable singer-actor
7 Mata Hari was one
9 Maps
11 Tiny vegetable
13 Singer Boone
14 Call ____ day: 2 wds.
15 Lower limb
16 Cut off
17 Actress Lupino
18 Opposite of pro

ACROSS
1 Short-lived fashion
4 Saucer's partner
7 "All men ____ created equal"
8 Holy Roman Empire: Abbr.
9 British air arm: Abbr.
10 "Act your ____!"
11 Pitcher's opponent
13 Durocher of baseball
14 Rots
17 Historic period of time
18 "Ready, ____, fire!"
20 Suit
21 F.D.R. measure: Abbr.
22 Golfer's gadget
23 Honor card, in bridge

5 Exhort
6 Nobleman
12 "____ for Two," old song
14 Skillful
15 Canal, lake or city
16 Beget
19 Chess piece

DOWN
1 Distant
2 Native of Syria
3 Embezzle
4 Having a changeable luster

Puzzle 1

ACROSS

1 Littleneck, cherrystone or steamer
5 Dish of leftovers
9 "I ___ a Parade"
10 Choir voice
11 Border; touch upon
12 Hit with the palm of one's hand
13 Quill or ballpoint
14 Gaze
15 Sing like young Bing
17 "St. Louis ___"
19 "___ For Two"
22 Regulation
23 Opposite of bought
24 Historic periods of time
25 Boy Scouts' outing
26 "The Way We ___"
27 Paradise

DOWN

1 Applaud
2 Part of the ear
3 Pertaining to uncles; also, unduly kind
4 Convened or encountered
5 Must: 2 wds.
6 Sausage-shaped
7 Actor having the leading role
8 Faith, ___ and charity
14 Distress call at sea
16 Della or Peewee
17 Beer or ale
18 Entice; tempt
20 Actress Sommer
21 Capital of South Yemen
23 Pronoun for a girl or a ship

Puzzle 2

ACROSS

1 Matterhorn is one
4 Young male horse
8 Peruse
10 To ___ (precisely): 2 wds.
11 Mania; itch; uncontrollable desire
13 Hew yews
14 Superlative ending
15 What sitters form
17 Actress Gardner
20 Pack pipe tobacco
23 Literary hack
26 "I cannot tell ___": 2 wds.
27 "The night ___ thousand eyes": 2 wds.
28 Be ahead in a race
29 "Tell it ___ in Gath"

DOWN

1 Part of a circle
2 Part of a bed
3 Walking tempo
4 Maltese or Siame
5 Will- ___ -wisp: hyph. wd.
6 Sediment
7 Examination
9 Pretty child
12 Make jubilant
16 Footway
17 "I Got ___ in Kalamazoo": 2 wds.
18 Low-lying tract
19 Song for Sutherland
21 Intend
22 Peon's mite
24 Old Glory color
25 Relative of a mouse

ACROSS

1 Fellow
5 Go away, feline!
9 Path
10 Native of Warsaw
11 Smell ___ (be
   suspicious):
   2 wds.
12 Chip for the poker
   pot
13 Affirmative
14 Vehicle for moving
   furniture
15 Racetrack officials
19 Constellation
20 Ponder
23 "Sail ___ Ship of
   State!": 2 wds.
24 Annoy
26 Word with Liberty
   or America
28 Read poetic meter
29 To ___ (exactly):
   2 wds.
30 Moreover
31 Robin's home
32 Encounter

DOWN

1 Kind of pigeon or
   pipe
2 Animals chased by
   hounds
3 Intercommunica-
   tions
4 Sandy, to Orphan
   Annie
5 Place featuring
   baths
6 Secret religious
   meeting
7 Part of a church
8 Adolescent years

16 Nickname Onassis
   had
17 ___ Tin Tin, movie
   dog
18 Keats's "Ode ___
   Nightingale":
   2 wds.
20 Caesar was one
21 Join; weld; fuse
22 Rub out
25 Something tied by a
   sailor or a
   preacher
27 Television ___
28 Houston or Snead

ACROSS

1 Leftovers from a fire
6 "Trinity" author
10 Depart
11 At no time
13 Active; strong
15 Actor Wallach
16 Explorer Johnson or female Spanish bear
17 Dover ___, fish dish
19 Letter before gee
20 Newly married man
22 Cubans' coin
25 Receives
26 Discolored, as if burned
30 Sergeant's superior officer: Abbr.
31 Art gallery in London
32 Green vegetable
35 Chemist's workshop, for short
37 Of the woods
39 Not affected by passion or pain
41 Dickens' forte
42 Roof edge
43 Cassettes

DOWN

1 Besides
2 Defeats a bidder at bridge
3 Guffaw
4 First woman
5 Touch or smell is one
6 Stowe's "___ Tom's Cabin"
7 Concerning
8 "___ Got Sixpence"
9 Choose
12 Schisms
14 Atomic particle
18 Rim
20 Fight in an arena
21 That is: Latin abbr.
22 Tugs
23 Piece of property containing an elaborate house
24 Joan of Arc: Abbr.
27 Knight's weapon
28 Consumed
29 Entice
32 Stage convenience
33 Vacationer's delight
34 Pub drinks
36 ___ constrictor
38 "Was it a vision ___ waking dream?": Keats (2 wds.)
40 Four, to Caesar

ACROSS
1 Headgear for the Mets
5 Scrooge's exclamation
8 Word with grease or room
9 Poe's one-word bird
11 Curtain fabric
12 Site of University of Maine
13 The art of attaining happiness
15 Highway: Abbr.
16 Very young child
17 Letter after cee
18 Word on a towel
19 Overhead railways, for short
22 Superlative suffix
23 Voice of America: Abbr.
26 Creeping
29 More uncommon
30 Jai alai basket
31 Used up
32 Singer Smith and actress Jackson
33 Harden, as cement
34 Mast on a ship

DOWN
1 Three-base hit
2 Dwell or tolerate
3 Actress Negri of silent films
4 Darling
5 Heifer's home
6 Shun
7 Therefore
8 Always
9 Underground parts of some plants
10 Facial feature
14 Wet; dewy
19 Makes a fluff
20 Vaults
21 Binge
23 Scene; view
24 Horse opera
25 Word said with a sigh
27 Camper's dwelling
28 Harvest the crops

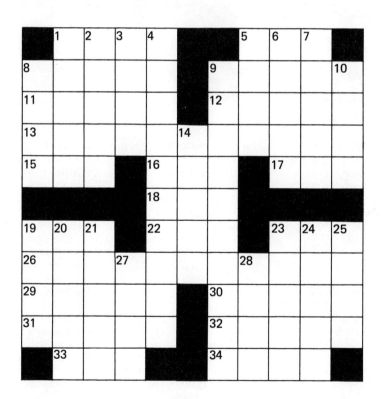

ACROSS
1 Aid
7 Mineral springs
11 Batter's or golfer's position
12 Snare
13 Poker player's prize
14 Exists
15 Bygone days
16 "Say It Isn't ___"
17 Nursery school attendees
19 Heavy weight
20 Jack and Jill's burden
22 Deputy or F.B.I. man
24 Inventor Whitney
25 Woman's neckpiece
26 Machinations
28 Containers for ashes, flowers, etc.
30 Have the sniffles
31 Story
33 Ma's partner
35 Saucy girl
37 Behold!
38 Not against
39 Rip
40 Where to see art, relics, etc.
42 British queen
43 Qualities in one's favor

DOWN
1 Vipers
2 Condescend
3 Took a chair
4 "___ God we trust"
5 Pretender to scholarship
6 Examine
7 Pen for pigs
8 Variable
9 Burr
10 Exhausted; used up
17 Cause to slope or slant
18 Gritty; sandy
21 Giving forth a soughing sound
23 Author Vidal
26 Spaghetti, macaroni, etc.
27 Kind of shower
29 Part of a teapot
32 ___ Mater
34 Hemingway's "A Farewell to ___"
36 Prefix with fix
38 Charge
41 Steamship: Abbr.

CHAPTER 18

Test Yourself

Here are one hundred spelling demons. In each case you have a choice between a correctly spelled word and a misspelling. Check the one that is correct. The answers appear on p. 438, in the Appendix.

A score of 90 percent or better is *excellent;* 80–89 percent is *good;* 70–79 percent is *fair.* If you fall below 70 percent, you should brush up on your orthography.

1. asinine	assinine	31. resuscitate	resusitate
2. innane	inane	32. asphixiate	asphyxiate
3. existance	existence	33. sylogism	syllogism
4. toboggan	tobbogan	34. renascence	renasence
5. develop	develope	35. accummulate	accumulate
6. occurrence	occurence	36. vacinnate	vaccinate
7. surprize	surprise	37. anoint	annoint
8. indispensible	indispensable	38. irrelevant	irrevelant
9. accommodate	accomodate	39. sacharine	saccharine
10. silouette	silhouette	40. tarpalin	tarpaulin
11. harrass	harass	41. baboon	babboon
12. procede	proceed	42. vacillate	vaccilate
13. tattooed	tattoed	43. privilege	privelege
14. saddist	sadist	44. persistent	persistant
15. vermillion	vermilion	45. violoncello	violincello
16. personell	personnel	46. souvenir	souvenier
17. seize	sieze	47. mayonaisse	mayonnaise
18. adolescence	adolesence	48. jodphurs	jodhpurs
19. daguerreotype	daguerrotype	49. dilletante	dilettante
20. stupify	stupefy	50. perserverance	perseverance
21. embarassed	embarrassed	51. ersatz	erzats
22. supercede	supersede	52. sublety	subtlety
23. innoculate	inoculate	53. Chihuaha	Chihuahua
24. resistance	resistence	54. auxilliary	auxiliary
25. inate	innate	55. paraphernalia	paraphenalia
26. mocassin	moccasin	56. copywright	copyright
27. masochist	masachist	57. stilleto	stiletto
28. titillate	tittilate	58. glockinspiel	glockenspiel
29. reconnoiter	recconnoiter	59. impresario	impressariao
30. bookeeper	bookkeeper	60. Scandanavian	Scandinavian

61. deleterious	deliterious	81. villify	vilify
62. flagelate	flagellate	82. battalion	battallion
63. picnicked	picniced	83. nickel	nickle
64. weird	wierd	84. concensus	consensus
65. permissible	permissable	85. exhilirate	exhilarate
66. momento	memento	86. committment	commitment
67. innocuous	inocuous	87. brethren	brethern
68. Fahrenheit	Farenheit	88. liqueur	liquer
69. ecstasy	ecstacy	89. separate	seperate
70. phenominal	phenomenal	90. geneology	genealogy
71. liaison	liason	91. sacreligious	sacrilegious
72. cacchinate	cachinnate	92. mackerellike	mackerelike
73. changable	changeable	93. knicknack	knickknack
74. Renaissance	Renaisance	94. connoisseur	connoiseur
75. siege	seige	95. inadvertent	inadvertant
76. mausaleum	mausoleum	96. iridescent	irridescent
77. rococo	roccoco	97. desireable	desirable
78. ladled	ladeled	98. dichotomy	dicotomy
79. obeisance	obesiance	99. seersucker	searsucker
80. permanence	permanance	100. Pharaoh	Pharoah

THE MORE THE EERIER

There was a time when the only accepted plural for *deer* was *deer;* more than one *trout* was still *trout.* But so many hunters and fishermen insist on adding the usual *s* that W-3 now accepts *deers* and *trouts.*

In Rome a road was an *iter,* and the plural was *itinera.* Medical men got hold of the word and described it as a brain channel. Sure enough, *iters* evolved. Whenever I use that plural in a crossword puzzle, Latin scholars scream to high heaven.

Once upon a time, too, the army had various kinds of *courts-martial.* Now W-3 and other dictionaries accept *court-martials.* And, believe it or not, W-3 accepts even *crisises.* Strangely, *brother-in-laws* and *sister-in-laws* are still taboo, as well as *oxes.*

Cupfuls, handfuls and other such measurements are still preferred, but if you would rather pluralize the first syllable, W-3 gives the okay.

Interestingly, W-2 once yielded to popular usage too. It allowed *seraphs* as an alternative for *seraphim, matrixes* for *matrices* and *focuses* for *foci.* But it held the line on the plural of *locus.* In that case, *loci* and the Romans' *loca* were cited. No *locuses*—and none in W-3 either!

Here are ten singular nouns. You are asked to spell the presently accepted plural for each. The answers are on p. 438, in the Appendix.

1. knight-errant	4. hypothesis	7. jackanapes
2. talisman	5. pelvis	8. cinerarium
3. manservant	6. embryo	9. auspex
		10. monsieur

HATES AND FEARS

The Greek root *mis-miso* means "hate."
Match the following "hate" words with the definitions. The answers appear on p. 438, in the Appendix.

1. misoxene	a. one who hates marriage
2. misoneist	b. one who hates strangers
3. misocapnist	c. one who hates mankind
4. misosophist	d. one who hates beards
5. misopedist	e. one who hates innovation
6. misologist	f. one who hates children
7. misogynist	g. one who hates tobacco smoke
8. misanthrope	h. one who hates women
9. misogamist	i. one who hates argument
10. misopogonist	j. one who hates wisdom

The Greek root *phobia* means "fear."
What kind of fears are the following?
See p. 439, in the Appendix.

1. agoraphobia	6. toxiphobia
2. acrophobia	7. herpetophobia
3. heliophobia	8. triskaidekaphobia
4. gynephobia	9. nosophobia
5. thanatophobia	10. ochlophobia

FIVE OF A KIND

Below are five words that have three things in common. Examine them carefully and see if you can find all three similar elements. The answer is on p. 439, in the Appendix.

hearth
neon
ranger
rover
tart

IRRELIGIOUS

Here are ten people associated with churchly activities. Surprisingly, all of them can be defined in secular terms. Can you match the two columns? The answers appear on p. 439, in the Appendix.

1. bishop	a. rose-colored starling or man-of-war fish
2. cardinal	b. calf too young for veal
3. nun	c. card game
4. deacon	d. kind of buoy
5. priest	e. bird, color or woman's cloak in the eighteenth century.

6. Pope Joan f. kind of beetle
7. sexton g. strong purple
8. acolyte h. African weaverbird
9. pastor i. follower
10. monsignor j. short club to stun or kill a captured fish

BUILDING VOCABULARY

Five vocabulary tests are given below. In each case choose the word or phrase that most closely defines the underlined word at the left.

90–100 You should compile your own dictionary.
80–89 You qualify as an editor.
70–79 You qualify as an English teacher.
60–69 You ought to write a book.
50–59 You ought to read a book.
49–40 You ought to read lots of books.
Below 40 percent You may wish to tear up this book.

The answers are on p. 439 in the Appendix.

VOCABULARY TEST—#1

1. *scarify* a. frighten b. reduced to dross c. hunt insects d. scratch
2. *sobriquet* a. card game b. bunch of flowers c. nickname d. serious essay
3. *syncope* a. harmony b. elision of letters c. union of parties d. simile
4. *thrasonical* a. euphonious b. rational c. short-tempered d. boastful
5. *benedict* a. bachelor b. hermit c. newly married man d. anything well said
6. *factotum* a. adding machine b. clique c. general handyman d. copy
7. *veridical* a. green b. lofty c. truthful d. manly
8. *factitious* a. artificial b. quarrelsome c. divisive d. fragile
9. *farrago* a. shrew b. mixture c. veterinary d. a sort of grain
10. *termagant* a. scolding woman b. final session c. monster d. deserter
11. *vitiate* a. adhere b. corrupt c. enliven d. convert into glass
12. *perfunctory* a. indifferent b. useful c. precise d. prompt
13. *pariah* a. sycophant b. outcast c. upstart d. rampart
14. *meretricious* a. tawdry b. well deserving c. southerly d. fruity
15. *proem* a. preface b. verse c. offspring d. preemption
16. *sententious* a. sagacious b. terse c. aged d. full of feeling
17. *flatulent* a. level b. noisome c. pretentious d. verbose
18. *traduce* a. lead across b. vituperate c. lead astray d. slander
19. *enervate* a. weaken b. make strong c. mollify d. repair
20. *majuscule* a. steward b. precept c. capital letter d. staff of office

VOCABULARY TEST—#2

1. *prawn*   a. light carriage b. tool c. shrimp d. baby food
2. *magma*   a. monkey b. molten rock c. Greek letter d. largeness
3. *gibus*   a. jest b. small mast c. rodent d. opera hat
4. *biggin*   a. tea cup b. grafted fruit c. enlargement d. nightcap
5. *pharos*   a. Egyptian crown b. lighthouse c. chariot d. bird's nest
6. *meable*   a. penetrable b. laughable c. tillable d. traceable
7. *giglet*   a. ship's boat b. frivolous girl c. dance hall
   d. strangulation
8. *firkin*   a. cask for butter b. sweet pickle c. high shoe d. waistcoat
9. *moiety*   a. hardness b. softness c. plethora d. half
10. *abigail*   a. headdress b. aunt c. lady's maid d. type of skirt
11. *purlieu*   a. French soldier b. street c. outskirts d. stew
12. *marplot*   a. thrust b. interferer c. damaged property d. agate
13. *agnomen*   a. surname b. patronymic c. shepherds d. epithet
14. *cabal*   a. horseman b. occult doctrine c. intrigue d. phaeton
15. *widgeon*   a. hybrid pigeon b. duck c. fence rail d. dam
16. *precent*   a. lead in singing b. go before c. counterfeit d. ninety-
   nine
17. *goliard*   a. minstrel b. javelin c. magician's wand d. gray whale
18. *gibbous*   a. apelike b. deathly c. jocular d. protuberant
19. *aeneous*   a. heroic b. white with age c. having a brassy color
   d. pastoral
20. *acescent*   a. steely b. becoming sour c. perfumed d. growing
   strong

VOCABULARY TEST—#3

1. *peculate*   a. embezzle b. congeal c. sin d. trade cattle
2. *levigate*   a. stutter b. lighten a burden c. grind into powder
   d. strengthen
3. *boniface*   a. innkeeper b. newly married man c. pretty girl
   d. holy person
4. *enchorial*   a. musical b. hooklike c. native d. repetitive
5. *plangent*   a. royal b. beating noisily c. schematic d. easily
   understood
6. *dotation*   a. endowment b. excessive love c. fixed point d. tax
7. *abecedary*   a. imported raisin b. primer c. simpleton d. nursery
   rhyme
8. *acclinate*   a. accustom b. recline c. slope upward d. come to a
   point
9. *fimbriate*   a. scale b. fringed c. grind d. rave
10. *ampulliform*   a. electric b. obese c. dilated d. attractive
11. *precative*   a. sinning b. beseeching c. rubbing d. dangerous
12. *adminicle*   a. growing on b. group c. auxiliary d. warning
13. *tramontane*   a. foreigner b. farmer c. rugged d. wavering
14. *acuminate*   a. united b. cloudy c. high d. pointed
15. *festination*   a. window dressing b. happiness c. haste d. gluttony

16. *adscititious*   a. fortunate b. wise c. supplemental d. founded on truth
17. *lexiphanicism*   a. pretentious phraseology b. legally sound practices c. legibility d. overuse of dictionaries
18. *tralatitious*   a. on the side b. singsong c. figurative d. migratory
19. *adiaphorous*   a. expanding when heated b. transparent c. widespread d. indifferent
20. *impignorate*   a. pawn b. strike against c. make insinuations d. involve

VOCABULARY TEST—#4

1. *garniture*   a. embellishment b. fee c. preparation of salads d. gaudiness
2. *cadastre*   a. corpse b. register of taxable property c. framework d. fairy's wand
3. *jejune*   a. trite b. complicated c. barren d. merry
4. *terrapin*   a. earthy deposit b. turtle c. cement flooring d. rampart
5. *caseous*   a. hard b. cheesy c. chancy d. conditional
6. *fulgurate*   a. flash b. explode c. menace d. become smoky
7. *torose*   a. like a bull b. very dry c. muscular d. sluggish
8. *ubiquitous*   a. transitory b. extraordinary c. interrogative d. omnipresent
9. *gargoyle*   a. ugly woman b. monster c. water spout d. clown
10. *trencher*   a. slice b. porcelain plate c. blade d. food supply
11. *caballine*   a. inspirational b. chivalrous c. mystical d. intriguing
12. *shamefaced*   a. recalcitrant b. immodest c. brazen d. bashful
13. *fuliginous*   a. shining b. sooty c. complete d. fleeing
14. *brash*   a. arrogant b. impetuous c. sharp d. timorous
15. *whiffle*   a. sneeze b. scent c. vacillate d. inveigle
16. *dissemble*   a. take apart b. disguise c. vary d. oppose
17. *cincture*   a. half decade b. enclosure c. extraction d. limitation
18. *perorate*   a. speak at length b. pierce c. philosophize d. digress
19. *purfle*   a. tinge b. adorn a border c. bend in two d. filch
20. *funambulist*   a. shyster lawyer b. undertaker c. ropedancer d. marathon runner

VOCABULARY TEST—#5

1. *rogatory*   a. dissolute b. seeking information c. deprecative d. supplicatory
2. *dispendious*   a. excusable b. hanging down c. costly d. bountiful
3. *nubilous*   a. lumpy b. relating to marriage c. nebulous d. uncertain
4. *holograph*   a. handwritten document b. treatise on saints c. homonym d. inscription
5. *picaresque*   a. scenic b. artful c. wandering d. roguish
6. *desultory*   a. downcast b. jumping away c. rambling d. disparaging

7. *prorogue*   a. adjourn b. extend c. defend d. beseech
8. *argot*   a. market place b. watchful guardian c. merchant vessel
    d. slang
9. *nugacious*   a. without sanction b. precious c. trivial d. moronic
10. *lambent*   a. milky b. smooth c. flickering d. lying hidden
11. *viduity*   a. panorama b. grasslands c. widowhood d. kinship
12. *lamia*   a. harvest festival b. vampire c. bird of prey d. priest
13. *gingival*   a. pertaining to the gums b. heedful c. sharp and spicy
    d. of joints
14. *harbinger*   a. forerunner b. port c. street cleaner d. long speech
15. *homiletical*   a. pastoral b. domestic c. in consonance d. advisory
16. *execrate*   a. slander b. curse c. daub d. force out
17. *ululant*   a. wavy b. excessive c. wailing d. onomatopoetic
18. *shallot*   a. small boat b. small onion c. twilled material d. castle
19. *inexorable*   a. inevitable b. cruel c. disadvantageous
    d. unyielding
20. *gossamer*   a. powerful hawk b. filmy substance c. type of linen
    d. tinsel

WORD ORIGINS

Choose the word in each group which does not come from the same root as the others. The answers appear on pp. 439 and 440, in the Appendix.

1. sediment   sedition   sedentary   session
2. volatile   volume   voluble   involute
3. voice   invoice   vowel   advocate   invoke
4. magnate   major   mayor   mastodon   majesty
5. vaunt   vain   advantage   vanity   evanescent
6. cockade   peacock   coquette   cockatrice
7. convalesce   valance   valiance   valedictory   avail
8. heredity   hesitate   adhere   cohesion   inherent
9. devolve   revolt   vault   evolution   volition
10. impede   expedite   pedagogue   sesquipedalian
11. trait   traitor   attract   contraction   treat
12. joke   jest   jeopardy   jewel
13. enjoy   gaudy   jubilee   rejoice
14. allege   legend   collect   coil   legible
15. league   college   colleague   legate   legacy
16. deviate   diverge   envoy   voyage   trivial   impervious
17. vestige   vestigial   investigate   invest
18. money   mint   monetary   minatory   admonition   monitor
19. minute   minuend   menu   miniature   diminish   minuet
20. ligature   ally   liable   league   beleaguer

ETYMOLOGY TEST

Choose the word in each group which does not come from the same root as the others. The answers appear on p. 440, in the Appendix.

1. annoy, nuisance, noisome, ennui, odious
2. spiral, spirit, conspire, sprite, sprightly
3. trite, attrition, nutrition, terse, try, triturate
4. desolate, sole, console, solitaire, sullen
5. effigy, finger, fingent, fiction, faint, feign
6. infant, infantry, fate, fairy, nefandous, profane
7. popular, poplar, people, pueblo, populous
8. poetaster, disaster, astral, asterisk
9. sally, exile, consult, insult, resilient
10. censure, incense, candid, candidate, incendiary
11. explicit, duplex, deploy, supple, supply, apply
12. plausible, exploit, explode, applause, applaud
13. moribund, moratorium, mortgage, mortify, mortician
14. terrible, terrestrial, terrine, tureen, subterranean
15. science, nescient, scintillate, omniscient, conscience
16. recondite, ensconce, condiment, abscond
17. provide, envy, vise, visit, visa, review
18. auxiliary, augment, authentic, author, auction
19. inquest, require, acquisition, requiem
20. aspire, prosperous, despair, desperate

OUT AND DOWN

Here is a new anagrams puzzle with an interlocking feature. To the right of each word, fill in an anagram using all the letters. To start you off, the answer to the first word is ORACLE.

When you finish, look at the first letters of the words you have filled in. They should form an anagram for ROASTING.

The answers appear on p. 440, in the Appendix.

COALER _____   HEEDING _____

ANTLER _____   GOBELIN _____

RUGGED _____   HORNETS _____

LAMINA _____   ROTATES _____

SCANAGRAMS

In each of the couplets below, one of the words is an anagram for the word to be filled in. To give you a start, the word to be unscrambled in the first couplet is CANOE.

The answers appear on p. 440, in the Appendix.

1. *Caution, Hiawatha!*
   Your frail canoe may quickly tip
   If you should take that _____ trip!

2. *Until the Fur Flies*
   A girl who wears a _____ may
   Attempt to look a bit blasé.

3. *Beware the Ides*
   March has a certain _____ about it,
   Though Caesar's ghost will surely doubt it.

4. *Where Is the Rascal Cook?*
   Said Papa, and his voice was gruff:
   "This steak _____ not to be so tough!"

5. *The Whole Truth*
   The timid witness did not curse,
   And yet he _____. Now, was that worse?

6. *Olympics*
   For athletes strong and simon-pure
   The _____ wreath has great allure.

7. *How to Succeed ...*
   If you should aspire to jobs that are higher,
   Then _____ the boss though you may be a liar.

8. *Under the Christmas Tree*
   Now, listen, you can almost hear
   The _____ tinkling in your ear.

9. *School Daze*
   The dullard, _____, and the pest
   Can make a teacher need a rest.

10. *B.C. Burner*
    'Tis _____ that Mauna Loa
    Erupted once in the time of Noah.

A MAD, MAD WORLD

Can you match the manias in Column 1 with the definitions in Column 2? A score of 80 percent or better qualifies you as a maniac. The answers are on p. 441, in the Appendix.

1. dipsomania		a.	inordinate passion for music
2. melomania		b.	abnormal desire for food
3. phaneromania		c.	fad involving imitation of painted porcelain
4. sitomania		d.	delusions of grandeur
5. eleutheromania		e.	madness for postage stamps
6. potichomania		f.	excessive sexual desire
7. erotomania		g.	alcoholism
8. theomania		h.	zealous pursuit of freedom
9. megalomania		i.	morbid habit of picking at a superficial body growth, as biting fingernails
10. timbromania		j.	delusion that one is God

LOVERS

Match the words in Column 1 with the definitions in Column 2. The answers appear on p. 441, in the Appendix.

I

1. aelurophile		a.	lover of books
2. audiophile		b.	lover of wine
3. bibliophile		c.	antiquarian
4. cinephile		d.	glutton
5. cynophilist		e.	lover of cats
6. discophile		f.	lover of dogs
7. gastrophile		g.	devotee of movies
8. nemophilist		h.	lover of woods
9. oenophilist		i.	collector of phonograph records
10. paleophilist		j.	hi-fi fan

II

1. philosopher		a.	lover of the beautiful
2. philodespot		b.	lover of God
3. philodox		c.	lover of tyranny
4. philogynist		d.	lover of learning
5. philocalist		e.	one who loves his own opinion
6. philiater		f.	one devoted to the practical arts
7. philozoist		g.	lover of wisdom
8. philomath		h.	lover of women
9. philotheist		i.	lover of animals
10. philotechnist		j.	one interested in medical science

ALTERNATES FOR DEMOCRACY

Here are ten forms of government. From the list below choose the correct word for each type of rule. The answers appear on p. 441, in the Appendix.

1. rule by riffraff or gangsters
2. government by the worst people
3. rule of the majority
4. government by the military
5. government by workers
6. rule by harlots
7. government by aged persons
8. government by the wealthy
9. rule of gold
10. government by upstarts

aristocracy	ergatocracy	kakistocracy	oligocracy
arithmocracy	gerontocracy	monocracy	plutocracy
autocracy	hagiocracy	neocracy	pornocracy
chrysocracy	hierocracy	ochlocracy	stratocracy

WHO'S IN CHARGE?

Here are ten different leaders. From the list below, choose the correct word for each V.I.P. The answers appear on p. 441, in the Appendix.

1. chief of a clan
2. ruler of a church
3. head of an unorthodox sect
4. chief magistrate of a modern Greek province
5. toastmaster
6. leader of a revolt
7. one of the few who have the power
8. chief of a sacred order
9. commander of a thousand men
10. governor; viceroy

anarch	heresiarch	nomarch	polemarch
chiliarch	hierarch	oligarch	scholarch
ecclesiarch	matriarch	patriarch	symposiarch
exarch	monarch	phylarch	tetrarch

SPECIALTIES

Here are ten fields in which people specialize. From the list below choose the correct word for each of the studies, arts or sciences. The answers appear on p. 441, in the Appendix.

1. science of kissing
2. study of birds' nests
3. art of engraving on precious stones
4. study of mollusks
5. scientific study of ants
6. obstetrician's field
7. study of mosses
8. catalogue of saints
9. art of treating fractures
10. bell ringer's art

agmatology	cytology	glyptology	myrmecology
areology	dendrology	hagiology	oenology
caliology	enigmatology	malacology	philematology
campanology	gerontology	muscology	tocology

THE PROGNOSTICATION VOCATION

Here are ten ways of predicting the future. From the list below choose the correct word that applies to each of forecasting method. The answers appear on p. 441, in the Appendix.

1. prophecies based on flights of birds
2. use of smoke to tell the future
3. rolling dice to see what is ahead
4. forecasting by observation of animals
5. divination via playing cards
6. employment of mathematics by seers
7. auguries based on movements of mice
8. conjectures arising from watching serpents
9. predictions based on random literary extracts
10. fishing for tomorrow's events via fish

arithmancy	cartomancy	myomancy	sciomancy
bibliomancy	cleromancy	ophiomancy	stichomancy
capnomancy	ichthyomancy	ornithyomancy	zoomancy

A PENNY FOR YOUR THOUGHTS

Complete the word in Column 2 according to the clue given in Column 1. The correct answers appear on p. 441, in the Appendix.

1. a reddish cent   ru _____
2. a bright, shining cent   lu _____
3. a cent causing evil   ma _____
4. a cent just appearing   na _____
5. a cent at rest   qu _____
6. a rather old cent   se _____
7. a vanishing cent   ev _____
8. a blackish cent   ni _____
9. a greenish cent   vi _____
10. a lustful cent   co _____
11. a somewhat woody cent   li _____
12. a whitish cent   al _____
13. a cent that changes color   ir _____
14. a cent going out of use   ob _____
15. a taciturn cent   re _____
16. a flowering cent   fl _____
17. a cent breaking out afresh   re _____
18. a frothy cent   sp _____
19. a soothing cent   de _____
20. a cent wasting away   tab _____
21. a cent tinged with red   ruf _____
22. a glassy cent   hya _____
23. a slightly swollen cent   tum _____
24. a cent approaching whiteness   can _____
25. a rather smooth cent   gla _____
26. a scintillating cent   ig _____
27. a cent turning yellow   fla _____
28. a concealed cent   del _____
29. a rather tawny cent   ful _____
30. a cent becoming obscure   la _____

A LEAGUE OF NATIONS

Complete the word in Column 2 according to the clue given in Column 1. The correct answers appear on p. 441, in the Appendix.

1. a nation of violent outbursts — de _____
2. a nation of thinkers — ra _____
3. a nation of fortune-tellers — di _____
4. a nation filled with hatred — ab _____
5. a meditative nation — ru _____
6. a nation of travelers — pe _____
7. a scheming nation — ma _____
8. a dilatory nation — pr _____
9. a nation of thunderous denunciations — fu _____
10. a nation of interdependent links — co _____
11. a guffawing nation — ca _____
12. a nation capable of metapsychosis — re _____
13. a forgiving nation — co _____
14. a prophetic nation — va _____
15. a hasty nation — fe _____

THE ANT COLONY

Here is a list of "ant" words designed to build and strengthen your vocabulary. The answers appear on p. 442, in the Appendix.

1. a sinful ant — pe _____
2. a green ant — ve _____
3. a nonchalant ant — ins _____
4. a biting ant — mo _____
5. a kissing ant — os _____
6. a howling ant — ul _____
7. a flying ant — vo _____
8. a penetrating ant — po _____
9. a disagreeing ant — discr _____
10. a submissive ant — ob _____
11. a swimming ant — na _____

12.	a voracious ant	cor _____
13.	a bellowing ant	bl _____
14.	a helping ant	adj _____
15.	a second-sighted ant	cl _____
16.	a nonconforming ant	rec _____
17.	a powerful ant	pu _____
18.	a rustling ant	su _____
19.	a glittering ant	cor _____
20.	a scourging ant	fla _____
21.	a crying ant	cl _____
22.	a twinkling ant	sc _____
23.	a harsh ant	str _____
24.	a feigning ant	si _____
25.	a blunt ant	he _____
26.	a hostile ant	oppu _____
27.	a lustrous ant	cha _____
28.	a yawning ant	osc _____
29.	a gaudy ant	cli _____
30.	a night-walking ant	no _____
31.	a night-wandering ant	no _____
32.	a creepy ant	hor _____
33.	an ant playing a small role	fig _____
34.	a drooping ant	nu _____
35.	a boring ant	ter _____
36.	a nest-building ant	ni _____
37.	a shiftless ant	fai _____
38.	a priestlike ant	hi _____
39.	a ghostly ant	rev _____
40.	a wildly dancing ant	Cor _____

FIND THE STRANGER

In each of the following groups, choose the one word that does not belong with the others. The correct answers appear on p. 442, in the Appendix.

I

1. charlatan, chauvinist, empiric, mountebank
2. cacophony, callithump, charivari, euphony
3. arcane, recondite, patent, cabalistic
4. noisome, mephitic, blatant, noxious
5. pilose, hirsute, pilgarlic, shaggy
6. fatuous, flagrant, heinous, flagitious
7. thrall, hedonist, serf, helot
8. sciolist, casuist, sophist, equivocator
9. bodkin, buskin, eyeleteer, stiletto
10. iridescent, cymophanous, delitescent, opalescent

II

1. salamander, triton, gerrymander, newt, eft
2. perjuror, taradiddler, pseudologist, cicerone, ananias
3. garand, gibus, gatling, bowie, derringer
4. Nesselrode, tartuffe, napoleon, flan, frangipane
5. depone, depose, testify, certify, execrate
6. meritorious, tawdry, brummagem, meretricious, specious
7. salmagundi, olio, gallimaufry, pilpul, potpourri
8. endemic, exiguous, indigenous, autochthonous, natal
9. miscreant, poltroon, caitiff, dastard, recreant
10. jargon, lingo, jingo, dialect, cant

THE BLOCKBUSTER

Caution! Do not take this test if you have a weak heart. It's fiendishly calculated to drive the most placid of people up the wall. If you score 50 percent, consider yourself a pansophical savant.

The answers, if you dare or care to look, appear on p. 442, in the Appendix.

1. *pandiculation*
    a. ability to speak several languages
    b. a stretching of the body, as after a long sleep
    c. a confusion of noises
    d. a complete code of the laws of a country
2. *ponticello*
    a. change in the register of a boy's voice
    b. bridge of traverse nerve fibers
    c. musical instrument used in the Middle Ages
    d. member of an Italian council of priests

3. *gallinipper*
   a. French barfly
   b. fowl related to the Bantams
   c. sail used only in a fierce storm
   d. large mosquito or bedbug
4. *lentiginous*
   a. freckled
   b. fasting
   c. having leafy stalks
   d. living in still waters
5. *auscultation*
   a. the act of vaulting, as with a pole
   b. the effect of turbulence in the air
   c. the act of listening, as with a stethoscope
   d. a breaking away from orthodox practices
6. *chrematistics*
   a. garbled data, as from a computer
   b. the study of wealth
   c. the art of producing liqueurs
   d. selective study of passages from various authors
7. *peristeronic*
   a. pertaining to spiral shells
   b. relating to pigeons
   c. having a beautiful back
   d. of Vitamin D
8. *omphaloskepsis*
   a. meditation while staring at one's navel
   b. treatise on the verses of troubadours
   c. cynic's view of life
   d. sexual impotence
9. *usufructuary*
   a. one enjoying the profits of another's property
   b. person who eats only fruits
   c. arsonist
   d. jack-of-all-trades; factotum
10. *philematology*
   a. the study of the works of Saint Paul
   b. discourse on love
   c. branch of numerology dealing with words
   d. the art of kissing
11. *leiotrichous*
   a. wearing a chaplet
   b. creeping up slowly on prey
   c. having straight smooth hair
   d. muscular

12. *hermeneutic*
    a. mystical
    b. interpretive
    c. solitary
    d. pertaining to saints
13. *cameralistics*
    a. candid photography
    b. art of secret arbitration
    c. study of mechanical gears
    d. science of public finance
14. *sillographer*
    a. parodist
    b. draftsman
    c. writer of satires
    d. person with erratic handwriting
15. *malversation*
    a. hubbub
    b. lisping
    c. corrupt administration
    d. incorrect rhyming
16. *nemoricole*
    a. cabbagelike
    b. pertaining to the stone flies
    c. living underground, as a worm
    d. inhabiting groves
17. *oblivescence*
    a. the act of forgetting
    b. gradual shading
    c. dimness
    d. approach to death
18. *gerontogeous*
    a. crippled
    b. relating to the eastern hemisphere
    c. senile
    d. having a sexual attraction toward older people
19. *hypocorism*
    a. pet name
    b. arterial dysfunction
    c. abnormal sensitivity of the skin
    d. satanic doctrine
20. *eudaemonical*
    a. pertaining to exorcism
    b. hellish; infernal
    c. living in a haunted house
    d. producing happiness

APPENDIX

CHAPTER 1

SOME ENGLISH WORDS THAT COMBINE
GREEK ROOTS
(The words marked with an
asterisk combine three roots.)

anthropodermic—consisting of
human skin

anthropogenesis—study of certain
aspects of man's origin and
development

*anthropogeography—study of man's
distribution on earth

anthropolatry—deification or
worship of man

anthroponymy—study of personal
names

astrolatry—worship of heavenly
bodies

astrometry—science of measuring
celestial bodies

astronomy—science dealing with
size, composition, motion, etc., of
heavenly bodies

*astrophotograph—photograph of a
heavenly body

bibliogenesis—production of books

bibliography—list of writings on a
particular subject

bibliolatry—excessive devotion to
books

biogenous—produced from living
organisms

*biogeography—study of the
distribution on earth of plants
and animals

biography—written history of a
person's life

biometrics—statistical study of
biological phenomena

bionomics—ecology

cosmogenesis—study of the creation
of the world or universe

cosmography—description of the
world or universe

cosmopolis—large city inhabited by
people from all over the world

cosmopolitan—common to or
representative of many parts of
the world

cryptogenic—of obscure or unknown
origin, as a disease

cryptogram—secret message

cryptography—art of preparing or
decoding secret messages

cryptometer—instrument for
determining the hiding power of
a paint

cyclometer—instrument for
measuring arcs or recording
revolutions of a wheel

dermatograph—surgeon's or
allergist's crayon; instrument for
producing markings on the skin

doxographer—compiler of extracts on
ancient Greek philosophers

geography—science dealing with the
earth and its life

geometry—branch of mathematics

geophoto—picture taken from an
airplane

geopolitics—study of the
interrelationship of geography
and politics

graphometry—science of determining
constants in handwritings

heterodox—heretical

heterogeneous—differing in kind

heterography—spelling different
from standard usage

heterometric—characterized by a
diversity of meter

heteronymous—subject to or
involving different laws of
growth

heteronymy—subordination to the
law of another

homogeneous—of a similar kind or
nature

homogenize—to make homogeneous

homograph—one of two or more words spelled alike but differing in derivation, meaning or pronunciation

homonym—a homophone or homograph

hydrocycle—vehicle for riding on water

hydrogen—lightest of the elements

hydrograph—mechanism for recording changes in water levels

hydrography—study of seas, lakes, rivers, etc.

hydrolatry—worship of water

hydrometer—instrument for measuring specific gravity of a liquid

hydronymy—names of bodies of water

megacycle—one million cycles per second (unit of radio frequency)

megalopolis—very large city

metronome—clockwork device that taps out a tempo

microcosm—miniature universe

microcyclic—short-cycled

*microgeographic—localized on earth

micrograph—instrument for executing very small writing

*microphotograph—small photograph

*microphotometer—instrument for measuring amount of light transmitted or reflected by small areas

nomogenesis—a theory of evolution

nomography—the art of drafting laws

*photobiography—history of a person's life in photography

photogenic—produced by light; suitable for being photographed

*photogrammetry—mapmaker's or surveyor's science, using aerial photographs

photograph—picture obtained by photography

photometer—instrument for measuring luminous intensity

*photomicrograph—photograph of a magnified image of a small object

MYRIADS OF METERS

The Greek metron (measure) is an especially rich source for names of apparatus or instruments of measurement.

acidimeter—strength of acids

actinometer—heat of the sun's rays

alcoholometer—alcoholic content of a liquid

altimeter—height above land or sea

ammeter—strength of electric current

anemometer—a wind gauge

areometer—a hydrometer

arithmometer—a calculating machine

atmometer—rate of exhalation of moisture

audiometer—hearing

barometer—pressure of the atmosphere

bathometer—ocean depths

bolometer—very exact measurement of heat

calorimeter—heat

chondrometer—a balance for weighing grain

chronometer—an accurate watch or timekeeper

clinometer—angles of elevation, slopes of strata, etc.

colorimeter—density of color

comptometer—a calculating machine

craniometer—skulls

cryometer—low temperatures

cyanometer—depth of atmospheric tint

cyclometer—circles or distance traveled by a cycle

cymometer—length and frequency of waves in wireless telegraphy

cyrtometer—the curves of a chart

dasymeter—the density of gases

dendrometer—trees

densimeter—specific gravity

diaphanometer—atmospheric transparency

drosometer—fall of dew

dynameter—magnifying power of telescopes

dynamometer—energy exerted by living beings or machines

echometer—duration of sounds

elaeometer—specific gravity of oils

electrometer—electrical force

eudiometer—quantity of oxygen in air

floodometer—the height of floods

fluviometer—rise and fall of a river

galvanometer—intensity, etc., of electric currents

gasometer—a large reservoir for storage of gas at gasworks

glaciometer—rate of motion of glaciers

graphometer—a surveyor's instrument for taking angles

gravimeter—specific gravity of bodies

heliometer—a delicate astronomical measuring instrument

hodometer—a distance measurer for wheeled vehicles

hydrometer—specific gravities, or for measuring velocity or discharge of water

hyetometer—a rain gauge

hygrometer—atmospheric moisture

hypsometer—a thermometrical instrument for determining altitudes

kinesimeter—bodily movements

kryometer—low temperatures

lactometer—specific gravity of milk

litrameter—specific gravities of liquids

logometer—a scale for measuring chemical equivalents

macrometer—distant or inaccessible objects

magnetometer—magnetic forces

manometer—elastic force of gases

micrometer—instrument used with telescope or microscope for measuring minute distances

nilometer—rise and fall of a river, especially the Nile

odometer—mileage

oleometer—purity, etc., of oils

ombrometer—a rain gauge

oometer—birds' eggs

opisometer—curved lines

optometer—range of vision, etc.

orometer—height of mountains

oscillometer—the roll of a ship

osmometer—acuteness of sense of smell

pantometer—angles, elevations, distances, etc.

pedometer—distance walked

phonometer—sound-wave vibrations

photometer—relative intensity of light

planometer—a gauge for plane surfaces

pluviometer—a rain gauge

pneumatometer—quantity of air taken in or given out at one breathing

psychrometer—atmospheric humidity

pulmometer—lung capacity

pulsimeter—beat of the pulse

pulsometer—vacuum pump for raising water

pycnometer—density of liquids or solids

pyrometer—high temperatures

radiometer—the effects of radiant energy

rheometer—force, etc., of the circulation of the blood

saccharimeter—quantity of sugar in any solution

salimeter—the salinity of a solution

salinometer—amount of brine in marine engine boilers

434

scintillometer—stellar scintillation
seismometer—a seismograph
sensitometer—the sensitiveness of photographic plates
sillometer—speed of a ship
sonometer—testing sounds
spectrometer—deflection of rays by a prism
speedometer—speed of machinery, etc.
sphygmomanometer—blood pressure in an artery
spirometer—lung capacity
stactometer—a pipette for counting drops of a liquid
stadiometer—a form of theodolite (surveying instrument)
stethometer—the chest during respiration
tachometer—speed
tachymeter—rapid surveying
taseometer—structural strains
tasimeter—minute variations in pressure, etc.
taximeter—for registering fare due in cab
thalassometer—a tide gauge
thermometer—temperature
tintometer—for determining tints
tonometer—a tuning fork
trechometer—distance covered by a vehicle
tribometer—sliding friction
tronometer—a delicate seismometer
udometer—a rain gauge
vaporimeter—pressure of gases
variometer—variations of magnetic force
velocimeter—velocity
viameter—distance traveled
vibrometer—vibrations
vinometer—alcoholic strength of wine
viscometer—viscosity of liquids
voltmeter—voltage
volumeter—volume of a gas
zymometer—degree of fermentation

CHAPTER 2

SOLUTION TO "LATIN MOTTOES" QUIZ

1—g, 2—d, 3—a, 4—j, 5—h, 6—c, 7—e, 8—f, 9—b, 10—i.

SOLUTION TO "LATIN HYMNS" QUIZ

1. "Be Present, Ye Faithful"
2. "Lamb of God"
3. "Thou Shalt Sprinkle" (really an anthem rather than a hymn)
4. "Hail, Mary"
5. "Day of Wrath"
6. "Glory Be to God on High"
7. "Glory Be to the Father"
8. "Now Thou Lettest Depart"
9. "The Mother Was Standing"
10. "So Great, Therefore" (also the last two stanzas of a Eucharistic hymn)

TRANSLATION OF THE "LATIN" POEM:

"I say, Billy, here's a go,
Forty buses in a row.
O, no, Billy! Them is trucks!
What is in 'em? Peas and ducks!"

CHAPTER 5

ROOTS AND THEIR DERIVATIVES

ag, act (ig)—act, agendum, agent, agile, agitate, ambiguous, coagulate, cogent, exact, exigent, fumigate, fustigate, interaction, intransigent, levigate, litigate, navigate, objurgate, prodigal, purge, retroaction, transact
cad, cas—accident, cadaver, cadence, cadent, cascade, case, chance, chute, decay, deciduous, incident, occasion, recidivism
cap, capt, cept, cip—cable, capable, capacious, capstan, caption,

captious, captive, captor, capture, catch, chase, accept, anticipate, conceive, concept, deceive, except, inception, incipient, receive, receptive, recipient, susceptible

clud, clus—clause, cloister, close, conclude, exclude, exclusive, include, inclusive, occlude, preclude, recluse, seclusion

cur, curr, curs—concourse, concur, corridor, courier, course, currency, current, curriculum, cursive, cursory, discourse, excursion, incur, intercourse, occur, precursor, recourse, recur, succor

fac, fact, fect, fic—affect, affection, artifact, beatific, benefactor, benefit, comfit, confection, counterfeit, defect, deficient, deficit, discomfit, edifice, effect, efficacious, efficient, facile, facsimile, fact, faction, factitious, factor, factory, factotum, factual, faculty, fiction, fictitious, imperfection, infect, malefactor, manufacture, officiate, perfect, proficient, profit, refectory, rubefacient, sacrifice, satisfaction, suffice, sufficient

frag, fract—fracas, fraction, fractious, fracture, fragile, fragment, fragmentation, frangible, infraction, refract, saxifrage, suffrage

leg, lect, lig—collection, diligent, election, elegant, eligible, intelligence, lectern, lecture, legend, legible, legion, neglect, negligent, sacrilege, select

mit, miss—admittance, commission, commit, commitment, committee, compromise, demit, dismissal, emissary, emit, intermission, intermittent, manumit, mass, mess, message, missal, missile, mission, missionary, noncommittal, omit, permission, premise, promise, remiss, remit, submit, surmise, transmission

pend, pens—append, appendix, compendium, compensate, depend, dispense, expend, expenditure, expensive, impend, pendant, pendulous, pensive, peso, penthouse, perpendicular, propensity, suspend, suspense

plic, pli—application, complaint, complicate, duplicate, explicate, implicate, imply, plait, pliant, replicate, supplication

sed, sid, sess—assess, assiduous, dissident, obsess, preside, president, possess, reside, residence, residual, seance, sedentary, sediment, session, siege, subside, subsidy, supersede

sent, sens—assent, consensus, consent, dissension, insensate, presentiment, resent, scent, sense, sensible, sensibility, sentence, sententious, sentient, sentimental, sentinel

solv, solu, solut—absolute, absolution, absolve, dissolve, dissolute, insoluble, insolvable, resolve, solve, solvent, soluble

ten, tin, tent—abstain, abstention, contain, content, continence, continent, continue, detain, detention, entertain, lieutenant, maintain, obtain, pertain, pertinacious, pertinent, retain, retention, sustain, sustenance, tenable, tenacious, tenant, tenement, tenet, tennis, tenon, tenor, tenure

volv, volu—convoluted, convolution, devolve, evolution, evolve, involute, involve, involvement, revolution, revolve, vault, volt, voluble, volume

CHAPTER 7

ANSWERS TO "CITIES OR TOWNS" TEST

1—f, 2—j, 3—a, 4—c, 5—h, 6—b, 7
—d, 8—i, 9—e, 10—g.

CHAPTER 11

Below is the list of words to be
inserted in the tale "In Vino,
Veritas," which appears on p. 320.

1. paternal	8. sommelier
2. anecdotage	9. acquiesced
3. aggrandize	10. somniferous
4. extricate	11. somnolent
5. indigent	12. propensity
6. vintners	13. mythomania
7. oenologists	

IN WINE THERE IS TRUTH

My grandfather on my father's side
has reached the advanced age that is
accompanied by a strong tendency to
reminisce and talk about incidents in
one's past life. Recently he related the
story of how he had once decided to
make some extra money in order to
get himself out of financial problems
that were causing him to worry about
eventually becoming as poor as a
church mouse.

Grandpa had two friends who
owned a wine company and also were
experts in the art of making the stuff.
So he asked them if they would allow
him to be one of their tasters. He figured it would be the first step toward
becoming a waiter in charge of the
wines at a restaurant or club.

Well, Grandpa's friends agreed to
his proposal, but the plan backfired.
It seems that the wine caused him to
become drowsy! He kept dozing off on
his regular job as a con man at carnivals. Worse yet, he discovered that
whenever he fell into a sleepy state
he would forget his natural inclination to fool people with his lies, and
he would actually tell customers the
truth!

CHAPTER 12

ANSWERS: TO EPONYM QUIZ

1. William Ewart *Gladstone*
2. *Geronimo*
3. *Garrison* finish
4. *Nicotine*
5. Colonel *Bogey*
6. Smoke pipe for a ship's kitchen
7. a crayon
8. condom
9. Thomas *Hobson*
10. *"Jim Crow"*

CHAPTER 13

ANSWERS TO "PRESENT AND FORMER
NAMES"

1—g, 2—d, 3—a, 4—j, 5—b, 6—i,
7—c, 8—f, 9—e, 10—h.

CHAPTER 17

SOLUTIONS TO PUZZLES

Page 406 top

H	A	M	■	T	A	P
A	L	A	■	H	I	E
D	I	S	C	E	R	P
■	■	C	A	W	■	■
H	Y	A	L	I	N	E
E	A	R	■	L	A	W
S	P	A	■	D	Y	E

Page 406 bottom

D	A	M	■	F	O	G
O	R	O	■	A	R	A
C	E	N	T	R	A	L
■	■	T	A	R	■	■
E	L	E	G	A	N	T
P	E	R	■	G	O	O
I	D	O	■	O	D	E

Page 407 top

Page 407 bottom

Page 408 top

Page 408 bottom

Page 409

Page 410

Page 411

Page 412

CHAPTER 18

ANSWERS TO SPELLING TEST

1. asinine	35. accumulate	68. Fahrenheit
2. inane	36. vaccinate	69. ecstasy
3. existence	37. anoint	70. phenomenal
4. toboggan	38. irrelevant	71. liaison
5. develop	39. saccharine	72. cachinnate
6. occurrence	40. tarpaulin	73. changeable
7. surprise	41. baboon	74. Renaissance
8. indispensable	42. vacillate	75. siege
9. accommodate	43. privilege	76. mausoleum
10. silhouette	44. persistent	77. rococo
11. harass	45. violoncello	78. ladled
12. proceed	46. souvenir	79. obeisance
13. tattooed	47. mayonnaise	80. permanence
14. sadist	48. jodhpurs	81. vilify
15. vermilion	49. dilettante	82. battalion
16. personnel	50. perseverance	83. nickel
17. seize	51. ersatz	84. consensus
18. adolescence	52. subtlety	85. exhilarate
19. daguerreotype	53. chihuahua	86. commitment
20. stupefy	54. auxiliary	87. brethren
21. embarrassed	55. paraphernalia	88. liqueur
22. supersede	56. copyright	89. separate
23. inoculate	57. stiletto	90. genealogy
24. resistance	58. glockenspiel	91. sacrilegious
25. innate	59. impresario	92. mackerellike
26. moccasin	60. Scandinavian	93. knickknack
27. masochist	61. deleterious	94. connoisseur
28. titillate	62. flagellate	95. inadvertent
29. reconnoiter	63. picnicked	96. iridescent
30. bookkeeper	64. weird	97. desirable
31. resuscitate	65. permissible	98. dichotomy
32. asphyxiate	66. memento	99. seersucker
33. syllogism	67. innocuous	100. Pharaoh
34. renascence		

ANSWERS TO "THE MORE THE EERIER"

1. knights-errant
2. talismans
3. menservants
4. hypotheses
5. pelvises or pelves
6. embryos
7. jackanapeses
8. cineraria
9. auspices
10. messieurs

ANSWERS TO "HATES AND FEARS" MIS, MISO

1—b, 2—e, 3—g, 4—j, 5—f, 6—i,
7—h, 8—c, 9—a, 10—d.

PHOBIAS
1. of open spaces
2. of heights
3. of sunlight
4. of women
5. of death
6. of being poisoned
7. of reptiles
8. of the number thirteen
9. of catching a disease
10. of crowds

ANSWERS TO "FIVE OF A KIND"
1. Each word begins and ends with the same letter.
2. Each word forms a new word when the first letter is dropped.
3. Each word forms another new word when the last letter is dropped.

ANSWERS TO "IRRELIGIOUS" QUIZ
1—h, 2—e, 3—d, 4—b, 5—j, 6—c,
7—f, 8—i, 9—a, 10—g.

ANSWERS TO VOCABULARY TESTS
#1 1—d, 2—c, 3—b, 4—d, 5—c, 6—c, 7—c, 8—a, 9—b, 10—a, 11—b, 12—a, 13—b, 14—a, 15—a, 16—b, 17—c, 18—d, 19—a, 20—c.
#2 1—c, 2—b, 3—d, 4—d, 5—b, 6—a, 7—b, 8—a, 9—d, 10—c, 11—c, 12—b, 13—d, 14—c, 15—b, 16—a, 17—a, 18—d, 19—c, 20—b.
#3 1—a, 2—c, 3—a, 4—c, 5—b, 6—a, 7—b, 8—c, 9—b, 10—c, 11—b, 12—c, 13—a, 14—d, 15—c, 16—c, 17—a, 18—c, 19—d, 20—a.
#4 1—a, 2—b, 3—c, 4—b, 5—b, 6—a, 7—c, 8—d, 9—c, 10—d, 11—a, 12—d, 13—b, 14—b, 15—c, 16—b, 17—b, 18—a, 19—b, 20—c.
#5 1—b, 2—c, 3—c, 4—a, 5—d, 6—c, 7—a, 8—d, 9—c, 10—c, 11—c, 12—b, 13—a, 14—a, 15—d, 16—b, 17—c, 18—b, 19—d, 20—b.

ANSWERS TO "WORD ORIGINS"
(The root(s) common to the related words in a group is enclosed in parentheses.)
1. sedition: from *se*, aside, and *ire*, to go (*sedere-sessus*, to sit)
2. volatile: from *volare*, to fly (*volvo, volutus*, to roll)
3. invoice: from Fr. *envoyer*, to send, or *envois*, things sent (*voc, vok*, to call)
4. mastodon: from Gr. *mastos*, breast, and *dont*, tooth (*magnus*, great; comparative of *magnus* is *major*)
5. advantage: from Fr. *avant*, before (*vanus*, empty)
6. cockatrice: from Lat. *caucatrix*, crocodile (*coccus*, seed)
7. valance: from Fr. *avaler*, to go down (*valere*, to be strong)
8. heredity: from *hereditas*, heirship (*haereo, haesus*, to stick) When you hesitate you get *stuck!*
9. volition: from *volere*, to wish (*volvo, volutus*, to roll)
10. pedagogue: from *pais, paidos*, boy (*pes, pedis*, foot)
11. traitor: from *tradere*, deliver or betray (*traho, tractus*, to draw or drag)
12. jest: from *gerere*, to bear or carry or accomplish (*jocus*, joke)
13. jubilee: from Heb., *yobel*, blast of a trumpet, or grand sabbatical year announced by trumpet blast (*gaudere*, to rejoice)
14. allege: from ex-*litigare*, to quarrel or sue (*legere* [L], to gather or read)
15. league: from *ligare*, to bind (*legare*—to depute or send, as a deputy)
16. diverge: from *vergere*, to bend (*via*, a way or road)
17. invest: from *vestire*, to clothe (*vestigare*, to trace)

18. minatory: from *minae*, projections or threats (*monere, monitus,* to warn) N.B. The Romans coined money in the temple of Juno Moneta!
19. miniature: from *minium,* a brilliant red (*minuere,* to lessen)
20. beleaguer: from A.-S. *leger,* bed (*ligare,* to bind)

N.B. Strangely enough, *colleague* and *league* are from two different roots.

ANSWERS TO ETYMOLOGY TEST

(The root(s) common to the related words in a group is enclosed in parentheses.)
1. nuisance: from *nocere,* to hurt or harm (*odium,* hatred)
2. spiral: from *spira,* a coil or twist (*spirare,* to breathe)
3. nutrition: from *nutrire,* to nourish or nurse (*terere, tritus,* to rub or wear out)
4. console: from con-*solari,* to comfort (*solus,* lonely or alone)
5. finger: from A.-S. *finger*—same meaning (*fingere, fictus,* to form or invent) *Fingent* means "molding" or "fashioning" (pronounced "fin-jent").
6. profane: from pro-*fanus,* a temple (*fari, fatus,* to speak) *Nefandous* means "unfit to speak of."
7. poplar: from *populus,* a poplar tree (*populus,* people)
8. poetaster: from Gr. *poies,* a maker, and *aster,* a suffix meaning "inferior" (Gr. *aster,* a star)
9. consult: from *consulere,* to consider (*salire,* to leap)
10. censure: from *censére,* to value or tax (*candére,* to be glowing white)

N.B. candidates for office in Rome were clothed in glittering white robes.
11. supply: from sub-*plere,* to fill (*plicare, plicitus,* to fold)

12. exploit: from *plicare,* to fold (*plaudere, plausus,* to applaud or beat)
13. moratorium: from *morari,* to delay (*moriri, mortuus,* to die)
14. terrible: from *terrére,* to frighten (*terra,* earth)
15. scintillate: from *scintilla,* a spark (*scire,* to know)
16. condiment: from *condire,* to pickle (*condere,* to lay up)
17. vise: from *vitis,* a vine (*videre,* to see)
18. authentic: from Gr. *authentes,* one who does anything with his own hands (*augere, auctus,* to increase)
19. requiem: from re-*quies,* quiet (*quaerire, quaesitus,* to seek or search
20. aspire: from ad-*spirare,* to breathe (*sperare,* to hope)

ANSWERS TO "OUT AND DOWN"

ORACLE
RENTAL
GRUDGE
ANIMAL
NEIGHED
IGNOBLE
SHORTEN
TOASTER

NOTE: The first letters of the above words form ORGANIST, which is an anagram for ROASTING.

ANSWERS TO SCANAGRAMS

1. OCEAN   CANOE
1. SABLE   BLASÉ
3. CHARM   MARCH
4. OUGHT   TOUGH
5. SWORE   WORSE
6. LAUREL   ALLURE
7. PRAISE   ASPIRE
8. TINSEL   LISTEN
9. CHEATER   TEACHER
10. REPUTED   ERUPTED

ANSWERS TO "A MAD, MAD WORLD"

1—g, 2—a, 3—i, 4—b, 5—h, 6—c, 7—f, 8—j, 9—d, 10—e.

ANSWERS TO "LOVERS"

I

1—e, 2—j, 3—a, 4—g, 5—f, 6—i, 7—d, 8—h, 9—b, 10—c.

II

1—g, 2—c, 3—e, 4—h, 5—a, 6—j, 7—i, 8—d, 9—b, 10—f.

ANSWERS TO "ALTERNATES FOR DEMOCRACY"

1. ochlocracy
2. kakistocracy
3. arithmocracy
4. stratocracy
5. ergatocracy
6. pornocracy
7. gerontocracy
8. plutocracy
9. chrysocracy
10. neocracy

ANSWERS TO "WHO'S IN CHARGE?"

1. phylarch
2. ecclesiarch
3. heresiarch
4. nomarch
5. symposiarch
6. anarch
7. oligarch
8. hierarch
9. chiliarch
10. exarch

ANSWERS TO "SPECIALTIES"

1. philematology
2. caliology
3. glyptology
4. malacology
5. myrmecology
6. tocology
7. muscology
8. hagiology
9. agmatology
10. campanology

ANSWERS TO "THE PROGNOSTICATION VOCATION"

1. ornithyomancy
2. capnomancy
3. cleromancy
4. zoomancy
5. cartomancy
6. arithmancy
7. myomancy
8. ophiomancy
9. stichomancy
10. ichthyomancy

ANSWERS TO "A PENNY FOR YOUR THOUGHTS"

1. rubescent
2. lucent
3. maleficent
4. nascent
5. quiescent
6. senescent
7. evanescent
8. nigrescent
9. virescent
10. concupiscent
11. lignescent
12. albescent
13. iridescent
14. obsolescent
15. reticent
16. florescent
17. recrudescent
18. spumescent
19. demulcent
20. tabescent
21. rufescent
22. hyalescent
23. tumescent
24. canescent
25. glabrescent
26. ignescent
27. flavescent
28. delitescent
29. fulvescent
30. latescent

ANSWERS TO "A LEAGUE OF NATIONS"

1. detonation
2. rationation
3. divination
4. abomination
5. rumination
6. peregrination
7. machination
8. procrastination
9. fulmination
10. concatenation
11. cachinnation
12. reincarnation
13. condonation
14. vaticination
15. festination

442

ANSWERS TO "THE ANT COLONY"

1. peccant
2. verdant
3. insouciant
4. mordant
5. osculant
6. ululant
7. volant
8. poignant
9. discrepant
10. obeisant
11. natant
12. cormorant
13. blatant
14. adjutant
15. clairvoyant
16. recusant
17. puissant
18. susurrant
19. coruscant
20. flagellant
21. clamant
22. scintillant
23. stridulant
24. simulant
25. hebetant
26. oppugnant
27. chatoyant
28. oscitant
29. clinquant
30. noctambulant
31. noctivagant
32. horripilant
33. figurant
34. nutant
35. terebrant
36. nidificant
37. faineant
38. hierophant
39. revenant
40. Corybant

ANSWERS TO "FIND THE STRANGER"

I

1. empiric
2. euphony
3. patent
4. blatant
5. pilgarlic
6. fatuous
7. hedonist
8. sciolist
9. buskin
10. delitescent

II

1. gerrymander
2. cicerone
3. gibus
4. tartuffe
5. execrate
6. meritorious
7. pilpul
8. exiguous
9. miscreant
10. jingo

ANSWERS TO "THE BLOCKBUSTER"
1—b, 2—a, 3—d, 4—a, 5—c, 6—b,
7—b, 8—a, 9—a, 10—d, 11—c,
12—b, 13—d, 14—c, 15—c, 16—d,
17—a, 18—b, 19—a, 20—d.

Eugene T. Maleska is an educator, poet, and author who is currently the Crossword Puzzle Editor of The New York Times. *Now retired from teaching and school administration, Dr. Maleska has had a distinguished public school career spanning more than thirty-five years—primarily in New York City, where his last position was Community Superintendent, District 8, Bronx. He is the only person to have a New York City school named for him during his lifetime—the Eugene T. Maleska School, I.S. 174, Bronx.*

Born in Jersey City, New Jersey, Dr. Maleska received A.B. and M.A. degrees from Montclair State College and an Ed.D. from the Harvard Graduate School of Education. He has been the recipient of numerous awards and has been on the faculty of CCNY, Hunter College and the University of Vermont. His books include The Story of Education *(with C. Atkinson) and two volumes of poetry, and he has edited several successful series of crossword puzzle books, including* Simon and Schuster's Crossword Book of Quotations. *He is the editor of a new series,* Simon and Schuster's Crossquotes Omnibus *and in 1978 joined Margaret Farrar as co-editor of the most successful series ever published, the* Simon and Schuster Crossword Puzzle Book. *Most recently he has edited the* Simon and Schuster Book of Cryptic Crossword Puzzles.

Dr. Maleska lives in Massachusetts with his wife, Jean. The Maleskas have two grown children, Merryl and Gary.